Education Reform: The Unwinding of Intelligence and Creativity

EXPLORATIONS OF EDUCATIONAL PURPOSE

Volume 28

Series editors

Shirley R. Steinberg, *University of Calgary, Calgary AB, Canada*
Kenneth Tobin, *City University of New York, The Graduate Centre, New York, USA*

Editorial Board

Barrie Barrell, *Memorial University of Newfoundland, Canada*
Rochelle Brock, *University of Indiana, Gary, USA*
Stephen Petrina, *University of British Columbia, Canada*
Christine Quail, *State University of New York, Oneonta, USA*
Nelson Rodriguez, *College of New Jersey, USA*
Leila Villaverde, *University of North Carolina, Greensboro, USA*
John Willinsky, *Stanford University, USA*

Series Scope

In today's dominant modes of pedagogy, questions about issues of race, class, gender, sexuality, colonialism, religion, and other social dynamics are rarely asked. Questions about the social spaces where pedagogy takes place—in schools, media, and corporate think tanks—are not raised. And they need to be.

The *Explorations of Educational Purpose* book series can help establish a renewed interest in such questions and their centrality in the larger study of education and the preparation of teachers and other educational professionals. The editors of this series feel that education matters and that the world is in need of a rethinking of education and educational purpose.

Coming from a critical pedagogical orientation, *Explorations of Educational Purpose* aims to have the study of education transcend the trivialization that often degrades it. Rather than be content with the frivolous, scholarly lax forms of teacher education and weak teaching prevailing in the world today, we should work towards education that truly takes the unattained potential of human beings as its starting point. The series will present studies of all dimensions of education and offer alternatives. The ultimate aim of the series is to create new possibilities for people around the world who suffer under the current design of socio-political and educational institutions.

For further volumes:
http://www.springer.com/series/7472

Des Griffin

Education Reform:
The Unwinding of
Intelligence and Creativity

Des Griffin
Australian Museum
Frenchs Forest, NSW
Australia

ISSN 1875-4449 ISSN 1875-4457 (electronic)
ISBN 978-3-319-01993-2 ISBN 978-3-319-01994-9 (eBook)
DOI 10.1007/978-3-319-01994-9
Springer Cham Heidelberg New York Dordrecht London

Library of Congress Control Number: 2013953643

© Springer International Publishing Switzerland 2014
This work is subject to copyright. All rights are reserved by the Publisher, whether the whole or part of the material is concerned, specifically the rights of translation, reprinting, reuse of illustrations, recitation, broadcasting, reproduction on microfilms or in any other physical way, and transmission or information storage and retrieval, electronic adaptation, computer software, or by similar or dissimilar methodology now known or hereafter developed. Exempted from this legal reservation are brief excerpts in connection with reviews or scholarly analysis or material supplied specifically for the purpose of being entered and executed on a computer system, for exclusive use by the purchaser of the work. Duplication of this publication or parts thereof is permitted only under the provisions of the Copyright Law of the Publisher's location, in its current version, and permission for use must always be obtained from Springer. Permissions for use may be obtained through RightsLink at the Copyright Clearance Center. Violations are liable to prosecution under the respective Copyright Law.
The use of general descriptive names, registered names, trademarks, service marks, etc. in this publication does not imply, even in the absence of a specific statement, that such names are exempt from the relevant protective laws and regulations and therefore free for general use.
While the advice and information in this book are believed to be true and accurate at the date of publication, neither the authors nor the editors nor the publisher can accept any legal responsibility for any errors or omissions that may be made. The publisher makes no warranty, express or implied, with respect to the material contained herein.

Printed on acid-free paper

Springer is part of Springer Science+Business Media (www.springer.com)

Oscar enquired of Lucinda about the book she was reading. Montaigne, she said.

Mr. Borradaile felt his neck go prickly…Mr. Borradaile did not like this sort of talk at all. He was a practical man. His father had been a wheelwright…He imagined the young woman was being pretentious, using a foreign word for mountain where an English one would have done…

(It made Lucinda) remember things about Sydney she had forgotten. This man was rich and powerful. She did not know him, but she could be confident he would dine at Government House. He was a barbarian.

Oscar and Lucinda by Peter Carey
(University of Queensland Press, 1988)

The sixteenth century French philosopher Michel Eyquem de Montaigne (1533–1592) was sent by his father to get a good education so he could rise in society. He spent the last 30 years of his life writing about topics such as how to live and what it is to be a human being.

James Watson and Francis Crick were awarded the Nobel Prize in Physiology or Medicine in 1962 for discovery of the double helix structure of DNA published in the journal Nature on 25 April 1953, a discovery which has transformed biological and medical science. But the initial X-ray crystallography data on which the structure was based was produced by Rosalind Franklin and Maurice Wilkins at Kings College, London. (Wilkins was also awarded the Prize.)

Watson and Crick at Cambridge University spent their days talking to each other about the structure.

New information is revealed by correspondence brought together by Cold Spring Harbor scientists Alex Gann and Jan Witkowski. Franklin died in 1958 but in any event was not nominated for the Prize. (Rules of the Prize preclude award to deceased persons.)

There was concern that the distinguished American scientist Linus Pauling from CalTech would discover the structure first. Pauling was due to attend a scientific meeting in London at which Franklin and Wilkins data was to be presented. At the last minute, Pauling's passport was cancelled by the American State Department in the belief that he had Communist sympathies.

In any event Pauling, having regained his passport, toured English laboratories before proposing a three strand structure for DNA. He could have visited Franklin's lab but chose not to.

From Science in Action, BBC World Service, presented by John Stewart 25 April 2013.

Foreword

There are many books and many times. A good book can be written at the wrong time and its impact may be lost forever or for years. A bad book written at the right time can be destructive. And, what of this book?

When I first read drafts of *Education Reform: the Unwinding of Intelligence and Creativity* I was unsure. Might the political context date? Could the reactionary determination to push education back into twentieth century basics dissipate? Perhaps debates about school reform might become well informed, rational, and evidence-based? Any fear I had regarding the long-term currency of the book was obliterated today as I read an article in the *Daily Mail* by Michael Gove, UK Secretary of State for Education entitled, 'I refuse to surrender to the Marxist teachers hell-bent on destroying our schools: … the new enemies of promise …'

He wrote:

> But who is responsible for this failure? Who are the guilty men and women who have deprived a generation of the knowledge they need? Who are the modern Enemies Of Promise? …They are all academics who have helped run the university departments of education responsible for developing curricula and teacher training courses.

He concludes:

> The fight against the Enemies Of Promise is a fight for our children's future. It's a fight against ideology, ignorance and poverty of aspiration, a struggle to make opportunity more equal for all our children.
>
> It's a battle in which you have to take sides … (Gove 2013)

Then I knew *Education Reform: the Unwinding of Intelligence and Creativity* is the right book at the right time. A book that sees the same problems: ideology driving reform, ignorance and poverty, a struggle to make opportunity more equal for all our children. A book that helps us to see how this came to pass and a book that can inform what we might do about these challenges.

There is a war being waged, in education, let there be no doubt. There are battles being fought in policy, curriculum, pedagogy, and funding. It is a time to take sides and Griffin takes a side.

Unlike Gove, his argument does more than misinterpret and inappropriately apply a catching title from a book. In *Education Reform: the Unwinding of Intelligence and Creativity* Griffin takes us on a journey through key current educational debates. He examines the political contexts that shape education and society. He allows us to see why education research has so often failed to impact on developments in education. Where it has had impacted, he not only highlights successes but also shows how simplistic rendering of core values, principles, and research findings can be destructive rather than constructive.

Education Reform: the Unwinding of Intelligence and Creativity examines a field of education reform that has become increasingly politically charged. A space where Governments and Nations compete for scores on international tests. A place where doing well is not enough. No, each nation must beat the others and climb the international education league table, in much the same way that a nations sporting prowess is measured at 4-yearly intervals in the Olympic Games. In the popular media, education is too readily positioned as the source and solution for every social ill. And, the misguided belief prevails that every complex problem has a simple solution: that social and economic disadvantage is solved by academic rigor; and that if only young people were made to spell properly, economic success would follow. Griffin could have only outlined the problems and challenges we face and lamented the failure of society to invest intelligently in education. The book, in part no doubt, tells a tale of woe. Yet it is a book of hope. It invites us to re-engage with fundamental questions about what education is for and how education could be positioned to enhance the life experience of all citizens, why education is in servitude to demands that we cull the worthy from the unworthy. Unlike current so-called, educational reforms and educational revolutions, Griffin provides no simple recipe for how to do education better. Rather, Griffin invites all of us to engage in a well-reasoned, articulate, and evidence-based argument to create a better future with each coming generation. There is a war being fought and battles to be one. Which side are you on? *Education Reform: the Unwinding of Intelligence and Creativity* may help you to decide.

Sydney, 24 May 2013   Peter Aubusson

Reference

Gove, M. (2013). I refuse to surrender to the Marxist teachers hell-bent on destroying our schools: Education Secretary berates the new enemies of promise for opposing his plans. *Daily Mail*. Retrieved May 24, 2013 from http://www.dailymail.co.uk/debate/article-2298146/I refuse-surrender-Marxist-teachers-hell-bent-destroying-schools-Education-Secretary-berates-new-enemies-promise-opposing-plans.html

Preface

This book has its origins in comments about education made by influential persons in 2008. Rupert Murdoch, expatriate Australian, and media magnate, delivered the Boyer Lectures for the ABC in that year; Joel Klein was Chancellor of the New York City School system and had been invited to Australia by the then Minister for Education the Hon Julia Gillard to talk about education. What they had to say did not seem to make sense to me so far as the situation in Australia was concerned.

Their comments seemed to be along the familiar lines that Australians had to do better. Who could disagree with that? But the criticisms lacked resonance, they had more to do with the situation in the US from whence these people came as if, like many other things, we had lots to learn from that country and its policies and practices. Though Australia has developed very close relations with the US, seen particularly in the preparedness to join in armed conflict in Vietnam, Iraq, and Afghanistan, it is not the US.

The essays comprising the chapters try to draw out the various influences upon education. Those influences go well beyond school which absorbs most of the popular argument. The book is a summary of what a reasonably intelligent person with an interest and preparedness to be critical where necessary might conclude. The essays are not comprehensive surveys of any particular aspect of education, of teaching, or of learning. They are not grounded in the intellectual discourse of educational philosophy or any particular political philosophy (well not deliberately anyway) though they certainly do not accept current economic orthodoxy and its notions of small government, pursuit of self-interest, and the merits of competition as a driver of prosperity. Rather they try to traverse the myriad influences which bear on the eventual education outcomes which result from the experiences that every one of us goes through. Though schooling is the most obvious component of those experiences, it is not the be all and end all of education. That is the first point.

The essays traverse some fundamental aspects of economics because so much of what we do these days seems to depend on a certain view of economics; generally, it is a very wrong view but for some reason that view is accepted. They also traverse community issues and disadvantage because poverty and economic and social disadvantage, especially poverty, so strongly impedes achievement, not least through its influence on health. Whilst education can help overcome the burdens of poverty, other actions are also important: there is a view that it is not just poverty but a lack of opportunity for development, development of the individual especially, which is holding people back and limiting their social mobility. Increasingly even in the western world, people born into poverty die in poverty. That flies in the face of certain myths fundamental to societies such as that of the US. It is important to understand where one is and why, to acknowledge one's situation.

And the essays deal with the situations facing teachers, situations little different from those facing all employees, levels of trust in them and their professionalism, access to appropriate evaluation of their performance and to opportunities for advancement. That is tied up with views about economics and the views about the role of individuals in society and indeed the purpose of education.

Many of the essays deal with education as we are used to thinking about it, what is effective teaching, what makes for successful schooling. But first of all, what early childhood is like, what happens in those first few years and how that is so important in influencing what happens later. What is involved in the learning process and is education something that mainly goes on in school? The answer to the second question is no, yet it is schooling that absorbs most attention in the education debate. And again it is economics, or a certain view of it, which so influences both those processes, education in school and in life. Most especially it is the belief that people have which determines what we do, not necessarily any wider set of views which might be grounded in more substantial evidence.

It is the evidence which contradicts what many people seem to believe which is the core of this book. Quite simply, the most successful education outcomes derive from attention to basic issues of human rights and what characterizes humanity, a natural curiosity, and the ongoing amalgamation of new experiences into previous views, a wish to advance one's self and to have the opportunity to be involved in worthwhile pursuits. And it is based on the proposition that people with access to education generally have a good idea of what they want to get out of it. They respond to their own drivers, or try to. But how people behave is influenced by how they are treated and what is expected of them. Respect for the individual and high expectations are critical.

Unfortunately, there is a widely held contrary view that others know what is best for them. It recalls Charles Dickens' Mr. Gradgrind and his obsession about facts. Despite all the evidence to the contrary, there are still those who consider that transmission or rote learning or didactic education, the teacher at the front of the class, the students taking notes and being tested later on their recall of what was said, is what we should strive to return to. And that a return to basics, to literacy and numeracy, is vitally important. Forget creativity and the diversity of human interests and abilities and the variety of intelligences and the way relationships and experiences can strongly influence later outcomes!

Unequivocally, I take the view of people like philosopher John Rawls and economist Amartya Sen, that social justice means ensuring the opportunity for every individual to reach their potential and that so long as some do not have that opportunity, we have to strive to make it so. Indeed successful school systems are based on the proposition that every child can learn and that high standards should be set for every student. I also take the view that we can only understand enough to see what, at the moment, might be the truth by being prepared to challenge the current orthodoxy, even when that seems to have the authority of those in power. It is not always a comfortable situation. It is too often a prescription not followed.

So in this book reforms which emphasize concern for early childhood, school leadership, and respect for teachers are contrasted with ones based on standardized tests, private schools, and sacking bad teachers.

Clearly what works in certain circumstances, does not work in others. That is true of education as it is of most situations. Yet people are people, organizations are organizations, and societies are societies: similar beliefs and actions seem to produce similar outcomes though culture and history play a significant role. At the same time different societies provide lessons for us which challenge us to think about what we believe are appropriate in our own society.

Celebrated physiologist, bird watcher, and author Prof. Jared Diamond of the University of California is just one person who has recently alerted us to just how many lessons there are to learn from other societies in his book, *The World Until Yesterday; What Can We Learn From Traditional Societies?* (Viking 2012). In doing so he has illuminated the richness of humanity. Some anthropologists and advocates for traditional societies criticized his approach: that ought to encourage us to think about the arguments rather than reject his views out of hand! In truth anthropology can both illuminate humanity and divide it.

In a world dominated by neoliberalism and its promotion of choice and financial rewards the demand for accountability is shrill. But that accountability means metrics that unwind the most exciting aspects of teaching and learning—intelligence and creativity and the search for new relationships: innovation.

All those mantras about learning from the past and ultimately failing for not doing so are correct, but individual and collective actions can make a difference, even in the face of seemingly immovable obstacles. Unfortunately there are a very large number of obstacles. But the attempt to achieve the best must go on. This book might help to encourage that.

Acknowledgments

A number of people have provided encouragement and advice. In particular I want to thank Prof. Peter Aubusson from the University of Technology Sydney for his enthusiastic support for the project throughout.

Dr. Barry Jones AC and Prof. Lyn Yates of the University of Melbourne generously gave moral support to the publication as did Debbie Lee, publisher at the Australian Council for Education Research.

Several people read various parts of the manuscript and provided valuable comment. I thank Kimberley Pressick-Kilborn and John Buchanan of the University of Technology Sydney, Frank Talbot AM and Ken Cusson, both formerly of Macquarie University, Sydney, Prof. Chris Nash, Monash University, Tim Sullivan, now of the Australian War Memorial, Canberra and Emeritus Prof. George Hein of Lesley College, Cambridge, MA.

Trevor Cobbold of Save Our Schools, through his website postings and articles promoting the importance of public schools and everything to do with them is owed a great deal. Time and again his posts have alerted me to important articles which led on to other significant contributions by experts around the world. My friend Chris Curtis of Melbourne commented frequently and provided opinion on many matters concerning government policies and the history of education and schooling in Victoria as well as reading and commenting on some of the essays.

I would not have started on this project were it not for the opportunity to attend several annual meetings of the American Education Research Association and hear some of the world's leading experts whose addresses were so inspiring: David Berliner, Milbrey McLaughlin, Gloria Ladson-Billings, Lauren Resnick, Anthony Bryk, and many others. The contribution of many other experts to programs broadcast by ABC Radio National, especially 'All in the Mind', the 'Science Show' and 'Background Briefing' has been invaluable.

I want to acknowledge two people especially for their inspiring research and writing. The late Graham Nuthall, Emeritus Professor of Education at the University of Canterbury in Christchurch, New Zealand, studied children in the classroom. He examined what they actually did and said, what they said to each other. His research led him to challenge many of the current views about what constituted effective teaching and learning: "just because teachers are teaching doesn't mean students are learning."

The late Kenneth Rowe died tragically at Marysville, Victoria in the awful "Black Saturday" bushfires in 2009. He had been until a year before his death the leader of ACER's research into teaching and learning. His prodigious writing included some of the most precise critiques of education policy; at his funeral ACER's Chief Executive Prof. Geoff Masters recalled that Ken Rowe was not backward in letting people know what he thought. His statement, "Australian politicians and senior bureaucrats currently advocating the publication of performance information in the form of league tables are naively, and in typical fashion, stomping around in an uninformed epistemopathological fog" ought to be familiar to all who aspire to propose how we assess the effectiveness of teaching and learning.

I thank Prof. Lyn Yates (Melbourne University) for permission to quote from her inaugural professorial lecture and Dr. Bronwyn Bevan (The Exploratorium, San Francisco) for permission to quote from her forthcoming review of Deborah L. Perry's book *What Makes Learning Fun?: Principles for the Design of Intrinsically Motivating Museum Exhibits* (Walnut Creek CA: AltaMira Press, 2012) for the journal *Visitor Studies*.

Finally as always I thank Janette Griffin for her ongoing support and encouragement.

Contents

1 What Do We Expect of Education? 1
    1.1   The Value of Education 1
    1.2   Education: Its Purpose 3
    1.3   The Issues for Reform 4
    1.4   Economics, Community and Inequality 6
    1.5   Australia: Economic Background 6
    1.6   Education Reform in Australia 8
    1.7   Where Should We Start? 10
    1.8   The Questions to be Answered 11
    References 14

2 A Word on Economics 15
    2.1   Economics and Education Reform 15
    2.2   The Basics of Neoclassical Economics 16
    2.3   Individuals and Choice: Limits to Government 18
    2.4   Privatisation of Government Services 20
    2.5   The Global Financial Crisis and Its Consequences .. 21
    2.6   An Alternative View: Lessons from Behavioural
            Economics 25
    2.7   Reciprocity 26
    2.8   Mirror Neurons and Belongingness 27
    2.9   Neoclassical Economics: Adam Smith Made Small! .. 28
    2.10   The Consequences for Education 29
    2.11   The Irrelevance of Market Economics 31
    References 33

3 Community and Inequality: Part 1:
    Creating an Enabling Environment 37
    3.1   The Importance of Socioeconomic Status 37
    3.2   The Real Wealth of Nations: Human Development .. 40
    3.3   Unequal Society and Its Cost 42
    3.4   The Great Divergence: Why Nations Fail 44
    3.5   Personal Development, Home Environment
            and Child Wellbeing 47

		Urban Youth in the US and the UK	49
	3.6		
	3.7	Education Reform and Economic and Social Disadvantage	51
	References		51
4	**Community and Inequality: Part 2: Australia**		**55**
	4.1	Inequality in Australia	55
	4.2	Indigenous Australians	58
	4.3	Indigenous Education and the Home	59
	4.4	Community and Responsibility	60
	4.5	The Northern Territory Intervention	61
	4.6	Self Determination: Sovereignty Matters!	66
	4.7	Closing the Gap	67
	4.8	Hope for the Future?	69
	4.9	Overcoming Inequality: Self-Determination and Ending Discrimination	71
	References		73
5	**Early Childhood: A World of Relationships**		**77**
	5.1	The Critical Importance of Early Childhood	77
	5.2	Pioneer Studies of Early Childhood	79
	5.3	The Nature of Early Experiences	81
	5.4	An Environment of Relationships: Healthy Development	82
	5.5	Personal Development and the Home Environment	84
	5.6	Attachment Theory, Mothers Memories and Mothers Roles	86
	5.7	Policies on Parental Leave in Europe and Australia	88
	5.8	A National Early Childhood Development Strategy in Australia	89
	5.9	Economic Benefits of Early Childhood Intervention	91
	5.10	Early Childhood is the Critical Time	92
	References		93
6	**Effective Teaching and Learning Part 1: John Hattie, Graham Nuthall and Jonathan Osborne**		**97**
	6.1	The Importance of Teachers	97
	6.2	Some Initial Observations	99
	6.3	John Hattie: The Teacher, Not the School, Makes the Difference	100
	6.4	Productive Pedagogy	102
	6.5	Formative Evaluation	104
	6.6	Graham Nuthall, What Goes on in the Classroom?	106
	6.7	Learning Outcomes: TIMMS	110

	6.8	Jonathan Osborne and Argumentation in Science	111
	6.9	Knowledge of Effective Teaching and Learning is Ignored.	112
	References		113

7 Effective Teaching and Learning Part 2: Lessons from the US ... 115
    7.1   School Reforms in the US: Follow Through and Direct Instruction 115
    7.2   US Reforms: The Last 20 Years..................... 117
    7.3   The South Side of Chicago 118
    7.4   Nested Learning Communities and Accountable Talk 122
    7.5   Ricky DuFour and Professional Learning Communities..... 125
    7.6   Class Size Matters in Early Grades When Carefully Planned.................................. 126
    7.7   A Note on Homework............................. 128
    7.8   What do Children Want from School?................ 129
    7.9   Leadership, Student Engagement and Support 130
    References 132

8 Teacher Pay, Performance and Leadership 135
    8.1   The Call for Accountability 135
    8.2   Teacher Performance and Evaluation 138
    8.3   Merit Pay....................................... 140
    8.4   Teacher Certification, Evaluation, Career Paths and Rewards 142
    8.5   School Leadership: Leadership in Education 143
            8.5.1   Transformational Leadership 144
            8.5.2   Transformational Leadership in the School 145
    8.6   International Perspectives on School Leadership.......... 147
    8.7   Teacher Profession and School Leadership 148
    References 149

9 Public or Private Schools, Tests and League Tables, Parental Choice and Competition in Australia, the USA and Britain 153
    9.1   The Australian School System 153
    9.2   Australia and Government Funding of Independent Schools After 1996................................ 154
    9.3   Student Socioeconomic Background and School Environment 156
    9.4   The Rudd and Gillard Australian Governments and Independent Schools........................... 157
    9.5   Choice and Competition in the US School System 158
    9.6   Independent Schools in the UK 159
    9.7   Market Mechanisms 160

9.8	Tests and League Tables: A Democratic Right to Know?	161
9.9	Evidence is not Always Sufficient!	163
9.10	No Child Left Behind (NCLB)	163
9.11	Standardised Testing in the UK	166
9.12	Value-Added Tests	167
9.13	Intrinsic Motivation	168
9.14	Important Issues Missed	168
9.15	Effective Student Engagement and Ineffective Standardised Tests	169
References		171

10 Curriculum Matters ... 175
- 10.1 What Should Students be Taught? ... 175
- 10.2 A National Curriculum ... 178
- 10.3 The History Wars ... 180
- 10.4 Science Education for What? ... 182
- 10.5 Science Education in the European Union ... 185
- 10.6 Mathematics: Not Just Skills but a Discipline Requiring Understanding ... 186
- 10.7 Curriculum Reform Must Focus on Understanding and Intellectual Development ... 187
- References ... 189

11 Creativity to Free Choice Learning ... 193
- 11.1 What Creativity is ... 193
- 11.2 Creativity is What Makes us Human ... 195
- 11.3 The Arts in Schools ... 197
- 11.4 Reggio Emilia ... 198
- 11.5 Success and Failure at School ... 199
- 11.6 Organisations Encouraging Creativity and Innovation ... 200
- 11.7 Free Choice Learning: Learning in Informal Settings ... 201
- 11.8 Lifelong Learning and Public Broadcasting ... 204
- 11.9 Education Means Creativity Means much more than School ... 205
- References ... 206

12 International Comparisons ... 209
- 12.1 Misinformation and Urban Mythologies ... 209
- 12.2 Successful Schools ... 212
  - 12.2.1 Finland ... 213
  - 12.2.2 New Zealand ... 214
  - 12.2.3 China ... 216
  - 12.2.4 Singapore ... 217
  - 12.2.5 Japan ... 218

		12.2.6 Canada	219
		12.2.7 Korea	220
		12.2.8 Sweden	221
	12.3	Lessons from PISA 2009 for the US (and Other Countries)	223
	12.4	Successful Systems Share Common Feature: All Children Can Learn	225
	References		227
13	**Universities and Tertiary Education**		**229**
	13.1	Universities and Society	229
	13.2	Issues for Universities	230
		13.2.1 Issues of Access	232
		13.2.2 Corporatisation, Managerialism and Leadership in Universities	233
		13.2.3 What do University Students Know?	237
	13.3	Tertiary Education Reform in Australia	238
	13.4	The Bradley Review in Australia	240
	13.5	Assessing the Value of Universities	242
	13.6	Universities and Research: Why Can't We Have a Silicon Valley in Australia?	244
	13.7	Universities and Skills Training	245
	13.8	Teacher Training	246
	13.9	The Importance of Government Investment in Tertiary Education	246
	References		248
14	**Policy Development in Education and Schooling in Australia**		**251**
	14.1	Public Policy and the Education Debate	251
	14.2	Australian Students Educational Achievement	252
	14.3	The Rudd and Gillard Education Revolution	255
	14.4	The State and Territory Ministerial Declarations	255
	14.5	Australian Business	256
	14.6	Australian Literacy and Numeracy	256
	14.7	Testing Australian Students: NAPLAN and My School	257
	14.8	Improving Australian Teaching Standards	260
	14.9	The Gonski Review	261
	14.10	States Announce Their Own Education Policies	270
	14.11	Funding the Gonski Reforms; the National Plan for School Improvement	272
	14.12	Education Reform: A Future of Equity or a Future of Privilege?	276
	References		279

15 Concluding Essay: What Have We Learned and Where are We Going? ... 283
- 15.1 Centuries of Thought and Decades of Research: Critical Conclusions ... 283
- 15.2 Early Childhood ... 286
- 15.3 Schooling, Schools and Teaching ... 287
- 15.4 Community and Inequality ... 291
- 15.5 Universities and Other Places of Learning ... 297
- 15.6 Misinformation and Its Consequences ... 298
- 15.7 The Future of Australian Education Reform ... 299
- 15.8 Everything is Connected ... 303
- References ... 304

16 Postscript: Australian Educational Futures After the 2013 Federal Election ... 307
- 16.1 A New Australian Government: Policies Compared ... 307
- 16.2 The Human Development Report ... 310
- 16.3 Adult Literacy and Numeracy ... 312
- 16.4 Challenges for a New Government ... 313
- References ... 315

Index ... 317

Abbreviations

ACER	Australian Council for Educational Research
COAG	Council of Australian Governments
GFC	Global Financial Crisis
IMF	International Monetary Fund
NCLB	No Child Left Behind
NAPLAN	National Assessment Program for Literacy and Numeracy
NBN	National Broadband Network
NTER	Indigenous people in Australia's Northern Territory covered by the Australian Governments Intervention
OECD	Organisation for Economic Co-Operation and Development
PIRLS	Progress in International Reading Literacy Study
PISA	Program for International Student Assessment
TIMSS	Trends in International Mathematics and Science Study
UK	United Kingdom
UN	United Nations
UNDP	United Nations Development Program
UNICEF	United Nations Children's Fund
US	United States of America

Note: In referring to the governments of Australia, the terms Australian Government and Commonwealth Government are used interchangeably to refer to the Government of the Federation or Commonwealth of Australia, with preference being given to Commonwealth where the context refers to state and territory governments as well.

Chapter 1
What Do We Expect of Education?

1.1 The Value of Education

Education enriches our life immeasurably: socially, intellectually and economically. We are continually educating ourselves through learning, building our experiences into what we think we already know. We are constructing our own reality, our own world view. We see the past and the present and envisage the future through the prism of that world view. Life is a continual exercise in sensemaking. At its most fundamental education is about learning: the way teaching is pursued influences learning, in school and in any context in which a novice, a student of any age including a young child and even an older adult, interacts with an expert, such as a teacher, an authority in some endeavour or field of study or a parent, especially in the early years of a child's life.

Whilst the principal gains of education might be to ourselves, the gains to the community at large from more formal education, schooling and, if we are fortunate, preschool and university or college, are very substantial. Because of that, and because the learning is not a limited resource, education has been increasingly seen as something to which everyone is entitled and which the community ought to support financially as it does other common resources. In other words it is seen as a right, like liberty.

Article 26 of the United Nations Universal Declaration of Human Rights states, in part

'(1) Everyone has the right to education. Education shall be free, at least in the elementary and fundamental stages. Elementary education shall be compulsory. Technical and professional education shall be made generally available and higher education shall be equally accessible to all on the basis of merit.
(2) Education shall be directed to the full development of the human personality and to the strengthening of respect for human rights and fundamental freedoms. It shall promote understanding, tolerance and friendship among all nations, racial or religious groups…
(3) Parents have a prior right to choose the kind of education that shall be given to their children.'

Education shall be free and equally accessible! For all kinds of reasons but mainly obsession with notions about the nature of human behaviour derived from neoclassical economics, the education debate in some countries has become an argument mainly about rights of choice of school, about competition, incentives and accountability. For many, education comes at a cost. In some quarters teaching is still considered a matter of transmitting facts. For this and other reasons a standard curriculum is demanded. The view that the individual should be responsible for their own future, a common theme in the US and some other countries, leads to minimal intervention in areas such as preschool: that is considered a matter for families to deal with. Propositions that post-school education largely benefits the individual lead to universities and colleges charging fees for attendance.

On the other hand, especially in those countries where educational achievement, as assessed by international tests, is high governments have led policies attending to equity and supported by a community persuaded to the view that privileging some in the community but not others diminishes the quality of life in that community. The support extends to the economically and socially disadvantaged including those whose first language is not that of the country in which they now live. Choice of school is not an issue since all schools are public, competition and choice are not issues, accountability being replaced by a belief that teaching and teachers are important and should be highly qualified, trusted and appropriately remunerated. Equity in access to education is a major concern of the Organisation for Economic Cooperation and Development (OECD) in its Program for International Student Assessment (PISA) and disparities related to social and economic background and access to education are reported on in detail.

The fundamental issues are the life of the child, equity and the expectation that all schools will provide a quality education. Concern for the child also leads in a number of countries to universally available preschool and in some countries a relatively late start to school and relatively short hours of attendance. Trust in teachers leads to flexibility in curriculum content in later school years.

When we talk about education we mostly are talking about schools and schooling, about teachers and about curriculum. But schooling is not education or rather education is not just schooling. Many other issues impact on the eventual outcomes of education and particularly school. These include early childhood experiences within the family and friends of the family and other adults in the community, economic and social issues as well as urban planning, transport, housing and health policies as they are influenced especially by economic policies at government level.

These essays set out to explore educational developments and understandings in the strict sense—learning, teaching, schooling and the relevant organisational environment. They also address issues including economics, the nature of community and life matters, and the impact of social and economic conditions on educational outcomes. The argument is that the judgements about achievements in education cannot be separated from these other issues.

1.1 The Value of Education

What we expect of schools was well expressed by Foundation Chair of Curriculum in the Graduate School of Education at the University of Melbourne, Professor Lyn Yates, in her inaugural lecture (Yates 2005).

'If you read the press, or listen to the media, or read government inquiries on different topics, you'd be truly impressed with what schools can supposedly do if only they got their act together. No adult would live in poverty; students and teachers would be on task 24/7; there would be no bad drivers, no drunk drivers, no crime, no sexism or racism or discrimination of any kind; everyone would eat healthy diets and be active and slim; every particular school would be better than all its competitors, and every student would complete year 12 and get an ENTER score over 99 so they could all go on to do medical degrees at the University of Melbourne; although at the same time schools would also be producing a diverse range of enterprising young people who would fill the shortages in all the skilled trades (and in unskilled one's for that matter), and be entrepreneurs who would develop new inventions and turn around Australia's balance of trade.'

She continued, 'Schools *are* some of the most important social institutions we have, and they do have major effects both on individuals and on the shape of the culture and country we go on living in… But we do, routinely, have impossible expectations about schools, and blame them for not fulfilling impossible *and conflicting* hopes. The fact that some people don't do as well as others in schools isn't (or isn't just) a failing on the part of schools; it is part of what schools as a system *are set up to do*—to save universities and employers some of the burden of deciding for themselves who they will take on. If you don't in principle want some people to do worse than others, you don't set up final certificates that decide in advance what proportions can be awarded various grades, and you don't insist on a final tertiary entrance score that lists everyone on a relative standing from 1 to 100.'

1.2 Education: Its Purpose

Once upon a time the debate focused on the main purpose of education, what was expected to be achieved, who had access to it, what important knowledge should be acquired and by whom. Until early last century in many countries a broad education was the preserve of those who could afford it. Commonly, for ordinary working people, education amounted to the development of skills or trades. It was the upper classes of society and boys and young men who were considered likely to benefit from a broader education, one which took in the classics and classical languages Latin and Greek. And learning was generally held to be the accumulation of facts. But it was also held to be ability to reason and analyse.

Conversations about the nature and purpose of education are eternal and universal. Greeks Plato and Aristotle argued for special attention to the education of the future elite. English philosopher John Stuart Mill argued for the teaching of the classics at university and considered what we would call vocational training to not be something that should concern universities. Philosopher Bertrand Russell challenged some of the assertions of Plato and Aristotle. Understanding the nature of learning was advanced particularly by the very influential American education philosopher John Dewey who was concerned with concepts of democracy and social justice and had a strong commitment to naturalism, the view that life as it is lived contains all that exists (Hein 2012).

Swiss psychologist and natural scientist Jean Piaget (1896–1980), well known for his work studying children and his theory of cognitive development, declared in 1934 that only education is capable of saving our societies from possible collapse, whether violent, or gradual; 65 years later we have hardly begun to recognise how to give effect to such a view! Russian Lev Vygotsky, whose work was unfortunately hardly known in the west until the early 1960s, maintained that consciousness and cognition were the end products of socialization. Vygotsky contributed extremely important understandings about children's experiences and their learning processes. Vygotsky's views are now a major theme of education research. American Howard Gardner showed that intelligence was not just about literacy and numeracy but a great many other things. Knowledge of the brain and its development and the impact of the environment and the nature of learning have expanded enormously in the last decades, thanks to gains in the sciences of neurophysiology, psychology and behaviour.

These days however, the ongoing influence of the commercial sector and prevalent belief amongst its more vocal advocates that economic growth is essential to progress and increasing prosperity for everyone has meant that the main purpose of education is seen as developing skills useful for work. The view that those skills might be learned in the workplace, and therefore school and college might pursue a broader purpose such as communication, critical analysis and how to work together, is often ignored. The view that education in its broad sense is essential for participation in society, indeed a fundamental aspect of a participatory democracy, not simply a means of gaining employment, is thus marginalised.

1.3 The Issues for Reform

In the twenty-first century what do we now believe to be the major issues affecting education and what do we think we know? There are two areas where there is substantial awareness and agreement. First, educational achievement of the child is most clearly predicted by the socioeconomic level of the family, including parents educational achievement. Second, teachers make a contribution to educational achievement to a greater extent than any other factor apart from family background.

Why and how these two factors—socioeconomic background of the family and the teacher—have the influence they do is less clear, at least in debate, and very often the way they are treated does anything but improve educational gain.

1.3 The Issues for Reform

There are many who consider that a focus on education will by itself overcome socioeconomic disadvantage, even poverty. What is the evidence for this and what are those schools and other environments like where gains have been made despite disadvantage?

Whilst school years are the most common focus of the education debate, it is established, though not always acknowledged through policies and programs, that early childhood is a critical time and that the environment of the growing child is a significant factor. Why is this and what is the impact of the socioeconomic context? Children are universally acknowledged as creative and curious but how important is it that creativity be maintained and even developed within educational regimes?

Whilst teachers are acknowledged as important there are different views as to how their contribution might be enhanced, how their teaching might be more effective. Teachers are often thought to enjoy long holidays and work for only about 6 h a day: to have an easy life. What understanding do we have of the teaching environment, of the provision of opportunities for personal advancement in the workplace, of the nature of performance management and of the impact of various drivers such as salary and conditions, and of school leadership? How important relatively are content knowledge and pedagogy, the practice of teaching? What does learning in various environments, particularly the school classroom, actually involve?

In the age of the me-generation, the focus on the individual and responsibility, accountability is seen as more important. How can teachers and schools be held accountable and how can we understand the results of their contribution to eventual educational achievement and later outcomes? What can testing regimes tell us and what impact do they have on student and teacher behaviour? What conclusions can we draw about the achievement of students from different countries?

And though not everyone progresses to post secondary education, to what extent do colleges and universities contribute to society and to what extent should the individual contribute financially rather than the community through government funding? Is the way universities function likely to achieve superior results?

The key question in education is what is being learned and how, why does socioeconomic background and the family situation affect learning, what happens in the school class and what influences that? And to what extent is education and learning, not necessarily the same thing after all, benefitting the individual and, separately perhaps, the community and society.

As has been said already, schooling is only part of the education process. A very important point is that what happens at school is not the final determinant of every individuals future. Scores of people become successful in later life who were judged by their teachers to be unlikely to succeed. They include leading artists, Nobel prize-winning scientists, business people and politicians. In the end should we really be spending all this time worrying about school? A recent example is Sir John Gurdon, winner of the Nobel Prize for Physiology or Medicine in 2012 for work on conversion of mature cells to stem cells. At Eton College Gurdon came last in biology in a class of 250 and a report by his teacher described as ridiculous young John's wish to become a biologist.

Taking all these questions into account what reforms should we embark on, what policies should we seek to put in place and how much are we prepared to pay for those reforms?

1.4 Economics, Community and Inequality

As has already been pointed out, one of the few areas of agreement about education is that the socioeconomic background of the parents is the most important predictor of the child's educational achievement. In other words, children from poor backgrounds achieve to a substantially lower level than do children from high socioeconomic families. In a number of countries, both developing and developed, the gap in wealth and income has increased substantially in the last 30–50 years. Inequality is persistent, seen in the slow if any changes in social mobility within societies where disadvantage is actively exploited.

Historian and philosopher, the late Tony Judt (1948–2010) wrote the acclaimed *Postwar: A History of Europe Since 1945* which traversed the recovery of European countries after the horrors of World War 2. In *Ill Fares the Land*, written immediately before his untimely death Judt wrote, 'Inequality is corrosive. It rots society from within. The impact of material differences takes a while to show up: but in due course the competition for status and goods increases; people feel a growing sense of superiority (or inferiority) based on their possessions; prejudice towards those on the lower ranks of the social ladder hardens; crime spikes and the pathologies of social disadvantage become even more marked. The legacy of unregulated wealth creation is bitter indeed.'

It is not possible to discuss educational reform without considering these issues. Community and Inequality are addressed in two essays.

1.5 Australia: Economic Background

These essays deal with many countries and their education systems and experiences of reforms. Many of the essays compare the systems and the conditions of other countries with those in Australia. The principal focus though is Australia. It is as well to understand the situation of Australia early in the twenty-first century. That basically comes down to economics. That is especially relevant given the current obsession with economics and how we are going to pay for what we want.

Like many developed countries, Australia has embraced a market economic model based on neoclassical theories and neoliberalism, derived from it. Small government is promoted in favour of opportunities for the private sector. Every organisation should be business-like! The effects of the invasion of government practices by 'business principles' sometimes referred to as New Public Management (NPM), was shown in the 1970s and 1980s by the rush of every department and agency of government to compete its corporate plan with its 'key performance indicators'. In some cases the plans were written by consultants and had minimal consultation with staff so defeating the purpose; no-one in the lead departments read the plans! Many media commentators still have no idea about how organisations go about planning and what effective planning or strategy is…

Economically, Australia has performed well over the last several decades and particularly in the last several years: it has emerged from the Global Financial Crisis (GFC) substantially less affected than most other countries with the result that its economy has grown relative to many other countries. Reforms in the 1970s and 1980s in floating the dollar, removing tariffs on imports whilst retaining important controls over financial institutions contributed. So did stimulus funding provided by the Australian government following the crisis. However, reliance on the mining industry, export of raw material overseas and import of finished product continues. The manufacturing sector is weak. Australia's economy has been characterised as that of an oil-rich sheikhdom, not a modern diversified economy (a factor contributing to the relatively low increase in aggregate stock prices); it has the living standards of a prosperous industrialised country but the structure of a technologically undeveloped country (McAuley 2012a).

In Australia inflation is relatively low, interest rates provide opportunities for variation and unemployment is relatively low. In respect of the broad components of taxation Australia is about average (Tiffen and Gittins 2009, Table 5.4). However there has been a trend to the increasing wealth disparities seen also in some other countries: inequalities are quite severe in remote areas, in parts of all urban centres and amongst Indigenous peoples.

Australia is risk averse in respect of debt and budget deficits. Public debt is extremely small relative to that of other countries and government is certainly not large. Government debt as a percentage of GDP is half that of most OECD countries, almost a third of that of the Norway, Finland and the UK (UK) for instance and one-fourth that of the US (US): it absolutely is not an issue of concern (Tiffen and Gittins 2009, Table 5.6).

What is a concern is the notional liability in respect of development of infrastructure in transport and communications, infrastructure which would contribute substantially to increasing productivity. Were Australian governments to reach the average of OECD countries they could borrow $300 billion or more. They don't because they are terrified of the judgements of international rating agencies, those people who promoted the value of financial derivatives offered by numerous institutions that collapsed in 2008! Instead government leaders talk about fiscal discipline and living within our means, as if they were running a household, but not their house since that would have required them to acquire debt!. These attitudes contribute to, though they do not determine, a reluctance to invest in programs with long-time horizons, goals to be achieved in future decades rather than next year or the year after.

Private debt, ultimately owed to overseas financial institutions, is quite large and has gone mostly to increasing the value of private housing rather than public infrastructure. House prices are high relatively to the rest of the world and housing affordability is at a very low level! A major contributor to that is, negative gearing, the ability of investors to write off the rental income of the property they rent out against the operating costs including the mortgage. Tax revenue foregone is some $40 billion every year!

There is an obsession with efficiency. That translates to productivity which is affected by issues such as organisational leadership and levels of training. A survey by Ernst and Young in 2011 found that 54 % of workplace respondents identified people management as the biggest factor influencing productivity yet organisations such as the Business Council of Australia continue to proclaim that government regulations are responsible for declines in productivity (McAuley 2012b; Irvine 2012).

Because most of the funding for education comes from government there is one other matter which should be dealt with. Business calls for smaller government. However, the size of government bears no relationship to international competitiveness. In most of the countries in the top ten of international competitiveness, general government outlays as a percent of GDP are one and a half times that in Australia! (McAuley 2012a); Switzerland was number one in competitiveness ranking in 2011 with a government outlay as a percent of GDP the same as Australia's. Australia has anyway slipped from 15th OECD country to 21st in the last 5 years. It also remains low in ranking of innovation.

A special essay expands on the issues of economics, economic theory and its consequences.

1.6 Education Reform in Australia

Education reform in the last 15 years at the Australian Government level has focused on provision of choice, as part of the agenda of small government through financial support to independent schools which benefitted those already economically and socially advantaged. The disadvantaged have not benefitted, despite early claims that they would. Public schools must enrol all who seek to do so and therefore were left with the rest including disabled and Indigenous students, particularly in remote areas. In the debate accountability means standardised tests, and financial incentives, bonuses or merit pay for 'better' teachers, have been to the fore. Bad teachers should be sacked! It is difficult to do so because of the power of unions we are told.

Australia participates in international student assessments, particularly the OECDs Program PISA. It also takes part in a couple of other international assessments which do not assess precisely the same issues as PISA does. The Australian Council for Educational Research (ACER) undertakes very detailed and comprehensive analyses of the results of these international tests. Since 2008 a national test, the National Assessment Program—Literacy and Numeracy or NAPLAN has been conducted. All children in Australian schools in alternate school years from years 3 through 9 sit the Assessment on the same days. The tests are in Reading, Writing, Language Conventions (Spelling, Grammar and Punctuation) and Numeracy. The media comments on the results of all these tests: often the commentary is misleading, not least because writers are not acquainted with the fundamentals of statistics!

Whilst the States have constitutional responsibility for education the Australian Commonwealth Government has played an increasingly active role since the early 1970s, especially in universities and more recently in schools. Recent reform has proceeded in the context of Australian federalism. Though Australia became a federated nation in 1901, the level of cohesion in policy amongst the states and with the Commonwealth is seldom evident: indeed at the 2012 mid-year meeting of the Council of Australian Governments (COAG) just elected Premier of Queensland Campbell Newman declared the days of cooperative federalism were over! Clearly it is not just economics which influences the outcomes of education reform! When COAG met in April 2013 to discuss education reform they did not reach agreement and many in the commentariat suggested COAG be disbanded.

The last 40 years in Australia have seen profound changes in every level of the education system. Melbourne University's Professor Richard Teese points out that States equivocation about Australian Government funding of education—'it might erode their rights'—were moderated through the expansion of activity after World War 2 (Teese 2011). The Whitlam government established an interim Committee for the Australian Schools Commission chaired by Professor Peter Karmel in December 1972. It was intended to examine the needs of schools and advise on school financing. The Committee's recommendations advocated needs-based funding to ensure that all schools achieved minimum acceptable standards. As a result Australian Government recurrent funding was extended to non-government schools. Special funding programs were introduced for disadvantaged schools, special education, teacher professional development and innovation. Triennial grants to the States for recurrent and capital costs as well as for targeted programs began in 1973 and continued through the 1980s, variously modified.

From 1976 grants to non-government schools were linked to the average cost of maintaining students in government schools. In Teese's words, these systems did not survive the tensions of competing political agendas… By the time the enrolment effects of Commonwealth policies had become evident, no framework existed for either managing choice or integrating the efforts of Commonwealth and State and Territory governments around agreed national priorities. Nor was there any clear view of the respective roles of Commonwealth and State/Territory governments in the funding of schools and the framing of educational policy. The result is a plethora of arrangements typical of much of Australia's ongoing government programs at all levels in many areas of public policy and substantial confusion about the multiplicity of ways of funding (Dowling 2007).

An extended essay summarises recent policy development in Australia. Another, drawing on OECD studies, compares the achievements of various countries.

1.7 Where Should We Start?

My interest in seeking a greater understanding of the progress in education reform most recently was heightened by the statements made by two visitors to Australia in 2008. Expatriate Australian, US citizen and media magnate Rupert Murdoch, delivering the fourth of his Boyer lectures on ABC Radio National in November 2008, reminded Australians, 'The unvarnished truth is that in countries such as Australia, Britain, and particularly the US, our public education systems are a disgrace'. Murdoch went on to express concern that 'lesser schools are leaving far too many children innumerate, illiterate, and ignorant of our history. These are the people whose future I am most concerned about…' He called for more corporate involvement from business leaders 'who knew better than government officials what skills were needed for people to get ahead in the twenty-first century'. Poor performance could not be accepted any more than bad coffee.

Then New York City Education Department Chancellor Joel Klein, interviewed just before his visit to Australia in November 2008, pointed to a stagnant New York education system despite a doubling of investment in education reform. He described the New York education system as 'having a dysfunctional culture which could not be saved just by more money'. He asserted that he was transforming the system on 'a backbone of accountability'. Klein left New York City education in 2010 to join Rupert Murdoch's organisation, initially to join the investigation of allegations of phone hacking in Britain and eventually to head the education operations of News Corporation. Klein's New York school reforms later ended up as farce with his claims of achievements shown to be incapable of substantiation.

The endorsement by then Education Minister Julia Gillard and Prime Minister Kevin Rudd of the statements of Murdoch and Klein, implying agreement with the reforms in the US, continue to be regarded by anyone familiar with the US education scene as very odd and indeed inappropriate! But then the landscape has changed in the last 4 years!

Australia tends to look overseas for solutions, especially to the US and before that to the UK, in almost everything. Still! But the fact is that in the US numerous very costly interventions over the last 20 or so years have led to little apparent gain in student achievement. Expenditure per student and time spent by teachers are greater than in other countries. It had been observed that from 1980 to 2005 in the US spend per student increased by 73 % and the student-to-teacher ratio declined by 18 % but little improvement was seen in student results. The administration of President George W Bush responded in 2001, by adopting with bipartisan support, legislation entitled 'No Child Left Behind' (NCLB). It mandated ongoing improvement as measured by standardised tests in literacy and numeracy. Creativity and education expert Sir Ken Robinson reminds audiences that such a program gives the lie to the proposition that Americans do not understand irony.

The Obama administration adopted a new program, 'Race to the Top' which amongst other things encouraged new charter schools funded by government but also supported privately. In his 2011 State of the Union address President Obama claimed the program to be 'the most meaningful reform of our public schools in a generation'. Early in 2013 he promised to introduce universal pre-school.

In the UK, reforms under the Blair Labour Government achieved mixed results. Private organisations were offered the opportunity to run schools ('academies'), an office for standards in education (Offsted) was established, performance-related pay was introduced, contracts awarded to companies to devise criteria for assessing teacher effectiveness, consultants were hired to train head teachers how to assess their staff and so on. Debate about effectiveness of the reforms was frequent. Improvements seemed illusory. Problems were identified with the testing regime which led some to claim they diminished the capability of young people leaving school to function effectively in the workplace.

The new coalition government in Britain, dominated by the Conservative Party elected in 2010, continued some of the Blair and Brown Labour governments reforms and not others: academies are to be encouraged, university student fees are to be increased.

What is clear about the new accountability regime which has been introduced in some other countries including Norway and Italy is that it has represented a considerable opportunity for business, not just in the traditionally rich text book industry but in books about testing and how to pass tests, in coaching and in areas relating to emerging demands placed on teachers such as tests for competency and emotional intelligence.

Australia seldom looks for inspiration to Europe or Asia except in relation to economic gain. That is more than unfortunate! In Finland, in some other European countries and some South East Asian countries, different strategies to improve education emerged. Educators from all over the world have flocked to Finland to seek understanding of the system which produced the world's top performing students in international tests for the last 15 years or so but did not necessarily implement changes in their own countries when they returned. When Finland's director of education, Pasi Sahlberg, visited Australia in 2012 he made the important point that Finland did not set out to design its education system to be the best but to ensure equity in the system.

1.8 The Questions to be Answered

A major conclusion from the research for these essays is that there is a wealth of literature on education and all relevant issues. It is unfortunately not always referenced and sometimes when it is, entirely wrong conclusions are drawn. The essays on Australian policy and on international comparisons therefore seek to elucidate the major elements of reforms in various countries and identify those strategies which have led to improvements.

Almost every day some influential person or group claims education to be of extraordinary importance for the future. Yet the next day, funding is reduced because of the alleged need to trim government budgets. Or some other reason. The view that teachers are important does not translate to high relative salaries and improved conditions.

It is extraordinary surely that governments can consider it economically and politically sensible to subsidise the manufacture of aluminium, the growing of corn to turn it into corn syrup and drilling for oil but not subsidise investment in education, urban planning and other areas including decent public housing which would reduce crime, increase health and wellbeing, increase employment and in the end increase government revenue.

Education doesn't finish at school or even university. And even more importantly, it isn't simply what the student knows at the end of the day that determines whether our education system is successful. Creativity is in greater demand than ever because of the vast array of challenges that face us but the nature of it and its links with innovation are mostly not understood.

Society can go on spending vast amounts of money in unproductive activities such as policing, imprisonment and other forms of control as well as large social security outlays. Or it can instead invest in overturning the factors which are contributing to disadvantage and all the destructive outcomes of it, outcomes the cost of which we refuse to recognise, or worse leave others to pay!

In the end education arguably is where our attempts to chart a meaningful future and work out how to meet the ever greater challenges have to start. We aren't making a good fist of it in many countries, not least because we aren't thinking deeply about what is happening in those systems where students really are successful and how their approaches might be applied locally taking account of whatever differences are important. We aren't thinking about how as a collection of communities we might work out sensible ways of reaching appropriate conclusions about how to achieve agreement on what we want of the world. We are denying our humanity. In some countries truth is being overwhelmed by pre-Enlightenment dogma. That education should be a free publicly funded system precisely because the benefits are overwhelmingly to the public domain is put aside and the right to have a choice of school promoted as a democratic right.

Far more attention is needed to the learning environment, the influence of teachers, parents, peers and the perceived values of society, to the nature of society, perceptions of social justice and the influence of economic and political views on the capacity of mothers in their earliest nurturing of the young child and on young adolescents as they emerge into adulthood. More understanding is needed of how we judge success, how leaders exercise judgement. Everyone agrees that education is important but that isn't enough!

We complain that young people can't spell but ignore the huge consequences of the poor judgements made every day by those with influence. Intellectual laziness

1.8 The Questions to be Answered

is common: even professionals engaged in knowledge work, especially in areas less exposed to market competition or hindered by central control, are often too busy to access the latest literature outside their own area of expertise and so do not seek different solutions from seemingly unrelated disciplines and fields of knowledge even when they would provide innovative ways to advance. Pursuing agreement rather than exploring and encouraging constructive dissent is too common in decision-making. What others say prevails over independent analysis.

Two examples. Almost everyone has enthusiastically embraced social media but government and business in many areas have hardly taken advantage of the way information technology and communication (ICT) can contribute to an improved worklife from working from home to better time management to facilitation of meetings. Too much time is spent in government on ensuring compliance with process so as to avoid charges of waste. Inadequate judgement is common in hiring staff, in performance management and in strategic planning and too much time is spent on exercises like psychological profiling, branding and interpreting the views of focus groups and the popular media.

The National Broadband Network (NBN) in Australia is intended to bring faster internet speeds to everyone through fibre rather than cable which was used in the past; the capital outlay by the Commonwealth Government is substantial. It receives constant criticism, usually referring to other countries and technological alternatives. But the comparisons are often problematic or invalid: many other countries are investing in high speed internet. The view is promoted that the NBN is government waste though by how much seems lately to be difficult to calculate. In the process the potential of the NBN to revolutionising healthcare, micromanaging energy distribution through the smart grid and facilitating access by children in remote schools to teachers anywhere in the world are ignored (Ross 2012).

What can all this say about the success of our education system and the judgement of the critics? Sociologist James March, who collaborated with Nobel economics prize-winner Herbert Simon, pointed out that problems are often put together with whatever solutions are around at the time (March 1982). At the moment those solutions turn out to rest on the failures of the judgement by the market and the commentary of economists whose opinions are often wrong and based on information seldom revealed. More of humanity is ignored than can be sustained.

In thinking about education, and any other important issue of public concern, we might recall that rationality has lately provided the means by which we got here but creativity illuminated the goals for which we might strive and the strategies to reach them.

Distinguished Australian scientist, one-time science adviser to the British Government and President of the Royal Society, Lord Robert May, presented the 2007 Lowey Lecture on Australia and the World (Williams 2007). In talking of the critical issues facing us he said, 'We're faced with problems that are both unprecedented and serious caused by human numbers and associated impacts exceeding the globe's sustainable limits. The problems are not yet insuperable. But to solve them we require a paradoxical mixture; not only the questioning fact-based spirit of the Enlightenment to acknowledge the problems and seek solutions to them, but also people and institutions showing high levels of cooperative behaviour, the evolutionary origins of which may well be associated with inflexible and authoritarian beliefs and structures which are antithetic to such a questioning spirit.'

References

Dowling, A. (2007). *Australia's school funding system*. Melbourne: ACER. Retrieved August 28, 2012, from http://www.acer.edu.au/documents/PolicyBriefs_Dowling07.pdf

Hein, G. (2012). *Progressive museum practice: John Dewey and democracy*. Walnut Creek: Left Coast Press.

Irvine, J. (2012, May 25). More fiction than fact in talk of poor productivity. *Sydney Morning Herald*.

March, J. G. (1982). Theories of choice and making decisions. *Society, 1982*, 29–39.

McAuley, I. (2012a). *The Australian economy will our prosperity be short-lived?* Albert Park: The Australian Collaboration. Retrieved September 8, 2012, from http://www.australiancollaboration.com.au/pdf/Essays/The-Australian-Economy.pdf

McAuley, I. (2012b, October 8). Why are we living beyond our means? *New Matilda*.

Ross, N. (2012, April 27). The coalitions NBN: Cheaper or a false economy. *ABC The Drum* Retrieved October 12, 2012, from http://www.abc.net.au/technology/articles/2012/04/27/3490479.htm

Teese, R. (2011, September 30). From opportunity to outcomes. The changing role of public schooling in Australia and national funding arrangements. *Australian Policy Online*. Retrieved September 12, 2012, from http://apo.org.au/research/opportunity-outcomes-changing-role-public-schooling-australia-and-national-funding-arrangem

Tiffen, R., & Gittins, R. (2009). *How Australia compares* (2nd ed.). Melbourne: Cambridge University Press.

Williams, R. (presenter) (2007 December 1). Robert may and our greatest challenge ever. *ABC RN The Science Show*. Retrieved October 13, 2012, from http://www.abc.net.au/radionational/programs/scienceshow/robert-may-and-our-greatest-challenge-ever/3290620

Yates, L. (2005 June 7). *What can schools do? knowledge, social identities and the changing world*. Inaugural professorial lecture. Melbourne university faculty of education deans lecture series 2005. Retrieved August 28, 2012, from www.edfac.unimelb.edu.au/news/lectures/pdf/lynlecture.pdf

Chapter 2
A Word on Economics

Economists are not some innocent technicians who did a decent job within the narrow confines of their expertise until they were collectively wrong-footed by a once-in-a-century disaster that no one could have predicted… Economics as it has been practised in the last three decades has been positively harmful for most people.

British political philosopher, author and former School Professor of European Thought at the London School of Economics John Gray (2010) reviewing Ha-Joon Chang's book, 23 *Things They Don't Tell You About Capitalism.*

Capitalism is best conceived and practised, runs the theory, by hunter-gatherer bankers and entrepreneurs owing no allegiance to the state or society. This is nonsense. Business and the state co-generate wealth in a system of complex mutual dependence. Markets are beset by mood swings and uncertainty which, if not offset by government action, lead to violent oscillations. Capitalism without responsibility or proportionality degrades into racketeering and exploitation.

Will Hutton (2011). The ailing euro is part of a wider crisis. Our capitalist system is near meltdown. *The Observer* 18 September.

2.1 Economics and Education Reform

There seem to be two worlds in which education reform, along with everything else, proceeds. In one a purely statistical and theoretical view of economics prevails. In the other sociology, a view informed by studies of the social interaction of people. To move from the former view to the latter is to enter through a kind of 'green door' from a society dominated by individual utility maximisation to one more concerned with social value, one which recognises the sometimes irrational behaviour of people. One is based entirely in theory and has a utility related to its alleged predictability derived from sophisticated mathematics, a predictability which in most cases is at best difficult to test. The other is supported by extensive research on what people value and what they do not and how they actually behave and how that is influenced by their stated values.

This essay reviews the various approaches to economics and especially considers the nature of neoclassical economics and its consequences, ultimately for the advance of society at large and particularly education. I review the basic approaches of neoclassical economics and then the evidence for its failures and inadequacies. I believe it is clear that not only has neoclassical economics led to substantial inequities and disruptions in society but driven education reforms in a wholly negative direction largely favouring the more privileged in society. In the final analysis, neoclassical economics does not appropriately describe human society and human behaviour. That is a view in fact held by many prominent economists and supported by research.

If any reader thinks this essay is too harsh or not relevant, they might take the time to watch at least the trailers of the films, *The Inside Job*, *Company Men* and *The Corporation*. There are many comments on economics and the world of commerce far harsher than anything I say in this essay. It has been observed, for instance by Madeleine Bunting in *The Guardian* of 30 May 2011 that *Inside Job* does for banking what *An Inconvenient Truth* did for climate change.

Economics as a discipline is not to be uniformly distrusted: much of it is based on well analysed empirical data, even over the long run. Much of it is intellectually challenging. But the economics which dominates society in most western countries is not like that and the popular economic commentary which dominates much of the media, especially the daily diet of 'analysis' of movements, actual or predicted, of various indicators and issues such as government budgets, is often worse! The carefully reasoned analysis found in print media such as the *New York Review of Books* and the business pages of some of the broadsheets seldom gets to the front page and certainly seldom reaches the minds of politicians or some so-called think tanks whose conclusions are overwhelmed by their preconceived ideologies.

2.2 The Basics of Neoclassical Economics

Whilst economics is in reality a mixture of sociology and statistics, the prevailing view over the last 40 or so years has largely ignored sociology and the statistics have become sophisticated, even arcane. Moreover what is readily analysed and for which there is substantial data is the focus whilst the more difficult and the rare event is put aside. Humans are viewed as rational utility maximisers motivated principally by financial incentives, competition is considered to drive people and therefore organisations towards efficiency and therefore lower prices for goods and services.

The market is self regulating and ultimately acts as a clearing house reconciling conflicts, economic growth is the path to society's greater wealth and the solution to problems such as the need for more jobs. Deleterious consequences, such as increasing inequality, are seldom considered. Government intervention is eschewed. Neoclassical economics has driven the agenda of public policy, usually referred to as neoliberalism, for several decades.

As a matter of course, costs of transactions which cannot be directly charged, particularly those which would seem to apply generally such as public goods like water and forests, are considered to be externalities and are not counted in the pricing. Pollution produced by coal fired power stations is not included in calculating the cost to the energy generator, and therefore is not charged to the consumer: consequently the cost has to be met at a later time, usually by the government, in other words the public.

Where the resource is not replaceable there is no brake on its consumption. This situation is captured by the well known phrase, 'capitalise the gains and socialise the losses': the transfer of billions of dollars from governments to banks to stave off likely financial collapse following the GFC is an example. Many of these activities receive government subsidy whilst at the same time those who benefit declaim against subsidies for other activities. The result is a distortion of choice. Heavily subsidised sport is often compared with less well subsidised arts activities, a frequently expressed view being that the arts should pay for themselves.

Consumption is favoured as the engine of growth and a larger population is needed to help achieve that. Innovative technology is believed to arise to solve any problems which might emerge. Individuals are favoured over communities. Individuals are considered responsible for their future welfare other than in exceptional circumstances. That growth in consumption cannot continue indefinitely seems not apparent to those economists whose opinions are quoted every day in the media as various statistics are reeled off to a seemingly ignorant population.

Professor John Quiggin of the University of Queensland has summarised five significant ideas central to neococlassical economics which have little or no basis in fact but continue to be treated as valid (Quiggin 2010):

- the notion that the period beginning in 1985 was one of unparalleled macroeconomic stability which has been comprehensively refuted by the GFC,
- the efficient market hypothesis which asserts that the prices generated by financial markets represent the best possible estimate of the value of any investment which has been shown to be absurd by events such as the dot-com bubble, macroeconomic analysis should not be concerned with observable realities such as booms and busts but with theoretical consequences of optimizing behaviour by rational actors—branded by Paul Krugman as mistaking beauty for truth,
- the trickle down hypothesis which supposes that polices benefitting the wealthy will eventually help everyone which was conclusively refuted by postwar experience and the extraordinarily limited economic mobility in countries like the USA (and the experience of the last several decades in which inequities in wealth have increased enormously),
- privatisation, the notion that nearly any function undertaken by government would be done more effectively and efficiently by the private sector which has simply replaced public monopoly with private monopoly whilst numerous commercial entities have had to seek government bailouts.

2.3 Individuals and Choice: Limits to Government

The theoretical base of neoclassical economics derives from the writings of a number of economists, especially at the University of Chicago, who had arrived there from Europe, most particularly Austria, in the years after the close of the First World War (Judt 2009). They had experienced the failure of a centralised economy: therefore a different economic model was needed. Notable among them were Friedrich Hayek and Joseph Schumpeter. Milton Friedman of the University of Chicago became the principal promoter of neoclassical economics after the Second World War and received the Nobel Prize for his efforts. These views found fertile ground in a country with an ideology grounded in individual freedom and choice and a belief that commerce must be free from government 'interference'.

Social democracy, its advocacy for intervention by government at appropriate times, such as when benefits to the community would not otherwise be provided and its concern for the community at large including those less fortunate, as advocated by the English economist John Maynard Keynes, was left behind in the latter day striving for individual gain.

Private enterprise in the context of neoliberal philosophy is considered inherently able to perform more efficiently than government. Government is believed to be a brake on, to crowd out, the free operation of business and the market which itself is (asserted to be) self regulating. Indeed business, including the media, is said to be self-regulating, even in the face of appalling invasions of privacy through hacking of personal phones, not to mention frequent failures to report issues bearing on important matters because of political positions adopted by particular media. Attempts by government to even consider regulation are attacked as unnecessary intrusions into the market and as attacks on free speech. When numerous financial institutions grossly overreached themselves governments rushed to bail them out: the ordinary citizens who suffered through loss of their houses as a result of foreclosures and so on were largely ignored, left to fend for themselves.

The first responsibility of business enterprises is now considered to be the generation of wealth for shareholders, not the provision of goods or services to customers at an optimal quality and price, which once was seen as the purpose. A tension is asserted to exist between the motivation of executives on the one hand and the shareholders. Boards, representing the shareholders, therefore need performance targets to assist oversight and ensure transparency and accountability.

Managerialism—management in every enterprise is a management function—has become dominant in government over the last 30 years supported by business lobby groups. Senior executives are appointed on fixed terms and enrolled in merit pay schemes. Investment in training and development is poor; all but core functions are outsourced. Public–private partnerships for infrastructure projects are favoured though they ended up costing more than they would have if they were managed within government, partly because of unfavourable interest rates on debt. Guarantees to pay the commercial partner in the event of loss and excessively optimistic financial estimates mean increasing government debt (Walker and Walker 2008). Substantial downsizing led to significant loss of corporate memory and inability to manage complex contracts. Financial matters and corporate functions have achieved greater prominence.

All of this has led, in some countries, to an undermining of democratic government through the marginalisation of parliament and parliamentary accountability by the head of government and senior ministers and advisors (Foster 2005). UK Prime Minister Tony Blair replaced cabinet by 'prime ministerial government', Australian Prime Minister Kevin Rudd was notable for the way he and three other Ministers controlled all cabinet decisions (Marr 2010).

Above all effectiveness has been conflated with efficiency, microeconomic reform such as holding wages down, reducing extra allowances for overtime and so on, has led to decline in commitment to the enterprise and therefore a decline in productivity (Gittins 2011a). Despite this these strategies continue and so does the drive to reduce employee benefits. No reference was made to the substantial evidence about these matters when the Business Council of Australia and others praised the decision of Fair Work Australia to allow employees to trade off their holidays and other benefits for higher wages.

In Australia, Prime Minister Gillard agreed February 2012 to establish a Business Advisory Forum, 'to advise governments on how best to coordinate and progress the remaining areas of competition and regulatory reform; and to nominate new areas of regulatory reform that will help lift productivity and drive investment' (Anon 2012).

By way of contrast, in many European countries governments still provide high levels of social welfare without negative consequences for the economy and productivity levels. Interestingly, French people spend more time eating and more time sleeping than the average for people in OECD countries and have amongst the very highest life expectancy. As widely reported, in the 2010–2011 global competitiveness ranking compiled by the World Economic Forum France was ranked 15th, having risen 15 places in 5 years, ahead of Australia (which had fallen 5 places in 5 years); the US was fourth after Switzerland, Sweden and Singapore. By 2012 Switzerland was first followed by Singapore and Finland, then Sweden; the US was 7th and Australia 20th ahead of France.

Importantly there is increasing interest in constructing an index representing many different aspects of life to sit alongside such strictly economic indicators as Gross National Product or GDP which measures only economic performance and that somewhat unreliably. Compilation of an index of social progress for Australia has recently started; the OECD began publishing its 'better life index' in 2011 (Gittins 2011b). Yet neoclassical economics consistently emphasises choices relating to material goals and links pursuit of such goals to happiness. Much of the striving for material goods amounts to no more than a seeking of positional goods, things which relate only to attaining status in the eyes of others. Things are acquired to impress others whom one doesn't know very well and who actually don't care anyway.

2.4 Privatisation of Government Services

The consequences of these changes have been disastrous in some cases and led to declines in quality of service in most cases!

In Bolivia the World Bank made water privatization a condition of a loan to the government. The public water system was privatized in 1997, sold to a water company owned by a consortium led by the French water giant Suez, the World Bank and others. (A report in 2005 on water privatisation in Latin America by Puerto Rican journalist Carmelo Ruiz Marrero is featured on numerous websites.). Nine years later the Bolivian government cancelled the contract with Aguas del Illimani following several days of public protests in El Alto, a satellite city of La Paz, at overcharging of customers and failure to invest enough to expand water services to poor neighbourhoods; costs to connect to the system exceeded more than half a year's income at the Bolivian minimum wage. Similar outcomes have occurred in other countries.

The clever salesmanship and development of sophisticated mathematically-based financial instruments sold in complicated ways to other enterprises and eventually to investors who ended up losing their money and their property is a typical outcome of the GFC. In Jefferson County in Alabama USA, the county seat of which is the city of Birmingham, a sewage system project originally estimated to cost around $250 millions ended up costing several billions after complicated interest rate swaps were arranged by corrupt country officials and bank officers. County employees lost their jobs, a number of people were paid ongoing bribes, the banks ended up being fined, sewage rates were increased; at the end the county was left with a debt equal to more than $4,000 per resident. In November 2011 leaders of the Jefferson County voted to file for a $4.1bn bankruptcy, the costliest US municipal failure ever (Anon 2011).

The notion that in general, the private sector performs more efficiently than government is an exaggeration and in some cases, wrong! A comprehensive study by Christopher Stone at the Centre for Policy Development in Australia shows that in terms of technical efficiency, doing the same job more cheaply, the stripping out of expertise in government agencies in order to contract out the work led to projects costing more than when technical expertise was retained (Stone 2013a, b). Analysing the much criticised 'Building the Education Revolution' or BER, wrongly characterised by some as wasting a lot of money, costed significantly more in New South Wales and Victoria which had to rely entirely on external contractors than in Queensland which has maintained a relatively strong public works skills capacity.

Private schools, private hospitals and private health insurance, for instance, are not more efficient than single public systems. Public–private partnerships are more expensive and the private sector certainly does not address 'dynamic efficiency', such as investing in high speed rail. Unfortunately in Australia, risk-averse governments won't either, continuing to build roads when clearly public transport would achieve much greater efficiency with less cost to the environment. And certainly regulations and work practices are not better enforced in the private sector, quite the reverse.

Stone concludes, 'Our public sector suffers the plight of the anorexic. No matter how thin it gets there are voices saying it's too fat. Do we really want a size zero government? The word 'efficiency' is often misused to mean 'cuts', and some cuts to public services can end up costing us much more than they save. When it comes to privatisation or outsourcing, too many of our politicians have tunnel vision. They can only see the private sector as efficient and are blind when it fails…' The benefits and disadvantages of outsourcing and privatisation need to be carefully considered instead of adopting endless cuts to the public sector through 'a blind faith in market solutions'

2.5 The Global Financial Crisis and Its Consequences

The GFC has significantly increased unemployment in many countries including the US and Europe. That has been further exacerbated by the response of governments to the huge debt incurred through their bail out of banks and other actions. Many banks in those countries had loaned excessive amounts of money for purchase of housing, often without proper consideration of the alibility of borrowers to repay the loans. When housing prices crashed as a result of bank's risky lending, many borrowers found their debt greatly exceeding the revised value of their housing. In many cases they remained liable for the debt even when their home was resumed by the lender.

Revisions of legislation which might limit the recurrence of further actions of the kind which led to the GFC met with strong opposition from the financial industry. However, financial institutions resumed their payment of large bonuses to executives not long after governments bailed them out.

A legion of economic writers, Nobel Prize winning economists and others, have filled the pages of scholarly journals, newspapers, magazines and the radio airwaves and television screens with commentary pointing to the failure of the financial system and its economic base. Paul Krugman, Professor of Economics at Princeton University, 2008 Nobel Prizewinner and *New York Times* columnist, observes, 'the economics profession went astray because economists, as a group, mistook beauty, clad in impressive-looking mathematics, for truth. Until the Great Depression, most economists clung to a vision of capitalism as a perfect or nearly perfect system. That vision wasn't sustainable in the face of mass unemployment, but as memories of the Depression faded, economists fell back in love with the old, idealized vision of an economy in which rational individuals interact in perfect markets, this time gussied up with fancy equations.' (Krugman 2009).

Influential lobbyists work hard to convince governments that they themselves should reduce expenditures and deficits, that excessive control of financial institutions would produce serious distortions and economic hardship. Professor Andrew Kakabadse, Professor of International Management Development at

Cranfield University School of Management in the UK and author of the book *The Elephant Hunters* (Lake, Kakabadse and Kakabadse 2008) about the GFC, told Phillip Adams, presenter of the ABC RN program *Late Night Live* in October 2008 that senior managers reporting their concerns about the future consequences of sophisticated financial instruments such as credit default swaps and the like can be informed by their executives and boards that their concern is misplaced and not conducive to further employment.

Staff of financial entities and officials at the highest levels, as well as academic economists, have failed to consider the possibilities of unlikely events. A week of intense discussions amongst leading academic economists at a workshop on modelling financial markets in 2008 (Collander 2008) concluded, 'The economics profession appears to have been unaware of the long build-up to the current worldwide financial crisis and to have significantly underestimated its dimensions once it started to unfold. In our view, this lack of understanding is due to a misallocation of research efforts in economics... The economics profession has failed in communicating the limitations, weaknesses, and even dangers of its preferred models to the public.'

Those conclusions closely resemble the views of Nassim Taleb, essayist, mathematical trader and author of *The Black Swan*. Taleb's central belief is scepticism about the predictability of markets and people's biases in the attribution of skills, how we are fooled by randomness (Taleb 2004). 'Much of what happens in history', he notes, 'comes from Black Swan dynamics, very large, sudden, and totally unpredictable outliers, while much of what we usually talk about is almost pure noise. Our track record in predicting those events is dismal; yet by some mechanism called the hindsight bias we think that we understand them. We have a bad habit of finding 'laws' in history (by fitting stories to events and detecting false patterns); we are drivers looking through the rear view mirror while convinced we are looking ahead.' Taleb advances these ideas in his latest book, *Antifragile*. (See Sect. 11.2)

In February 2008, the President of the French Republic, Nicholas Sarkozy, unsatisfied with the present state of statistical information about the economy and the society, asked three leading economists, Joseph Stiglitz, Amartya Sen and Jean Paul Fitoussi to create an investigative Commission, subsequently called 'The Commission on the Measurement of Economic Performance and Social Progress' (Stiglitz, Sen and Fitoussi 2009).

The Commission concluded that the low level of public trust in official figures has a clear impact on the way in which public discourse about the conditions of the economy and necessary policies takes place.

Three years on from the depths of the GFC, problems remained which had not been born by financial institutions. Madeleine Bunting (2011) writing in *The Guardian* newspaper proclaims that 'outrage against the banks is no longer a leftwing hobby as the fact that the greed and irresponsibility of some in the financial community were the cause'. Bunting observes '… finance has intertwined itself intimately into the political process in both the US and the UK.' In many cases banks are failing to meet their targets of lending agreed with governments who bailed them out.

Lobbying has ensured some crucial reform initiatives hit the buffers (Taibbi 2011b). Senior executives in the Securities and Exchange Commission in the US authorized systematic destruction of the records of preliminary investigations of possible crimes by financial institutions, where decisions had been made not to proceed further. Those executives are frequently appointed to senior positions in the companies which the SEC had been investigating.

In November 2011 Nobel prizewinner and Columbia University professor Joseph Stiglitz, noted economic analyst Nouriel Roubini and biographer of Keynes Robert Skidelsky, writing on the Project Syndicate website, all strongly criticised the increasing inequality brought about by the exercise of political influence and the anti-competitive practices of financial institutions (Stiglitz), strongly urged easing of monetary policy by the European Central Bank to reflate the Eurozone periphery and criticised fiscal austerity (Roubini) and urged that a growth strategy be adopted by the Europeans (Skidelsky). All criticized the refusal of the German Government and the European Central Bank to take a more interventionist role. Paul Krugman, in numerous articles in the *New York Times*, has consistently urged similar approaches.

The austerity budgets adopted by peripheral economies of the European Union have meant shrinkage of the economy: yet an expansion of the private sector was anticipated by some economists as justifying the austerity! That in turn has meant a decline in jobs—employment prospects in the UK have been described as the worst for almost a year (Allen 2011): large numbers of skilled young professionals are leaving for South America and Australia. Quite how the decline in the professional workforce will assist economic growth in later years remains a puzzle to put it mildly. As well, poorer people are in some cases abandoning their very young children, no longer able to care for them (Hadjimatheou 2012). In the US survival through the economic downturn for some pensioners has meant selling their pensions for a lump-sum payment. Repayment of debt is treated as a moral issue. One of the alternative ways in which a country's debt could be dealt with is to institute a scheme comparable with the US system of Chapter 11 bankruptcy which would allow writing off of old debt and borrowing to finance new growth (Kuttner 2013).

And when glaring errors are found in the methods and forecasts made by economists, workarounds are found and nothing much changes. JP Morgan's "London Whale" venture went bad because modellers divided by a sum instead of an average; the calculations leading to the view that once government debt reached 90 % of gross domestic product economic growth dropped off was shown to be due to an Excel spreadsheet error (Krugman 2013a, b) which was uncovered by an economics student! These revelations had little effect. In the case of the miscalculation of the impact of government debt, the economists involved, Carmen Reinhart and Kenneth Rogoff of Harvard, faced criticism from the start, yet have continued to promote their views. But as Paul Krugman observed, another dubious piece of economic analysis will be found to be canonised by the 'usual suspects' and the depression will go on. 'Policy makers abandoned the unemployed and turned to austerity because they wanted to, not because they had to.' The proposition that governments should not spend more than they gain in revenue is astonishingly pervasive: the view is that countries that run up large debt, such as Greece, Spain, Portugal and Ireland, have to be punished. The consequences have been disastrous.

The head of the International Monetary Fund (IMF), Christine Lagarde, expressed great concern at the policies of the UK government but it made little difference. Chancellor George Osborne was told to invest more in social housing, schools and road repairs (Elliott 2013). Early in 2013 the IMF revealed that whereas they had previously asserted that for every dollar governments reduced their budgets, economic growth would be reduced by half that, in fact the impact was three times greater, $1.50 instead of 50c. Did European countries halt their austerity measures which have driven millions into unemployment? No. These developments were not recalled either when the Grattan Institute in Australia in late April 2013 forecast years of government debt at all levels; other analysts rushed to agree. Commentators spoke in authoritative voices pointing out that belts would have to be tightened: Australians had come to expect too much from governments! The relatively tiny level of government debt and the relatively small budget deficits were ignored. It was all reduced to the frame of our household!

Equities markets are supposed to be responsive to economic trends and be self regulating. Four years after the research was first announced, statements are appearing that 'the world could be heading for a major economic crisis as stock markets inflate an investment bubble in fossil fuels to the tune of trillions of dollars' (Carrington 2013). A report by Nicholas, Lord Stern of the UK pointed out that almost all investors and regulators were failing to take note of the research by scientists at Potsdam Institute for Climate Impact Research in Germany, published in 2009 (Meinshausen et al. 2009; Eickemeier 2009), which concluded less than a quarter of the proven fossil fuel reserves can be burnt and emitted between now and 2050, if global warming is to be limited to two degrees Celsius (2 °C).

A report, *Unburnable Carbon* 2013, prepared by the Carbon Tracker Initiative and the London School of Economics' Grantham Research Institute (Hutton 2013) showed that stock markets worldwide are cumulatively valuing coal, oil and energy companies' huge reserves of fossil fuels as if they will all be burned and every year spending billions of dollars on finding new reserves. In other words, there is either a carbon bubble with investors and companies wildly over-speculating on the value of owning fuel reserves that can never be burned, or nobody believes there is the remotest chance that the world will stick to the limits on fossil fuel use congruent with containing global warming.

Novelist and writer on ethnography, history, and social theory Richard Sennett points to the way these countries deal with this unemployment: leave it to voluntary associations (Sennett 2011). He points out that different solutions are found along Europe's northern rim—in Scandinavia, Germany and the Netherlands. There governments have protected established companies, especially small companies, providing capital for growth when banks won't lend it. Norway and Sweden have made concerted efforts to include young people in starter jobs; youth unemployment stands at about 8 %. Germans put big resources into youth training schemes; the Dutch effectively supplement the wages of part-time employees.

Factories in these countries have long explored how to deal humanely with automation, and tried in many different ways to counteract the outsourcing of jobs.

A survey of 11,000 people in 23 countries in late 2011 found unemployment to be the world's fastest-rising worry (Gregory 2011). Welfare changes imposed by the UK government have impacted those least able to afford them. Of the jobs lost in the aftermath of the GFC a disproportionate number have been one's in construction, manufacturing and high finance, jobs traditionally occupied by men (Rosin 2012). The lessons of President F.D. Roosevelt in overcoming the Great Depression of the 1930s in the US have been ignored (Bennett and Walker 2011).

2.6 An Alternative View: Lessons from Behavioural Economics

Studies by Daniel Kahneman, winner of the Nobel Prize in Economics in 2002, and Amos Tversky, contradict the claim that the freest market produces the best economic outcome but rather than being the rational individual, maximizing utility in an institutional vacuum imagined by the market model they are real people (Kuttner 1997). 'People will typically charge more to give something up than to acquire the identical article… People help strangers, return wallets, leave generous tips in restaurants they will never visit again, give donations to public radio when theory would predict they would rationally "free-ride", and engage in other acts that suggest they value general norms of fairness. To conceive of altruism as a special form of selfishness misses the point utterly.'

Economist George Akerlof, Professor at the University of California Berkeley, shared the 2001 Nobel Prize for Economics with Joseph Stiglitz. In a celebrated address in 2007 he pointed out that the omission of people's normative behaviour from economists' models results in quite important deviations of predictions from behaviour which is actually observed: positive economics privileges models without norms… He concludes 'Economic decisions may not be as duplicable as biological processes, but the basic reason why science intensively studies the microscopic applies to economics as well. The individual economic unit, be it a firm, a consumer, or an employee, behaves the way it does *for a reason.* And if these actors behave as they do for a reason, we can expect to find those reasons from the structures that we see in close observation; and because of those structures their behavior will also tend to be duplicated.' (Akerlof 2007)

Studies of behavioural economics have attracted increasing attention (Cassidy 2008, McAuley 2010). They show that people tend to be subject to mental quirks and biases including inertia, overconfidence and loss aversion.

Levels of cooperative behaviour and reciprocity, perception of and tolerance for inequalities in society differ amongst people, especially between Asian societies and western societies. Whilst intrinsic self esteem as expressed by association of self with positive events and feelings may not differ, extrinsic self-esteem expressed as preparedness to admit positive feelings about one's self differ substantially, being low in east Asian societies and high in western societies (Mitchell 2010). Statistics compiled by the OECD (2011) and by Gert Hoffstede, Dutch pioneer in his research of cross-cultural groups and organizations, available on his website, elucidate these points.

Tim Jackson, Professor of Sustainability at the University of Surrey, pointed out in his Deakin Lecture in Melbourne in 2010 (Jackson 2010) 'Prosperity without Growth' that the concept of prosperity as an ongoing drive for growth is inconsistent with human nature. He observed that in fact prosperity is not about income growth but about health of family, trust of friends, security of one's community, participation in the life of society '… just asking people in the street tells you that prosperity… is about some sense perhaps of having a meaningful life and a hope for the future… 'there is no evidence in social psychology that we really are the narrow, materialistic, selfish, individualistic consumers that the economy would have us believe that we are. Social psychology talks much more about tensions between selfishness and other regarding behaviour. It talks about tensions between novelty seeking and conservation and tradition. All of these poles of these traditions, matter… We evolved as much as social beings as we did as individual beings. We evolved as much in laying down the foundations for a stable society as we did in continually pursuing novelty… The consumer economy', Jackson concluded, 'has preferred novelty-seeking selfish behaviour because that is what we need to keep the system going.'

Jackson quoted French President Sarkozy, launching the Commission on the Measurement of Economic Performance and Social Progress: 'The financial crisis doesn't just free us to imagine other models, future worlds. It obliges us to do so.'

David Brooks, political analyst for the *New York Times* and PBS NewsHour (Brooks 2011) pointed to the contribution of geneticists, neuroscientists, psychologists, sociologists, economists, and others over recent decades who have made great progress in understanding the inner working of the human mind… 'The cognitive revolution of the past 30 years provides a different perspective on our lives, one that emphasizes the relative importance of emotion over pure reason, social connections over individual choice, moral intuition over abstract logic, perceptiveness over I.Q.'

Sociologist James March observed some time ago, rather than making rational choices people indulge in normative decision making: they ask what sort of person am I, what would a person like me do in a situation like this, and they do it! (March 1982).

2.7 Reciprocity

Researchers at the Economics Program and the Program on Cultural and Social Dynamics at the Santa Fe Institute studied the way people deal with reciprocity, the response to gift giving and the extent to which obligations are created through that (Heinrich et al. 2005). Using well-known games to explore co-operation they studied the way in which self-interest works, or doesn't, in 15 small-scale societies—most of them indigenous—around the World. Together they exhibit a wide variety of economic and cultural conditions.

In one game (called Ultimatum), a 'proposer' was provisionally assigned an amount of money or equivalent goods equal to a day or two's wages and makes an offer to the 'respondent' who may accept the proportion offered or reject it. If accepted the players receive the proposed amounts, if rejected they receive nothing. The market economic model, based on the primacy of self interest, would predict a high rate of rejection of any offer significantly less than half the available amount. That has been found in experiments in advanced societies where such offers are rejected and so neither of the participants gains a reward.

In small scale societies participants' reactions reflected the everyday reactions reflected the everyday situations with which they were familiar. Most offers were accepted so long as they were at least a quarter of that available; generous offers were rejected where it was considered that unreasonable reciprocal obligations in future encounters would be created. The wide variation in the behaviour reflected the extent to which the different societies were involved in regular sharing and trading situations, that is the extent to which the market was integrated into their activities.

Many people respond to nice behaviour of others by being nice to them and more cooperative. 'Conversely, in response to hostile actions they are frequently much more nasty and even brutal' (Fehr and Gachter 2000a, b). Moreover, 'free riding generally causes very strong negative emotions among co-operators and there is a widespread willingness to punish the free riders…. this holds true even if punishment is costly and does not provide any material benefits for the punisher… the more free riders deviate from the cooperation levels of the co-operators the more heavily they are punished. They can avoid or reduce punishment by being more cooperative. Punishment opportunities lead to less free riding.'

Studies of the behaviour of Capuchin monkeys reveal loss aversion, a tendency to choose strategies which result in minimal loss over those which result in greater losses even if they also result in greater gains (Chen et al. 2006). This behaviour is part of 'Prospect Theory' as developed by Amos Tversky and Daniel Kahneman.

Neoclassical economics posits that financial incentives drive improved performance. However, this is not so in all domains in all situations. It is fair to say that billions of dollars have been wasted by governments and business in paying huge bonuses to executives, all justified by the assertion that it is necessary to attract the best talent! In some years the bonuses were so substantial that they raised the index of inflation leading to a rise in interest rates which impacted less advantaged people.

2.8 Mirror Neurons and Belongingness

Humans are inherently social animals. Social research shows concern for others to be a major feature of humans and indeed many other social animals. Studies of so-called mirror neurons which fire when the animal acts *and* when it watches another animal performing the same act strongly suggest facilitation of social behaviour and very likely empathy. Mirror neurons were first found in the ventral premotor cortex, an area near the front of the brain, of macaque monkeys by scientists at the University of Parma in Italy. Subsequently, in April 2010, scientists at the University of California Los Angeles reported mirror neurons in other regions of the human brain, those involved in vision and in memory (Anon 2010). Other social animals show evidence of concern about the welfare of others of their species but in humans this characteristic is much more developed.

Distinguished neurophysiologist V.S. Ramachandran of the University of California San Diego considers the elucidation of the role of mirror neurons will 'do for psychology what DNA did for biology' providing 'a unifying framework and help explain a host of mental abilities that have hitherto remained mysterious and inaccessible to experiments including the development of tools and of speech, amongst other things' (Ramachandran 2000).

Numerous other studies support these conclusions about the sociality of humans. Roy Baumeister of Western Case University and his colleague Mark R Leary (Baumeister and Leary 1995) concluded that evaluation of the empirical literature supports the proposition that there is a need to form strong, stable interpersonal relationships. 'Belongingness' as they call it, appears to have multiple and strong effects on emotional patterns and on cognitive processes. Lack of attachments is linked to a variety of ill effects on health, adjustment, and well-being.

2.9 Neoclassical Economics: Adam Smith Made Small!

Economists, and politicians, like to refer to Adam Smith, the eighteenth century Scottish philosopher and author of *The Wealth of Nations*. Smith, they say, considered freedom to pursue one's own self-interest to be one of the three things that make us more prosperous, in a general sort of way. (The other two were specialization, which Smith called division of labour; and freedom of trade: Smith was an ardent anti-mercantilist.) Amartya Sen points out Smith was concerned not only with the sufficiency of self-interest at the moment of exchange but also with the wider moral motivations and institutions required to support economic activity in general. Sen (2010) observed, While some men are born small and some achieve smallness, it is clear that Adam Smith has had much smallness thrust upon him.

When Smith referred to self-interest what he meant was that it was a good idea for individuals to try to better themselves: Smith was writing in a time when the overwhelming majority of people were living in extremely poor conditions in almost every way. To give self-interest the emphasis it is given today—a kind of Darwinian survival of the fittest—is to completely ignore the context in which Smith wrote. Smith did not mean to imply an emphasis on the individual to the exclusion of others; he did not mean that competition should be the driving force of the human condition.

American writer and satirist, and biographer of Adam Smith, P.J O'Rourke, talking on NPR Radio's Talk of the Nation on January 8 2007, pointed out, that in the chapter 'Of the Wages of Labour', in book 1 of *The Wealth of Nations*, Smith remarked in a tone approaching modern irony, 'Is this improvement in the circumstances of the lower ranks of the people to be regarded as an advantage or as an inconveniency to the society?'

'Smith wasn't talking about Gordon Gekko in Wall Street, laughs O'Rourke, He was talking about poor crofters in Scotland. At the time he was writing, the majority of people the world over had no capacity to exercise self-interest. They were serfs, slaves, peons working for pitiful wages. All their behaviour was subject to the will of others.' (Walsh 2008). By self-interest, Smith meant having a chance to better themselves, to improve their standards, have the liberty to start a business without interference by the rich and powerful.

In an extensive critique of the way in which contemporary economics has diminished modern humanity, historian Tony Judt (2009) notes that Americans would like their child to have improved life chances at birth, their wife or daughter to have the same odds of surviving maternity as women in other advanced countries as well as full medical coverage at lower cost, longer life expectancy, better public services and less crime.

When told that these things are available in Austria, Scandinavia, or the Netherlands, but that they come with higher taxes and an 'interventionary' state, many of those same Americans respond: 'But that is socialism! We do not want the state interfering in our affairs. And above all, we do not wish to pay more taxes… it is incontrovertible that social democracy and the welfare states face serious practical challenges today'.

Judt points to 'remarkable achievements' to the credit of the welfare state such as, in the case of the neo-Keynesian governments of the postwar era, their success in curbing inequality. 'With greater equality there came other benefits. Over time, the fear of a return to extremist politics—the politics of desperation, the politics of envy, the politics of insecurity—abated.' But, Judt observes, the reasons for the welfare state had been forgotten by the 1960s and it was all neglected by the 1970s.

2.10 The Consequences for Education

Neoclassical economics has become the driver for education policy in countries such as the US, UK and Australia, as well Norway and Italy and some other countries including recently to an extent, Sweden. This has meant, at the very least, advocacy of performance indicators in the form of standardised test scores, merit pay for teachers (based on students' test scores), choice through independent schools and oversight by community representatives on school boards. In some cases, for instance in England, business enterprises now manage schools and provide basic services.

The benefits of education to the community at large from advanced education are ignored as is the fact that development of teachers' expertise is not acquired in a few months from the time the need for such expertise is acknowledged. What is also ignored are the many apparently successful experiments in education of less advantaged students, in the US for instance. Rather, the views of those people which conform to neoclassical ideology are promoted. For example, much attention was paid in Australia shortly after the election of the Rudd government to the views of media magnate Rupert Murdoch and the then Chancellor of the New York school system, Joel Klein, as reported in the Introductory essay to this book. Little attention was paid to the views of experts from the UK such as Cambridge University Emeritus Professor Robin Alexander, principal author of the Cambridge Primary Education Review established by the UK government or Sir Ken Robinson, one time chair of the National Advisory Committee on Creative and Cultural Education, also established by the UK government.

Sometimes, neoliberal views which intrude upon the education scene, especially at school level, are referred to under the heading of 'New Public Management' (NPM). In all cases, the introduction of NPM has generated tensions between education as a social good and as something freely available to all and the notion of schooling as a commodity, its utility measured by the extent to which it prepares students for work and is accountable for the extent to which it does so.

These tensions have been studied in a number of countries including the UK, Norway and Italy (Hall et al. 2013). In the UK, specifically England, NPM has severely weakened the former basis of education over several decades including particularly during the time of the Blair Labour Government. England is now appropriately described, according to David Hall and colleagues from the University of Manchester, as having a 'post-welfarist' public education. Education is regulated in order to provide performance data that serve education markets and is viewed as being about 'passing on the correct knowledge and moral values to future generations'.

In Norway the main tensions are between education as underpinned by socially democratic ideologies linked to notions of equity, participation and comprehensive education and competition, marketisation and privatisation; conservative parties seek to privatise education whilst opposing political parties seek to overturn such trends, according to Jorunn Møller and Guri Skedsmo of the University of Oslo (in Hall et al. 2013). The professional autonomy of teachers has been overturned and principals are seen as managers. In Italy, tensions are manifested as struggles between managerialist accountability and performance control on the one hand and welfarist arrangements on the other, according to Emiliano Grimaldi and Roberto Serpieri of Naples' University Fedrico II (in Hall et al. 2013).

What seems to not be obvious to those advocating these reforms is that whilst they promise more freedom from control they produce more bureaucracy and centralised direction. Even worse, far from leading to improvements in education, they diminish the outcomes. As elaborated elsewhere, education, especially schooling, becomes nothing more than a process for producing people suitable for basic tasks in enterprises dominated by routine where on the job training is

2.10 The Consequences for Education

minimal because the expectation is that people will arrive to be recruited fully equipped. Should they not be, then clearly the education system is at fault and greater accountability is required to fix it up. And more didactic teaching is required, not the student-centred approach advocated by so many. Arguably, the entire notion of neoliberalism and NPM is a fraud!

Reforms of education in those countries whose students perform well in international tests—Finland, Korea, Singapore, provinces of Canada such as Ontario and so on—do not follow these prescriptions. These are issues taken up in other essays, especially as they relate to effective teaching and learning and the conditions of employment of teachers.

In the end, what has neoclassical economics and NPM contributed to the advance of society and education over the last 60 years of extraordinary focus on economics combined, in some countries, with a neoconservative approach to politics exemplified most especially by the US but in many European countries as well? Some commentators, such as one time advisor to the President of Estonia and Senior Legislative Analyst in the US Congress Wolfgang Dreschler (2005) and London School of Economics Professor Patrick Dunleavy (Dunleavy et al. 2005), have pronounced NPM to be dead: their judgements unfortunately have been premature!

Many economists point to the millions in some countries lifted out of poverty over the last several decades. But against that must be put the millions still living in poverty in India, sub-Saharan Africa and South America, the failure of developed countries to meet the Millennium Goals and the increasing disparity in wealth in many of the most highly developed countries, termed by Paul Krugman the Great Divergence. One detailed analysis has concluded that the exploding rise in wealth by a tiny percentage of the population has been due mainly to various failures in the education system and political influence—Wall Street and corporate boards' pampering of the Stinking Rich in particular deregulation and lowering of taxes followed by limitations on unions or decline of labor but not immigration, race or gender or computers (Noah 2012).

Considerable attention has been paid to the recent study of the origins of power, prosperity and poverty by MIT economist Daron Acemoglu and Harvard political scientist James Robinson (Acemoglu and Robinson 2012). Their thesis, supported by analysis of societies from Roman times to the present is, No society which organizes the economy to benefit just 10 % of the population will generate prosperity. To grow and become prosperous the most critical thing a society must do is to harness its talent and human potential which is widely disbursed in the population.

2.11 The Irrelevance of Market Economics

Academic economists have focused on refining econometric analyses for which there is substantial data rather than rare events concerning human behaviour which have very important, often negative, consequences. All the evidence from studies of behaviour, sociology and neurobiology shows humans to be anything but the utility maximisers, money-driven individualistic creatures that neoclassical economics posits.

Markets are not the efficient mechanisms claimed for them. Continuous economic growth is unsustainable. Increasing the wealth of the already rich does not increase overall prosperity. Privatisation of government assets and functions have replaced public monopoly with private monopoly and produced no greater efficiency.

Government and the private sector together generate prosperity and are involved in a complex system of mutual independence. Provision of social services by government in Nordic and European countries has led to more equitable societies.

Will Hutton (2012b) of *The Guardian* has recently pointed to the failure of the three interlocking pillars of British capitalism. Editor in Chief for the Australian online magazine *Business Spectator* Alan Kohler (2012) reported a major business conference as delivering one overriding theme—that most of the world, if not all of it, is now governed by rich elites who are just out to look after themselves—oligarchies.

Joseph Stiglitz in his new book *The Price of Inequality: The Avoidable Causes and Invisible Costs of Inequality* describes how unrestrained power and rampant greed are writing an epitaph for the American dream (Roberts 2012). Stiglitz writes, 'Paying attention to everyone else's self-interest—in other words to the common welfare—is in fact a precondition for one's own ultimate wellbeing… it isn't just good for the soul; it's good for business.'

Social scientist Robert Putnam, author of *Bowling Alone* about the increasing move away from social activities reveals, according to Will Hutton, that class is becoming ever more important as a determinant of outcomes in American life; it now trumps race, he argues, and the differences can be observed very early on in the children of different classes (Hutton 2012a). The middle class now spends more on children's enrichment activities, so important for psychological wellbeing and character building, in fact 11 times more, than families at the bottom.

Harvard philosopher Michael Sandel has pointed to everything being priced and commodified: 'We have drifted from a market economy to being a market society.' (Aitkenhead 2012).

That regular economists whose forecasts of economic indicators seem irredeemably wrong continue to be heard is surely a matter of great concern. Of even greater concern is the fact that much attention is paid to proponents of the current orthodoxy, whilst the fact that the basis of many of their judgements such as the relationship of debt as a proportion of Gross National Product to future economic growth turn out to be based on simple arithmetic errors (Krugman 2013) are glossed over and the fact that many academic economists chose not to explore the difficult issues of economics are not even mentioned publicly!

Distinguished American author and columnist William Pfaff, reviewing Francis Fukuyama's *The Origins of Political Order: From Prehuman Times to the French Revolution*, wrote, 'I am not myself aware that human character and conduct today display any general improvement over that recorded in the historical past. That men and women are morally improved from what they were at the beginning of recorded history has yet to be demonstrated.' (Pfaff 2011).

Propositions inherent in neoclassical economics, with its focus on maximising utility and the primacy of financial rewards as a major motivator that are predicated on the treatment of humans as competitive, self-regarding creatures are at complete variance with all the evidence from behavioural economics, psychology and sociology. Studies of reciprocity, mirror neurons and belongingness and many other studies show, as Tim Jackson says, 'We evolved as much as social beings as we did as individual beings…'

The adoption of neoclassical economic models and their outgrowth—neoliberalism and New Public Management (NPM)—has played a major part in undermining the attempts at reform of education in a number of countries including Australia and some countries in Europe, but most especially the US and the UK.

Progress in education reform will not be achieved whilst neoliberalism (and NPM) prevails. Politicians, often with the help of sections of the media and with the support of some sections of the business community, lack the preparedness to honestly address the continually emerging understanding of teaching and learning and the nature of effective organisations including the nature of genuine and authentic school leadership!

References

Acemoglu, D., & Robinson, J. (2012). *Why nations fail. The origins of power. Prosperity and poverty*. New York: Crown.
Aitkenhead, D. (2012, 27 May). Michael Sandel: We need to reason about how to value our bodies, human dignity, teaching and learning. *The Guardian*.
Akerlof, G. (2007, January 6). The missing motivation in economics presidential address to the American Economic Association, Chicago.
Allen, K. (2011, 14 November). UK jobs market faces slow, painful contraction. *The Guardian*.
Anon (2010, April. 13). First direct recording made of mirror neurons in human brain. *Science News*. Retrieved 2 June 2013, from http://www.sciencedaily.com/releases/2010/04/100412162112.htm
Anon (2011, 10 November). Jefferson county in Alabama faces bankruptcy. BBC News.
Anon (2012, 6 March). Govt unveils new business advisory forum. *Business Spectator*.
Baumeister, R., & Leary, M. R. (1995). Need to belong: Desire for interpersonal attachments as a fundamental human motivation. *Psychological Bulletin, 117*, 497–529.
Bennett, M., & Walker, R. (2011, 25 November). The Jobs crisis: What did roosevelt do that Obama should? *Truthout*.
Brooks, D. (2011). *The social animal: The hidden sources of love, character and achievement*. New York: Random House.
Bunting, M. (2011, 30 May). Outrage at the banks is everywhere. So why aren't there riots on the streets? *The Guardian*.
Chen, M. K., et al. (2006). How basic are behavioural biases? Evidence from Capuchin Monkey Trading Behaviour. *Journal of Political Economy, 114*, 517–537.

Carrington, D. (2013, July3). Policymakers say a higher price is essential to encourage more greenhouse gas reductions across Europe's industry. *The Guardian.*

Cassidy, J. (2008, June 12). Economics: Which Way for Obama? *New York Review of Books.*

Collander, D. et al. (2008). The financial crisis and the systemic failure of academic economics. 98th Dahlem Workshop. Retrieved 18 August 2012, from http://ideas.repec.org/p/kie/kieliw/1489.html

Dreschler, W. (2005, 14 September). The rise and demise of the new public management. *Post-Autistic Economics Review* 3. Retrieved 8 April 2008, from http://www.paecon.net/PAEReview/issue33/Drechsler33.htm

Dunleavy, P., et al. (2005). New public management is dead—long live Digital-Era Governance. *Journal of Public Administration and Theory, 16,* 467–494.

Eickemeier, P. (2009). On the way to phasing out emissions: More than 50% reductions needed by 2050 to respect 2°C climate target. Retrieved 17 October 2010, from http://www.pik-potsdam.de/news/press-releases/on-the-way-to-phasing-out-emissions-more-than-50-reductions-needed-by-2050-to-respect-2b0c-climate-target

Elliott, L. (2013, 22 May). Austerity is a task for another day, IMF tells George Osborne. *The Guardian.*

Fehr, E., & Gachter, S. (2000a). Fairness and retaliation: the economics of reciprocity. CESifo Working Paper 336.

Fehr, E., & Gachter, S. (2000b). Cooperation and punishment in public goods experiments. *American Economic Review, 90,* 980–994.

Foster, C. (2005). *British Government in Crisis or The Third English Revolution*. Oxford and Portland: Hart Publishing.

Gittins, R. (2011a, 15 August). Maybe economic reform is worsening productivity. *Sydney Morning Herald.*

Gittins, R. (2011b, 8 December). There's so much more to wealth than money. *Sydney Morning Herald.*

Gray, J. (2010, 29 August). 23 things they don't tell you about capitalism by Ha-Joon Chang. *The Observer.*

Gregory, M. (2011, 12 December). Unemployment is world's fastest-rising fear—survey. BBC.

Hadjimatheou, C. (2012, 10 January). The Greek parents too poor to care for their children. BBC.

Hall, D. et al. (2013). Educational reform, modernisation and the new public management: Perspectives from Europe. American Education Research Association Annual Meeting, San Francisco 27th April-1st May, ms.

Heinrich, Joseph, et al. (2005). Economic man in cross-cultural perspective: Behavioural experiments in 15 small-scale societies. *Behavioral and Brain Sciences, 28,* 795–815.

Hutton, W. (2011, 18 September). The ailing euro is part of a wider crisis. Our capitalist system is near meltdown. *The Observer*

Hutton, W. (2012a, 15 July). Born poor? Bad luck. You have won last prize in the lottery of life. *The Observer.*

Hutton, W. (2012b, 23 September). The key pillars of our economy need reshaping. Starting with finance. *The Observer.*

Hutton, W. (2013, 21 April). Burn our planet or face financial meltdown. Not much of a choice. *The Observer.*

Jackson, T. (2010, 6 July). Prosperity without growth. ABC big ideas. Retrieved 18 August 2012, from http://www.abc.net.au/tv/bigideas/stories/2010/07/06/2945103.htm

Judt, T. (2009, December 17). What Is living and what is dead in social democracy? *New York Review of Books.*

Kohler, A. (2012, 13 August). The moral bankruptcy of our ruling classes. *Business Spectator.*

Krugman, P. (2009, September 2). How did economists get it so wrong? *New York Times.*

Krugman, P. (2013a, 19 April). Excel depression. *New York Times.*

Krugman, P. (2013b, 6 June). How the case for austerity has crumbled. *New York Review of Books.*

Kuttner, R. (1997). The limits of markets. *The American Prospect, 31,* 28–41.

References

Kuttner, R. (2013, 9 May). The debt we shouldn't pay. *New York Review of Books*.

Lake, A., Kakabadse, A., & Kakabadse, N. (2008). *The elephant hunters: Chronicles of the moneymen*. Basingstoke: Palgrave Macmillan.

March, J. G. (1982). Theories of choice and making decisions. *Society, 1982*, 29–39.

McAuley, I. (2010). When does behavioural economics really matter. A paper presented to the Australian Economic Forum. Retrieved 18 August 2012, from http://www.home.netspeed.com.au/mcau/academic/confs/bepolicy.pdf

Marr, D. (2010). *Power trip: The political journey of Kevin Rudd*. Quarterly Essay 38. Melbourne: Black Inc.

Meinshausen, M., et al. (2009). Greenhouse gas emission targets for limiting global warming to 2°C. *Nature,*. doi:10.1038/nature08017

Mitchell, N. (presenter). (2010, 7 August). Challenging stereotypes: Culture, psychology and the Asian self. ABC RN All in the Mind. Retrieved 18 August 2010, from http://www.abc.net.au/radionational/programs/allinthemind/challenging-stereotypes-culture-psychology-and-the/3017858

Noah, T. (2012). *The great divergence*. New York: Bloomsberry Press. (first published in 10 parts in the online magazine *Slate* in 2010).

OECD. (2011). Society at a glance 2011—OECD social indicators. Paris: OECD. Retrieved 18 August 2012, from www.oecd.org/els/social/indicators/SAG

Pfaff, W. (2011, 24 November). How much progress have we made? *New York Review of Books*.

Quiggin, J. (2010, October 15). Five Zombie economic ideas that refuse to die. *Foreign Affairs*.

Ramachandran, V. S. (2000). Mirror neurons and imitation learning as the driving force behind "the great leap forward" in human evolution. Retrieved 2 June 2013, from http://www.edge.org/3rd_culture/ramachandran/ramachandran_index.html

Roberts, Y. (2012, 13 July). The price of inequality by Joseph Stiglitz—review. *The Guardian*.

Rosin, H. (2012, 30 September). Are men an endangered species? *The Observer*.

Sen, A. (2010). Adam Smith and the contemporary world. *Erasmus Journal for Philosophy and Economics*. 3(1), 50–67.

Sennett, R. (2011, 9 September). Americas inhumane approach to labour problems will finish Obama. *The Guardian*.

Stiglitz, J. E., Sen, A., & Fitoussi, J.-P. (2009). Report by the commission on the measurement of economic performance and social progress. Retrieved 18 August 2012, from www.stiglitz-sen-fitoussi.fr/

Stone, C. (2013a). *False economies. Decoding efficiency*. Canberra: Centre for Public Policy.

Stone, C. (2013b). *False economies. Doing more with less*. Canberra: Centre for Public Policy.

Taibbi, M. (2011b, August). Is the SEC covering up Wall Street crimes? *Rolling Stone,* 17.

Taleb, N. (2004, April 19). Learning to expect the unexpected. *The edge*. Retrieved 18 August 2012, from http://www.edge.org/documents/archive/edge136.html

Walker, B., & Walker, B. C. (2008). *Privatisation: Sell off or sell out The Australian experience*. Sydney: Sydney University Press.

Walsh, J. (2008, 7 January). PJ O'Rourke: The original Republican Party Reptile is back. *The Independent*.

Chapter 3
Community and Inequality: Part 1: Creating an Enabling Environment

3.1 The Importance of Socioeconomic Status

Family socioeconomic background is the most important determinant of educational attainment: lower status means low achievement. This is confirmed by a multitude of data but often ignored in the education debate. Too often economic growth and education are promoted as the way out of poverty: however, data from worldwide surveys show that to be unrealistic (OECD 2008). Governments are thereby excused from any significant action to address the principal causes of poverty and inequality. This essay traverses evidence about poverty and its impact on education, the experiences of children in poor families and the costs to society at large.

Poverty leads to poor health, is accompanied by relatively little environmental and intellectual stimulation. Poor neighbourhoods have limited access to playgrounds and libraries. High levels of unemployment contribute to poverty and to relatively high levels of violence in the home. And schools in high poverty areas are generally poorly resourced, poorly maintained and staffed by teachers less qualified than in schools in higher socioeconomic areas; teacher turnover is often high. Poverty, unsurprisingly, because it leads to additional stress as people try to cope with the immediate problems of managing to live within a very small budget, absorbs more mental energy than in other people, leading to a cognitive deficit equivalent to a loss of 13 IQ points, according to recent research by Anandi Mani at the University of Warwick in the UK and others (Jha 2013).

Children of parents enjoying high socioeconomic status grow up in a supportive and stimulating environment where resources such as books, libraries and playgrounds are easily accessible and interaction with highly supportive parents is frequent and challenging. At least that is the situation in many countries. Children living in poverty attend school less often. Large enrolments of children from low social and economic backgrounds place special demands on schools and their teachers. Average socioeconomic levels of children in class have a profound influence on the achievement of individual students, no matter their own background, as discussed in the essay on Public or Private schools.

In many developed countries inner urban areas are typified by concentrated poverty, exacerbated by changing economic conditions (Wilson 2008–2009). Declining opportunities in rural areas or in neighbouring countries bring people to seemingly economically better locations in cities or to emigration. But the opportunities for employment often fluctuate or change more permanently, suddenly throwing many people out of work. Employment conditions which allow payment of wages at levels below the poverty line, and which tie medical insurance to employment, further exacerbate the situation. In many countries there may not be a minimum wage or, if it is, it is fixed by the legislature and adjusting the minimum wage may take a long time. In any event, it is by no means uncommon for firms to employ people on wages below the defined poverty level.

At times of economic stress, opponents of immigration complain that immigrants take the jobs of natives. But in fact businesses often use the preparedness of immigrants to accept low wages to drive wages down: it is that which contributes to increasing unemployment amongst the resident population.

In the US the minimum Federal wage is fixed by Congress which has frequently failed to make adjustments; the giant retailer Wal-Mart pays many staff below the minimum wage and as a result those employees are in receipt of federal income relief (Ehrenreich 2006): in effect this is a taxpayer subsidy to Wal-Mart.

Over the last 100 years in the US large numbers of African Americans migrated from the southern plantations to the industrial north. At the same time more affluent whites moved to the suburbs. The cities became dissected by freeways, discrimination in housing finance led to poorer families being unable to gain reasonable housing. Explicit racial policies led to ageing infrastructure in mostly black neighbourhoods and as jobs were casualised and exported unemployment increased. Schools in inner city black neighbourhoods were neglected.

For young black males in the inner city the Code of the Street, the rules of behaviour devised to achieve manly pride through the right look, speaking the right way and wearing the right clothes, only reinforced their subordinate position and perpetuated poverty (Anderson 1994).

The changes at one school in India exemplify how poverty impacts on school attendance (Ruthven 2010). Many people would be surprised to be told that many schools in developed countries are in a similar situation! The renovations of a local government school in Nizamuddin in India included a renovated toilet block with separate cubicles for girls and boys. Dropout rates had been high, especially among girls. The lack of toilets was seen as the primary reason since there was no private place where they could relieve themselves… After the introduction of the new toilets in the Nizamuddin school, female dropout rates declined dramatically: girls now make up 55 % of the pupils. In September 2012 India's Supreme Court ordered all schools must be provided with toilets and drinking water within 6 months; 40 % of schools do not have any toilets.

Robert McNamara, former President of the World Bank, speaking to Governors in 1973 said, '.. critics of additional assistance to the poorer nations, when citing the needs of their own cities and countryside, fail to distinguish between two kinds of poverty: what might be termed relative poverty and absolute poverty' (McNamara 1973).

'Relative poverty means simply that some countries are less affluent than other countries, or that some citizens of a given country have less personal abundance than their neighbors..

'But absolute poverty is a condition of life so degraded by disease, illiteracy, malnutrition, and squalor as to deny its victims basic human necessities. It is a condition of life suffered by relatively few in the developed nations but by hundreds of millions of the citizens of the developing countries represented in this room.'

The research of Jean Anyon, Professor of Social and Educational Policy at the City University of New York, elaborates the notion that academic inequality is not a function of the underachieving poor but rather of the macroeconomics of the US. She has pointed out (Anyon 2005) that '.. despite stated intentions, federal and metropolitan policies and arrangements generally restrict opportunities available to city residents and neighborhoods.

'.. job, wage, housing, tax, and transportation policies maintain minority poverty in urban neighborhoods, and thereby create environments that overwhelm the potential of educational policy to create systemic, sustained improvements in the schools.' Minimum wage statutes yield full-time pay below the poverty level, affordable housing and transportation policies segregate low-income workers of color in urban areas whilst industrial and other job development are in far-flung suburbs that public transit routes do not reach.

Despite the fact that low-income individuals desperately need a college degree to find decent employment, only 7 % obtain a bachelors degree by age 26. So, in relation to the needs of low-income students, urban districts fail their students with more egregious consequences now than in the early twentieth century.

On 3 August 2012 the US the Children's Defense Fund released its report *The State of America's Children* (Edelman 2012). There are 16.4 million poor children in rich America of whom 7.4 million live in extreme poverty. 'Most public school students and more than three out of four Black and Hispanic children, who will be a majority of our child population by 2019, are unable to read or compute at grade level in the fourth or eighth grade and will be unprepared to succeed in our increasingly competitive global economy. Nearly eight million children are uninsured... More children were killed by guns in 2008–2009 than US military personnel in both the Iraq and Afghanistan wars to date. A Black boy born in 2001 has a one in three chance of going to prison in his lifetime; a Latino boy a one in six chance of the same fate.'

The report continued, 'Millions of children are living hopeless, poverty- and violence-stricken lives in the war zone's of our cities; in the educational deserts of our rural areas; in the moral deserts of our corrosive culture that saturates them with violent, materialistic, and individualistic messages; and in the leadership deserts of our political and economic life where greed and self-interest trump the common good over and over.' The most basic human supports needed to survive are not there: millions of children are left behind. Parents alone cannot provide for them at a time of deep economic downturn, joblessness. 'Low wage jobs place a ceiling on economic mobility for millions as Americas dream dims.'

In the 5 years to 2008, poverty and inequality grew in two-thirds of OECD countries, especially Canada, Germany, Norway and the US. In the other third, particularly Greece, Mexico and the UK, the gap between rich and poor decreased (OECD 2008). A recent report observes, 'Global efforts to reduce poverty have been moderately successful over the last 20 years, with extreme poverty declining in certain areas of rapid economic development [However]… Debilitating poverty continues to afflict ever-increasing numbers of people in the regions of Sub-Saharan Africa and Southern Asia' (Sowey 2011).

The extraordinary and increasing gap in wealth in developed countries is a major feature of the last 30 or so years. More people are left behind in an ever-changing world economy. But that trend is not inevitable: governments can close the gap with effective social policies. The price of inequality is a waste of human resources: a large proportion of the population able to work are trapped in low-paid, low-skilled jobs or out of work. Greater involvement of local populations in decision-making may contribute to significant poverty reduction (Bonfiglioli 2003). However, for the most part poverty is not a choice people make: people born into poverty die in poverty.

In Europe the financial situation is leading to a potential reversal of the prospect that children will do better than their parents did (Bauman 2012). 'Nothing has prepared them for the arrival of the hard, uninviting and inhospitable new world of downgrading of results, devaluation of earned value, volatility of jobs and stubbornness of joblessness, transience of prospects and durability of defeats, stillborn projects and frustrated hopes and chances ever more conspicuous by their absence… it doesn't happen often that the plight of being outcast may stretch to embrace a whole generation. Yet precisely that may be happening in Europe now.'

As 2013 advanced jobs continued to be lost in several industries including the financial industry and many parts of the economies of European countries continued to decline, even return to recession. Meanwhile in the UK, unemployment rose to 2.5 million and large numbers of Conservative politicians voted to express regret at the fact that the Queen's speech to the Parliament did not acknowledge the possible departure of the country from the European Union.

3.2 The Real Wealth of Nations: Human Development

In 2010 the United Nations Development Program (UNDP) published its 20th Annual Human Development Report, titled *The Real Wealth of Nations: Pathways to Human Development* (United Nations 2010). The Report series was launched in 1990. Its goal was to put people at the centre of development, to go beyond income in assessing peoples long-term well being. As such it was influenced by the thinking of Nobel Prize winning economist Amartya Sen who has been a leader in elaborating the notions of freedom and justice through a focus principally on the

3.2 The Real Wealth of Nations: Human Development

individual rather than the community. In Sen's view individual claims to freedom are to be assessed in terms of the freedoms the individual actually enjoys to choose the lives they have reason to value. This is different from the utilitarian view of ethics promoted by John Stuart Mill and Jeremy Bentham that society should seek the greatest good for the greatest number of people.

Over the 40 years from 1970 to 2010 average increase in school enrolment around the world was almost the same in countries whether growth was negative or positive. Growth of a global consensus for universal education likely reflected deeper political processes at home. Democratisation is a factor in some countries and urbanisation is a key positive influence on changes in education and income. Trade had no significant impact on income but a positive correlation with health and education. Constraints on executive power had positive effects on education and income but not health.

> 'People are the real wealth of a nation.' With these words the 1990 Human Development Report (HDR) began a forceful case for a new approach to thinking about development. That the objective of development should be to create an enabling environment for people to enjoy long, healthy and creative lives may appear self-evident today. But that has not always been the case.

Overview, UN Human Development Report 2010.

Policies which redress gender inequity contribute to human development because women generally have poorer health and lower educational attainment than men. However, women have a higher propensity to invest in their children than do men.

Strong institutions as assessed by levels of corruption, rule of law, quality of the bureaucracy and internal conflict, together with higher government spending on wages, goods and services is conducive to faster progress in human development. Improved literacy leads to improved life expectancy, improved health predicts improvement in school enrolment.

Markets can be very inadequate in providing public goods such as security, health and education because firms may simply want cheap labour with no more than basic skills Firms producing cheap labour-intensive goods or exploiting natural resources may not want a more educated workforce. Markets are necessary but they are not enough.

The Real Wealth of Nations notes, 'The past 20 years have seen substantial progress... Most people today are healthier, live longer, are more educated and have more access to goods and services. And there has been progress also in expanding people's power to select leaders, influence public decisions and share knowledge. Yet not all sides of the story are positive. Progress has varied: in regions such as Southern Africa and the former Soviet Union there have been periods of regress, especially in health.'

One of the most important conclusions is that a significant correlation between economic growth and improvements in health and education is lacking. Whereas many economists regard income growth as fundamentally important in driving improvements that is not so! 'The correlation [between income growth and non-income Human Development Index (HDI) or HDI excluding the income measure] is remarkably weak and statistically insignificant.'

Countries more often become top performers on the HDI scale through exceptional progress in health and education due to unprecedented increase in the cross-country flow of ideas, not through fast income growth. Many of these innovations have enabled countries to improvements at low cost. 'In other words, over time progress has come to depend more on how countries exploited these ideas—with differences among countries traceable, in part, to variations in institutions and in the underlying social contract.'

The dramatic decline in poverty levels in developing countries of the South often overshadows the increasing inequality in developed countries of the North. Moreover, the pace of development continues to vary substantially with countries such as India, once thought of as likely to rival China in economic growth, faces severe problems. Obsolete university curricula and continuation of the traditional teaching method of rote learning produces students who are good at memorising but deficient in analytical skills as well as English (Dhillon 2013). Underinvestment in technical education continues: India has only 11,000 vocational training schools compared with China's 500,000.

Distinguished economist Amartya Sen continues to express outrage at the defective development in India which is a consequence of class, caste and gender discrimination which leads, for instance, to the fact that planning requirements for urban condominium development contain no requirement that toilets be provided for servants (Bunting 2013). Sen points to 50 % of children who are stunted because of undernourishment and 50 % of women who suffer anaemia for the same reason. Modern India is a disaster zone in which millions of lives are wrecked by hunger and by pitiable investment in health and education services.

3.3 Unequal Society and Its Cost

One of the most important studies of the severe negative effects of inequality is by Richard Wilkinson from the University of Nottingham and Kate Pickett from the University of York (Wilkinson and Pickett 2010). Lynsey Hanley's (2009) review of their book *The Spirit Level* commences, 'We are rich enough. Economic growth has done as much as it can to improve material conditions in the developed countries, and in some cases appears to be damaging health. If Britain were instead to concentrate on making its citizens incomes as equal as those of people in Japan and Scandinavia, we could each have seven extra weeks' holiday a year, we would be thinner, we would each live a year or so longer, and we'd trust each other more.'

Hanley noted the life-diminishing results of valuing growth above equality in rich societies.. the shorter, unhealthier and unhappier lives, the increased rate of teenage pregnancy, violence, obesity, imprisonment and addiction, destruction of relationships between individuals born in the same society but into different classes and its depletion of the planet's resources through driving consumption.

Whilst America is one of the world's richest nations, with among the highest figures for income per person, Americans have the lowest longevity of the developed nations and a level of violence–murder, in particular–off the scale. 'Of all crimes, those involving violence are most closely related to high levels of inequality—within a country, within states and even within cities. The inequality in the US extends not least to the practices of imprisonment and management of jails, another stark contrast with practices in various European countries, especially those of Nordic states (Larson 2013). Greater openness and more humane conditions in Nordic prisons are accompanied by recidivism rates one-half to one-third those in the US.

For some, mainly young, men with no economic or educational route to achieving the high status and earnings required for full citizenship, the experience of daily life at the bottom of a steep social hierarchy is enraging. Many of these people are recruited into the US army with catastrophic impacts on citizens in countries where US forces are fighting such as Iraq and Afghanistan. It is a practice engaged in for decades, one which led the Rev. Martin Luther King Jr to protest the Vietnam War when he saw young blacks returning to a life of ongoing discrimination.

The countries with the lowest inequality are Japan, the Nordic countries of Finland, Sweden, Denmark, Norway and some European countries including Belgium, Austria, Germany and Spain: in those countries homicides, mental illness and teenage births are low and life expectancy high. And it is students from Nordic countries and some European countries that do best in international tests like PISA, conducted by the OECD and TIMSS conducted by the International Association for the Evaluation of Educational Achievement as pointed out in the essay comparing educational achievements in different countries (Chap. 12)!

One of the most important contributors to equality is the community's concern for the disadvantaged and less fortunate, the way what is usually termed welfare is provided. In many European countries the government takes responsibility for unemployment relief, for medical insurance and a variety of schemes to support those such as older people, those with disabilities and so on through income support. In Germany for instance government also has in place provisions to lessen the impact of financial downturns in companies which otherwise would lead to unemployment.

Whilst there are varying amounts of criticism of such welfare payments and various schemes have been introduced to limit payment, especially for the unemployed, the contrast with the US and countries strongly influenced by American practice and belief is stark. In the US much of the welfare is provided by the employer. In particular, this applies to health insurance so that loss of employment means loss of medical insurance which can mean access to medical care is nearly impossible. Life expectancy for African Americans is significantly less than for whites mainly because they are unable to afford medical care: it has little to do with violence.

People's feelings about their level of control over their own destiny have an important impact on their health. Stresses in the workplace flowing from trying to cope with jobs over which employees feel they have little control cause huge financial losses. VicHealth in Australia found that preventable stress costs more than $8,000 an employee and $730 million a year to the Australian economy. This includes costs of government subsidised health services and medication (Anon 2010; VicHealth 2006).

The long-tem deleterious consequences of job stress were documented by Professor Michael Marmot, MRC Research Professor of Epidemiology and Public Health at University College, London and colleagues from that University in the Whitehall study of British civil servants (Marmot 2001; Bosely 2008). People from higher socioeconomic levels of society were found to be more able to cope with stresses because of the networks of relationships they had formed in their early life. The lack of strong relationships meant that those at lower socioeconomic levels were less able to deal successfully with stress.

3.4 The Great Divergence: Why Nations Fail

Since around 1980 the significant divergence in wealth in the US has been substantial. Around the 1920s the richest 1 % of American families accounted for about 18 % of the nation's income. Today they account for 24 %. Income started to become more equal after the Great Depression of the 1930s and that situation obtained through the 1970s, a period of increasing prosperity termed the 'Great Compression'. But in the 1970s wages stagnated and inflation grew rapidly. The share of income going to the top 0.1 % (those earning more than $1 millions) increased fourfold in the last two decades. The conclusions from studies of this 'divergence' are the same as drawn by Wilkinson and Pickett and others: the gains are to the more equal societies and costs of inequality are substantial.

Journalist Timothy Noah's (2012) analysis of the reasons for the Great Divergence lead him to the view that the principal contributors to it have been various problems with the education system, especially declines in levels of college graduation—the disparities are least for those with college degrees or more—and some other factors. These come down to the actions of the super rich in one form or another and include deregulation of the financial industry and reduction in taxes. 'Wall Street and corporate boards pampering of the Stinking Rich is responsible for 30 %.' As Noah says, 'most of these factors reflect at least in part things the federal government either did or failed to do'. Noah refers to studies by economist Richard Freeman showing that unions play a significant part in reducing income inequality. Increased restrictions on organized labor through federal legislation promoted by wealthy interests account for 20 %. Immigration and tax policy are each responsible for 5 % and trade for 10 %. Race, gender and transformational technology are not responsible for any of the disparity.

The divergence has also been studied by Claudia Goldin and Lawrence F. Katz of Harvard University. They found that the majority of the increase in wage inequality since 1980 can be accounted for by rising differences in wages for workers with different educational attainments (Goldin and Katz 2007). 'Relative demand shifts favouring more-educated workers have not been particularly rapid since 1980. Instead growth in the supply of skills slowed considerably after 1980, and the wage structure, in consequence, widened. The deceleration in the relative supply of skills of the working population came about largely from a slowdown in the growth in the educational attainment of US natives for cohorts born since 1950.'

The increase in unskilled immigration accounts for only a small part of the post-1980 slowdown in skill supply growth. Computerization and foreign offshoring have changed the nature of skill demand though the overall rate of growth in relative demand for more-skilled workers does not appear to have accelerated since 1980. The consequence is a polarization of labor demand: 'inequality has rapidly increased in the top half of the distribution while there has been little or no change in the bottom half'.

Daron Acemoglu, economist of the Massachusetts Institute of Technology and political scientist James A. Robinson of Harvard have documented the profound impact of inequality around the world from Roman times to the present in *Why Nations Fail* (Acemoglu and Robinson 2012). Their thesis can be summarised succinctly: 'No society which organizes the economy to benefit just 10 % of the population will generate prosperity. To grow and become prosperous the most critical thing a society must do is to harness its talent and human potential which is widely disbursed in the population.' In other words, prosperity results from the ability of the average person to benefit from their contribution.

When Spanish conquistadors invaded Central and South America they demanded the indigenous people work for no reward and supply the invaders with gold. Rulers of African countries oppressed the people and profited from slavery. More recent rulers of Mexico violated people's property rights and granted monopolies and favours to supporters. History has an impact well beyond its time. In recent times however, Chinese leader Deng Xiaopeng and his allies, despite opposition from some quarters, overturned the collective ownership of agricultural land and industry and allowed individuals to benefit from any surplus of their production thus lifting millions out of poverty. At the same time however, widespread corruption has meant a rapid increase in the gap between rich and poor. It is the nature of political institutions which determines prosperity.

But it should not be forgotten that [substantial economic problems] arise in many countries, especially developing countries, from two practices by companies and other nations which are supposedly engaged in assisting their development. Firstly, many countries including the US and China, through their aid programs, employ their own nationals in the development projects which they fund. At the completion of the project, citizens of the country receiving the aid have gained no advancement in their skills whatsoever. There is little difference from colonialism where citizens were employed in lowly jobs such as servants and working in plantations.

Inasmuch as skill development, a component of education, advances the community, this form of aid is of almost no value other than the gaining of infrastructure which in most cases only benefits the rich and foreign corporations.

Many corporations are engaging in various strategies which minimise the tax paid in the countries in which they operate. Corporate tax avoidance is big business and CEO rewards for facilitating it are still on the rise. A recent study found that 280 of the most profitable corporations in the US avoided a staggering $223bn in federal taxes over a period of 3 years, with more than half of this total tax subsidy going to just 25 companies (Share the Worlds Resources 2012). The organisation Share the Worlds Resources calculates that, 'As a minimum step toward ending all forms of global tax avoidance, clamping down on tax havens and preventing corporate trade mispricing could raise more than $349bn globally each year [and] preventing illegal tax evasion, strengthening tax systems in the Global South and adopting more progressive taxation policies in rich countries could raise billions more dollars of government revenue each year.'

Whilst tax evasion and tax minimisation especially affect developing countries they also have an impact on developed countries including the UK, US and Australia, the governments of which are increasingly expressing concern and in some cases conducting inquiries. Companies such as Apple and Google are setting up companies in countries with low tax rates such as Ireland. During the last decade, tax havens helped facilitate the illicit flow of an estimated $6.5tn out of wealthy countries, the majority of which occurred through the manipulation of profits and costs by multinational corporations, a practice known as trade mispricing. In Africa total tax evasion loss slightly exceeds spending on health care and in South America healthcare spending is significantly less than total tax evasion loss. Capital flight from the 1970s through 2010 has cost South Korea $779 billion, Mexico $417 billion and Indonesia $331 billion.

Zambia and Mongolia are taking action to try to combat tax avoidance by multinational companies, saying they lose billions of dollars every year (Robinson 2013). Mongolia has had a treaty with the Netherlands, signed in 2002 allowing payment of dividends to the Netherlands free of tax. Numerous companies subsequently set up subsidiaries registered in the Netherlands and were therefore able to benefit from the treaty! The OECD asserted that unilateral action could be dangerous.

On average poverty affects 11 % of the world's population: it is rising amongst children and youth and falling amongst the elderly. The OECD documented the growing inequality between rich and poor in its 2011 report, *Divided We Stand*. Poorer households are losing more or gaining less. The growth that has occurred in developed economies has benefitted the rich more than the poor, so widening the gap (OECD 2013). A key driver has been the number of low-skilled and poorly educated who are out of work. Children and young adults are now 25 % more likely to be poor than the population as a whole and single-parent households are three times as likely to be poor. Without the increased taxing and spending on social benefits in developing countries the rise in inequality would [obviously] be more rapid.

3.5 Personal Development, Home Environment and Child Wellbeing

The close relationship between educational achievement and social and economic advantage are direct and feed through to the entire way of life, starting with early childhood and relationships with parents and relatives and continuing through the opportunities that the home environment provides (Rampell 2009). In disadvantaged communities, the home environment is of much lower quality. This is taken up in the essay on early childhood.

The experiences and economic situation of the parents, including their experiences of schooling, are critical. For all children, irrespective of economic background, the physical conditions of the school, the facilities and diversity of opportunity to participate in a variety of activities in a safe and supportive environment responsive to their needs, are critical. One would think the latter was so self-evident that attention would be paid to it.

UNICEF and the Innocenti Research Centre released a comprehensive report on child wellbeing in February 2007 (UNICEF 2007). It observed, 'The true measure of a nation's standing is how well it attends to its children—their health and safety, their material security, their education and socialization, and their sense of being loved, valued, and included in the families and societies into which they are born.' For some countries the report is more than startling.

There is no obvious relationship between levels of child well-being and GDP per capita. The Czech Republic, for example, achieves a higher overall rank for child well-being than several much wealthier countries. European countries dominate the top half of the overall league table, with the Netherlands, Sweden, Denmark and Finland claiming the top four places. The US comes second to last in the equity league table.

The Report brought 40 indicators together under the headings poverty, family relationships and health from the years 2000 through 2003. Its assessment of 'wellbeing' was guided by the UN *Convention on the Rights of the Child*. Commenting on the Report Professor Sir Al Aynsley-Green, Children's Commissioner for England said, 'We are turning out a generation of young people who are unhappy, unhealthy, engaging in risky behaviour, who have poor relationships with their family and their peers, who have low expectations and don't feel safe.' (Anon 2007). Many commentators recognised that these results did not happen overnight but were the consequence of 20 or 30 years of lack of investment in children. Little progress has been made however!

The UK ranked 17th in 'educational well-being' and was last in respect of 'family and peer relationships' and 'behaviours and risks'. Long term underinvestment in issues affecting children including reduced expenditure on education and child health services, have led to UK children suffering greater deprivation and worse relationships with their parents than in the other 20 countries surveyed. More young people smoke, abuse drink and drugs, engage in risky sex and become pregnant at too early an age than in the other countries.

Poverty in Britain has trebled since 1979: one in four children now live below the poverty line. Barnardos reported in 2005 that in some wards in the UK over 90 % of children lived in poverty (Sharma 2005). Ten years ago the UK Treasury reported, 'Children from disadvantaged backgrounds are much less likely to succeed in education… On difficult to let estates, one in four children gain no GCSEs (the national average is one in twenty) and rates of truancy are four times the national average…' (Davies 1999).

Attitudes to children in Britain are very negative: almost half of British adults consider children to be 'violent and starting to behave like animals' (Anon 2011). In a Barnardo survey as many thought children who get into trouble need help as disagreed; one in four said those children who behaved badly were beyond help by the age of 10.

In July 2009, the Report *Unleashing Aspiration* in the UK was released (Toynbee 2009; Wintour 2009). The Social Mobility Panel found that class has become more rigid, incomes of rich and poor had drawn farther apart and the result was that most people's destiny was decided at birth. 'The ladders up from bottom to top have grown higher. The barriers preventing the rise of interlopers have grown higher, while the safety net preventing even the dimmest privileged children from slipping downwards has grown stronger.'

Professors Jack Shonkoff, founding director of the Center of the Developing Child at Harvard University, Bruce McEwan of Rockefeller University in New York and W. Thomas Boyce, University of British Columbia, Vancouver, reported on some recent scientific advances concerning development in early childhood (Center on the Developing Child 2009). Early life experiences are incorporated into the body and build a foundation not only for later achievement in school and eventual economic productivity, but also for lifelong physical and mental health.

This means that our growing national investment in early childhood services should not be viewed solely through the lens of school readiness. When these programs augment the provision of enriched learning opportunities with the effective reduction of toxic stress, they also serve as promising vehicles for health promotion and disease prevention across the lifespan.

'There is a kind of biological embedding if you will, a biological fingerprint that is left by experiences of growing up in disadvantage, and there are both short term changes in the biology of children who are exposed to those kinds of settings, but there appears to be longer term changes as well.' (Mitchell 2011). Toxic stress occurs when people don't have the personal resources perhaps, the social support system. As McEwan says, 'Stress is really something where you don't have control. And then the paradox about the body is that the body produces chemicals, hormones, like cortisol and adrenalin and we also produce inflammatory cytokines when were stressed, it affects our metabolic hormones'. Amongst the many researchers on how all this leads to suicide is Professor John Mann of Columbia University (Mitchell 2008). Provision of appropriate caring during early childhood, good education, adequate social opportunity and secure housing are matters of social justice.

3.6 Urban Youth in the US and the UK

Research by Professor Milbrey McLaughlin of Stanford University and colleagues over several decades reveals features of the lives of young adolescents very different from what is often portrayed (McLaughlin and Irby 1994; McLaughlin 2000). Young adolescence is the time when they begin to make decisions about such dangerous behaviours as alcohol consumption, drug use, sexual activity and gang involvement. They face far more risks than did their parents in earlier times; they do not become mature adults without assistance. Everyone has a stake in their healthy development.

Out of school young adolescents choose community-based programs which provide enriching and rewarding experiences, opportunities to socialise with peers and with adults, opportunities to learn to set and achieve goals, resolve disputes peaceably, acquire life skills, all programs which contribute significantly to learning and development. There they participate in activities where they feel valued, respected and challenged in positive ways. Students point to a number of improvements schools could make that would help them to be more successful such as additional counselling, appreciation of different learning styles, a better rapport with teachers. As well they seek better access to textbooks and computers outside of class, a quiet place to do homework and adults to work with them in a positive fashion.

Following the general election in the UK severe budget reductions were imposed by the new coalition government. Many analyses have shown that it is the poorer sections of society that will suffer, especially because of the negative impact on the welfare programs funded by local councils.

In August 2011 riots erupted in a number of English cities following the shooting by police of a young male initially believed to be carrying a weapon and threatening police, an assertion later acknowledged as incorrect. Cars were trashed and burned, stores were looted, young people were run down by a car whilst trying to save another person. Prime Minister James Cameron and others talked of a breakdown in family life and of parents failing to control their children and instil into them a sense of right and wrong. Police were given extra powers to arrest and charge people behaving in a grossly disorderly manner.

In the aftermath little attempt was made by authorities to recall the numerous reports which had pointed to the severe outcomes of poverty, inequality and neglect though some commentators did indeed point to these issues (Toynbee 2011a, b). The riots crystallised the fear and loathing felt by the older and wealthy. Magistrates were advised to disregard normal sentencing guidelines and deal harshly with young people arrested during the riots (Bowcott and Bates 2011).

Amongst the numerous comments seeking to explain the reasons for the riots two can be noted. Camila Batmanghelidjh, who has spent decades working with poor and disenfranchised youth, acknowledged the mayhem was unacceptable but pointed to social factors: 'the divide between the rich and the poor exacerbates the problem, things that erode young people's sense of dignity and keeps shaming them, repeatedly, into the corners of society… [so that] violence becomes the currency of survival'; and many neighbourhoods are propped up by the drug trade, violence in effect becoming the norm (Ross 2011). Overcrowding, economic decline, high unemployment, violence within the community are all issues.

In November 2012 there were reports that local authorities in London were preparing to send thousands of homeless families to live in temporary homes outside the capital, in defiance of ministerial demands that people should continue to be housed locally (Butler and Ferguson 2012). Councils are acquiring properties in locations outside London to cope with an expected surge in numbers of vulnerable families presenting as homeless as a result of welfare cuts from next April. They say rising rents in London coupled with the introduction next April of stringent benefit caps leave them in an impossible position, with no option but to initiate an outflow of poorer families from the capital by placing homeless households in cheaper areas, often many miles from their home borough.

In early 2013 leading architects in the UK warned that future homeowners could end up living without enough space or light (Booth 2013). The Government proposes to loosen planning rules leading, in the opinion of the Royal Institute of British Architects, to permission for 'another generation of poor-quality homes'. The average UK home is smaller than ones in France, Spain, Ireland, Denmark, Australia and the US.

Barbara Ehrenreich, author of the book *Nickel and Dimed* (New York: Picador, 2001) about her experience posing as an unemployed person trying to find work, wrote of the extensive criminalisation of poverty in America (Ehrenreich 2011). Families attempting to cope with worsening economic situations tended to cut back on health care, food and often increased the number of people living together. The food stamp program now reaches 37 million people, up about 30 % from pre-recession levels.

Governments defund services that might help the poor but increase law enforcement. Criminalisation of poverty is widespread: ordinances are promulgated designed to drive the destitute off the streets by outlawing sitting, loitering, sleeping or lying down in public places, begging, even jaywalking, littering or carrying an open container. A 62 year old ordained minister Eric Sheptock, wheelchair bound because he was shot in the spine in Vietnam, was taken off to prison by police visiting the shelter where he was staying looking for men with outstanding warrants: Sheptock had previously been issued with a warrant for criminal trespassing, that is sleeping on the streets!

The consequences of the failures beginning in Wall Street financial institutions in 2008 have been huge (Taibbi 2011). No executive has been jailed. That is not to say that law enforcement has fallen away. In Ohio last month, a single mother was caught lying about where she lived to put her kids into a better school district; the judge in the case tried to sentence her to 10 days in jail for fraud, declaring that letting her go free would demean the seriousness of the offenses.

3.7 Education Reform and Economic and Social Disadvantage

Attention to improving educational achievement requires attention to removing the causes of economic and social inequality. Poor children grow up in a social and physical environment of little stimulation, attend poorly resourced schools with high teacher turnover and are often poorly fed. Their physical and mental health is poor and in later life they are more likely to be unemployed, poorly housed and involved in criminal activities and substance abuse. Life expectancy is low.

Substantial proportions of the populations of developed countries live in poverty. The media reinforces the perception that the poor are deliberately antisocial and involved in crime, unwilling to attend school or get work and are happy to subsist on welfare. Substantial research shows that failure to address the causes of poverty contributed to the failure of the program 'No Child Left Behind'. Deliberate campaigns by the very wealthy have contributed significantly to the increasing gap in wealth between the super rich and the poor in developed economies.

The GFC which began around 2008 has had huge effects on young people particularly as well as on single-parent families. Young people are expected to play a major role in the future yet we are not asking them what they think and we mostly pay little attention to the circumstances in which they grow up. Austerity policies in many countries are driving young people into long-term unemployment. The ranks of the homeless increase, the women among them almost invisible.

It is extraordinary surely that governments can consider it economically and politically sensible to subsidise the manufacture of aluminium, the growing of corn to turn it into corn syrup and drilling for oil but not fund actions in urban planning and education which would reduce crime, increase health and wellbeing, increase employment and in the end reduce government outlays.

As a recent report, *The High Cost of Low Educational Performance—The Long-Run Economic Impact of Improving PISA Outcomes* (Hanushek and Woesman 2010) observes, 'While governments frequently commit to improving the quality of education, it often slips down the policy agenda. Because investing in education only pays off in the future, it is possible to underestimate the value and the importance of improvements'.

The second essay discusses inequality in Australia, especially the situation facing Indigenous Australians.

References

Acemoglu, D., & Robinson, J. (2012). *Why nations fail: The origins of power, prosperity and poverty*. New York: Crown.
Anderson, E. (1994, May). The code of the streets. *The Atlantic*.
Anon. (2007, February 14). UK is accused of failing children. *BBC News*.
Anon. (2010, October 6). Job stress drains $730 m from economy. *Sydney Morning Herald*.

Anon. (2011, November 3). Many adults think children are feral, survey finds. BBC.
Anyon, J. (2005). What "Counts" as educational policy? Notes toward a new paradigm. *Harvard Educational Review, 75,* 65–88.
Bauman, Z. (2012, May 31). Downward mobility is now a reality. *The Guardian.*
Bonfiglioli, A. (2003). *Empowering the poor: Local governance for poverty reduction.* New York: United Nations Capital Development Fund.
Booth, R. (2013, April 16). Social housing standards review could worsen rabbit-hutch Britain. *The Guardian.*
Bosely, S. (2008, November 8). Michael Marmot: Leader in the social determinants of health. *The Lancet,* 372(9650), 1625. Retrieved September 7, 2012 from http://www.thelancet.com/journals/lancet/article/PIIS0140-6736%2808%2961675-X/fulltext
Bowcott, O. & Bates, S. (2011, August 15). Riots: Magistrates advised to disregard normal sentencing. *The Guardian.*
Bunting, M. (2013, July 17). Amartya Sen: India's dirty fighter. *The Guardian.*
Butler, P. & Ferguson, B. (2012, November 4). Homeless families to be expelled from London by councils. *The Guardian.*
Center on the Developing Child. (2009, June 2). Roots of adult disease traced to early childhood adversity. Media release. Center on the Developing Child. Harvard University. Retrieved September 8, 2012 from http://developingchild.harvard.edu/
Davies, N. (1999, September 14). Poverty is the key – not just an excuse. *The Guardian.*
Dhillon, A. (2013, September 11). Where did the great dream go? *The Age.*
Edelman, M. W. (2012). *The state of America's children 2012.* Washington, DC: Children's Defense Fund. Retrieved October 11, 2012 from http://www.childrensdefense.org/newsroom/child-watch-columns/child-watch-documents/the-state-of-americas-children-1.html
Ehrenreich, B. (2006, August 25). Wal-Mart licks Its wounds. *Alternet.* Retrieved September 7, 2012 from http://www.alternet.org/story/40784/wal-mart_licks_its_wounds
Ehrenreich, B. (2011, August 9). Tomgram: Barbara Ehrenreich. On Americans (Not) Getting By (Again). *TomDispatch.* Retrieved September 7, 2012 from http://www.tomdispatch.com/archive/175428/
Goldin, C., & Katz, L. F. (2007). Long-run changes in the wage structure: Narrowing, widening, polarizing. *Brookings Papers on Economic Activity, 2,* 135–165.
Hanley, L. (2009, March 14). The Way we live now. *The Guardian.*
Hanushek, E., & Woessmann, L. (2010). *The high cost of low educational performance the long-run economic impact of improving PISA outcomes.* Paris: OECD.
Jha, A. (2013, August 30). Poverty saps mental capacity to deal with complex tasks, say scientists. *The Guardian.*
Larson, D. (2013, September 24). Why scandinavian prisons are superior. *The Atlantic.* Retrieved September 28, 2013 from http://www.theatlantic.com/international/archive/2013/09/why-scandinavian-prisons-are-superior/279949/
Marmot, M. (2001). Inequalities in health. *New England Journal of Medicine, 345*(2), 134–136. Retrieved September 7, 2012 from http://www.mindfully.org/Health/Inequalities-In-Health-Marmot.htm
McLaughlin, M. W. (2000). *Community counts: How youth organizations matter for youth development.* New York: Public Education Network. Retrieved September 7, 2012 from http://publiceducation.issuelab.org/resource/community_counts_how_youth_organizations_matter_for_youth_development
McLaughlin, M. W. & Irby, M. A. (1994). Urban sanctuaries. *Phi Delta Kappa, 76*(4), 300–306.
McNamara, R. S. (1973). Address to the Board of Governors by President. World Bank Group. Nairobi, Kenya. September 24. Retrieved September 7, 2012 from http://www.juerg-buergi.ch/Archiv/EntwicklungspolitikA/EntwicklungspolitikA/assets/McNamara_Nairobi_speech.pdf
Mitchell, N. (presenter). (2008, January 26). The neurobiology of suicide. *ABC RN All In The Mind.* Retrieved September 7, 2012 from http://www.abc.net.au/radionational/programs/allinthemind/the-neurobiology-of-suicide/3226244

Mitchell, N. (presenter). (2011, January 1). Stressed out the powerful biology of stress mastering the control factor part one. *ABC RN All in the Mind*. Retrieved September 7, 2012 from http://www.abc.net.au/radionational/programs/allinthemind/stressed-out-the-powerful-biology-of-stress/2959284

Noah, T. (2012). *The great divergence*. New York: Bloomsberry Press (First published in 10 parts in the online magazine *Slate* in 2010).

OECD. (2008). *Are we growing unequal? New evidence on changes in poverty and incomes over the past 20 years*. Paris: OECD. Retrieved September 7, 2012 from http://www.oecd.org/social/soc/41494435.pdf

OECD. (2013, May 15). *Crisis squeezes income and puts pressure on inequality and poverty…* Retrieved May 16, 2013 from http://www.oecd.org/els/soc/OECD2013-Inequality-and-Poverty-8p.pdf

Rampell, C. (2009, August 27). SAT scores and family income. *New York Times Business Day*.

Robinson, M. (2013, May 23). Tax avoidance: Developing countries take on multinationals. *BBC News*.

Ross, M. (2011, August 11). Blame for riots turns to UK social system. *ABC News*. Retrieved September 1, 2011 from http://www.abc.net.au/news/2011-08-10/society-role-in-london-riots/2833168

Ruthven, M. (2010, May 13). Excremental India. *New York Review of Books*.

Share the Worlds Resources. (2012). *Financing the global sharing economy*. August. Retrieved May 25, 2013 from http://www.stwr.org/about/overview.html

Sharma, N. (2005, July 25). Breaking the cycle of child poverty, *BBC*.

Sowey, M. (2011). *Global poverty*. Albert Park: The Australian Collaboration. Retrieved September 7, 2012 from http://www.australiancollaboration.com.au/pdf/Essays/Global-poverty.pdf

Taibbi, M. (2011, February 16). Why isn't wall street in jail? *Rolling Stone*.

Toynbee, P. (2009, July 20). Equal opportunity is fantasy in any society this unequal. *The Guardian*.

Toynbee, P. (2011a, August 12). Moral outrage at rioters fixes nothing: The only remedies are liberal. *The Guardian*.

Toynbee, P. (2011b, August 19). How sad to live in a society that won't invest in its young. *The Guardian*.

UNICEF. (2007). *Child poverty in perspective: An overview of child well-being in rich countries*. Florence: UNICEF Innocenti Research Centre Report. Retrieved September 7, 2012 from http://www.unicef.org/media/files/ChildPovertyReport.pdf

United Nations. (2010). *Real wealth of nations: Pathways to human development. United nations human development report 2010* (20th Anniversary ed.). Chapter 3. New York: United Nations. Retrieved September 7, 2012 from http://hdr.undp.org/en/reports/global/hdr2010/

VicHealth. (2006). Workplace stress in Victoria – developing a systems approach. Retrieved September 7, 2012 from http://www.vichealth.vic.gov.au/workplacestress

Wilkinson, R., & Pickett, K. (2010). *The spirit level: Why more equal societies almost always do better*. London: Allen Lane.

Wilson, W. J. (2008–2009). The political and economic forces shaping concentrated poverty. *Political Science Quarterly, 123*, 555–571.

Wintour, P. (2009, July 21). Britain's closed shop…. *The Guardian*.

Chapter 4
Community and Inequality: Part 2: Australia

4.1 Inequality in Australia

The first essay on community and inequality dealt with the principle determinants of poverty and the consequences in home life for educational futures and reviewed comprehensive reports on child wellbeing and inequality, especially.

This second essay deals exclusively with inequality in Australia, especially the situation facing Indigenous Australians. Some specific programs to address the basic issues contributing to long standing negative outcomes offer considerable hope after decades of neglect.

Inequality between the very rich and the very poor is increasing in Australia, though not as drastically as in some other countries. Ongoing investment in extractive industries such as mining and the high exchange rate of the Australian dollar has exacerbated the decline in manufacturing and some other parts of the economy including tourism. Legislation restricting organised labour, especially in the last 14 years, has helped continue a trend of declining union membership. The practice of 'fly-in fly-out', adopted by several mining companies in Western Australia and Queensland, has impacted on families. For indigenous people in some areas however, the mining industry has generated considerable employment and revenue to Land Councils through mining royalties.

Ongoing drives for efficiency in business and in government have led to substantial layoffs of employees though unemployment rates have remained at a level substantially below that of several other advanced economies. At the same time remuneration for business executives has continued to increase substantially. And very high housing prices in Australia, fuelled by the ability to write off expenditures on housing for rental purposes from taxes (known as negative gearing), have led to serious and ongoing declines in housing affordability generally as well as very substantial government losses of revenue through the taxes foregone amounting to $40 billion, as already pointed out!

UNICEF delivered another report in 2011 on children in Australia (Child Rights Taskforce 2011). *Listen to the Children* found that for the most part, Australia had not developed child-sensitive laws, policies, initiatives and systems; and

Government bodies had not learned how to consult effectively with children on the full range of issues that affect children's lives. 'Australia currently supports children using a traditional welfare model. Australia delivers assistance to vulnerable children and provides benefits to families but too often, Australia does not ask children about what they think and need. The current approach falls short of Australia's obligations under the Convention of the Rights of the Child…'.

The UNICEF findings for Australia included high levels of infant mortality, high teenage pregnancy and weak family relationships. Findings in respect of indigenous children were particularly poor: only Mexico and Turkey, of OECD countries, have worse levels of deprivation. School achievement is relatively positive with Australia ranking in the top 20 % of OECD nations in reading, maths and science. School achievement for Indigenous young Australians is in the bottom 10 % with ratings better than only Mexico and Turkey. In 2006 7.2 % of Australian children reported having fewer than 11 books in their home.

The Report identified three groups especially disadvantaged by the policy failure: Aboriginal and Torres Strait islander children, children in out-of-home-care and children of asylum seekers who remain in detention facilities in direct contravention of the UN children's convention. Australia collects no data on the reasons why children are placed in care and has no legal remedies for breaches of child rights!

A partnership of unions and the Brotherhood of St Laurence initiated a study, assisted by the Australian Research Council, of people living low paid in Australia. Masterman-Smith and Pocock (2008) point out that most of the people who end up in low paid work are women. They are concentrated in occupations such as cleaners in hotels and workers in child care centres—surprisingly considering the importance of such centres—or providing day care in the home for children of highly paid parents. Many of them are single parents or are in relationships which lack the level of mutual support which go to make a rewarding relationship. If they are women they may also have to do the unpaid housework for the family. By and large those on low pay also lack entitlements such as recreation leave, paid sick leave and flexible working hours, which usually means short notice of what hours are to be worked on any day; all this creates further strain. Low paid workers paying rent often face stress over rent levels and in some Australian cities additional stress because of shortage of rental accommodation.

Many of those on low pay are in fact relatively highly qualified: skilled tradespeople clean schools and offices, experienced school teachers and mental health workers are child minders. They may have tertiary qualifications at diploma or some other first qualification level but see upgrading to a higher degree requires a financial outlay unlikely to be adequately rewarded through a higher level job at higher pay. Low pay is not a transitory experience for many!

The Brotherhood of St Lawrence's 2010 study followed 138 young people from diverse backgrounds throughout their lives (Taylor and Gee 2010). All were born in inner Melbourne, and at 18 the majority (87 %) lived in Melbourne, with some in regional Victoria or interstate. At the end of the year they turned 18, 77 % had completed Year 12 VCE (Victorian Certificate of Education certifying completion of secondary school); 7 % had completed other Year 12 (VCAL, the work-related equivalent of the VCE); 6 % were still at school and were planning to complete Year 12; and 10 % had left school without completing Year 12.

Their pathways differed according to family income. While 98 % in high-income families and 86 % in medium-income families completed VCE, only 44 % of young people from low-income families did. However 15 % from low-income families had completed other Year 12 qualifications, and 15 % were still at school planning to complete Year 12. A quarter from low-income families (26 %) had left school early, but all children from high-income families stayed on.

Taylor and Gee found that social inclusion in education relates not only to completing Year 12, but also to academic achievement which influences tertiary education options. Young people from high-income families had higher average tertiary entrance (ENTER) scores (81.2) than those from medium and low-income families (69.6 and 68.8). (Scores are scaled from 0 to 99.95.) Higher scores at age 18 were positively associated with the following factors at age 16: family factors (high family income, parents with tertiary qualifications, positive family relationships), and school factors (self-rated academic achievement, getting on well with teachers, school engagement) and wellbeing. These results undoubtedly reflect the different experiences in early life influenced by socioeconomic circumstances of the families as described in the first essay. (In the sample 33 % were from low-income families, 26 % from medium and 41 % from high-income backgrounds.)

Unemployment and the working poor are not new phenomena. The experiences of the working poor were explored in Australia by Elisabeth Wynhausen, a senior and well respected journalist (Wynhausen 2006). Inspired by Barbara Ehrenreich's book *Nickel and Dimed—On (Not) Getting By in America* Wynhausen took 9 months leave from the newspaper *The Australian.* Her experiences were published as *Dirt Cheap: Life At The Wrong End of the Job Market* (Pan Macmillan, Sydney, 2005). Employers were not interested in whether she had a criminal record, but only whether she could be available for work at any time. She found, as expected, difficulty in living on the minimum wage. But as well she found painful loss of identity and status.

Workplaces were typified by a culture of hostility and suspicion, workers behaved as if competing with one another and were prepared to sell out their fellow workers if that was needed to keep their job; they accepted their state of powerlessness, workplace conditions dangerous to their health and safety and low pay. Applying for jobs was time-consuming and costly and once employed she had to learn a diversity of skills: training was generally inadequate. She observed many people even in jobs paying above average wages stay in jobs with low satisfaction and that will not further their career because financial security is more important.

In late 2012 the Australian Council of Social Services (ACOSS 2012) reported that in 2010, 2.27 million Australians (almost 13 % of all people or one in eight) were living below the poverty line (50 % of median income or $358 for a single adult and $752 for a couple with two children). This included 575,000 (over 17 % of all children). Twelve per cent of people in capital cities and 13 % outside capital cities were living in poverty. Perhaps disturbingly, despite economic growth over the previous 7 years from 2003 (averaging 0.77 % pa), the proportion of people in poverty rose by a third of a percent. (The poverty line of household disposable income is the most austere poverty line widely used in international research; were the figure of 60 % used, that applying in Britain and the European Union, the figure for people in poverty would rise to 3.7 million people!).

The situation is especially dire for people in unemployed households, between 63 and 73 % living below the poverty line depending on where the line is set. These figures include social security payments; the income figure is arrived at after deducting housing costs. Though those living in poverty come from a diverse background they all aspire to a normal life with secure income, to be respected and to have a place in society.

4.2 Indigenous Australians

Aboriginal and Torres Strait Islander people in Australia, as in many countries where the indigenous inhabitants have been overrun by a later colonising people, suffer severe economic and personal disadvantage. Cultural practice and language have been suppressed, educational opportunities denied, very young children removed from their families. Unemployment or employment in low paid and menial jobs are the norm. Later life is characterised by higher crime rates and high levels of incarceration, poor health and low life expectancy, suicide, alcohol and drug abuse.

There are high levels of conflict including violence within families, high level of pregnancies amongst unmarried women and so on. In particular, school attendance is often low and irregular. It is important to note that social dislocation is an outcome for people on the margin no matter their race! In some of these issues the incidence amongst non-Indigenous people is as high yet the levels of arrest and of incarceration of Indigenous people remain very much higher than for others. A similar situation exists in the US for African Americans and in many societies.

It is clearly established that the experiences of early childhood have a profound effect on later life. Aboriginal children and adolescents are over nine times more likely than other children and young people to be in out-of-home care (Yeo 2003). The conditions under which many Indigenous women grew up is important: it needs to be acknowledged that, in some cases, denial of educational opportunities, recalled experience of forced removal, relative deprivation and physical abuse is an element in the behaviour toward their own children. A cycle is established in which the experiences of young children influence their later behaviour as parents which influences their treatment of their children which in turn.... Positive feedback: escape seems nearly impossible!

If the behaviour of Indigenous children in remote communities, including their participation in schooling, is to be properly addressed the situation of Indigenous women surely needs very special attention. That women are often the ones taking the most direct action to counteract unacceptable social behaviour, often by men, and who oppose the disruptive availability of liquor outlets, is an additional reason for special support of them.

Remote areas pose critical problems for all young people. The solution to lack of employment and other opportunities is likely to be seen to be moving to cities, as it has for decades in all countries. There the attendant problems are crowded living, no employment and a likely slide into crime and/or substance abuse. The costs end up being borne by the community through government expenditures on health costs, policing and similar largely unproductive activities. It would surely be better for governments to subsidise various programs to support regional development and people on the margin anywhere, instead of repeating rhetoric about the solution being individual responsibility!

Treating government funded schemes involving employment in community work such as maintaining areas around towns (Community Employment Development) as work for the dole and not proper employment eliminates important opportunities which can contribute to a feeling of being useful as well as improving the physical and social environment. Providing housing for homeless people in the end costs less than the usual actions of treating them in hospitals, housing them in jails or other ways which end up doing nothing to reduce the homelessness or its causes. People accommodated in reasonable conditions bring hope to their future and often abandon some of their previous unsatisfactory habits; they develop new confidence in themselves and their future.

4.3 Indigenous Education and the Home

Analysis by ACER of Australian Indigenous performance in PISA from 2000 to 2006 reveals that across the three PISA cycles, Indigenous students have performed at a substantially statistically lower average level in reading, mathematical and scientific literacy than their non-Indigenous peers (De Bortoli and Thomson 2010). ACER's Lisa De Bortoli and her colleagues found, 'More than one third of Indigenous students did not achieve Level 2 in reading, mathematical or scientific literacy.' (Level 2 is the base level at which students are considered able to demonstrate competencies that will enable them to actively participate in life situations.) Only 12 % of Indigenous students were able to achieve the highest levels of reading literacy, and no more than 5 % achieved the highest level in mathematical and scientific literacy. In the PISA 2009 tests 35–40 % of Indigenous students did not achieve the proficiency benchmarks compared to 14 % of all students.

The situation at home is critical. Fewer parents of Indigenous students, compared with non-Indigenous families, had attended post-secondary education and many had not completed secondary school. Indigenous students are more likely to live in single parent families, less likely to possess items of family wealth, less likely to have access to the required books and materials or to have a quiet place to study. Initiatives to improve the education of Indigenous students through educational policy have to date had little effect.

If Indigenous students had attended preschool it was most likely to have been for no more than 1 year. They were significantly less likely to be interested or engaged in reading than their non-Indigenous peers and males in particular were little interested in reading. They reported significantly lower levels of confidence in their abilities to handle tasks effectively. These differences were found when self-efficacy was assessed generally, as well as when self-efficacy was assessed in relation to mathematics and science, though that was not so when it came to levels of effort and persistence in studying.

There were no important differences in use of various learning strategies such as memorisation but Indigenous students reported lower preferences for competitive learning environments than did non-Indigenous peers. Students' interaction with teachers and the disciplinary climate of their classes were no different. And Indigenous students start school at a disadvantage compared with their non-Indigenous peers. Whether the real reasons for the low attendance at school is understood by policymakers and many commentators is not clear.

4.4 Community and Responsibility

As part of the development of a course about Aboriginal young people for school counsellors in New South Wales Anthony Hillin and Rob McAlpine from the New South Wales Institute of Psychiatry visited remote communities in New South Wales (Hillin et al. 2008). Their meetings with Aboriginal women were interesting. Sitting in a circle out in the open with 10 Aboriginal women they listened to the talk. After nearly 2 h they had hardly mentioned anything which seemed relevant. 'The women appear hesitant and a little formal. We have identified some people we know in common. The women have talked about other things, including the river and food. Anything but young people! There's been much good-natured joking about each other's fishing prowess: who caught the biggest yellowbelly and how many people got a feed out of it' (Hillin 2010).

'As time goes on, the diameter of the circles in the conversation reduces and there's more focus on young people. One of the women tells us: "My Billy's been in trouble at school and they just chucked him out." Other women name grandchildren who dropped out or have been excluded from school. One volunteers: "School don't know how hard it is for us to go up there". We ask them to tell us more to help us understand. "Some of us don't read so well… When we were at school they hit us for speaking language". Gradually the floodgates open. Tears and anger flow as the women describe their own and their family's difficult experiences at school, in hospitals and in other services.'

Prior to 1972 New South Wales government schools were able to exclude Aboriginal children on racial grounds, including home conditions or substantial community opposition. But they had attended school. They weren't only punished for speaking Aboriginal language; all traditional practices were discouraged. 'Like many indigenous grandparents these women are playing a significant role in parenting their grandchildren. Each said something about how their own humiliating experiences at school made it emotionally difficult for them to attend meetings with school staff when their grandchildren were experiencing problems' ('They think it's because we don't care about our kids').

In 2012 the New South Wales Minister for Education, Adrian Piccoli, announced a new program of support for remote schools including those with high Indigenous enrolment. Teaching in language would be important and if nearby pre-schools did not exist, the government would build one.

In Australia overall, outlays on services per capita, including education, for Indigenous peoples can be as low as 47 % of that for non Indigenous communities. The consequences are particularly evident in the Northern Territory where almost 30 % of the population and 40 % of school children are Indigenous. But it is also evident in Queensland and Western Australia which have high proportions of Indigenous citizens; New South Wales has the highest absolute number of Indigenous citizens who are, however, a much smaller percentage of the total population.

4.5 The Northern Territory Intervention

The largest Aboriginal communities live in cities, especially Western and South Western Sydney with over 28,000 Indigenous people. These areas are, on recent Australian Bureau of Statistics figures, among the most socioeconomically disadvantaged communities in the country.

A new policy of 'Intervention' in prescribed settlements of Australia's Northern Territory (NT) was launched by the Howard Government as the Northern Territory National Emergency Response Act (NTER) following the release of a report, *Little Children are Sacred*, by the Northern Territory Board of Inquiry into the Protection of Aboriginal Children from Sexual Abuse. The legislation was enacted within months of the calling of the 2007 General Election. The Howard Government was defeated at that election; the Intervention was continued in most respects by the subsequent Rudd and Gillard governments. There is substantial debate about the effectiveness of the policy which sought to respond to high levels of domestic violence, including abuse of children, and alcohol and substance abuse and low levels of school attendance. The policy included, amongst other things, the quarantining of welfare for Aboriginal people in certain circumstances including failure of parents to ensure their child's attendance at school, encouragement of home ownership which was believed to reduce poverty and the granting of land tenure through leases to the government and conditional access to public housing (Behrendt 2010). The practical effect of the application of the legislation was suspension of the Commonwealths Racial Discrimination Act or RDA and to deem acts pursuant to the NTER and related legislation to be special measures. Certain Northern Territory and Queensland legislation dealing with discrimination was likewise excluded.

The RDA does provide, *inter alia*, for suspension of the Act in circumstances generally understood to apply to positive measures taken to advance the human rights of certain racial or ethnic groups or individuals by redressing historical disadvantage and creating more favourable conditions or conferring benefits on a particular racial group (Australian Human Rights Commission). Measures characterised as special measures are protected from challenge by those outside the racial or ethnic group who cannot access the measure or do not benefit from them.

Professor Larissa Behrendt, of the Jumbunna Indigenous House of Learning at the University of Technology Sydney, points out that Aboriginal communities of urban areas all over Australia are more disadvantaged than many of the Aboriginal communities being targeted by the Commonwealth government. Prominent Indigenous people including Cape York leader Noel Pearson and Professor Marcia Langton of Melbourne University support the Intervention.

Professor Helen Hughes of the Australian Centre for Independent Studies pointed to the low achievement of Indigenous children in the NT who complete school with severely deficient numeracy and literacy skills (Hughes 2008). She identified inequitable school faculties, inappropriate curriculums and inadequate teaching as major contributors to the situation. But, she asserted, 'the principal causes of the absence of literacy and numeracy are not physical shortcomings but separate Aboriginal curriculums and substandard teaching. Aboriginal and Torres Strait Islander children that live in the open Australian society and attend mainstream schools perform as well as their peers.' She urged all primary schooling to be brought up to mainstream standards with fully equipped schools, mainstream curriculums [sic] and full time qualified resident teachers. Teacher accommodation and additional training would be required.

Four years later Helen Hughes and Mark Hughes released a further report *Indigenous Education 2012* (Hughes and Hughes 2012). They noted that the Commonwealth Government had replaced the target of educational equality for Aboriginals [sic] and Torres Strait Islanders with what they labelled as a 'soft target' of halving the gap between Indigenous and non-Indigenous students by 2018. They repeated some of the criticisms of Indigenous education infrastructure and staffing of the 2008 report by Helen Hughes.

They asserted, 'Governments and education departments refuse to face the evidence that school ethos and classroom instruction are at the heart of education problems. The failure to reform welfare also contributes to high failure rates through low expectations and attendance rates.' They recommended school principals be given sufficient autonomy in staffing and budgeting as well as after schools and vacation programs and be held accountable for students' results. Training for the unemployed should be linked to actual job offers; pretend vocational training and jobs should be abolished.

Responding to the report by Helen and Mark Hughes, Bill Fogarty (Research Associate at the National Centre for Indigenous Studies at the Australian National University) emphasised the relationship between levels of attainment and social and economic disadvantage including infrastructure and access to government services (Fogarty 2012). 'These factors are not excuses for poor outcomes. They combine to constitute the reality within which teachers, students and parents battle every day to raise literacy and numeracy standards.' He pointed also to the prevalence of hearing loss, a feature of life in situations of poverty, as mentioned (in the later chapter in this book) in the discussion of testing and the understanding of educational achievement. He recalls a study of education expenditure in Wadeye, an Aboriginal community on the western edge of the Daly River Reserve formerly known as Port Keats. There underspending on education totalled over $3 million per annum: for every dollar spent on a child elsewhere in the Territory, only 47 cents was spent on a student in Wadeye. He also mentions previous reviews which found that almost half of the money designated for Indigenous education was in fact going into the Territory's Treasury as 'on costs'.

Fogarty does strongly support proper funding and servicing, standardised attendance data and addressing of truancy. But he advocates attention to 'known factors of success such as community partnership and a mix of direct and indirect instruction' as well as genuine commitment from all levels of government.

ARC Australian Professorial Fellow at the Centre for Aboriginal Economic Policy Research at the Australian National University Jon Altman is one of the people who have studied Indigenous economic development. Altman's research extends over the past 33 years. He has strongly criticised the Intervention and in late 2011 commented on its impact (Altman 2010, 2011). The Government had reported that since 2007–2008 Indigenous hospitalisation rates NT-wide had increased from 229 per 1,000 to 262 per 1,000. Recorded school enrolment and attendance had declined from 64.5 % in February 2009 to 62.7 % in February 2011. Income support recipients had increased from just on 20,000 in June 2009 to nearly 24,000 in June 2011. Reports of child abuse in NTER communities (communities covered by the Intervention) had increased from 174 in 2007–2008 to 272 in 2010–2011; as had domestic violence reported incidents, from 1,612 to 2,968. Confirmed attempted suicide/self harm incidents increased from 109 in 2007–2008 to 227 in 2010–2011 in NTER communities.

Commenting on the persistent Aboriginal employment problem in mid 2012, Altman (2012) observed that though there was a slight drop in Aboriginal unemployment it was insignificant. The gap between Indigenous and non Indigenous unemployment appeared, according to Bureau of Statistics (ABS) figures, to have stagnated. Altman pointed out that the ABS figures showed Indigenous unemployment in regional areas was almost four times that of non-Indigenous people and in remote areas it was more than five times as great. He pointed to policies in other countries which imagined huge numbers of unemployed and marginalised people would magically find work, policies that were decimating livelihoods and communities through valorisation of formal work and training and provision of social spending only where the unemployed participated in 'supervised workfare'.

Altman noted that in Maningrida in the Arnhem Land region of the Northern Territory, the unemployed are deemed as being irresponsible subjects whose welfare income needs to be managed and whose expenditures closely monitored by the nanny state… An unprecedented massive housing construction phase that has just ended has delivered 100 public houses in 'new sub', as locals call it, but it has delivered neither bankable skills nor sustainable jobs for local people. He concluded by observing that the alternative to this kind of policy failure would be 'basic income support, which could unleash individual productivity and entrepreneurship in myriad unconventional ways to improve livelihoods and well-being'.

Behrendt (2010), reviewing the NT Intervention and its outcomes 3 years on, points to a study in Halls Creek in Western Australia linking welfare payments to school attendance which found the attitudes of parents of Aboriginal children were only one of the factors that affected school attendance. Quality teaching and general school culture play a central role in the attendance and performance of Aboriginal children. The housing situation in Halls Creek—where overcrowding is a critical problem—hardly provides an environment where families can be 'school ready'. Is the failure to address this overcrowding an example of negligence?

Behrendt pointed out that there is no evidence to show that linking welfare to behavioural change is effective. In fact, 'the imposition of such punitive measures in an already dysfunctional situation will exacerbate the stress on households. The goal of improved attendance may be better achieved by the introduction of breakfast and lunch programs; programs that bring the Aboriginal community, especially Elders, into the schools; Aboriginal teacher's aides and Aboriginal teachers; curriculum that engages Aboriginal children; and programs that blend the development self-esteem and confidence through engaging with culture with programs that focus on academic excellence.'

Speaking at the Wheeler Centre, Melbourne on 23 March 2011 Behrendt (2011) cited numerous examples of successful community-school driven projects. She also pointed out that Indigenous women in some towns in New South Wales will indeed take direct action to deal with substance abuse and school truancy whereas in other towns a feeling that they are not noticed or consulted can be the excuse for no action.

The 2011 evaluation of trends in education as a result of the Intervention (Rothman et al. 2011) in NTER communities noted that one of the reasons given to justify the Intervention was the poor educational outcomes of Aboriginal children: they were seen as being at the heart of the exclusion of Aboriginal people from confidently participating in their own culture or mainstream culture. This report for the Commonwealth Department responsible for Indigenous Affairs compiled by researchers from the Australian Council for Education Research (ACER) found that many children entering school in the NT are at a distinct disadvantage when compared to other children across Australia. The report was based on 3 years of data.

The substantial challenges facing education of Indigenous children in the NT are not assisted by the fact that only 3 % of teachers in the Territory and four of the 150 school principals were of Indigenous origin though Indigenous people make up almost a third of the Territory population; almost half of teachers serving NTER communities covered by the Intervention had been in their current job for less than 1 year indicating a turnover considerably greater than for all Territory schools. On average a teacher stays at NTER schools for some 8–10 months! The report referenced an independent review of teaching which found that a highly coordinated and consistent approach to professional development in curriculum, pedagogy and assessment was paramount (Rothman et al. 2011, p. 300, footnote 862).

Housing for teachers had been increased in the 3 years to 2011 and the Territory Government had implemented a wide range of professional development opportunities. Though funding had been provided for new classrooms it was considered impossible to assess the quality of the infrastructure. A universal meals program was introduced at a cost of over $40 million over 4 years. Further support was given to early childhood programs under the Partnership Agreement on Early Childhood Education.

Assessment of educational outcomes in NTER communities concluded that there had been some progress in reading as assessed by NAPLAN, the nationwide program of standardised tests: the percentage of Year 3 students above the national minimum standard in reading increased from 28 % in 2008 to 41 % in 2010. Small increases in the proportion of students at or above the national minimum standard were found in Years 5, 7 and 9. However, while the results for Year 3 were impressive, results for Indigenous children continue to remain far behind the results for all Territory schools and all students in Australia. Numeracy results were less impressive, the results in writing much lower. Participation rates increased. School enrolment rates—estimates at the time of reporting, which must be viewed with caution—were that some 2,000 or 13 % of Indigenous school age children were not enrolled and showed little or no improvement over the years 2006–2010 except for middle years (7 through 9). Low enrolment mainly involves older children. There are also differences in attendance rates by age, the highest rates being at the Primary level; attendance rates declined over the period covered by the report!

Rothman and colleagues concluded that there was some improvement in some outcomes. However, the ability of the Intervention to contribute to continued improvement in younger peoples educational outcomes will depend, they said, in large part on the extent to which the measures applied are integrated with other initiatives in the Territory: in other words the initiatives introduced must become part of the mainstream.

Rhetoric takes over in the hardest areas of reform instead of genuine policy development and implementation. One of the responses to Aboriginal children's poor test scores in NAPLAN has been to demand more teaching in English: in October 2008 the Territory Education Minister announced that the first 4 hours of every school day all schooling were to be conducted in English.

Bilingual education means children learning to recognise the letters of the alphabet in their own language which makes it easier to learn to read in English: as at September 2008 there were eight schools in the Territory with bilingual programs. What is extraordinary is the failure of people advocating teaching in language other than the first language of the student to recognise that language is integral to identity; languages are fast disappearing, restricting language is a strategy of control! Of course being able to communicate in the language most commonly spoken is important. On the other hand, many Indigenous people already are multilingual!

4.6 Self Determination: Sovereignty Matters!

At issue in much of this debate about Indigenous policy is the question of whether, or to what extent, identification of Indigenous peoples with their own tradition and maintenance of contact with cultural tradition is significant in either improving behaviour and social and economic conditions or instead stands in the way of what is seen as improvement. Generally in all cases where western peoples have entered the country of Indigenous peoples, the new arrivals have seen one of their roles to be establishing rules by which the original inhabitants should behave. The outcomes have been poor to tragic at least initially and in many cases this continues to the present.

In Australia, as *Sydney Morning Herald* columnist Adele Horin (2011) wrote, referring to various opposing views, 'The relentless barrage of bad news about indigenous Australians is at odds with signs of unambiguous improvement in important aspects of their lives. For decades we have heard a depressing story of policy failure in Aboriginal affairs, buttressed by media images of drunken Aborigines, their broken-down homes and mangy dogs… [Yet] progress has been made. Horin notes, It is often assumed traditional culture is the stumbling block to achievement. [But]… the reverse is generally true.'

Horin noted that 35 years of research by academics from the Australian National University found absolute and relative improvement for Aboriginal people in economic and jobs growth, education, school retention, home ownership and declining fertility rates, improvements which held true also for the 10 years to 2006.

Michael Dockery of Curtin University in Western Australia analysed 'indicators of attachment to Indigenous culture', including language spoken at home, ability to speak an Indigenous language, identification with clan, tribal or language group, recognition of and living in or visiting homeland, attendance at or participation in cultural events and social activities (Dockery 2010). The respondents came from remote and very remote locations, regional towns and major cities in Australia.

Dockery wrote, 'While intense debate continues regarding the direction that Australian policy should take in addressing Indigenous disadvantage, or in closing the gap, there are two points upon which there can be little disagreement: 1. Our policies to date have been a dismal failure, and 2. The deplorable circumstances in which many Indigenous peoples continue to live require urgent attention.'

Dockery's research found strong evidence of a positive effect of cultural attachment on socioeconomic outcomes… Strong attachment leads to significantly better self-assessed health. Those with weak or moderate cultural attachment are the most likely to have been arrested in the past 5 years relative to both those with minimal or strong attachment… 'Finally, those with strong cultural attachment are significantly more likely to be in employment than those with moderate or minimal attachment.'

Dockery's research was based on the 2002 NATSISS (National Aboriginal and Torres Strait Islander Social Survey) data comprising responses from 9,359 individuals, all of Indigenous descent, from 5,887 different households.

4.6 Self Determination: Sovereignty Matters!

George Williams, Anthony Mason Professor of Law at the University of New South Wales, has pointed to a fundamental flaw in the latest changes to the nature of the NT Intervention (Williams 2011). Aboriginal people want a say about the use of alcohol, how they spend their money, about ownership of their land and about the health of their children. Williams referred to the Harvard Project on American Indian Economic Development (Harvard Project 2010) which '.. has run hundreds of research studies over more than two decades on what does and does not work in Native American communities. Its most important finding is that "sovereignty matters".'

Williams points out, 'The evidence in the US and Australia shows time and again that redressing disadvantage in the longer term depends upon indigenous people having the power to make decisions that affect them. They must be responsible for the programs designed to meet their needs, and must be accountable for the successes and failures that follow.'

The Harvard Project's headline finding is that when Native Americans 'make their own decisions about what development approaches to take, they consistently out-perform external decision makers on matters as diverse as governmental form, natural resource management, economic development, health care and social service provision. Improvements in education, employment and quality of life must be achieved by policies and programs owned and developed by the indigenous people affected. The hard work must be done by Aboriginal people.'

But if development is to take hold, assertions of sovereignty must be backed by capable institutions of governance. The Harvard project found that capable institutions of governance are developed through adoption of stable decision rules and establishment of fair and independent mechanisms of dispute resolution. 'Culture matters. Successful economies stand on the shoulders of legitimate, culturally grounded institutions of self-government… Leadership matters. Nation building requires leaders who introduce new knowledge and experiences, challenge assumptions, and propose change.'

4.7 Closing the Gap

The Australian Parliament's House of Representatives Standing Committee on Aboriginal and Torres Strait Islander Affairs reported in June 2011 on Indigenous youth in the criminal justice system (House of Representatives Standing Committee on Aboriginal and Torres Strait Islander Affairs 2011). Twenty years after the Royal Commission into Aboriginal Deaths in Custody Report the incarceration rate of Indigenous Australians is worse. 'Indigenous juveniles are 28 times more likely than non-Indigenous juveniles to be incarcerated, despite Indigenous peoples representing only 2.5 % of the Australian population. This is a shameful state of affairs.'

The incarceration rate in Victoria has remained steady but there are higher rates in Western Australia and the NT according to Australian Bureau of Statistics figures (Vowles 2011). In Western Australia Aboriginal people are 19 times more likely to be in gaol than are non-Aboriginal people. Deaths in custody have increased by nearly 50 % in the decade to 2008 compared with the decade to 1989 and are especially high in New South Wales and Queensland (Ting 2011). The rate of deaths in custody for non Aboriginal people is slightly more than for Aboriginal people but the incarceration rates are radically different.

'Indigenous social and economic disadvantage have contributed to the high levels of Indigenous contact with the criminal justice system. Sadly, the Committee found there is intergenerational dysfunction in some Indigenous communities which presents a significant challenge to break the cycle of offending, recidivism and incarceration.'

Dr Don Weatherburn and colleagues at the NSW Bureau of Crime Statistics and Research report (Weatherburn, Snowball and Hunter 2006), 'The analysis shows that the Indigenous respondents to the NATSISS were far more likely to have been charged with, or imprisoned for, an offence if they abused drugs or alcohol, failed to complete Year 12 or were unemployed. Participating in the Commonwealth Development Employment Scheme (CDEP) appears to reduce the risk of being charged (compared with being unemployed). Other factors that increase the risk of being charged or imprisoned include: experiencing financial stress, living in a crowded household and being a member of the 'stolen generation''.

The Committee found that current policy for COAG's Closing the Gap Strategy did not include a National Partnership Agreement dedicated to the Safe Communities Building Block, nor did it include specific targets relating to justice.

Of specific relevance to education are these findings of the Committee (paragraphs 2.38–2.40): Children who have access to a good quality education and who are supported and directed by their parents to attend school are likely to develop the necessary knowledge, skills and social norms for a productive and rewarding adult life.

'The difference in educational attainment between Indigenous and non-Indigenous Australians is a powerful determinant of the overrepresentation of Indigenous youth in the justice system'. 'Indigenous children are less likely than non-Indigenous children to have access to, or participate in early childhood education. The gap in preschool learning opportunities means that many Indigenous students will be disadvantaged from their very first day at school.'

In August 2011, Gary Banks and Robert Fitzgerald of the Productivity Commission and Professor Mick Dodson of the Australian National University launched *Overcoming Indigenous Disadvantage*. The latest trend data assembled in the report (Martin 2011; Wilson 2011) showed improvement in only 13 of the 45 indicators monitored by the government. In another 10 the report found no real improvement. In seven it found outcomes to be going backwards. This is 4 years after the NT Intervention and 2 years after then Prime Minister Rudd pledged to close the gap!

The report notes, 'Not everything that matters can be captured in indicators, and some information is better presented in words, rather than numbers. In particular, community level change may not show up in aggregate data. The main report includes examples of things that work—activities and programs that appear to be making a difference, often at the community level…'

Analysis of the things that work, together with wide consultation with Indigenous people and governments, identified the following 'success factors':

- cooperative approaches between Indigenous people and government—often with the non-profit and private sectors as well
- community involvement in program design and decision-making—a bottom-up rather than top-down approach
- good governance—at organisation, community and government levels
- ongoing government support—including human, financial and physical resources.

4.8 Hope for the Future?

In this ongoing consideration of Australian Indigenous education little attention is given in the media to positive developments such as the work of the Indigenous Literacy Foundation which aims to raise literacy levels and improve the lives and opportunities of Indigenous Australians living in remote and isolated regions. This is done by providing books and literacy resources to Indigenous communities and raising broad community awareness of Indigenous literacy issues.

Young Sydney Aboriginal man Jack Manning Bancroft recently started AIME, Australian Indigenous Mentoring Experience, which provides young graduate students to help Indigenous children. This goes to the heart of the problems identified by ACERs study of Indigenous educational performance as researched by Lisa De Bortoli and colleagues mentioned above. AIME provides dynamic educational programs that give Indigenous high school students the skills, opportunities, belief and confidence to finish school at the same rate as their peers. AIMEs website states that the program has proven to dramatically improve the chances of Indigenous kids finishing school.

AIME also connects students with post Year 12 opportunities, including further education and employment. At each site, AIME operates a Core Program and an Outreach Program. The Core Program targets local Indigenous high school students located within 30 min drive of a participating university campus. The Outreach Program extends the AIME experience to Indigenous high school students within 2–3 h of a participating university campus. AIME is supported by a number of distinguished Australians.

The Heads Up 2010 conference, the first Indigenous and Social Circus conference and professional development project was held in July 2010. Over 50 Indigenous and community circus artists from all over Australia gathered in Sydney for the conference (O'Brien 2009). Many artists who spoke attested to the incredible benefits of circus programs and gave accounts of their personal and professional experiences that made profound differences to their lives.

Noel Tovey, who opened the conference, spoke about his experience as an Indigenous artist. Tovey was born in the slums of Melbourne in 1933 (as reported in the Australian Biography 2006). He suffered sexual abuse, was abandoned by his parents at age six, was bashed and bullied for being black and ended up on the streets. 'In Pentridge Jail at the age of 17, he contemplated suicide—but the voices of his ancestors prevented him and helped turn his life around'. He cited the arts as his saviour, strengthening and promoting Indigenous culture on a personal, spiritual and social level. At age 24 he was dancing in Sadlers Wells in London and became principal dancer and an acclaimed choreographer. He returned to Australia in 1991: his experience gave him the opportunity to connect more deeply with his Aboriginal heritage and contribute to the Indigenous community. As well as sitting on various boards and committees and teaching, he continues as a writer and theatre director. Many other stories were told at the conference of young Indigenous people becoming a success through artistic engagement.

Jack Buckskin is a Kaurna man living in Adelaide, South Australia. He grew up in South Australia's Adelaide Plains not knowing his traditional language and culture. The language was thought to have disappeared a century ago but has been revived by linguists. Buckskin started learning the language in 2006 and now leads the teaching of Kaurna language and culture offered as evening classes at two sites in Adelaide and through the School of Languages. Eight Aboriginal languages are taught at various schools technical colleges and universities in South Australia. Buckskin's mission to renew interest in the language and culture is the subject of a film by Dylan McDonald.

These stories go to that vitally important element in all people, self confidence, a feeling of being worthwhile!

Tony Abbott, Leader of the Opposition Coalition addressed the Sydney Institute in March 2013. He noted the significant and growing numbers of well-educated, highly articulate and successful Aboriginal people. 'We need to become more familiar with these success stories even as we lament that they are still too rare.' He promised that should the Coalition be elected to government in September 2013, Indigenous affairs would be a responsibility of the Department of Prime Minister and Cabinet: he would be Prime Minister for Indigenous Affairs!

He began, 'There may come a time, perhaps some decades hence, when we can be relaxed and comfortable about the circumstances of indigenous Australians—but it's not now'. Our failure to come to grips with this remains, in Paul Keating's resonant phrase, a stain on our nation's soul.' He gave support to after school education of Indigenous children in indigenous culture. He also spoke of truancy officers administering on the spot fines instead of quarantining welfare payments to encourage attendance at school, publishing reliable school attendance data, increasing incentives for teachers to undertake longer-term postings to remote Indigenous communities.

4.9 Overcoming Inequality: Self-Determination and Ending Discrimination

Inequality is increasing in Australia, despite economic growth. Government and private sector policies on employment, including wage policies, provision of maternity/paternity leave and social services programs affecting the disadvantaged all have influences on each other and on health and education. Inequality is especially affecting children and Indigenous peoples of all ages, especially in remote areas. Addressing the inequities in education and the failures in educational achievement requires simultaneously addressing the other causes of poverty and disadvantage.

Social service programs are mostly inadequately funded in Australia as in the US, the UK and many other countries. This contributes to about one in eight people in Australia, including 17 % of children, living in poverty. In Australia well over 50 % of unemployed people live in poverty; remote communities are especially at risk.

In Australia, Indigenous children, children in out-of-home-care and children of asylum seekers are especially vulnerable. This is a similar to the situation in other countries. In the US, Canada, New Zealand and Australia, occupation of country by colonising people from Europe has been accompanied by violence, exploitation, forced removal of children from their families, deprivation of educational opportunity, denial of the right to speak their language and so on. Some of those policies have continued even to the most recent times!

That the Commonwealth Government's Intervention in the Northern Territory has been beneficial is a strongly contested proposition. Provision of quality teaching and adequate resources for schools are significant issues for Indigenous children in remote locations. Even availability of writing materials are a problem, let alone books. High levels of incarceration of Indigenous people continue decades after Royal Commissions even though levels of substance abuse and minor crime are no greater than for non-Indigenous people. Substantial readily accessible research reveals severe negative effects of parental incarceration on children, often leading to socially unacceptable behaviour later in life by those children.

The recommendation by the Royal Commission into Aboriginal Deaths in Custody that as far as possible people, if they are to be imprisoned, be located as close as possible to their family seems not to have been implemented. Conditions within prisons make visits by family very difficult or even rule it out. A very unsatisfactory situation indeed exists in Australia in respect of prison conditions, a situation entirely unlike that in Scandinavian countries (Larson 2013).

The measures introduced in some states in response to perceived socially unacceptable behaviour by Indigenous people continues to result in very negative outcomes. People severely affected by excessive consumption of alcohol are taken to police stations where they may be severely mistreated, even bashed. They could be taken to hospital instead! The measures applied in the NT Intervention, such as quarantining welfare payments to force school attendance are ones that would not be applied to other communities except in the most extraordinary of circumstances. That is why the Howard Government originally removed the Racial Discrimination Act from application in the NTER. Those measures are grounded in views about Indigenous life, beliefs and reasons for behaviour which seldom have any relationship to reality. Demanding attendance at schools which are poorly staffed and resourced and at which it appears that it is appropriate to marginalise Indigenous culture seems more than a hard ask!

To assert that families have little or no interest in the future of their children flies in the face of evidence from normal conversation. At the 1997 conference commemorating the 30th anniversary of the passing of the 1967 referendum which recognised Indigenous Australians as citizens by removal of words from the Australian Constitution which discriminated against them, the then Governor-General, Sir William Dean, reported his wife as saying to him that Aboriginal women wanted for their children exactly what she wanted for her children.

Chris Graham, award-winning journalist and former managing editor of *Tracker* magazine, examined the voting patterns at identifiably Aboriginal voting booths in the 7 September 2013 general election (Graham 2013). He found that on average 71 % of the vote at these booths was for the Australian Labor Party with swings against candidates for the Abbott-led Coalition averaging around 12 %. The underlying trend in the seat of Lingiari, which takes in all of the communities affected by the Intervention, favoured the ALP. Graham concludes that the evidence from the 2013 and 2007 elections shows that whilst there is a preference for Labor amongst Aboriginal people there is no persistent preference for any major party: but overwhelmingly Aboriginal people do not want Tony Abbott as the Prime Minister for Aboriginal Affairs. Two issues got mainstream airing through the campaign: Abbott's plan to appoint a National Indigenous Council and the probable removal of $40 millions from Aboriginal Legal Aid. Graham's concluding observation is that overwhelmingly Aboriginal people want genuine self-determination where a distinct people choose their own leaders, make their own laws, govern their own lives.

Placing authority for control of their affairs in the hands of Indigenous peoples can lead to many of the consequences being at least significantly overcome. That is shown by the Harvard study and by the experience of countries such as New Zealand and Canada. Maintaining connection with tradition and continuing to speak language are also significant. It is very unfortunate that some influential persons advocate marginalising language as if it was holding back educational achievement! Various community programs involving Indigenous youth show promise. The evidence for this is strong: it is known to Australian governments.

Many fine plays by, and involving, Indigenous people, as well as novels, poetry, music and dance, have been contributed by Indigenous Australians: these have become more prominent and appreciated in the last 20 or so years as has the interest in, purchase and exhibition of Indigenous art, now recognised in Australian and overseas as significant contemporary creativity, not 'primitive art'. Many of the literary and graphic contributions deal with a hideous past. Many of them, even when they concern violence and deprivation, nevertheless contain extraordinary humour and hope.

In 2013, a play *The Secret River*, based on the novel of the same name by Kate Grenville and adapted for the stage by Andrew Bovell, opened at the Sydney Theatre Company. It tells the story of William Thornhill and his wife, transported to Sydney from England as convicts, early settlers with their children on the Hawkesbury River north of Sydney. Thornhill's early fears of Aboriginal people progress to appreciation of them but end in appalling tragedy as egged on by villainous settlers he participates in the massacre of the local people.

Distinguished Director Neil Armfield wrote in the introduction to the program notes, 'The Secret River is a difficult story to tell. For all the beauty, dignity and depth of this tale, it keeps leading into dark places. Four weeks into rehearsal it is hard to direct with your eyes stinging with tears. It takes us back to a moment in our country's narrative when a different outcome, a different history, was possible. Or at least imaginable, where those who came might have listened and learnt from those who were here, might have found a way of living here on this land with respect and humility. Instead, enabled by gunpowder and fed by ignorance, greed and fear, a terrible choice was made. It is a choice that had formed the present. Nine generations later, we are all living with its consequences. The lucky country is blighted by an inheritance of rage and of guilt, denial and silence.'

The history of Indigenous peoples in Australia is unique unto itself. But there are parallels with other countries and there are commonalities in the way we deal with 'the other'. Time and time again people of the dominant culture seek to resolve the problems which emerge from domination and marginalisation by populist myths and implementation of strategies derived from those myths, myths about intelligence, motivations, relationships and world views. There is instead so much to learn from the rich diversity of humanity. As Armfield says though listening and learning might have been a consequence of Europeans arriving in Australia, the relationship with Indigenous peoples has instead been destroyed by ignorance and more. As many have said we do not face an Indigenous problem, we face a non-Indigenous problem.

It is not just education which is needed to overcome the consequences!

References

Altman, J. (2010, June 21). NT intervention three years on: Government's progress report is disturbing. *Crikey*. Retrieved September 7, 2011 from http://www.crikey.com.au/2010/06/21/nt-intervention-three-years-on-governments-progress-report-is-disturbing/

Altman, J. (2011, November 1). Evidently: A new intervention? *Tracker*. Retrieved September 7, 2012 from http://tracker.org.au/2011/11/evidently-a-new-intervention/

Altman, J. (2012, August 10). Rethinking the persistent indigenous employment problem. *Crikey*. Retrieved May 11, 2013 from http://www.crikey.com.au/2012/08/10/rethinking-the-persistent-indigenous-employment-problem/

Australian Human Rights Commission. (2013). *The suspension and reinstatement of the RDA and special measures in the NTER*. Retrieved October 2, 2013 from http://www.humanrights.gov.au/publications/suspension-and-reinstatement-rda-and-special-measures-nter-1

Behrendt, L. (2010). Sharing the luck. Closing the evidence gap. In M. Davis & M. Lyons (Ed.), *More than luck*. Canberra: Centre for Policy Development. Retrieved September 7, 2012 from http://morethanluck.cpd.org.au/more-than-luck-ebook/rethinking-closing-the-gap/

Behrendt, L. (2011). Overcoming indigenous disadvantage video. Retrieved September 7, 2012 from http://wheelercentre.com/dailies/post/1d33b68500fb/

Child Rights Taskforce. (2011). *Listen to Children*. Child Rights NGO Report Australia. Retrieved September 7, 2011 from http://www.unicef.org.au/downloads/Advocacy/Listening-to-children-single-web.aspx

De Bortoli, L. & Thomson, S. (2010). *Contextual factors that influence the achievement of Australia's Indigenous students: Results from PISA 2000-2006*. Melbourne: ACER. Retrieved September 7, 2012 from http://www.acer.edu.au/documents/PISA2006-Indigenous.pdf

Dockery, A. (2010). Culture and wellbeing: The case of indigenous Australians. *Social Indicators Research, 99*, 315–332.

Fogarty, B. (2012, July 3). Indigenous education report misses the big picture. *The Conversation*. Retrieved April 12, 2013 from http://theconversation.com/indigenous-education-report-misses-the-big-picture-8024

Graham, C. (2013, September 13). Prime minister for indigenous affairs? hardly. *ABC The Drum*. Retrieved September 16, 2013 from http://www.abc.net.au/news/2013-09-12/graham-prime-minister-for-indigenous-affairs/4951900

Harvard Project. (2010). *What works. Where. and Why? Overview of the Harvard project on American Indian economic development*. Retrieved September 7, 2012 from http://hpaied.org/

Hillin, A. (2010, August 1). Walking the Path Together; ABC RN Ockham's Razor. Retrieved September 7, 2012 from http://www.abc.net.au/rn/ockhamsrazor/stories/2010/2967985.htm

Hillin, A., et al. (2008). A model for consultation with Aboriginal stakeholders about young people's mental health and wellbeing: The NSW school-link training program. *Australasian Psychiatry, 16*, 326–332.

Horin, A. (2011, July 16). Respect helps to bridge the gap. *Sydney Morning Herald*.

House of Representatives Standing Committee on Aboriginal and Torres Strait Islander Affairs. (2011). *Doing time—time for doing: Indigenous youth in the criminal justice system*. Canberra: The Parliament of the Commonwealth of Australia.

Hughes, H. (2008). *Indigenous Education in the Northern Territory*. CIS Policy Monograph 83.

Hughes, H. & Hughes, M. (2012). *Indigenous Education 2012*. Centre for Independent Studies Policy Monograph 129. Retrieved April 19, 2013 from http://www.cis.org.au/publications/policy-monographs/article/4223-indigenous-education-2012/

Larson, D. (2013, September, 24). Why Scandinavian prisons are superior. *The Atlantic*. Retrieved September 29, 2013 from http://www.theatlantic.com/international/archive/2013/09/why-scandinavian-prisons-are-superior/279949/

Martin, P. (2011, August 25). Indigenous population still falling through gap. *Sydney Morning Herald*.

Masterman-Smith, H., & Pocock, B. (2008). *Living low paid; the dark side of prosperous Australia*. Crows Nest: Allen & Unwin.

O'Brien, K. (presenter). (2009, June 16) Education systems too narrow: Sir Ken Robinson interviewed by Kerry O'Brien. ABC TV 7.30 Report. Retrieved August 23, 2012 from http://www.abc.net.au/7.30/content/2009/s2600125.htm

Rothman, S. et al. (2011). Enhancing education. In *northern territory emergency response evaluation report 2011* (pp. 292–331). Canberra: Dept of Families, Housing, Community Services and Indigenous Affairs (FaHCSIA).

Taylor, J. & Gee, N. (2010). Turning 18 pathways and plans. *Life Chances Study stage 9*. Retrieved September 7, 2012 from http://www.bsl.org.au/pdfs/TaylorGee_Turning_18_pathways_and_plans_2010.pdf

Ting, I. (2011, April 15). Why are deaths in custody rising? *Crikey*. Retrieved September 8, 2012 from http://www.crikey.com.au/2011/04/15/deaths-in-custody-20yrs-after-a-royal-commission-why-are-fatalities-rising/

References

Vowles, E. (presenter). (2011, April 19). Twenty years on from aboriginal deaths in custody report. *ABC RN The Law Report*. Retrieved September 8, 2011 from http://www.abc.net.au/radionational/programs/lawreport/twenty-years-on-from-aboriginal-deaths-in-custody/3008344

Weatherburn, D., Snowball. L., & Hunter, B. (2006). The economic and social factors underpinning Indigenous contact with the justice system: Results from the 2002 NATSISS survey. *Crime and Justice Bulletin,* 104: 1–16. Retrieved September 8, http://www.lawlink.nsw.gov.au/lawlink/bocsar/ll_bocsar.nsf/vwFiles/cjb104.pdf/$file/cjb104.pdf

Williams, G. (2011, July 5). Latest chapter ignores the fatal flaw in territory intervention. *Sydney Morning Herald*.

Wilson, L. (2011, August 2). Gillard holds hope for change on indigenous disadvantage. *The Australian*.

Wynhausen, E. (2006, December 30). Slippery slopes of the job treadmill. *The Australian*.

Yeo, S. S. (2003). Australia bonding and attachment of Australian aboriginal children. *Child Abuse Review, 12*, 292–304.

Chapter 5
Early Childhood: A World of Relationships

'… one of the things that we know is that literally from the time they're born, infants have capacities to empathise with the emotions and internal states of other people, and by the time they're 18 months old, perhaps even a bit younger, children show signs of altruism. So that they'll actively act to help another person achieve their ends or achieve their goals. By the time they're 2-1/2, a really striking set of studies, young children seem to be able to discriminate between purely conventional roles and genuinely moral ones.

'By the time they're 2-1/2… young children seem to be able to discriminate between purely conventional roles and genuinely moral one's….[in many ways] young children are actually smarter, more imaginative, more caring and even more conscious than adults.'

Professor Alison Gopnik, University of California, Berkeley (in Saunders 2011).

5.1 The Critical Importance of Early Childhood

The earliest years of a child's life are critical. Investment in time and money then returns substantial benefits to the child and the family and to the community and society generally. Whilst the social, economic and educational background of the family are the most significant predictors of the child's achievement in later educational life at school and beyond, this is not something inevitable. What is abundantly clear is that the social background, the environment in which they grow up influences the relationships they form and their capacity to pursue life's choices later.

A recent OECD review observed, 'Among the immediate factors turning governmental attention to ECEC issues are: the wish to increase women's labour market participation; to reconcile work and family responsibilities on a basis more equitable for women; to confront the demographic challenges faced by OECD countries (in particular falling fertility rates and the general ageing of populations); and the need to address issues of child poverty and educational disadvantage' (OECD 2006). Referring to the fact that the child's well-being and learning are core goals of early childhood services, problems are identified with children younger than 3 being assigned to services with 'weak developmental agendas'. A challenge exists in many countries to focus more on the child, and to show greater understanding of the specific developmental tasks and learning strategies of young children.

The OECD's *Education at a Glance* for 2012 says 'A growing body of research recognises that early childhood (pre-primary) education improves children's cognitive abilities, helps to create a foundation for lifelong learning, makes learning outcomes more equitable, reduces poverty, and improves social mobility from generation to generation. Enrolling pupils in early childhood education can also mitigate social inequalities and promote better student outcomes overall. Many of the inequalities that exist within school systems are already present when pupils enter formal schooling and persist as pupils progress through the school system.' (OECD 2012)

Much of the debate about education focuses on the school, some of it on university or other tertiary institutions. Meanwhile, the increasingly substantial research on early childhood remains largely ignored. Later interventions, such as at school or later, most often take a great deal more effort to achieve results. If we want to significantly increase the educational outcomes of young people intervention we must start in the early months of life. In other words this focus in the education debate on schools, on teachers and on curricula, is like trying to catch the proverbial horse after it has escaped the stall. Along with creativity and the impacts of social and economic inequity, early childhood is what we should be attending to in the debate.

The physical and social aspects of the environment strongly influence the relationships with the primary carer, generally the mother. That environment affects cognitive development with significant implications for later life. The mother's behaviour and attitudes are influenced by her recalled experiences of her early life. The relationships with the father or other principal carers are strongly influenced by their economic situation. Requirements that both carers work, especially if the child is then looked after by a relative, will likely lead to minimum development with all the consequences in later life. On the other hand, if the child is looked after by experienced and trained early childhood educators the gains are likely to be substantial, especially in the case of children from low socioeconomic background. In the case of children from an advantaged social and economic background, on the other hand, the gains from child-care will be supplementary.

Relationships of the child with the mother from the earliest hours of life in the outside world significantly affect cognitive ability. Cognitive ability, contrary to earlier views, varies significantly with variations in the environment with major impacts obvious in the first year and certainly by age 5. Provision of substantial and varied stimulation of the young child through reading, games, creative activities such as art and music, and dance, languages and much else contributes significantly to the individual's eventual ability as an older child and adult. Educational experiences in later life amplify the gains made in early childhood.

Above all it is clear that development of relationships and of social and emotional skills for cooperating with others is essential.

The basics of early childhood neurophysiology and behaviour are summarised in numerous articles and books (Bransford et al. 1999). 'Children are born with certain biological capacities for learning. They can recognize human sounds, distinguish animate from inanimate objects, and they have an inherent sense of space, motion, number, and causality... The environment supplies information, and equally important, provides structure to the information, as when parents draw an infant's attention to the sounds of her or his native language'.

Children actively engage in making sense of their worlds and can reason with the knowledge they understand. Children are problem solvers, generating questions and seeking novel challenges. They also develop knowledge of their own learning capacities. Adults are critical in promoting children's curiosity and persistence by directing children's attention, structuring their experiences, supporting their learning attempts, and regulating the complexity and difficulty of levels of information for them.

The infant brain is hard-wired for relationships and the optimal growth and development of the human brain in the early years is largely dependent on the nature and quality of a child's few and most important human relationships (Aber 2007). '...Infants from families in the top income quintile are born healthier, stay healthier, develop language skills faster, and experience fewer serious problems of self-regulation and social-emotional development than infants from families in the bottom income quintile'.

5.2 Pioneer Studies of Early Childhood

The two best known studies of intervention in early childhood are the Highscope Perry Preschool Study and the Carolina Abecedarian study, also described at the website Social Programs that Work (2012): both dealt with poor children.

The High/Scope Perry Preschool Project (2012) assessed whether high quality preschool programs could provide short and long-term benefits to children living in poverty and at risk of failing in school. A total of 123 children from African American families living in Ypsilanti Michigan were randomly divided into two groups, one providing a high quality active learning preschool program and the other receiving no program at all. Their status was assessed annually at ages 3 through 11, then on three occasions up to age 27.

The program was an open framework of educational ideas and practices based on the natural development of young children, the child development theories of Piaget and Vygotsky, the progressive educational philosophy of John Dewey and recent work in cognitive-development psychology and brain research (Promising Practices Network 2009). Children were recognised as active learners who learn best from activities they themselves plan, carry out and reflect on. Adults arrange interest areas in the learning environment and join in children's activities, encouraging them to make choices and solve problems. Children are encouraged to engage in curriculum activities that encompass all areas of intellectual, social and physical development.

Children from entering families were matched on initial IQ test scores, socio-economic status and percentage of boys and girls and one of each pair assigned to the treatment or control program. There was low attrition in the program and socioeconomic data was collected at 15 years old to determine whether the groups were still similar and differences controlled for in the analysis.

The study concluded that participation in high quality active learning preschool programs creates a framework for adult success, seemingly through experiences which allowed positive interaction with other people and tasks. Organised in-service training for preschool staff and an efficient workable method of parent inclusion and involvement were amongst the defining aspects of the high quality preschool experience as was good administration, valid and reliable developmentally appropriate assessment and monitoring and reasonable adult to child ratio.

Intellectual performance at age 7 was higher than in the control group, school achievement at age 14 was higher and general literacy at age 19 was higher. At age 27 those in the group given the preschool program differed significantly from the control group in level of schooling completed, monthly earnings and home and second car ownership and had significantly fewer arrests and fewer were in receipt of social services. 'Over the lifetimes of the participants, the preschool program returns to the public an estimated $7.16 for every dollar invested'.

A recent detailed evaluation of the Program based on numerous studies noted there were significant differences between the program and control group at age 19 in respect of employment, and economic self-sufficiency (Promising Practices Network 2009). At age 27 nearly three times as many program participants owned their own home and a significantly lower percentage of program participants had received social services in the previous ten years. Differences were also found in involvement in group or gang fights or levels of arrest. At age 40 program participants were more likely to have health insurance.

Professor James Heckman of the University of Chicago, a Nobel prize-winner in economics known for his work on statistics and labour economics, has been involved also in research on early childhood, together with other scientists. Independently (Heckman et al. 2009) he examined the claims of substantial economic benefit of the High/Scope Perry Preschool program. Whilst noting that previous studies had ignored compromises that occurred in the randomization protocol and did not report standard errors they found that there were generally statistically significant gains for the program for both males and females, with economic returns that were above the historical rate of return on equity; benefit-to-cost ratios supported the conclusion.

The Carolina Abecedarian Project (2012) was initiated in 1972. 'It provided educational child care and high-quality preschool from age 0-5 to children from very disadvantaged backgrounds (most raised by single mothers with less than a high school education, reporting no earned income, 98 % of whom were African–American). The child care and preschool were provided on a full-day, year-round basis; had a low teacher-child ratio (ranging from 1:3 for infants to 1:6 for 5-year-olds); and used a systematic curriculum of educational games emphasizing language development and cognitive skills'.

A total of 111 children participated and were randomly assigned to four groups, one of which involved no 'treatment'; one child care only/preschool, one school-age only and one both preschool and school-age 'treatment'. At age 21 children receiving only school-age attention differed from those receiving no special 'treatment' only marginally. Those receiving child care/preschool 'treatment' differed significantly from those receiving no 'treatment': an increase in reading achievement of 1.8 grade levels and in math achievement of 1.3 grade levels. There were modest increases in IQ. Impact on adult life was similar to that for the High/Scope Perry Pre School study in respect of school and college education and employment.

An important though less often cited study was conducted by Margaret McCain and Fraser Mustard for the government of Ontario in Canada (McCain and Mustard 1999; Garrett 1999). *The Early Years Study: Reversing the Real Brain Drain* brought together neurophysiology, developmental psychology and education and many other disciplines. The study focused on children starting from the time of birth. The study showed how much IQ was influenced by the amount of stimulation the child received in the first 24 months of life, particularly the first 12 months.

Part 2 of the Early Years Study was published in 2007 (McCain et al. 2007). The Council on Early Childhood Development ceased operation late 2010!

Professor Mustard was an 'Adelaide Thinker in Residence' in 2007, a program funded by the South Australian government which brought numerous experts from overseas to address and report on major initiatives. In his report on his residence (Fraser Mustard 2007) he advocated communication of the new knowledge emerging about early brain development and its effect on lifelong behaviour, learning and health and as well more involvement in gathering reliable and comprehensive data about early childhood development and learning. He called for raising the standards of education and training for all staff in higher education engaged in disciplines that affect the development of infants and young children, continuing development of universal early child development and parenting centres linked to local primary schools and supporting vulnerable families.

5.3 The Nature of Early Experiences

Professor James Heckman of the University of Chicago, a Nobel prize-winner in economics known for his work on statistics and labour economics, has been involved in research on early childhood and psychologists have brought studies of other animals to bear on the understanding of early childhood in humans (Knudsen et al. 2006). These included neurobiologist Professor Eric Knudsen of Stanford University whose laboratory studies of neural mechanisms of learning and attention use the barn owl as a model system. Other collaborators included Professors Judy L. Cameron (University of Pittsburgh) and Jack P. Shonkoff (Harvard University).

Knudsen and colleagues assert that the uniquely powerful nature of early experiences is central to the principles which unify the economic, developmental psychology and neurobiology perspectives on early environment. Skill development and brain maturation are hierarchical processes in which higher level functions depend on, and build on, lower level functions. The capacity for change in skill development and neural circuitry is highest early in life and decreases over time. Early experiences influence cognitive and social skills and brain maturation.

'Language is an example of a cognitive skill that is acquired readily in early life but requires great effort and is never learned as thoroughly as an adult. The dependence of language learning on age holds for first languages and second languages and for spoken languages and sign languages. Learning the language before age 7 gives the best results and early learning begets later learning. In the first stage of language learning, young children learn to discriminate among acoustically similar sounds (phonemes) that convey different meaning. This is critical: the next stage involves learning to segment phonemes into words. Sound segmentation is critical, in turn, to attaching meaning to words and finally to deriving meaning from grammar and syntax'.

Knudsen and colleagues noted that monkeys which lack close nurturing relationship with the primary caregiver—usually the mother—early in life respond aberrantly to social signals in later life and do not integrate well into social groups. The representation of cues in the auditory space map of owls is individually customized through experience. Manipulations of experience that alter auditory orienting behaviour also alter the functional properties of neurons in this circuit. The magnitude of the changes induced by experience is greatly influenced by the age of the owl. And in kittens, changes in the visual cortex which take place if vision in one eye is restricted during the sensitive period of early life become resistant to change and persist into adult life. Early learning establishes brain architecture which affects functional plasticity in adulthood.

5.4 An Environment of Relationships: Healthy Development

A number of James Hickman's colleagues are members of the National Scientific Council on the Developing Child at Harvard University. The Council was established in 2003 as a multi-disciplinary collaboration of scientists and scholars from universities across the US and Canada designed to bring the science of early childhood and early brain development to bear on public policy decision-making. The Council strongly advocates investment in improving quality of life of disadvantaged children during the early childhood years: failure to so invest in early life makes cognitive development in later life more difficult and more expensive. The health of the mother during pregnancy and involvement of the mother in early years of the child's life is critical!

5.4 An Environment of Relationships: Healthy Development

The Council, in their first 'working paper' stated, 'Healthy development depends on the quality and reliability of a young child's relationships with the important people in his or her life. Even the development of a child's brain architecture depends on the establishment of these relationships' (National Scientific Council on the Developing Child 2004). 'Young children experience their world as an environment of relationships; those relationships affect the intellectual, social, emotional, physical, behavioral, and moral aspects of later development and lay the foundation for later outcomes such as self-confidence and sound mental health, motivation to learn and achievement in school.' They also are critical to later life in such areas as the ability to control aggressive impulses and resolve conflicts in nonviolent ways and knowing the difference between right and wrong and to developing the capacity to form and sustain casual friendships and intimate relationships, ultimately to be a successful parent.

However, 'there is no scientific evidence to support the belief that frequently rotating relationships with large numbers of adult caregivers provides valuable learning opportunities in the early years of life... prolonged separations from familiar caregivers and repeated detaching and re-attaching to people who matter is emotionally distressing and can lead to enduring problems'.

Nurturing, stimulating, and reliable childcare requires skills and other personal attributes on the part of the caregivers. Improved wages and benefits affect staff turnover. School readiness must include the capacity to form and sustain positive relationships with other children and adults and the social and emotional skills for cooperating with others. 'Childhood education must strive to involve young children in reciprocal learning interactions with teachers and peers and it should capitalize on children's natural interests and intrinsic drive to learn, rather than follow an adult-determined agenda.' As has been said on numerous occasions, young children learn best in an interactive, relational mode rather than through rote instruction. Environmental influences can actually affect whether and how genes are expressed (National Scientific Council on the Developing Child 2010).

The finding by the Centers for Disease Control and Prevention in the US concerning breast feeding in the first year of life by American mothers (Bakalar 2010) is very interesting in the context of the Harvard Council's studies. 'Breast-feeding practices vary widely across race and ethnicity. More than 80 % of Hispanics and Asians begin breast-feeding, but only 74 % of whites and 54 % of non-Hispanic blacks do so. The higher the education level of the mother, the more likely she is to breast-feed... There were sharp geographical differences as well: in 13 states, most in the Southeast, the differences between blacks and whites were more than 20 %'.

Of further interest is the fact that because breast-feeding confers a large number of benefits to mother and child, a high prevalence of breast-feeding is viewed as an important public health goal by the Department of Health and Human Services which considers that if 90 % of mothers breast-fed exclusively for at least six months, the US would save $13 billion in medical costs and prevent 911 deaths every year.

Studies using data from the UK also show benefits of breastfeeding including cognitive development of the child and fewer behavioural problems (Quigley et al. 2009). Those mothers who breast-fed four months were older, better educated and from a higher socioeconomic level than those mothers who formula fed. But when the data were controlled for these and other differences there was still a 30 % lower risk of behaviour problems associated with prolonged breastfeeding. The data does not include mothers from non-white or mixed-ethnic backgrounds (Quigley et al. 2011).

5.5 Personal Development and the Home Environment

Recent research gives extremely strong support to the importance of early childhood and the relationships with parents and resulting environment in their influence on later educational achievement. Reported by Lehrer (2012) on his blog on *Wired*, research by Eliot Tucker-Drob of the University of Texas at Austin reinforces earlier research. Tucker-Drob investigated the relative contributions of 'nature and nurture' to early educational achievement using a national sample (in the US) of 1,200 identical and fraternal twins born to 600 families of various incomes and ethnicities in 2001. The fact that identical twins, who share 100 % of their genes, and fraternal twins, who share 50 % were studied is vitally important.

The relative genetic and environmental influences on achievement at age five could be compared both for those children who had been enrolled in preschool and those who were not. In twins family environmental factors (that is nurture) accounted for about 70 % of the variance in test scores for children who did not attend preschool but only about 45 % of variance among children who did attend preschool. The reason for the differences is that denial of an enriched environment to young children, typified by lots of stress, few books and little variation in conversation, amounts to a lack of nurture which holds back their nature: they are unable to reach their full genetic potential. Preschool closes the gap between the experiences of wealthy and poor children making whatever differences remain—nature—more important.

Tucker-Drob's earlier work gives further support to the importance of parents' socioeconomic status. A study of 750 pairs of American twins given a test of mental ability at the age of 10 months and then again at the age of 2, found that the home environment was the key variable for 10-month-olds across every socioeconomic class. For 2-year-old children from poorer households, however, the decisions of parents still mattered. Home environment accounted for approximately 80 % of the individual variance in mental ability among poor 2-year-olds; the effect of genetics was negligible. For 2-year old children from wealthy households genetics determined performance for 50 % of all variation in mental ability.

Very young children are housebound, their lives dictated by the choices of their parents. But as wealth increases, the choices adults make play a much smaller role in determining the mental ability of their children because their environment is already very stimulating: they are constantly surrounded by a variety of interesting and different things and attention by their parents (and other adults). Lehrer concludes, 'The greatest luxury we can give our children, it turns out, is the luxury of being the type of parent that doesn't matter at all'. In the long run the fretting which some well-off parents go through matters little. For children of poor families it is critical: preschool helps make the difference.

As so many earlier studies of early childhood have found, it is the children of poorer families who benefit most from the stimulation of quality preschool. Closing the gap between the later educational achievement of children of low and high socioeconomic background is in the very first instance a matter of preschool. Waiting until the child is at school means a much greater effort and likely less gain!

The developmental inequalities between children of different backgrounds emerge almost immediately they are born: '.. even the mental ability of 2-year-olds can be profoundly affected by the socioeconomic status of their parents. The end result is that their potential is held back. Early childhood intervention is a first step in ensuring every child has a chance to reach their potential!'

The reasons for the close relationship that exists between poor educational achievement and social and economic advantage are direct. Those advantages feed through to the entire way of life, starting with early childhood and the relationships with parents and relatives and continuing with the opportunities that the home environment provides (Rampell 2009).

In disadvantaged communities, the home environment is of much lower quality and the schools attended are characterised by less well-qualified and experienced teachers, teacher turnover is high and school facilities are significantly poorer.

Amongst the significant issues with children at disadvantage are the experiences and economic situation of the parents including their experiences of schooling. And for all children, irrespective of economic background, the physical conditions of the school, the facilities and diversity of opportunity to participate in a variety of activities in a safe and supportive environment responsive to the needs of the children, are critical. One would think the latter was so self-evident that attention would be paid to it.

How the home situations in different social class (regardless of race) affect student performance has been documented by sociologists for decades. Research by Annette Lareau of the University of Maryland and (the late) John U. Ogbu of the University of California Berkeley reviewed by Richard Rothstein of the Economic Policy Institute in Washington DC (Rothstein 2004) is amongst that supporting such conclusions.

Middle-class children are encouraged from an early age to negotiate with their parents over what to wear or eat, to question adult statements if they seem implausible, and to interact with adults as equals, for example to describe their symptoms to paediatricians. Money tends to be less frequently discussed so it seldom occurs that the child's ambitions might be blocked by a lack of money.

Working-class children have no such sense of entitlement. Most of them, black and white, speak to adults only when spoken to; they are not expected to express opinions that challenge what adults say. Money is a frequent topic of conversation at home, and children become aware early of the limits to their futures.

Middle-class parents organize a hectic schedule of after school activities for their children, the children earn trophies and parental praise for their performances which promotes teamwork and easier relations with strangers. Working-class children mostly stay in their neighbourhoods, playing games only among themselves.

Middle-class parents are more likely to encourage children to figure out problems for themselves. Working-class parents are more likely to tell them what to do. Whilst both middle- and working-class parents encourage their children to read, and read aloud to their young children, middle-class parents are more likely to read themselves so showing the importance of reading by their own behaviour. Middle-class parents more frequently intervene in schools when they feel it to be in their children's interest to do so. In high school middle-class white parents are aggressive in guiding their children's decisions on curriculum.

And by no means the least important difference is that in middle-class families children become familiar with a wide vocabulary (of 'academic' English) because of the ongoing conversations. They have a head start over children from poorer backgrounds on this score alone which influences performance in almost every other area of education.

5.6 Attachment Theory, Mothers Memories and Mothers Roles

The study of the relationships between the very young child and its parents is known as attachment theory. One of the earliest studies was conducted by British psychologist, psychiatrist and psychoanalyst John Bowlby after the Second World War. Bowlby was born into an upper middle-class family; his mother thought that special attention to children would lead to them being spoiled and the young Bowlby normally saw his mother only one hour a day after teatime. His primary carer was a beloved nanny who left the family when Bowlby was 4. As was common in upper middle-class English society of the time Bowlby was sent to boarding school at age 7.

After the second world war Bowlby studied patterns of family interaction in healthy and pathological development: he focused specially on how attachment difficulties were transmitted from one generation to the next. Bowlby posited that 'the inheritance of mental health and mental ill health through the medium of family microculture… may well be far more important than is their inheritance through the medium of genes. In other words it is not so much the actual experience of the mother's early childhood relationships with her parents but the way in which a mother considers her own historical relationship with her primary caregiver, which is central to the development of her own child's attachment'.

Bowlby's work on delinquent and affectionless children led to the conclusion that the infant and young child should experience a warm, intimate, and continuous relationship with his mother (or permanent mother substitute) in which both find satisfaction and enjoyment. There was mutual rejection of Bowlby's work by psychoanalysts on the one hand and on the other by Bowlby of current psychoanalytical explanations for attachment. Bowlby drew on studies of animal behaviour (ethology) in developing explanatory hypotheses for his observations. Bowlby's research in turn influenced later studies of animal behaviour on primates.

Psychotherapist and writer Dr Jessica Zucker, in a blog at This Emotional Life (Zucker 2012), reviewed research conducted by, amongst others, the late Stephen Mitchell of New York University, Mary Main of the University of California (Berkeley) and colleagues. That research revealed that 'what was important was not whether the parent has been deprived or nurtured as a child, but the degree of coherence versus incoherence in the parents subsequent memory of her childhood'. The organization of a mother's narrative and how it has been processed over the years is the most crucial predictor of attachment style, rather than actual lived experiences.

The Minnesota Longitudinal Study of Parents and Children led by Dr L. Alan Sroufe of the University of Minnesota is tracing the course of individual development to understand the factors which guide it toward good and poor outcomes (University of Minnesota website).

A number of evolutionary anthropologists including Sarah Blaffer Hrdy have challenged the notion that in rearing the child, the mother 'goes it alone' (Koner 2011). Hrdy argues that social support has been crucial to human success and that compared with other primates humans are uniquely cooperative. The ethnological record shows that the mother at home alone with an infant or toddler is a new one in human experience.

The late Beatrice Whiting and John Whiting, Harvard anthropologists, were amongst the first cultural anthropologists to do systematic cross-cultural studies of childhood. They found in their studies that even the closest mother-infant relationships were embedded in a dense social environment. In !Kung hunter-gather society in Botswana the child on the mother's hip is part of the entire social world of the mother. When the mother is standing, the infant can look right into the eyes of 'desperately maternal 10- to 12-year-old girls who frequently approach and initiate brief, intense, face-to-face interactions, including mutual smiling and vocalization.' At other times they are passed from hand to hand around a fire for similar interactions with one adult or child after another, kissed everywhere, on their faces, bellies, genitals and sung to, bounced, entertained, and encouraged. They are even addressed at length in conversational tones long before they can understand words.

This 'cooperative breeding' is compatible with the notion of the centrality of the single caregiver of which Bowlby wrote: the mother or primary caregiver should be more important but need not be exclusive.

The 'Longitudinal Study of Australian Children' (LSAC), entitled 'Growing Up in Australia', initiated by the Australian Government and managed by the

Australian Institute of Family Studies, commenced early 2004 is investigating the areas of health, education, childcare, family functioning, child functioning and socio-demographics in the lives of 10,000 children and their families. The longitudinal Study of Indigenous Children, *Footprints in Time,* launched in April 2008 continues. Results from these studies complement those reported above.

5.7 Policies on Parental Leave in Europe and Australia

The quality and affordability of childcare are major issues in determining parental leave in many European countries. So is the flexibility of employers in providing opportunities for the mother to return to work without disadvantage relative to the gains which had been achieved to the time when the mother left work to give birth. There is substantial variation amongst European countries in all these matters. For instance mothers in the UK have fewer work opportunities and less childcare support than mothers in a number of European countries and they have to pay more than in other European countries.

A UNICEF study (Frean 2008) suggested that government policies on maternity leave and childcare provision could be at odds with 'today's knowledge of the critical developmental needs of the very young child'. The UNICEF report cited research from Britain and the US suggesting that children who spend too long in formal childcare at too young an age may suffer from long-term effects, including behavioural problems, aggression, antisocial behaviour, depression and an inability to concentrate—although the effects are thought to be relatively small.

In Australia in low and middle income families the combined effect of fathers working long hours and mothers working has been found to be children spending significantly less time in language-related activities (Brown et al. 2007; Horin 2010). In high income families, parental employment hours had no impact on children's time use. Thus for children at greatest risk of poor developmental outcomes, developmental opportunities may be enhanced by strategies that reduce levels of long work hours by fathers.

In Australia, progress in implementing a meaningful policy has also been slow. The Australian Government introduced a paid parental leave scheme in 2009 (Australian Government 2009a). From 1 January 2011 new parents who are primary carers of a child born or adopted after that date receive taxable payments at the level of the Commonwealth minimum wage for a maximum period of 18 weeks. To be eligible the primary carer must have been in paid work continuously for at least 10 of the 13 months prior to the expected birth or adoption of the child and undertaken at least 330 h of paid work in the 10 month period. The payment is means tested. Various other conditions apply. From January 2013 the scheme was expanded to provide for partners of the primary carer to receive two weeks government funded parental leave at the minimum wage. Tony Abbott, as Opposition Leader, promised an alternative scheme to provide leave at the salary they would normally receive, funded by a levy on business. In early 2013, criticisms of Abbotts proposals were made by some members of the Coalition and some business advocates.

At the end of 2008, the Australian company ABC Learning, which provided out of school care for tens of thousands of children in 1,040 centres, went into administration and receivership after a $1 billion shortfall. The media reportage of the company's collapse generally focused on child-care issues. Eventually, most of the centres were able to continue their work.

Commercial media focused on the possible rise in fees and asked whether parents would be likely to pay more. No mention was made on television news items of the importance of well qualified staff at childcare centres or of the need for high ratios of staff to children. No mention was made either of the support for the recommendations Government's proposals to increase staff training and staff numbers at childcare centres by Australian Community Children's Services.

5.8 A National Early Childhood Development Strategy in Australia

In 2009 the National Early Childhood Development Strategy, *Investing in the Early Years* developed under the auspices of the Council of Australian Governments (COAG) was launched (Australian Government 2009b). The Strategy noted the advances in neurobiology and related areas which have increased understanding of the importance of early childhood. The Strategy is a collaborative effort between the Commonwealth and the State and Territory governments to ensure that by 2020 all children have the best start in life to create a better future for themselves and for the nation. 'The strategy will guide Australia's comprehensive response to evidence about the importance of early childhood development and the benefits—and cost-effectiveness—of ensuring all children experience a positive early childhood, from before birth through the first eight years of life. National effort to improve child outcomes will in turn contribute to increased social inclusion, human capital and productivity in Australia. It will help ensure Australia is well placed to meet social and economic challenges in the future and remain internationally competitive'.

The Strategy notes areas of concern in Australia for children including low birth weight, childhood obesity and diabetes, children with a disability, social emotional and behavioural issues and child abuse. Birth weight of Indigenous children, more, than double the non-Indigenous rate, places Australia lowest in OECD countries.

The reform initiatives include a National Partnership Agreement to achieve universal access to quality early childhood education for all children in the year before school by 2013, a National Partnership Agreement on Indigenous Early Childhood Development to establish 35 new Children and Family Centres and increase access to relevant health services, a National Partnership Agreement on Preventive Health with a focus on chronic disease that commences in early childhood, a National Quality agenda for early childhood education and care, national workforce initiatives to improve the quality and supply of early childhood education and care workforce and a number of other relevant agreements and plans.

The OECDs *Education at a Glance 2012* notes, 'Participation rates in, and public funding for, early childhood education are relatively low in Australia compared with other OECD countries.' The almost 70 % enrolment in 2010, slightly less than in 2005, for Australia is no greater than in the US (69 %).

In 2010 Australia ranked 34th of 38 OECD and partner countries in early childhood education enrolment rates; in 2009 Australia ranked 32nd. The report also points to the less-than-systematic nature of early childhood education in Australia which does influence the accuracy of the data itself so that it is possible that elements of the system were left out of the figures, particularly information from the private sector (OECD 2012).

The National Partnership Agreement on Early Childhood Education, endorsed by the Council of Australian Governments in 2008, set a target for all children in the year before they attend formal schooling to have access to pre-school delivered by a university qualified early childhood teacher for 15 h a week, 40 weeks a year. The Commonwealth Government undertook to provide almost $279 million of a total of $955 million over the five year period leading up to 2013.

Trevor Cobbold points to statistics indicating a parlous state for pre-school education (Cobbold 2013). Only 71 % of children aged 4 in Australia attended a pre-school program in 2012. Nearly one in every three children misses out. In Tasmania, one in every two children misses out and in Australia's most populous state (NSW) nearly one in two miss out. There is huge variation in pre-school attendance across the country from 96 % of children aged 4 in Western Australia and 89 % in South Australia to only 59 % in New South Wales and 51 % in Tasmania. There is also a large variation in the hours attended. In Western Australia, 94 % attended for 10–14 h a week whilst between one in six and one in ten children attended for less than 10 h a week in most states and the ACT. As would be expected expenditure per child also varies widely, from $1,033 in the Northern Territory and $556 in Western Australia to $190 in New South Wales.

The New South Wales Government commissioned a review of government funding of early childhood education programs to be chaired by Professor Deborah Brennan of the Social Policy Research Centre of the University of New South Wales. The Brennan review (Brennan 2011) found that while there were measurable improvements in the quality and extent of early childhood education in New South Wales 'some important challenges' remained. Brennan noted that the Productivity Commission had reported that the State had the highest median weekly cost of preschool in Australia and that the participation rate remained below the target rate; provision of early childhood education in rural and remote areas faces particular challenges.

5.9 Economic Benefits of Early Childhood Intervention

In one particularly comprehensive paper Knudsen et al (2006 loc cit) note that 'The future success of the US economy will depend in part on well educated and highly resourceful workers who are capable of learning new skills so that they remain competitive in a continually changing global market. That success is in jeopardy because a growing fraction of the nation's workforce will consist of adults who were raised in disadvantaged environments, a segment of the population that has historically been less likely to attain high levels of education and skill development than the general population'.

Laurence Aber (loc cit) of New York University observes, '…Scientists identify specific pathways of influence, from social and environmental risk to developmental processes and outcomes. One major pathway leads from low family income to reduced parental investment of money and time and then to less than optimal cognitive and language stimulation and development. The second leads from high family material hardship to parental stress and harsh and disengaged parenting to non-optimal social and emotional development and mental health'.

Aber concludes that in the US both practice and politics in the last 30 years have failed to keep pace with the science of early child development. Demand for child care has grown as a work support and this has meant increased state and federal investments. But because politics has failed to learn from the science, programs supporting development in early childhood remain seriously underfinanced. Most of the total public expenditure on children in America is spent on K-12 education.

The Rand Corporation (Karoly and Bigelow 2005) found, 'Research has shown that well-designed early education programs serving disadvantaged children in the year or so prior to kindergarten entry can generate benefits to government and the rest of society that outweigh the costs of the program services. As a result of this evidence and the conviction that children benefit from structured programs preparing them for school entry, enthusiasm for public-sector investment in preschool education has been growing among business leaders, policymakers, and the public'.

The Rand Corporation Report estimated that a one-year high quality universal preschool program in California would give 'an annual rate of return of about 10 % over a 60 year horizon and assuming a 70 % participation rate each annual cohort of children would generate $2.7 billion in net present benefits to California society'.

Early childhood education in the US is somewhat less established than in other OECD countries, especially in Europe, where formal pre-primary education in the public school system is more often the norm (OECD 2012). 'On average across OECD countries, 84 % of pupils in early childhood education attend programmes in public schools or government-dependent private institutions.' In the U.S on the other hand just under half attend independent private programmes. Whereas children typically start school at 3 years or younger in OECD countries, in the US they typically start early childhood education at 4 years old, while in 21 other OECD countries, it is 3 years old or younger.

Preschool education in the US is extremely limited: enrolments were less than 2 millions in 2005 and have hardly increased since. There is considerable variation in quality of the programs. In twelve of the 38 states programs met fewer than five of the 10 research-based quality standards (including qualifications of the classroom teacher) identified by the National Institute on Early Education Research. 'In accordance with a philosophy of limiting government intervention in matters related to family, there is no overall national child or family policy, nor is there any one federal state department in charge of children's services.' (OECD 2006).

5.10 Early Childhood is the Critical Time

Early childhood intervention delivers a greater return on investment in terms of education, health and employment, especially for families of high economic and social disadvantage. It should not be considered child minding. It is of less benefit for children of families who are economically advantaged.

Around 50 % of the educational achievement of children at school is contributed by what the child brings to school: a substantial part of their subsequent achievement involves the relationships established in the early years of the child's life. The mothers recalled experience of her early childhood is an important element in her later parenting behaviour the mother.

The environment provided in the home in the early years is the principal determinant of the relationship between family socioeconomic status and the child's educational achievement. Children in socioeconomically advantaged homes are stimulated and encouraged and parents participate in ensuring involvement in creative and sporting activities such that later involvement by the parents has less effect than in the case of socioeconomically disadvantaged children.

For all of these reasons, clearly supported by quality research, programs supported by government in respect of parental leave during the early years of the child's life should be justified on the basis of achieving high quality experiences for the child. Justifications grounded in goals relating to attracting greater participation by women in the workforce, though not unimportant, surely cannot be the first consideration of any society focused on future success! The finding by the 2013 Human Development Report (United Nations 2013) that the mothers education is a more significant indicator of child wellbeing than the socioeconomic status of the family is a related matter of substantial importance. The longer term future of societies depends on attention to the wellbeing of girls and their education, not least their experiences in very early childhood and their experiences as mothers in the first years of their children.

Early childhood policies vary widely across countries with low government support in the US particularly. On February 14 2013 in Decatur (Georgia)

President Barack Obama elaborated his commitment to early childhood education. He emphasised the importance of qualified, highly educated teachers. He said, 'students [who attend preschool] don't just show up in kindergarten and first grade more prepared to learn, they're also more likely to grow up reading and doing math at grade level, graduating from high school, holding a job, even forming more stable families. This is not babysitting. This is teaching.' The statement on the White House website reads, in part, 'Expanding access to high quality early childhood education is among the smartest investments that we can make. Research has shown that the early years in a child's life—when the human brain is forming—represent a critically important window of opportunity to develop a child's full potential and shape key academic, social, and cognitive skills that determine a child's success in school and in life'.

The recently agreed policy framework for early childhood in Australia importantly aligns with practice in many other OECD countries. Special attention will be needed concerning children with disabilities and Indigenous children. Although there is an agreement between the Commonwealth and State and Territory leaders through the National Partnership Agreement on Early Childhood Education there is clearly a long way to go in some states.

Parental leave provisions including ability to return to work without disadvantage are an important element in the decisions that families make about having children. However, it is unequivocal that investment in early childhood learning has significance in respect of education which translates to substantial personal and societal gains in other areas.

Early childhood intervention sensibly cannot be seen as child minding, simply as making it easier for women to participate in the workforce or as somehow related to encouragement of women to have more children. In a world of ever decreasing resources relative to population justification of early childhood intervention as a way of increasing the birth-rate is irresponsible. Failure to recognise the link between early childhood intervention through participation in preschool taught by professionally qualified teachers and later educational attainment, especially in the case of children from disadvantaged families, is similarly irresponsible!

References

Aber, L. (2007). Changing the climate on early childhood. *American Prospect*. Retrieved August 21, 2012 from http://prospect.org/article/changing-climate-early-childhood

Australian Government. (2009a). *Australia's paid parental leave scheme*. Retrieved August 21, 2012, from http://www.deewr.gov.au/Department/Publications/Documents/PPLBooklet.pdf

Australian Government. (2009b). *Investing in the early years-a national early childhood development strategy*. Retrieved August 21, 2012, from http://www.deewr.gov.au/earlychildhood/policy_agenda/pages/earlychildhooddevelopmentstrategy.aspx

Bakalar, N. (2010). Despite advice. Many fail to breast-feed. *New York Times*.

Bransford, J. D., Brown, A. L., & Cocking, R. R. (Eds.). (1999). *How people learn: Mind experience and school. committee on developments in the science of learning*. Washington DC: National Academy Press.

Brennan, D. (2011). *Review of NSW Government funding for early childhood education*. Sydney: NSW Government Education & Communities Office of Education.
Brown, J., Bittman, M., & Nicholson, J. M. (2007). Time or money: The impact of parental employment on time that 4 to 5 year olds spend in language building activities. *Australian Journal of Labour Economics, 10*, 149–165.
The Carolina Abcedarian Project. (2012). Retrieved August 21, 2012 from http://projects.fpg.unc.edu/~abc/
Cobbold, T. (2013). The parlous state of pre-school education. *Save our schools*. Retrieved 17, April 2013 from http://www.saveourschools.com.au/national-issues/the-parlous-state-of-pre-school-education
Fraser Mustard, J. (2007). Investing in the early years: Closing the gap between what we know and what we do. Adelaide: Government of South Australia. Retrieved 4, October 2013 from http://www.thinkers.sa.gov.au/thinkers/mustard/report.aspx
Frean, A. (2008). Childcare is bad for your baby working parents are warned. *The Times*.
Garrett, K. (1999). Reversing the real brain drain. *ABC Radio National Background Briefing*. Retrieved August 21, 2012 from http://www.abc.net.au/radionational/programs/backgroundbriefing/reversing-the-real-brain-drain/3559904
Heckman, J. J. et al. (2009). *The rate of return to the High/Scope Perry Preschool Program*. NBER working Paper no. 15471 JEL No. D62,122,128.
High/Scope Perry Preschool Study. (2012). Retrieved August 21, 2012 from http://www.highscope.org/content.aspcontentid=219
Horin, A. (2010, 11 December). Long work hours leave little time for child's play. *Sydney Morning Herald*.
Karoly, L. A. & Bigelow, J. (2005). *The economics of investing in Universal Preschool Education in California,* a report for the David and Lucile Packard Foundation. Washington: Rand Corporation. Retrieved August 21, 2012 from http://www.rand.org/pubs/monographs/MG349/
Knudsen, E. I., Heckman, J. J., et al. (2006). Economic, Neurobiological and behavioral perspectives on building Americas future workforce. *Proceedings of the National Academy of Sciences, 103*, 10155–10162.
Koner, M. (2011, 8 December). It does take a village. *New York Review of Books*.
Lehrer, J. (2012). Does preschool matter. *Wired* . Retrieved August 21, from http://www.wired.com/wiredscience/2012/03/does-preschool-matter/
McCain, M. N., & Fraser Mustard, J. (1999). *Reversing the real brain drain early years study final report*. Toronto: Canadian Institute for Advanced Research.
McCain, M. N., Fraser Mustard., J & Shanker, S. (2007). *The early years study 2: Putting science into action*. Toronto: Council of Early Childhood Development. Retrieved August 21, 2012 from http://www.founders.net/fn/setup.nsf/files/Early-Years-Study-2-Putting-Science-into-Action-March-2007/$file/Early-Years-Study-2-Putting-Science-into-Action-March-2007.pdf
National Scientific Council on the Developing Child. (2004). *Young children develop in an environment of relationships*. Working paper No. 1. Retrieved August 21, 2012 from http://developingchild.harvard.edu/index.php/resources/reports_and_working_papers/working_papers/wp1/
National Scientific Council on the Developing Child. (2010). Early experiences can alter gene expression and affect long-term development: Working paper No. 10. Retrieved August 21, 2012 from http://developingchild.harvard.edu/index.php/library/reports_and_working_papers/working_papers/wp10/
OECD. (2006). *Starting strong II: Early childhood and care*. Paris: OECD. Retrieved October 18, 2012 from http://www.oecd.org/edu/preschoolandschool/startingstrongiiearlychildhoodeducationandcare.htm
OECD. (2012). *Education at a glance 2012 OECD indicators*. Chapter C. *How do early childhood education systems differ around the world?* Paris: OECD. Retrieved September 13, 2012 from http://dx.doi.org/10.1787/eag-2012-en

References

Promising Practices Network. (2009). HighScope Perry Preschool project. Santa Monica: Rand Corporation. Retrieved May 7, 2005 from http://www.promisingpractices.net/program.asp?programid=128

Quigley, M. A. et al. (2009). Breastfeeding is associated with improved child cognitive development: Evidence from the UK millennium cohort study. *Community Health*, 63(2), 8.

Quigley. M. A et al. (2011). Prolonged breastfeeding may be linked to fewer behaviour problems. University of Oxford Science: Health media release. Retrieved August 21, 2012 from http://www.ox.ac.uk/media/news_stories/2011/111005.html

Rampell, C. (2009, 27 August). SAT scores and family income. *New York Times Business Day*.

Rothstein, R. (2004). Must schools fail? *New York Review of Books*.

Saunders. A. (2011). The philosophical baby—Alison Gopnik. ABC Radio National Philosophers Zone. Retrieved August 21, 2012 from http://www.abc.net.au/radionational/programs/philosopherszone/the-philosophical-baby—alison-gopnik/2930714

Social Programs that Work. (2012). Retrieved August 21, 2012 from http://evidencebasedprograms.org/wordpress/1366/abecedarian-project/

University of Minnesota. (2012). The Minnesota longitudinal study of risk and adaptation. Retrieved April 21, 2012 from http://www.cehd.umn.edu/ICD/research/Parent-Child/default.html

United Nations. (2013). *Human development report 2013. The rise of the south: human progress in a diverse world*. New York: UNDP. Retrieved June 9, 2013 from http://www.undp.org/content/undp/en/home/librarypage/hdr/human-development-report-2013/

Zucker, J. (2012). Intergenerational transmission of attachment. *Blog at This Emotional Life*. Retrieved August 21, 2012 from http://www.pbs.org/thisemotionallife/blogs/intergenerational-transmission-attachment

Chapter 6
Effective Teaching and Learning Part 1: John Hattie, Graham Nuthall and Jonathan Osborne

'We should focus on the greatest source of variance that can make the difference—the teacher. We need to ensure that this greatest influence is optimised to have powerful and sensationally positive effects, but they must be exceptional effects. We need to direct attention at higher quality teaching, and higher expectations that students can meet appropriate challenges—and these occur once the classroom door is closed and not by reorganising which or how many students are behind those doors…'

John Hattie, Teachers Make a Difference (Hattie 2003)

6.1 The Importance of Teachers

Everyone, almost, agrees that teachers are the key element in the education of children in school. As a McKinsey report (Barber and Mourshed 2007) observes, the only way to improve student outcomes is to improve the quality of classroom teaching across an entire system. The best-performing systems around the world go to great lengths to ensure that all their teachers are well qualified and well prepared in the subjects they teach and have access to high-quality, ongoing professional learning opportunities.

These two essays exploring effective teaching summarise some of the most important research on effective teaching and highlight some case studies. In this first part I deal with a very important meta-analysis of education outcomes, a particularly interesting study of what goes on in the classroom and an examination of the importance of 'argumentation'.

What does the effective teacher do that makes the most difference and what other factors might be relevant? A few decades ago, the simplest received explanation was that teachers who were content experts were most likely to do the best job. Few now believe that: the evidence doesn't support it. That doesn't mean that content knowledge is unimportant, just that it isn't enough. Knowledge of superior teaching instruction is vital and that is not simply a matter of more experience. Cooperation between teachers is also very important.

The OECD Report *Teachers Matter* points out, 'Student learning is influenced by many factors, including: student's skills, expectations, motivation and behaviour; family resources, attitudes and support; peer group skills, attitudes and behaviour; school organisation, resources and climate; curriculum structure and content; and teacher skills, knowledge, attitudes and practices. Schools and classrooms are complex, dynamic environments, and identifying the effects of these varied factors, and how they influence and relate with each other—for different types of students and different types of learning—has been, and continues to be, a major focus of educational research' (OECD 2005).

… Improving the efficiency and equity of schooling depends, in large measure, on ensuring that competent people want to work as teachers, that their teaching is of high quality, and that all students have access to high quality teaching.

The largest source of variation in student learning is attributable to differences in what students bring to school—their abilities and attitudes, and family and community background… While 'teacher quality' is the single most important school variable influencing student achievement, qualifications, experience and tests of academic ability don't capture many of the important aspects of teacher quality. Other reports (Mulkeen et al. 2008) make the same point.

Selecting teachers on the basis of their education and qualifications only is unlikely to be appropriate. Again, this is true of recruitment generally in all domains, something that is very commonly ignored.

According to Professor Roy Killen of the University of Newcastle in Australia, reviews of effective teaching strategies conclude 'no single teaching strategy is effective all the time for all learners… teaching and learning are very complex processes influenced by many different factors only some of which are under the teacher's control and none of which is fully understood… Nevertheless… enough is known about teaching and learning to develop a well-founded set of principles on which to base systematic approaches to effective teaching'.

Killen (2007) points out that 'high quality learning has occurred when students are able to

- apply knowledge to solve problems
- communicate their knowledge to others
- perceive relationships between their existing knowledge and the new things they are learning
- discover or create new knowledge for themselves; and students
- retain newly acquired knowledge for a long time
- want to learn more'.

'If teachers want quality learning to occur in their classrooms, they must deliberately teach in ways that will enable and encourage students to engage in the intellectual activities that promote quality learning' (Killen 2007, p. 17). And 'What a student knows on some particular day is not an invariably an indication of what the student is capable of learning.

6.2 Some Initial Observations

The studies of teaching and learning and what makes them effective is vast, especially in the US. The focus in teacher training now is much more on pedagogy, on the nature of the teaching process. There are a number of recent reports which consider practices in many countries.

The considerable research tells us that the quality of the instruction makes the difference *and* more than that, that it is the interaction between the teacher and student, most especially the feedback the student gets, which is essential. The effective teacher not only monitors the student's performance, the ability to show they have understood what has been learned. Effective teachers also provide a challenging curriculum, not one brought to the level which it is thought all students might easily manage. As in most organisations, cooperation between teachers makes a significant difference as each one helps others. And two other things matter, the respect people in the community give the teacher—indeed the relationships between the school and the parent community particularly—and the leadership provided by the principal of the school.

Whilst there is an understandable demand for some kind of indicator of achievement, mere performance by school students remembering what it is they learned and being able to apply that to answering questions in a test hardly resembles living a life or working in an organisation. An alternative way of assessing best practice, for that is what we actually want to find out about, is to look at the processes which occur in the organisations that perform well according to whatever criteria we have chosen.

No set of measures are sufficient by themselves in the long run for the formulation of best practice. And in the case of schools we need to understand what it is that we actually want the student to do in later life as a result of whatever it is they have achieved at school. Training and knowledge are important but not sufficient any more than are social skills alone.

We have reliable national and international tests from students in a large number of countries and information about schools and teachers. Some countries, notably the US, have huge runs of statistics on all kinds of matters from test scores to teacher's qualifications to indicators for disadvantage, geographic location and other demographics in relation to such things as student gender and age. But rather than more measures, we need to look at the practices of the teachers and the relations between schools and governments and communities at the best performing 'benchmark' schools.

Numerous reports make clear that better schooling means ensuring competent people are recruited to the teaching profession and that motivation to teach is of fundamental concern as is ongoing professional development and effective leadership by the principal and senior teachers in the school. A focus on efficiency by, for instance, merging schools or classes defeats attempts to bring greater effectiveness to the task. In these many ways a school resembles other organisations and the factors which contribute to an effective teaching profession are much the same as those that lead to any effective organisation.

Media has tended to focus on the trivia of conflict between the various players in the debates. Parents are portrayed as being concerned that the school their children are attending is probably not up to scratch but that if they had some performance indicators they would be able to make better decisions. In May 2010 in New South Wales (Patty 2010), the NSW Federation of Parents and Citizens Associations asserted that the process of removing ineffective teachers should be quicker and more succinct. The (then) state government backed away from an earlier decision to give principals the authority to hire and fire teachers, in response to pressure from the NSW Teachers Federation. The Education Minister, Verity Firth, said every teacher deserved 'due process'.

Subsequently, at both State and Commonwealth level greater control by school principals over staff recruitment, and over budget matters, has become commonplace, as is reported in the essay on Australian policy (Sect. 14.10) (Though it is often asserted otherwise, the OECD analyses forming part of the PISA 2009 assessment do not provide evidence that greater autonomy in respect of these issues leads to higher educational achievement. Rather, it is control over the way the curriculum is taught that makes a difference, something seen especially in Finland).

Meanwhile the business community complains that their recruits are insufficiently prepared for work implying thereby that the education system is failing. Some companies have established their own tertiary education courses in frustration at what they perceive as inadequate performance by the existing system. Every organisation has a responsibility to train its staff and superior staff development is one of the hallmarks of superior organisations. Even computers do not arrive at work ready on day one to perform what is required of them. Inasmuch as employers pay their more qualified staff more it makes sense to invest in their training, a value-adding exercise!

The research on the nature of effective teaching all reaches very similar conclusions about attention to the student, use of tests and other assessments to improve teaching strategies (not judge schools), cooperation amongst students in the classroom, feedback to the student on their performance and setting of high standards of achievement along with the belief that all students can succeed.

6.3 John Hattie: The Teacher, Not the School, Makes the Difference

Professor John Hattie, recently of Auckland University and now Director, Melbourne Education Research Institute in the University of Melbourne Graduate School of Education, is renowned for his detailed survey of more than half a million studies on the what factors contribute to superior outcomes for the student.

His meta-analysis studies reveal that after what the child brings to the school experience—what he or she has learned in the first few years of life—the teacher contributes more than any other factor to student achievement. But it is the expert teacher, not simply the experienced teacher, who makes the great difference! Expert teachers engage students in learning and develop the students' self-esteem as learners. And it is certain things that the teacher does. Effective instruction and certain components of feedback, dialogue between the teacher and the student, contribute substantially.

Exemplary teaching means challenging interaction between teacher and student together with formative evaluation, that is use of frequent feedback to improve performance against already determined (and high) standards (and previous performance). That is what those reports, inquiries and studies which compare the education systems and practices of various countries make clear. And the better education systems and practices are most likely found where teachers are respected within the community.

Hattie's conclusion from his research is unequivocal! 'We should focus on the greatest source of variance that can make the difference—the teacher. We need to ensure that this greatest influence is optimised to have powerful and sensationally positive effects, but they must be exceptional effects. We need to direct attention at higher quality teaching, and higher expectations that students can meet appropriate challenges—and these occur once the classroom door is closed and not by reorganising which or how many students are behind those doors…' (Hattie 2003).

Hattie recognises six major sources of variance in student's educational achievement: the student, home, schools, principals, peers and teachers. Students themselves account for about 50 % of the variance. 'It is what students bring to the table that predicts achievement more than any other variable'.

The influences of home, schools and peers each account for between 5 and 10 % of the variance. The influence of principals is, according to Hattie, already accounted for in the school effect (We should also remember that home has already been influential in the early childhood situation and therefore is relevant to what the student brings to the classroom experience). As to peers, Hattie observes, it does not matter too much who you go to school with, and when students are taken from one school and put in another the influence of peers is minimal (of course, there are exceptions, but they do not make the norm).

Hattie identifies 14 important influences, each with effect sizes greater than 0.4, the average effect size of all influences. ('Effect size' is a way of quantifying the size of the difference between two groups: it is the standardised mean difference between the two groups, in other words, the difference between the means of two groups divided by the standard deviation (The standard deviation is a measure of the spread of a set of values in a sample). One feature of an effect size is that it can be directly converted into statements about the overlap between the two samples in terms of a comparison of percentiles. An effect size is exactly equivalent to a Z-score of a standard Normal distribution. For example, an effect size of 0.8 means that the score of the average person in the experimental group is 0.8 standard deviations above the average person in the control group, and hence exceeds the scores of 79 % of the control group. The paper by Coe (2002) is very useful).

These include feedback, instructional quality, direct instruction, remediation/feedback, challenge of goals, peer tutoring, mastery learning, homework, teacher style and questioning. These are all sourced to the teacher! The first two influences—feedback and instructional quality—like student's prior cognitive ability—have effect sizes of more than one; indeed feedback has an effect size of 1.13 according to Hattie's research. An effect size of one is equivalent to about a year of schooling at primary or elementary level.

Hattie also explored the difference that expert, not just experienced, teachers make. With a colleague, the literature on distinctions between expert and experienced teachers was reviewed and the findings sent to pre-eminent researchers and expert teachers in the field for comment, changes and input.

Five major dimensions of expert teachers were identified as a result of the consideration of the initial research findings. They were the ability to identify essential representations of their subject, guide learning through classroom interactions, monitor learning and provide feedback, attend to affective attributes and influence student outcomes. Expert teachers adopt a problem solving stance to their work, have high respect for students and are passionate about teaching and learning. They engage students in learning and develop in their student's self-regulation, involvement in mastery learning, enhanced self-efficacy, and self-esteem as learners. [They] aim for more than achievement goals and to motivate their students to master rather than perform, they enhance student's self-concept and self-efficacy about learning, they set appropriate challenging tasks, and they aim for both surface and deep outcomes.

Hattie defined surface learning as being more about the content (knowing the ideas, and doing what is needed to gain a passing grade), and deep learning as more about understanding (relating and extending ideas, and an intention to understand and impose meaning). 'The claim is that experts are more successful at both types of learning, whereas both experienced and expert teachers are similar in terms of surface learning.'

6.4 Productive Pedagogy

The extensive research conducted as part of the Queensland School Reform Longitudinal Study (QSRLS) resulted in research on productive pedagogy (Lingard et al. 2001) based on the authentic pedagogy model developed by Fred Newmann and his colleagues at the University of Wisconsin-Madison. Authentic pedagogy was framed as, 'Construction of knowledge through disciplined inquiry to produce discourse, products or performance that have value beyond success in school can serve as a standard of intellectual quality for assessing the authenticity of student performance' (Ladwig 2007). The findings contrast with the analyses of John Hattie.

QSRLS was commissioned by Education Queensland (EQ) and conducted by researchers from the School of Education, The University of Queensland, from 1998 to 2000. Detailed observations and statistical analyses were made of 975 classroom lessons offered in 24 EQ schools over 3 years. Possible relationships between school-based management practices and enhanced student outcomes, both academic and social, were investigated.

Four dimensions of Productive Pedagogy were identified: *Intellectual Quality* which referred to the level at which students engaged in learning activities that promoted thinking, *Connectedness* which referred to the extent to which students engaged with problems connected to the world beyond the classroom, *Social Support* which indicates a supportive classroom environment in which students influence the nature of the activities they undertake and *Recognition of Difference* indicating recognition and valuing of a range of cultures. Some common misbeliefs seemed to inhibit teachers from adopting productive pedagogies. Many school staff saw behaviour management as a policy issue having priority over classroom practices, yet QSRLS data suggested that effective behaviour management is inherent in productive classroom practice.

Degrees of Intellectual Quality, Connectedness and Recognition of Difference were all initially considered to be directly and positively associated with the extent of students' engagement with, and self-regulation of, their learning. High intellectual demand and social support were seen as important for improving student academic outcomes. Some teachers considered that the two must be traded off against each other, rather than being synergistic and mutually productive. Most teachers reported low levels of organisational support for their efforts, and schools varied significantly on forming professional learning communities.

In further statistical analysis of Productive Pedagogy Professor Ladwig (2007) acknowledged that although the notion of there being a dimension of pedagogy related to Recognition of Difference may well have theoretical justification, the productive pedagogy research could not offer empirical substantiation.

Alignment between curriculum, pedagogy and assessment had been hindered by inconsistencies between the policies and practices of Education Queensland, new syllabus requirements and diagnostic testing procedures introduced by Queensland Studies Authority. System support structures, such as District Offices, appeared uncertain of their functions and how they could help build the organisational capacities of schools. School administrators and teachers reported more systemic constraints than support. School Councils were not working productively.

Both school administrators and teachers shared a perception that school leaders had been pushed in a managerial, rather than a pedagogical, direction by contemporary educational policy. Within-school and external professional development were needed.

The recommendations of the QSRLS and the propositions of Productive Pedagogy were incorporated to an extent into the teaching practice in Queensland.

6.5 Formative Evaluation

I learned early in my enhanced interest in education (listening to a talk by Professor Paul Black of Kings College London) that student learning was most significantly advanced by formative evaluation, ongoing interaction between teacher and student in together reviewing performance and achievement (Black and Wiliam 1998a). On the other hand, summative evaluations, test results, count for relatively little. It is just like the wider world of which the organisation and the family unit are parts.

We are all much more likely to respond positively when those with whom we work and live take notice of and value our contribution, when what we are saying and doing is responded to, when we are encouraged to believe we can go on to greater things. And when we are trusted (Ghoshal and Moran 1996). Threats cause resentment and generate avoidance behaviour. Waiting until you are about to leave school to find out if you have made the grade is not very helpful, not only because it is rather late: it is certainly too late to suggest remedial action.

With colleagues including Dylan Wiliam, Black explored the influence of formative assessment through literature analysis and experimentation. Learning gains, as measured by improvements in test scores of pupils involved in the relevant innovation compared with a typical group of pupils in the same test, confirm the value of formative evaluation. Acknowledging that learning is driven by what teachers and pupils do in classrooms Wiliam and Black note however, 'In terms of systems engineering, present policies in the US and in many other countries seem to treat the classroom as a black box.' (Black and Wiliam 1998b),

Though admitting that both summative and formative assessment have essential roles in encouraging a wide range of teaching and learning, the Report *All Our Futures: Creativity, Culture and Education*, by a Committee chaired by Sir Ken Robinson (National Advisory Committee on Creative and Cultural Education 1999) noted 'By trying to use summative forms of assessment for all purposes, the education system downgrades the importance of formative assessment'. The Report refers to a study by Paul Black and Dylan William which reviewed 250 separate studies of the link between assessment and learning.

Initiatives designed to enhance the effectiveness of the way assessment is used in the classroom to promote learning was found able to raise student achievement by the equivalent of between one and two grades for an individual—and, for England as a whole, it was estimated they would have raised the country's position in the then most recent—the third_ TIMSS from the middle of the 41 countries involved to the top five. The gain for lower-achieving students was considered likely to be even more substantial.

With Helen Timperley (also of Auckland University), John Hattie explored the influence that feedback has (Hattie and Timperley 2007). Noting it as one of the most powerful influences on learning and achievement, Hattie and Timperley point out that feedback can be positive or negative depending on the type of feedback and the way it is given. 'Feedback is conceptualized as information provided by an agent (e.g., teacher, peer, book, parent, self, experience) regarding aspects of one's performance or understanding. A teacher or parent can provide corrective information, a peer can provide an alternative strategy, a book can provide information to clarify ideas, a parent can provide encouragement, and a learner can look up the answer to evaluate the correctness of a response. Feedback thus is a consequence of performance. As Paul Black and Dylan Wiliam concluded, the provision of challenging assignments and extensive feedback lead to greater student engagement and higher achievement'.

A synthesis of meta-analyses demonstrates that 'the most effective forms of feedback provide cues or reinforcement to learners; are in the form of video-, audio-, or computer-assisted instructional feedback; and/or relate to goals. Programmed instruction, praise, punishment, and extrinsic rewards were found to be the least effective for enhancing achievement. Indeed, it is doubtful whether rewards should be thought of as feedback at all'. In the model developed by Hattie and Timperley, feedback, to be effective, must specify the goals ('where am I going?'), progress toward the goal ('how am I going?') and activities to improve progress ('where to next?'). Written comments are more effective than grades, as shown by Black and Wiliam who demonstrated that classroom testing encourages superficial and rote learning, concentrating on recall of isolated details, usually items of knowledge which pupils soon forget... teachers do not generally review the assessment questions that they use and do not discuss them critically with peers, so there is little reflection on what is being assessed.

Obviously goals are more effective when students share a commitment to attaining them: that commitment needs to be nurtured and built and parents and teachers and peers are some of the agents that can influence that process. Feedback on progress cannot always be positive and therefore the feedback may not be welcome; tests and assessments are but one way of dealing with the issue and are not always effective. Feedback can provide information which opens up further possibilities for learning.

Feedback about the task is more effective when it leads to better ways of processing and understanding the material. Feedback about the process is most beneficial when it helps provide cues about how to go about finding suitable places and strategies to complete the task and leads to more challenging tasks and goals. Feedback directed at the personal level such as praise is rarely effective. Citing Paul Black and Dylan Wiliam, the point is made that 'when feedback draws attention to the self, students try to avoid the risks involved in tackling challenging assignments, to minimize effort, and have a high fear of failure to minimize the risk to the self'.

Feedback is not the answer but rather one answer: when combined with effective instruction in classrooms, Hattie and Timperley point out, it can be very powerful in enhancing learning. 'Students construct their worlds of learning and classrooms, and it is a major argument... that it is crucial for teachers to understand and appreciate that providing feedback is only a part of the equation... Feedback can only be built on something... it is what happens second'.

6.6 Graham Nuthall, What Goes on in the Classroom?

Effective teaching involves substantial attention to the student and that means understanding what it is that goes on in the classroom, the student's interactions with the teacher as well as with other students and the influence of previous perceptions and understandings (including parents and previous teachers). Graham Nuthall in New Zealand used video observation and microphones recording the conversations of the students (Nuthall 2004a). This led him to question many of the conclusions which other researchers have reached as to what constitutes effective teaching: much of that is reputational analysis, documenting the practices of teachers who have come to be regarded by other teachers as effective. Studies of the kind which Nuthall and colleagues conducted are amongst the most important in all these essays: recognising the truth of his comments is essential.

> 'An irony in the history of quantitative studies of schooling has been the failure of researcher's analytic models to reflect adequately the social organization of life in classrooms and schools. The experiences that children share within school settings and the effects of these experiences on their development might be seen as the basic material of educational research; yet until recently, few studies have explicitly taken account of the effects of particular classrooms and schools in which students and teachers share membership.'
>
> Raudenbush and Willms (1991)

The conclusion from the research by Graham Nuthall and Adrienne Alton-Lee from the 1980s through 2005 (Nuthall and Alton-Lee 1993) was that 'classroom learning could only be understood as a dynamic change process, in which each concept or belief had a life story of its own as it evolved in the mind of each student. Factors that affected the way a student first encountered a new concept were different from the factors that affected the subsequent elaboration and long-term storage of that concept' (Nuthall 1999).

What each student learns is unique to them. The nature of the interaction with content and its effects are shaped by the student's prior knowledge which means that student knowledge is constantly changing through personal and social cognitive processing arising from the need to manage experiences… New knowledge depends on inferring missing connections and identifying implicit information. Students engage 'in a process of inference and deduction in which both semantic and episodic recollections and related knowledge are used to justify a specific answer' (Nuthall and Alton-Lee 1993, p. 810).

Practicing making connections, identifying implications and noting differences leads to internalisation of the habit. The more time a student spends interacting with relevant content, the better is the learning (Interestingly Kandel 2001 joint winner of the Nobel prize for Physiology or Medicine, drew the same conclusion from studying learning in *Aplysia californica*, a marine snail (Kandel 2001)). The breadth of a topic is important in determining what is learned. 'Narratives provide powerful structures for the organisation of curriculum content in memory…

Interactive activities in which students work together in groups in ways that enhance their mutual dependence on each other's knowledge and skills may be another effective means of facilitating knowledge acquisition [because] sharing ideas during the process of integrating new knowledge makes accessible the background knowledge of all of the participants. Prior knowledge may be ambiguous, incomplete, fragmentary and complex' (Nuthall 1999, p. 335).

Analysis of students' classroom research and what is known about learning and memory processes led to a model of learning comprising several principles. Each time topic-relevant information or experience is encountered a representation of it is stored in working memory for a limited time and through semantic integration it becomes connected with other semantically-related experiences or if it does not it is lost from working memory. Once a sufficient number of semantically related representations become integrated into a single structure in working memory, the specific knowledge construct becomes established in long-term memory (Nuthall and Alton-Lee 1993).

Nuthall makes this most important statement: '… teaching is an art that requires, for its most effective expression, a solid basis of understanding of the learning process' (Nuthall 1999, p. 339). So much for the frequently made assertion that the problem with teachers is their poor content knowledge. Content is not unimportant, it just isn't sufficient. Nuthall's statement achieves support from other findings about the value of cooperation between teachers!

Another important finding by Nuthall is that there is no difference in the learning of low ability students and high ability students (Nuthall 2004b). 'Given the same experiences, they learned in the same way… the differences in ability are not about how people learn but are the result of the ways they manage their participation in classroom activities'. Research by Nuthall and colleagues found enormous differences in the ways pupils experienced the same classroom activities and consequently enormous differences in what they learned.

Though great attention is paid to teaching and what teachers do, Nuthall emphasises we do not really know a great deal about how students learn. He says, '…what the teacher needs to know about the minds and experiences of pupils is much more subtle and complex, but nevertheless necessary to genuinely effective practice. And our research makes it clear that it is never going to be achieved except through careful pupil or student-focused research in classrooms. Without this knowledge, fashions in teaching methods will continue to come and go without adequate justification. Attempts to reform the inequalities that now exist in the present system will continue to go round in circles'.

Nuthall's research provides as good evidence for the constructivist theory of education as any. (Notions of children developing an understanding of meaning-making based on prior understandings and the influence of experience is generally traced to Jean Piaget and John Dewey; the literature on constructivist education theory is vast, especially in the science education area; unfortunately some of it is still addressing validity of the theory, rather like research in geology still exploring whether Alfred Wegener's theory of tectonic plates is valid).

Summarising the results of over 30 years exploration of children's learning in classrooms Nuthall (2004a) says, 'Students interpret classroom activities in relation to their own goals, interests, and background knowledge, and they extract the information that is relevant to them... It is this ongoing process of making sense of and managing their participation in classroom activities that changes their knowledge, skills, and motivation, and creates the link between classroom activities and learning'.

> Jim (to Leigh): Um, well, what they did was they went to Antarctica and then they studied this big mountain, which had heaps of lava in it.
>
> Nathan: Yeah, if it had lava in it, it should be a volcano shouldn't it?
>
> Jim: Yeah.
>
> Nathan: Rock hard lava. Here it goes. I've got some lava in my hand.
>
> Jim: I'm going to give you a scoop of lava... (to Nathan, fooling around). Heaps and heaps and heaps and heaps of attempts to get into the inner core or inner...
>
> Nathan: They didn't make heaps (inaudible)
>
> Jim: Inner, inner whatever.
>
> Nathan: He doesn't know what he's talking about.
>
> Jim: Exactly. You hit it right on the forehead.
>
> Meanwhile, Jane talked to Jan and Leigh and focused on producing the summary.
>
> Jane (talking to Jan and Leigh): Well, it's how Kathy got the experience to go to Mount Erebus.
>
> Leigh (writing): Into the inner crater of
>
> Jane: Mount Erebus.
>
> Leigh (writing): Mount Erebus.
>
> (Nuthall 1999)

Nuthall notes the 'compelling evidence' of the continuing gap between research on effective teaching and the practice of teaching found by Professor Joel R. Levin at the University of Arizona and others. However, that research is seen often by teachers as too theoretical, too general to relate directly to the 'practical realities of classroom life'. On the other hand, researchers believe that research 'should shape practice directly'; they regard the conclusions from well-designed studies as proof that teachers should use the method in their classrooms. If the two are to come together in a mutually fruitful relationship, Nuthall says, then 'educators must critically examine how research can contribute directly to the problems of teaching. As Aristotle first suggested (and others have continued to assert), research methods should be suited to the problems they are intended to solve'.

Influence only works by gaining the attention of those to be influenced—in other words, the management of influence is the management of attention. Teachers are convinced that they develop their skills through recalling their own schooling experiences and through watching other teachers. Student behaviour and motivation, managing activities and resources within the limited time available are often the main concern of teachers. In our awareness of what students do in the learning process we start to understand what it is all about.

Writer Zadie Smith captures some of what Nuthall is talking about in a few words in her book *White Teeth*.

> *In the old age black was not counted fair*, continued Francis Stone in the catatonic drone with which students read Elizabethan verse. *Or if it were, it bore not beauty's name.*

> Irie put her right hand on her stomach, sucked in and tried to catch Millat's eye. But Millat was busy showing pretty Nikki Tyler how he could manipulate his tongue into a narrow role, a flute. Nikki Tyler was showing him how the lobes of her ears were attached to the side of her head rather than loose. Flirtatious remnants of this morning's science lesson: *inherited characteristics. Part One ...*

Zadie Smith, *White Teeth* (London: Penguin 2000)

In life the immediate often takes precedence over the important, as Barry Jones once said. More knowledge has little impact on day to day practice unless it becomes part of one's own experience. Nearly everyone has that experience. Nuthall reminds us, 'Teachers often feel that learning outcomes are unpredictable, mysterious and uncontrollable. It is not surprising to learn that teachers find studies most valuable when the studies give them a deeper understanding of this fundamental relationship'.

Nuthall concludes that the main reason why the practice of teaching remains largely uninformed by research-based knowledge is because researchers haven't clearly demonstrated how and why research can contribute more to practice than teachers trial and error, reflection and investigation of their own practice, they haven't clarified what, in the area of practical teaching problems, research should address and they haven't demonstrated a relationship between teaching and learning to teachers satisfaction.

Clearly it is important to keep in mind that research is important but better communication of its meaning is necessary if teaching is to benefit.

Nuthall criticises four common lines of research into what constitutes effective teaching. Case studies of 'best practice' provide a rich source of information about teachers commonly believed to be effective teachers. But they confuse best teachers and best teaching because the studies focus on those reputed to be a good teacher. An observer in a classroom cannot identify those behaviours which have a positive effect on student learning without knowing in advance what to look for. Studies which correlate the behaviour of teachers with measures of student learning are more reliable but the relative significance of each of the teachers behaviours is not usually identified, the semantic and social context of the behaviours is not examined and so on.

In Nuthall's view similar criticisms can be made of 'design experiments' in which high quality teaching programs are used to test learning theories: complex packages which produce results in one context are translatable to other contexts only with great difficulty.

Research involving teachers experimenting with and gathering information about their own classroom performance is useful, according to Nuthall, but again inconclusive unless the teacher knows what to look for to identify what is effective learning by the student. 'Teachers tend to look for and see only those factors that the common culture of teaching sees as significant.' Nuthall advocates research which independently identifies what students learn, involves systematic continuous observation and interviews, analyses connections between classroom activities and student experiences and learning, recognises the difficulties of generalisation and aggregation and connects explanatory theory to relevant evidence.

Direct observation of children in the classroom, and in other learning environments, is common and provides extraordinarily important insights. But it is hard to see what notice was taken by New Zealand politicians of Nuthall's important research when the decision was made to restructure school education as described elsewhere (Sect. 12.2.2). It was another example of ideology based on no evidence trumping educational research.

6.7 Learning Outcomes: TIMMS

A different international study, TIMSS, tested learning outcomes—that is knowledge as opposed to ability to apply the knowledge which is what PISA does—among three groups—middle primary, lower secondary, final year secondary—in 1995 and then re-tested lower secondary students in 1999. TIMSS conducted further studies in 2003 and 2006 (2007 in Australia) of year 4 and year 8 students and in 2011 (see Sect. 14.2).

Understanding the meaning and significance of international testing such as PISA and TIMSS requires consideration of the purpose of the questions asked and the nature of the questions themselves and their relevance to the syllabus being taught in the years leading up to the time the tests are administered, how both the questions and the syllabus relate to current knowledge and understandings. Since different countries have different syllabuses it is likely that the test scores will have different meanings.

In addition, teaching methods vary though obviously to the extent that some methods are superior it is vital to identify the features of those superior methods. One of the approaches to this was the TIMSS 1999 Video Study (IES 1999), a cross-national study of eighth-grade classroom mathematics and science teaching. The study involved videotaping and analysing teaching practices in more than one thousand classrooms in seven countries (Australia, the Czech Republic, Hong Kong (though a Special Administrative Region of the Peoples Republic of China Hong Kong was treated as a county for the sake of convenience), Japan, the Netherlands, Switzerland, and the US. Its goals included investigation of teaching practices and comparisons with those found in high-achieving countries, discovering new ideas about teaching and developing new teaching research methods and tools for teacher professional development and stimulating discussion among educators, policy makers, and the public.

The study was conducted by the National Center for Education Statistics, US Department of Education in conjunction with the International Association of the Evaluation of Education Achievement (IEA) under a contract with LessonLab Research Institute of Santa Monica, California.

The Study found that 'Despite some commonalities … each of the countries had a distinct approach to science teaching, providing students with different opportunities to learn science and different visions of what it means to understand science. Countries distinct approaches varied in the organizational features, content features, and the ways in which students were involved in actively doing science work in the science lessons'.

These kinds of studies can reveal difference between what teachers believe they are doing and what they are actually doing, such as continuing to teach in a traditional manner but believing they are meeting newly established standards. Culture has an influence on teaching methods and lesson format. However, those cultural differences do not overshadow commonalities of effective teaching!

6.8 Jonathan Osborne and Argumentation in Science

Argument and debate are common in science, yet they are virtually absent from science education. Professor Jonathan Osborne, now at Stanford University, points out that opportunities for students to engage in collaborative discourse and argumentation offer a means of enhancing student conceptual understanding and students' skills and capabilities with scientific reasoning (Osborne 2010, 2012). Since critical, rational scepticism is essential in science, educational practice which does not give opportunities to develop the ability to reason and argue scientifically is a weakness: 'knowing what is wrong matters as much as knowing what is right… Argumentation is the means that scientists use to make their case for new ideas.' Critique is not, therefore, some peripheral feature of science, but rather it is core to its practice.

Science education mostly lacks argument: 'in the rush to present the major features of the scientific landscape, most of the arguments required to achieve such knowledge are excised'. Science therefore comes across as a monolith of facts. This is consistent with the deeply held view that education is a process of transmission of knowledge as a set of unequivocal and uncontested facts transferred from expert to novice. 'However, in reality, education is a highly complex act where failure is the norm and success the exception… learning is often the product of the difference between the intuitive or old models we hold and new ideas we encounter'.

Research reveals some very interesting and important features of learning. For instance, groups holding differing ideas learn more than those who hold similar preconceptions. Improvements in conceptual learning occur when students engage in argumentation. Thus students asked to engage in small-group discussions significantly outperformed a group of control students in their use of extended utterances and verbal reasoning. Students studying genetics who engaged in discussion used biological knowledge appropriately significantly more often than a group that did not engage in discussion. And Osborne quotes a UK classroom study over 2 years of 30 lessons in 11 schools dedicated to the teaching of reasoning. Students' scores on tests of conceptual knowledge in the intervention schools were significantly better than those of the control sample and 2 years later, these students significantly outperformed a control sample not only in science, but also in language, arts and mathematics. That suggests this kind of program accelerates students' general intellectual processing abilities. The finding has been replicated many times.

It is most important, Osborne points out, that students be taught the norms of social interaction, to understand that the function of their discussion is to persuade others of the validity of their arguments. Skills which can be developed include the ability to formulate explanatory hypotheses to model phenomena and discriminate between supporting and contradictory evidence using argumentation to seek validity where appropriate and the application of statistical techniques.

In summary Osborne concludes, teaching students to reason, argue, and think critically will enhance students' conceptual learning. This will only happen, however, if students are provided structured opportunities to engage in deliberative exploration of ideas, evidence, and argument—in short, how we know what we know, why it matters, and how it came to be. Without such opportunity science seems hardly relevant, impenetrable. There are important complementarities with the work of Lauren Resnick at the University of Pittsburgh and colleagues on 'accountable talk' as described elsewhere (Sect. 7.4).

6.9 Knowledge of Effective Teaching and Learning is Ignored

There are thousands of articles by education researchers in scores of refereed journals, a seemingly never-ending number of daily newspaper articles and other media appearances which each year publish more information about schools, teachers and their interaction. To claim that we know little about what constitutes effective teaching does not accurately reflect the current state of knowledge. At the same time there is more to learn. The problem in policy development at the political level is not that we do not know enough but that what we know is almost completely ignored in favour of preconceptions!

Teacher quality and related matters will be the most important interventions once the child starts school. The quality of the interaction between teacher and student is critical. it is important to remember, however, that there are many other influences including other people and resources.

There can be little doubt that in many situations, leadership at government level makes a great difference to the extent that meaningful reform can occur. That is especially so in political environments where government plays a major role. Governments, and in the case of independent schools, the school boards, influence the quality of the teachers by helping to create an environment in which teachers want to teach and are recognised and respected for their contribution.

Important dimensions of expert teachers include representation of the subject, ability to guide student learning and provide feedback. Use of argumentation is important and relating content to student interest and knowledge increase learning. Understanding the dynamics of the classroom means recognising that learning is constructivist, a process of continual modification of previously held understandings.

Those who claim that we should return to more didactic approaches to teaching and learning and abandon child-centred approaches are simply ignoring the evidence, as will be evident from reading the second essay on the topic of teaching.

The second essay on Best Teaching examines a number of case studies in the US and some related matters including class size and homework.

References

Barber, M., & Mourshed, M. (2007). *How the world's best-performing school systems come out on top*. London: McKinsey & Company. Retrieved September 6, 2012, from http://www.mckinsey.com/clientservice/socialsector/resources/pdf Worlds_School_Systems_Final.pdf

Black, P., & Wiliam, D. (1998a). Assessment and classroom learning. Assessment in education: Principles. *Policy and Practice, 5*, 7–74.

Black, P., & Wiliam, D. (1998b). Inside the black box: Raising standards through classroom assessment. Retrieved September 5, 2012, from http://blog.discoveryeducation.com/assessment/files/2009/02/blackbox_article.pdf

Coe, R. (2002,12–14 September). It's the Effect Size. Stupid: What effect size is and they it is important presented at the Annual Conference of the British Educational Research Association. University of Exeter. England. Retrieved September 5, 2012, from http://www.leeds.ac.uk/educol/documents/00002182.htm

Ghoshal, S., & Moran, P. (1996). Bad for practice: A critique of the transaction cost theory. *Academy of Management Review, 21*, 13–48.

Hattie, J. (2003). Building teacher quality. Paper for Australian Council for Educational Research Annual Conference 2003. Retrieved September 5, 2005, from http://www.education.auckland.ac.nz/webdav/site/education/shared/hattie/docs/teachers-make-a-difference-ACER-%282003%29.pdf

Hattie, J., & Timperley, H. (2007). The power of feedback. *Review of Educational Research, 77*, 81–112.

IES. (1999). Highlights from the TIMSS 1999 video study of eighth-grade mathematics teaching. Institute of educations sciences. Retrieved October 15, 2012, from http://nces.ed.gov/pubs2003/timssvideo/

Kandel, E. R. (2001). The molecular biology of Memory storage: a dialog between genes and synapses. Nobel lecture December 8. 2000. Stockholm: The Nobel Prize in Physiology or Medicine 2000. Retrieved September 5, 2012, from http://www.nobelprize.org/nobel_prizes/medicine/laureates/2000/kandel-lecture.html

Killen, R. (2007). *Effective teaching strategies lessons from research and practice* (4th ed.). South Melbourne: Cengage Learning Australia.

Ladwig, J. G. (2007). Modelling pedagogy in Australian school reform. *Pedagogies, 2*, 57–76.

Lingard, R. L. et al. (2001). The queensland school reform longitudinal study: A strategy for shared curriculum leadership. In A. R. Thomas (Ed.). *Teachers manual*. Brisbane: Department of Education.

Mulkeen, A., Read, T., & Buchan, A. (2008). Providing effective and equitable opportunities to learn. In A. M. Verspoor with the SEIA Team (Eds.). *At the crossroads—choices for secondary education in sub-saharan Africa*. Chapter 7. *World bank Africa human development series*. Washington DC: The World Bank. Retrieved September 5, 2012, form http://siteresources.worldbank.org/INTAFRREGTOPEDUCATION/Resources/444659-1210786813450/Secondary_Education_At_the_Crossroads.pdf

National Advisory Committee on Creative and Cultural Education. (1999, May). *All our futures: Creativity. Culture and education. Report to the secretary of state for education and employment & the secretary of state for culture, Media and Sport*. Retrieved July 10, 2011, form http://sirkenrobinson.com/skr/pdf/allourfutures.pdf

Nuthall, G. (1999). The way students learn: Acquiring knowledge from an integrated science and social studies. *The Elementary School Journal, 99*, 303–349.

Nuthall, G. (2004a). Relating classroom teaching to student learning: A critical analysis of why research has failed to bridge the theory-practice gap. *Harvard Educational Review, 74*, 273–306.

Nuthall, G. (2004b). *Discovering the hidden realties of teaching and learning in the classroom*. Talk given at the launch of the Graham Nuthall Classroom Research Trust, University of Canterbury, May 5, 2004. Retrieved October 14, 2013, form http://www.nuthalltrust.org.nz/docs/GN_Trust_talk.pdf

Nuthall, G. A., & Alton-Lee, A. G. (1993). Predicting learning from student experience of teaching: A theory of student knowledge acquisition in classrooms. *American Educational Research Journal, 30*, 799–840.

OECD. (2005). *Teachers matter: Attracting. Developing and retaining effective teachers*. Paris: OECD. Retrieved September 5, 2012, form http://www.oecd.org/edu/preschoolandschool/attractingdevelopingandretainingeffectiveteachers-homepage.htm

Osborne, J. (2010). Arguing to learn in science: The role of collaborative. Critical discourse. *Science, 328*, 463–466.

Osborne, J. (2012). The role of argument: learning how to learn in school science. In B. J. Fraser et al. (Eds.), *Second international handbook of science education part two*. Dordrecht: Springer.

Patty, A. (2010, May 25). Streamline teacher sackings, say parents. *Sydney Morning Herald*.

Raudenbush, S. W., & Willms, J.D. (Eds.). (1991). *Schools. Classrooms and pupils: International studies of schooling from a multilevel perspective* (p. 9). New York: Academic Press. (quoted by Rowe, 2003).

Chapter 7
Effective Teaching and Learning Part 2: Lessons from the US

Part 1 of the essay on teaching dealt with some features of teaching practice considered to lead to effective learning. In this concluding essay I want to consider studies in the US, studies which are illustrative of the many local studies of school systems.

7.1 School Reforms in the US: Follow Through and Direct Instruction

First, some background on reforms in the USA.

In the USA, over the 25 years from 1980 to 2005, the McKinsey Report (Barber and Mourshed 2007) tells us, spending per student increased by 73 %, the student-to-teacher ratio in schools declined by 18 % and tens of thousands of initiatives were launched aiming to improve quality of education: however, actual student outcomes, as measured by the Department of Education's own national assessment program, stayed almost the same.

On the ground oversight in the US is provided by locally elected school boards with jurisdiction over school districts which are in turn faced with directives from state legislatures. Local election of members of the school boards is a feature unique to the system.

An example of US reforms in the last half century is provided by the Follow Through Project. In 1964 the US Congress passed the Economic Opportunity Act. One of the authorized programs was Headstart designed to assist children from disadvantaged backgrounds in their earliest years of schooling. Originally a summer program, it has been successively expanded. When it became evident that years of poverty could not be reversed by a few weeks of preschool President Johnson therefore requested in 1967 a program to "follow through" on Headstart.

When the Nixon administration's budget appropriations were reduced after 1968, before the program had started, Follow Through was transformed by the Department of Education into a systematic evaluation of different models of educating children. The result was envisaged as an elucidation of better ways to educate disadvantaged children. The longitudinal study involved 10,000 children from 120 communities in 51 school districts each year from 1968 through 1976 and continued as a service program until 1995 when funding ceased (Watkins 1995).

The Federal Office of Education contracted with developers, who then acted as sponsors, of various educational approaches or models for teaching young children. Twelve programs were chosen ranging from carefully controlled approaches through child-centred ones. A further 10 sponsors were added in subsequent years.

Complex evaluations of the outcomes of each program were undertaken, the data collected by Stanford Research Institute and analysed by Abt Associates, a consultancy company involved in research and program implementation in the fields of health, social and environmental policy, and international development. The programs were grouped into 'Basic Skills' which focused primarily on directly teaching fundamental skills in literacy and numeracy, 'Cognitive-Conceptual' focusing on 'learning to learn' and problem solving and 'Affective-Cognitive' which emphasised development of self-concept and positive attitudes to learning. The performance of groups of children from each model was compared with a comparison group not subject to that model. An effect was considered to be meaningful if the difference was both statistically significant and of at least one quarter standard deviation.

The major thrust of the reports by Cathy Watkins of California State University at Stanislaus is that not only did the models in the 'Basic Skills' group produce better learning outcomes but one of the models, Direct Instruction, had 'an unequivocally higher average effect on scores in the basic skills domain than did any other model'. She then proceeded to outline the way in which Direct Instruction was nevertheless not subsequently widely adopted by schools because, she says, it did not fit with the preconceived views of educators.

Direct Instruction (DI) is a highly structured approach to instruction designed to accelerate the learning of at-risk students (Promising Practices Network. 2005). Previously known as the DISTAR (Direct Instruction Systems for Teaching Arithmetic and Reading) program DI is based on the theory that learning is maximized when instructional presentations are clear, likely misinterpretations are eliminated, and generalizations are facilitated. Classroom teachers learn how to define tasks clearly, build toward more-complex concepts, use interactive lessons with large and small groups, use frequent praise for responses, and recognize and correct errors immediately. To maximize time spent on tasks, students are placed in instructional groups based on similar performance, and grouping may take place across classes and grades.

Direct Instruction has been evaluated and described by numerous researchers (Barbash 2012); importantly these have included consideration of long-term benefits (Gersten and Keating 1987). Amongst the evaluations is a meta-analysis by Promising Practices Network (loc. cit.). Promising Practices reports expansion of the program from basic skills to include social and physical sciences.

7.1 School Reforms in the US: Follow Through and Direct Instruction   117

DI is indeed 'old school': it includes teacher-led exercises, skills grouping, choral responding and repetition. It teaches fundamentals and then adds to those (Barbash loc.cit.). It confines students and teachers to a specific set of learning interactions. A number of studies that reported statistically significant results for DI were noted in which achievement was superior to that of other programs. But also noted was the fact that whilst the program receives a 'promising' rating, results of evaluation varied significantly and therefore 'overall evidence of DI effectiveness is limited'. It is not clearly established that DI is effective in later life in reducing or preventing juvenile delinquency though Gersten and Keating and some other studies found positive results.

In the end result it is important to note that the OECD in its PISA studies makes it clear that student engagement is critical.' PISA results show that mastering strategies that assist learning, such as methods to remember and understand or summarise texts and reading widely, are essential if students are to become proficient readers.' Practicing reading by reading for enjoyment is most closely associated with better outcomes when it is accompanied by high levels of critical thinking and strategic learning. Across OECD countries, students who have low levels of awareness about which strategies are most effective for understanding, remembering and summarising information are less proficient readers than those who have high levels of awareness about these strategies, regardless of their reading habits. 'In all countries, students who enjoy reading the most perform significantly better than students who enjoy reading the least.' (OECD 2010a, p. 12).

Watkins presents an important narrative about the politics of education. Project Follow Through involved many people and organisations and cost a lot of money. Its impact seems to have been limited indeed. This is typical of the education landscape of the US: large amounts of money are poured into specific programs but for various reasons the programs are largely though not entirely abandoned and other ones commenced. Political intervention is common. Self interest of certain education professionals also contributes to the outcome: that is an attribute not only of education!

7.2 US Reforms: The Last 20 Years

Diane Ravitch, in her book *The Death and Life of the American School System* (Ravitch 2010) provides a most useful summary of reforms in America. (I draw on her account in this summary.) In the late 1990s considerable attention was paid to achievements in the Upper East Side of New York City, which contained pockets of poverty and some wealthy areas. District Superintendent Anthony Alvarado introduced a reading program called 'Balanced Literacy' which integrates various models of instruction with assessment at its core. Described as requiring explicit skill instruction and 'authentic texts', it included interactive reading aloud shared with the teacher and shared writing, students practicing reading and writing following modelled reading and writing by the teacher. Students worked together to discover their own ways of solving problems, compared their solutions with those of other children: 'multiple solutions to problems were emphasized'.

One of the successful small schools in this program was Central Park East Secondary School established by Deborah Meier. Through what she called 'democratic education' she transformed several elementary and high schools involving the students and families in making these the kind of schools they want.

Alvarado encouraged those teachers who did not use Balanced Literacy to move to other districts; professional development was a daily routine. Improvements were considered to be 'dramatic' by the mid 1990s. Lauren Resnick of Pittsburgh and Richard Elmore of Harvard University pointed to 'heavy investment in professional development and determination to make every teacher and principal responsible for improving instruction.' Other researchers asserted that the improvements were due to rising SES levels of the students and that professional development did not appear to have an influence on student achievement. And some parents complained of children being 'stifled by constructivist methods'.

In 2001, a few years after Alvarado left New York District 2, newly elected Mayor Michael Bloomberg hired Joel Klein as Chancellor of the New York City school system. 'In his campaign Bloomberg vowed to gain control of the public schools and to make them successful. In June 2002 the state legislature transferred control of the public school system over to Bloomberg who in turn established the Department of Education (DOE) to manage the school system, so replacing the independent School Board.

Though successes were claimed by Klein, others, including Columbia University sociology graduate student Jennifer Jennings (blogging as 'eduwonkette'), pointed to severe statistical problems in the claims for achievement. So did Daniel Koretz, Professor of Education at Harvard University and one of the leading US experts in educational testing who characterised the methodology behind the reporting system as 'baroque' (Schemo 2008). The tremendous variation in schools grades from year to year were probably due to sampling and measurement error rather than school improvement (Cobbold 2008; Ravitch 2009; Otterman 2010). The 2010 test results for New York schools showed proficiency rates lower than they had been in 2006, when the state last overhauled grade school testing (Cobbold 2010).

Diane Ravitch, one time Assistant Secretary of Education in the George H.W. Bush administration (Ravitch 2010), once supportive of recent reforms, now vigorously opposes 'No Child Left Behind', the major reform of the last 20 years: none of the countries whose students perform to the highest levels in international tests have adopted the strategies which have been put in place in the US.

7.3 The South Side of Chicago

The south side of Chicago is in many ways a very difficult neighbourhood. But it has been the focus of ground breaking research by the University of Chicago research group. Their studies overwhelmingly concerned children from disadvantaged circumstances; most of the children were African American, all considered to contribute to poor educational achievement. The University of Chicago studies, like some other studies, show these disadvantages can be overcome. Their studies reveal the importance of developing relationships with the community.

Professor Stephen W. Raudenbush, Professor of Sociology and Chair of the Committee on Education at the University of Chicago, speaking at an American Education Research Association Conference, illustrated an aspect of effective teaching and learning with a story from China (Raudenbush 2009). '[The teachers in] MaPing Li's 1999 study of elementary mathematics instruction in China ... did not have advanced college degrees but they did have a good working knowledge of the mathematics they needed to teach and somewhat beyond. They had a common curriculum, common assessments, common instructional strategies. And they had a shared, systematic instructional system. They collaborated closely, sharing knowledge, expertise, and teaching plans, tested their students frequently and generated common strategies to overcome student misconceptions and advance instruction further. Their students displayed uniformly high levels of achievement. Expert teachers supported the least expert teachers and this developed the leadership capacities of the most expert.' Good knowledge is important but not enough: close collaboration of teachers around common goals is also important.

Raudenbush asserts 'powerful instructional systems require shared aims, shared assessment tools, shared instructional strategies, active collaboration, routine public inspection of practice, and accountability to peers... In this view, variability in teacher's expertise is highly visible and widely recognized, and novice teachers have strong incentives to seek out expert teacher's advice to advance their own expertise. School principals have incentives to increase the leadership responsibilities of the most expert teachers and to encourage growth in teacher expertise. Increased teacher expertise leads to greater responsibilities and higher compensation.' Raudenbush refers to this notion of teaching as shared, systematic practice.

He contrasts this with what he calls privatized, idiosyncratic practice, the received notion of teachers' work and teacher professionalism, according to which teachers' work has a high level of autonomy which is rarely open to public inspection (and may therefore lack rigour, testability or validity). Such a notion stands in the way of reforms which would drive improvement and equity.

The University of Chicago established the Center for Urban School Improvement (USI) to work with a small network of south side Chicago schools to improve literacy instruction. The inner urban kids demonstrated great intellectual energy but dealing with regular public schools was frustrating because of the restrictive bureaucracy. So USI set up a special elementary charter school which was free to shape teacher recruitment, curriculum design and instructional time to pursue ambitious intellectual goals. Staff of the Center studied schools through the 1990s and into the 2000s.

Anthony Bryk and colleagues (Bryk et al. 2010) note the 1990s as a period of 'extraordinary ferment and great optimism about schools in Chicago.' The Chicago School Reform Act (1988) devolved significant resources and authority to new Local School Councils which were intended to reform their schools. The power of the central bureaucracy to interfere in local initiatives was constrained. '… If local school professionals reconnected with the parents and communities they were supposed to serve, and if everyone were empowered to reform their schools, together they could be much more effective in solving local problems than some impersonal bureaucracy.' No explicit blueprint for improvement was set out in the 1988 Act: school community leaders were to develop their own plans to improve student learning.

In the schools studied by Raudenbush literacy instruction, developed through close cooperation with a number of outstanding practitioners and researchers, was built around a schoolwide formative assessment system known as STEP (Strategic Teaching and Evaluation of Progress). Every child was assessed every 10 weeks on a broad array of literacy skills, hierarchically arranged. Associated with each level was one or more required books for children to read, calibrated for difficulty. Associated with each level of STEP was a series of instructional strategies designed to get to the next level… work on word decoding, reading aloud, text comprehension, and lots of writing [combined] to create a coherent instructional system.

Every child's progress was recorded on a 'STEP wall' in the school's central office. Teachers of children lagging behind had help from the literacy coordinator who got experienced teachers to work with less experienced ones. So instruction was not left to the judgement of one teacher. Teachers whose students progressed gained expertise which was then used to help other teachers.

More expert teachers could contribute to revising the system to promote higher levels of learning. The logging of student achievement meant results were open to inspection. Raudenbush observes 'the system rewards advances in expertise, as it accords more responsibility to the more expert teachers… Teacher expertise is not a generic quality but rather a set of attainable skills and knowledge embedded in a well-defined instructional system. To be expert is to understand that system, to demonstrate skill in enacting it, and to develop the capacity to help other teachers enact the system effectively.'

USI later set up a second charter school which expanded instruction time and gave attention to extended tutoring for those who needed it and also embarked on an ambitious outreach program aimed at getting parents to understand the STEP system, their child's progress and understand their role in helping their child reach the next goal. (A charter school arrangement overcame bureaucratic problems which would have attended a regular public school.) Support staff were provided to help the small number of children whose parents lacked the resources to participate. The 'vice principal' became the 'director of parent and community engagement', got to know all the parents and siblings of each student.

Though Raudenbush admitted that evidence was limited he noted that '80 % of the first graduating class on their way to a 4-year college—in a system where most African American children don't even finish high school'.

Longitudinal studies of Chicago public elementary schools were conducted by University of Chicago education researchers as part of the Consortium on Chicago

School Research (CCSR). Penny Bender Sebring and colleagues, in their report on the Chicago schools, show how five 'community supports'—leadership, parent-community ties, professional capacity, student-centered learning climate, and ambitious instruction—influence a school's capacity for improvement (Sebring 2004).

They found links between professional staff of the school and parents and the community to be vitally important not least because support at home by parents of their children's learning contributed significantly to school improvement. Volunteer activity and participation in decision making by parents led to them becoming critical partners of the school. Of course the knowledge, skills, and dispositions of the faculty and staff, and their ongoing learning and professional growth are vitally important and so is a school-based professional community focused on developing instructional capacity across the school. Partnership and cooperation between teachers, parents, and community members provide the social resources needed to meet the challenges of improving school conditions and student learning.

'Leadership, acting as a catalyst, is the first essential support for school improvement.' Leadership is conceptualized broadly as being inclusive, with a focus on instruction and a strategic orientation. Leadership, in turn, stimulates development of the four other core organizational supports: parent-community ties, professional capacity of the faculty and staff, a student-centered learning climate, and ambitious instruction.

Although improving and stagnating schools were found in all communities, those with particularly strong social capital and low crime rates were likely to have schools with strong essential supports, whereas those with weak social capital were likely to have weak essential supports in their schools.

In a recent further elaboration of findings about reform in south Chicago, Bryk, now President of the Carnegie Foundation for the Advancement of Teaching, and colleagues at the University of Chicago emphasise the vital importance of the leadership style of the school principal and the principal's engagement with parents and school staff in achieving improvement (Bryk et al. loc.cit.). Introducing the book *Organizing Schools for Improvement* they compare two schools similar in the demographic features of community and students with subtle differences in local history and community: about half the men in each school neighbourhood aged sixteen and older did not work and about half the households receive some kind of aid such as food stamps. The two schools whose students had similar outcomes 6 years previously had later become quite different places. Differences in leadership style, sustained focus on instruction and teacher capacity building suggest themselves as being amongst the factors influencing outcomes. These are some of the essential supports already identified.

Whilst recognising that the key issue is how instruction is managed within the classroom, Bryk and colleagues acknowledge that the framework of essential supports focuses attention at the school level. 'If restructuring school organization matters, its effects must largely accrue through influencing the conditions under which teachers work and engage with students around subject matter in the classroom.' The Chicago studies do not address the process of individual student learning. However, the findings are critical to understanding best teaching practices. There are important parallels with reforms in New Zealand and in Sweden, as described in Chap. 12 'International Comparisons'. And as in the reforms described later in Illinois and California, it is leadership by the school principal in respect of teaching and learning which is critical, not autonomy in the administrative tasks of managing budgets and hiring staff.

7.4 Nested Learning Communities and Accountable Talk

Professor Lauren Resnick of the University of Pittsburgh is another of the many leading education researchers in the US. The habits of mind which influence beliefs about learning are acquired through socialisation, the process by which standards, values and knowledge of society are developed; it is a process influenced by other people who influence development during the child's life (Resnick and Hall 1998). Though socialisation is acknowledged in out of school settings such as the family, when it comes to more formally organised educational settings such as school its role is not usually acknowledged. Resnick talks of 'nested learning communities' in which students teachers, principals, and central-office administrators are all learners focused on improving their practice and becoming increasingly expert as conductors of learning communities in the classroom, the school, and the district (Resnick 2010). Since children's learning depends heavily on how well adults learn how to teach them, every adult is responsible for his or her ongoing professional growth.

'Children develop cognitive strategies and effort-based beliefs about intelligence—the habits of mind associated with higher-order learning—when they are continuously pressed to raise questions and accept challenges, to find solutions that are not immediately apparent, to explain concepts, justify their reasoning, and seek information.' Children need to be held accountable for this kind of intelligent behaviour. When they are not they come to believe that they are not considered smart and often accept that judgement. The hallmark of knowledge-based constructivist pedagogy is the paradoxical view that children become smart by being treated as if they already were intelligent.

In a short essay on 'Making America Smarter' Resnick (1999) points out that 'Americans mostly assume that aptitude largely determines what people can learn in school, although they allow that hard work can compensate for lower doses of innate intelligence. Our schools are largely organized around this belief. IQ tests or their surrogates are used to determine who has access to enriched programs. As a result, some students never get the chance to study a high-demand, high-expectation curriculum.' She points out that the results of achievement tests, instead of being compared with a standard of excellence, are used to compare students against each other which makes it difficult to see the results of learning and discourages effort. What is the point of trying, she asks, if no matter how hard one tries one still ends up in the same relative percentile rank?

A key point is that if students are held to low expectations they accept the judgement that inborn aptitude matters most and that they simply don't have the inherited capacity to do better. On the other hand, if they are treated as if they are intelligent they actually become so. Teaching demanding content engenders greater learning: they are able to 'bounce back in the face of short-term failures... In short, one's intelligence is the sum of one's *habits of mind.*' (original emphasis). That is shown by decades of research by social psychologists. To deliver the kinds of high-level academic achievement hoped for by everyone requires effort-based schools in which academic rigor and a thinking curriculum permeates the school day for every student. This is a fundamental point at the heart of the problems in learning faced especially by students from less advantaged backgrounds who attend schools with poorly trained teachers and poor resources. It is also a basis for objection to the mantra that standardised tests are the answer to improvement!

Resnick advocates an effort-based school to replace the assumption that aptitude determines achievement, clear expectations as to what is to be learned, recognition of authentic accomplishment, assessment that students find to be fair, abandonment of the proposition that knowledge can be taught without engaging the student—instead knowledge and thinking must be joined—and accountable talk which involves responses by each student to what other students have said and uses evidence in ways appropriate to the discipline and so on.

From the 'pedagogical core' of nested learning communities Resnick and Hall proceed to describe a school district in New York City with a high proportion of poor and non-English-speaking students that under the leadership of the superintendent and deputy has organised itself to promote and sustain a continuous upgrading of teaching practice. Teaching quality improved and student achievement rose. The University of Pittsburgh, through the Institute for Learning, has expanded this model to develop 'nested communities' of partnerships between schools and University.

In the role of orchestrator of the school-based learning community for teachers, school-based district principals observe and evaluate classroom practice, arrange professional-development opportunities, work out improvement goals with teachers, and assess whether goals are being met... 'In nested learning communities, instruction, management, and professional development are joined in a single set of aspirations, and the principal plays a pivotal role in the instructional-improvement process...'

In all her work Resnick emphasises competent performance as involving explanation and argumentation, discussion as discursive rather than question and answer and knowledge as distributed. In a thinking curriculum high cognitive demand is embedded in challenging subject matter and students are initiated into knowledge-based communities of participation. The key is the right classroom instruction embedded in a supportive organisational structure.

Resnick considers that 'despite the rhetoric of 21st century skills, we have by and large built our accountability system so that it actually suppresses the kind of learning that the 21st century calls for. Since the middle of the 20th century, the science of learning, and thus the underpinnings for trying to reach the gold star of knowledge-based reasoning for all Americans, has expanded substantially. The recommendations now coming from an expanded, multidisciplinary learning science community are substantially different from those of the first half of the 20th century.'

Learning theory has been transformed remarkably over the last century of its attempted application to schooling. Scientific research on learning has produced changed concepts of *knowledge* itself, new criteria for what counts as *competent performance* and as *intelligence,* new principles for *instruction,* and even new theories of how educational *organizations* work.

Resnick's accountable talk is a powerful approach to learning (Michaels et al. 2008; Alexander 2010). As Sarah Michaels of Clark University in Worcester, Massachusetts, Catherine O'Connor of Boston University and Lauren Resnick point out, accountable talk has been shown to result in academic achievement for a diverse population of students. Accountable talk emphasises the forms and norms that support and promote equity and access to rigorous academic learning. There are three dimensions: accountability to the learning community which involves listening to and responding to others and building their response to them, accountability to accepted standards of reasoning and accountability to knowledge, talk based on facts. That conversations have a profound influence on eventual outcomes is something known from organisational dynamics (Gratton and Ghoshal 2002).

Michaels and her colleagues give examples and illustrations of the success of accountable talk. It is true, as they point out, that some students unfamiliar with such approaches to conversation confronted by students who are, who have learned them at home, and control the discussion may find the situation difficult. But in classrooms where the process is used effectively teachers are able to build a culture that involves risk-taking and the 'explicit modeling and practice of particular talk moves on'. Over time new forms and norms of discourse develop and students begin to listen to one another, build on the ideas which emerge and participate productively. 'It is encouraging to think that if students are socialized early and intensively into these discourse norms in academic settings, they will internalize them and carry them into the civic sphere.' (Michaels et al. 2008, p. 295).

Emeritus Professor Robin Alexander of Cambridge University talks of 'dialogic teaching', how teachers as well as children talk (Alexander 2010). Alexander studied children in their classes in schools in England, France, Russia, India and Australia. His book, *Culture and pedagogy: international comparisons in primary education* (Oxford: Blackwell, 2000) is highly critical of the tendency to transplant policies and practices from one country to another with little understanding of the multi layered historical, cultural and political contexts of their origin (Zyngier 2004). The data is based on analysis of 36 lessons in 30 schools in the five countries. David Zyngier of Monash University, in his review of Alexander's book, says the study 'should clearly send the message to our policy movers, makers and shakers that there is no "magic bullet", no single pedagogy or pedagogical practice and no single definition of best practice'.

7.5 Ricky DuFour and Professional Learning Communities

The US school education scene over the last 40 years is typified by numerous experiments, very substantial research, a disregard by most politicians and much of the media of what is actually going on in schools and of the research. Much of the argument focuses on assertions that unions are resisting reforms; it also is frequently about notions of instruction, of disagreements about the effectiveness of student-centred learning as opposed to traditional didactic instruction.

The focus of the reforms varied. In some cases they were at the levels of the school and were district wide or local. In the case of much of the research they addressed what happened with the school class and the individual student. Most recently reforms have been at the district level. In that situation State officials seek to exercise particular influence. As education blogger Larry Cuban points out in his 21 February 2013 blog States have the constitutional authority to provide education and in pursuit of that have established districts and delegated authority to them to run schools. US education has been a decentralised operation for two centuries. The implementation of No Child Left Behind in essence recognised that.

Numerous studies, including those by the Chicago Group and Lauren Resnick, reveal features of successful schools and effective teaching which are stark contrasts with the rhetoric underlying reforms such as 'No Child Left Behind'.

Social Studies teacher Ricky Dufour in Illinois in the 1970s developed and implemented a transformative model, 'Professional Learning Communities at Work' (McLester 2012). Its core belief was that all students should have access to the most rigorous curriculum and that all of them should learn. This was counter to the common practices of the time. In the 1980s, DuFour implemented his student-centred model at Adlai Stevenson High School in Illinois. All incoming students were guaranteed support including a faculty advisor, a mentor from a more senior class, a weekly check with their counsellor and progress reports or grades every 3 weeks. If they struggled they were helped by their mentor. If they continued to struggle they were moved to a tutoring center and if still unsuccessful to guided study where staff monitored their work every day. From there, if they were still struggling they were put into a study skills class, mentored each day and the school partnered with their parents to give further help.

DuFour's experiments led to considerable improvements. Students receiving Ds and Fs dropped from 36 to 6 % and those earning As and Bs increased from 48 to 75 %. Du Four went on to become superintendent of Adlai Stevenson, retiring in 2002. The Department of Education described the school as the "most recognised and celebrate school in America" and won several awards.

The Professional Learning Communities at Work model is based on three big ideas. Ensure all students learn, which involves intervention such as peer mentoring, coaching and tutoring; establishing a culture of collaboration amongst school staff and a focus on results. The model emphasises the necessary role of leadership in building consensus, clarifying purpose and vision and putting in place structure which support teacher collaboration and overcome obstacles to student achievement.

The Sanger Unified School District is in the middle of California's Central Valley. Child poverty is two to three times the national average. Sangers test score gains surpassed average state gains over many years and reflect a district wide focus on learning (David and Talbert 2010). Sanger District Superintendent Marc Johnson leads the learning; he does not see his job as managing the program. Leaders at the school level see their role as learning leaders and their investment in strengthening leadership as the key to moving and sustaining the reform agenda. Exercising leadership requires understanding the culture of the school district. Reciprocal accountability is important: teachers expect to be held accountable for student achievement results and at the same time they hold their superiors accountable for providing the support they need.

Collaboration is highlighted, expertise and resources pooled to create a capacity bigger than the sum of isolated individuals. Teachers and principals seek continuous improvement and learn from reform practice and research. All of this follows the DuFour model of explicit practices, development of collaboration, data-driven decision-making and mutual accountability for student's success. Special attention is paid to students needing additional help.

Consultants Jane David (Bay Area Research Group) and Joan Talbert (Stanford University) wrote, 'There is nothing esoteric about Sangers focus on professional learning communities or direct instruction or English language development. What is unusual is the professional commitment with which they have taken on the challenge to teach all students to their potential and a corresponding set of strategic actions that both push and prepare educators to continually improve so that their students can do the same. This intensity, focus, and coherence is where the lessons for others lie.'

7.6 Class Size Matters in Early Grades When Carefully Planned

Whether class size makes a difference to student achievement is an often debated issue. The move to larger schools and classes is driven mostly by claims for efficiency. Aggregate statistics across entire schools seldom show any significant educational advantage for small classes or small schools.

Thus the OECD 'Education at a Glance' annual reports from the OECD consistently find no simple correlation between student/teacher ratio and performance. The 2008 report noted, for example, at the level of students within a classroom, the relationship between student achievement and class size may be negative if students in small classes benefit from improved contact with teachers. At the class or school level, however, students are often intentionally grouped such that weaker or disadvantaged students are placed in smaller classes so that they receive more individual attention.

The surveys of student outcomes undertaken by Professor Bill Mulford of the University of Tasmania and others found the larger metropolitan schools of over 900 students did not provide the environment most conducive for principal transformational and teacher distributive leadership or for student participation, although having a larger school was positively related to students academic self-concept (Mulford 2003). Students who traditionally struggle with school and students from disadvantaged backgrounds particularly benefit from smaller schools (Leithwood and Jantzi 2009).

A major review of the literature on class size by Bruce Biddle and David Berliner (Biddle and Berliner 2002) noted the considerable disagreement between various groups as to whether reducing class size has a positive effect on student achievement. Generally teacher groups assert that there is compelling positive evidence, conservative foundations that there is not good evidence and research tends to be mixed, partly because many of the studies involve small sample sizes. Other studies have been criticised for their methodology. For instance, economist Eric Hanushek who is committed to the notion that public schools are ineffective and should be replaced by a marketplace of competing private schools, concluded that differences in public school funding are not associated with education outcomes. Biddle and Berliner view Hanushek's responses to criticisms as quarrelsome and as ignoring the comments made.

In Tennessee's Project STAR (Student/Teacher Achievement Ratio), considered by Biddle and Berliner (2002) to be 'arguably the largest and best-designed field experiment ever undertaken in education studies' researchers were able to randomly assign students and teachers to variously sized classes at their kindergarten year and their achievement followed through to year 3. Nye and colleagues ensured statistically that any differences in Student Achievement Test (SAT) scores—which themselves were standardised—were not due to SES background: variance in reading ranged from 7 to 21 % and nearly twice as large in mathematics. The variance in student achievement in reading and mathematics which could be attributed to teachers was found to be substantial when compared with that between schools, particularly for mathematics, perhaps because it is more likely learned in school to a greater extent than reading. Policies which allow school choice don't take this into account.

'When planned thoughtfully and funded adequately, small classes in the early grades generate substantial gains for students, and those extra gains are greater the longer students are exposed to those classes… [those gains are retained] in standard size classrooms and in the upper grades, middle school, and high school… [the gains] are greater for students who have traditionally been disadvantaged in education.' Moreover students traditionally disadvantaged in education carry greater small-class, early-grade gains forward into the upper grades and beyond and those gains in early grades seem to apply equally to boys and girls. Evidence for similar gains in upper grades is inconclusive.

Biddle and Berliner also make this important statement: 'The theory also suggests a caution. Students are likely to learn more and develop better attitudes toward education if they are exposed to well-trained and enthusiastic teachers, appropriate and challenging curriculums, and physical environments in their classrooms and schools that support learning. If conditions such as these are not also present, then reducing class size in the early grades will presumably have little impact.'

Australian Productivity Commission Chairman Gary Banks in April 2010 called reducing class sizes in schools 'the most costly mistake' in education policy in recent years and that it amounted to 'stealing scarce resources from investment in teaching' and claimed that performance of teachers appears not to have been a priority of education policy' (Ferrari 2010). Such a view seems an excessive generalisation!

7.7 A Note on Homework

One of the common features of attending school is homework. As with out of school coaching some people attribute to homework a greater contribution to eventual learning outcomes than is reasonable. It is common in some countries to see kids on their way to or from school with huge bags filled with textbooks.

A popular article of a few years ago—in 2006—has some interesting comments about homework as it applies to children in the US (Wallis 2006; Bazelon 2006). An exhaustive review by the Duke University's Harris Cooper, considered the top homework scholar in the US, concluded that homework does not measurably improve academic achievement for kids in grade school. Cooper found that too much homework brings diminishing returns: students who do some homework in middle and high school score somewhat better on standardized tests, but doing more than 60 to 90 min a night in middle school and more than 2 h in high school is associated with lower scores.

In a number of countries whose students outperform students in the US in international tests, such as Japan and Denmark, teachers tend to assign less homework than do American teachers but in countries whose students do poorly—such as Greece, Thailand and Iran—teachers assign substantial amounts of homework. Whilst homework can help reinforce and amplify what the child has learned at school and provide an opportunity for parental support, it can also significantly reduce the time for building family relationships.

Interestingly a recent book about homework and attitudes to it in the US demonstrate again how successful school practices elsewhere are misconstrued (Johnson 2011). Amy Chua wrote, 'If a Chinese child gets a B—which would never happen—there would first be a screaming, hair-tearing explosion. The devastated Chinese mother would then get dozens, maybe hundreds of practice tests and work through them with her child for as long as it takes to get the grade up to an A.' What can be said is that education reforms in Asia with successful school systems emphasise a great deal more than cramming homework, something shown by the comparisons of various countries in the PISA 2009 exercise with the USA (OECD 2010b).

7.8 What do Children Want from School?

Compared with the vast amount of research on teacher behaviour and teacher effectiveness, curriculum issues and so on the amount of research on student's views on school is miniscule. It is referred to by people such as Ken Robinson in his advocacy for attention to creativity. It is to an extent at the heart of the criticism by Ivan Illich about how schools inculcate politically acceptable beliefs.

Two studies which explore students' opinions and wants might be mentioned. To some degree they complement the observations of Graham Nuthall described in an earlier essay. Dr David Zyngier of Monash University opens a review of children's views of education and schooling (Zyngier 2004) with a compelling question: 'Can you imagine studying something for 12 years and at the end you still haven't mastered it?' And he quite properly points out that many educators would still ascribe to the view that schools exist to meet student's needs but students themselves are seldom asked how they see their needs. He observes that teachers know from being in the classroom daily that the main thing students want when it comes to engaging education is to take education beyond the school walls.

Zyngier quotes David Reynolds, Middle Years Coordinator, Princes Hill Secondary College, 'For teaching and learning to work, the curriculum has to be challenging for all kids and connect students to the world around them.' Zyngier also quotes research which showed that students who develop strong relationships with teachers and other students are more likely to do well in their studies (Rothman and McMillan 2003).

Interviews of school children for a video, *What school kids want*, made by students from primary and secondary schools in the western suburbs of Melbourne brought forth a number of statements. Amongst other things kids wanted learning which created awareness and understanding of the needs of others through personal contact, involves allowing everyone to take greater responsibility for their own lives, working with others and inspiring them to take action and involves considering the effects on the environment, society and economy (both positive and negative).

Zyngier points out that if schools are simply training grounds for industry needs the essential skills of critical reasoning are often ignored, further disempowering students. Attention must be shifted from basic skills to incorporate intellectually challenging material that is relevant and connected to children's lives. Teaching has to acknowledge a range of learning styles and be conducted in a supportive environment.

The *Observer* and *Guardian* newspapers in the UK have run two competitions asking children to design the school of their dreams. The first, in 1967 attracted 1,000 entries, the second in 2001 received 15,000 responses (Birkett 2001). The ideal schools described by children were places that every child wanted to attend. They observed that at school there was a 'lack of positive happiness' amongst the children. 'And schools, they say, ought to be happy places.' One pupil wrote, 'Education should not close children's eyes to the wonder of learning as it presently does, but should give children the opportunity to feed their mind and never get tired of life before theirs has even begun.'

Trusted with the responsibility of redesigning their education, children are ready to meet the challenge. Edward Blishen, author of a book on the first competition observed, 'Juvenile irresponsibility was awfully hard to find'. A winner in the original 1967 competition, in 2001 a university drama teacher and judge for the 2001 competition observed, 'teachers and pupils all over the country realise that the system is outdated, that it does not allow decent expression of the values of creativity and independent thought that are needed in the new post-industrial world. Young people are not a problem that needs to be corralled and curfewed, but an incredible rich resource of wisdom and creative thinking that we should learn to listen to.'

The late Kenneth Rowe (2004) once observed, 'whereas students' literacy skills, general academic achievements, attitudes, behaviours and experiences of schooling are influenced by their background and intake characteristics—the magnitude of these effects pale into insignificance compared with class/teacher effects. That is, the *quality of teaching and learning provision* are by far the most salient influences on students cognitive, affective, and behavioural outcomes of schooling—regardless of their gender or backgrounds. Indeed, findings from the related local and international evidence-based research indicate that what matters most is *quality teachers and teaching, supported by strategic teacher professional development*!'

In concluding her extensive essay on the American education system, Diane Ravitch (2010) talked of a particular teacher.

'Mrs Ratcliffe was gruff and demanding, did not tolerate foolishness or disruptions. She had a great reputation among students. We studied the greatest writers of the English language, poems and essays—Shakespeare, Keats, Shelley, Wordsworth, Milton and others. She did nothing for our self-esteem. She challenged us to meet her exacting standards… Proper English and accuracy mattered. She encouraged everyone to do better. She went beyond just teaching literature and grammar: she was also teaching characters and personal responsibility. These are not the sorts of things that appear on any standardized test.'

7.9 Leadership, Student Engagement and Support

Reforms in the US over the last 20 years have involved a variety of programs. Generally, in public schools, they involved explicit instruction as to how the teaching was to be undertaken and as well had assessment using standardised tests at their core. The No Child Left Behind program (NCLB) introduced by the George W Bush administration was based on a program in Houston, Texas the results for which had been distorted. NCLB failed to achieve its goals which were unrealistic anyway, its title an example of American irony. Most of these reforms have failed to show gains in educational achievement. Reforms were delivered top down and sought outcomes in the short term. NCLB is further considered in the context of the campaign of standardised testing and accountability (Sect. 9.10).

One must proceed with caution in drawing conclusions about the applicability of programs which claim success in one country to the situation in another country. Nevertheless there are some broad themes which characterise successful programs. This will also be brought out in Chap. 12 dealing with international comparisons.

An overriding theme is student engagement! It seems that not everyone who should be aware of the necessary conjunction between knowledge and understanding and the essentiality of active involvement of students for learning to occur. A second point is that investment of time is necessary to achieve results, as in all endeavours. Unfortunately, that seems often to have been in short supply. A common theme of reform in the US is the involvement of individuals and private sector organisations including philanthropic foundations in advocating and funding reforms based on ideology with little reference to evidence. That theme continues with prominent people still maintaining that there is no significant link between poverty and educational achievement. Thus some of the reforms attempted in New York and California have simply not achieved the results claimed, something that is dealt with also in other chapters dealing with independent schools.

The studies of schools in the south side of Chicago are widely regarded as demonstrating the vital importance of leadership, professional development for teachers and cooperation amongst them, community engagement especially involving parents, a student-centred learning climate and ambitious instruction. Reforms in schools in south Chicago involved shared aims and instructional strategies and active collaboration between expert and novice teachers along with close involvement with local communities including parents. Formative assessment assisted students to progress through successive levels of learning.

Leadership is the first essential support for school improvement. Effective schools create an environment conducive to academic work. Ambitious coherent instruction and a curriculum coordinated across the school are important. A challenging teaching and learning environment, one which is high in cognitive demand which recognises the student as capable, leads to educational gains with long term retention and transfer to other domains.

The vital importance of student engagement through accountable talk which recognises that treating children as capable of learning leads to high levels of achievement is emphasised by Lauren Resnick and colleagues. Accountable talk places demands on the student; it pays attention to the learning community, standards of reasoning and facts.

The work of Rick Dufour and others in Illinois and California point up the importance of supporting students having difficulty learning, a feature typical of successful school systems in many countries. Again, leadership is critical! And it is leadership in respect of the learning and support of the teachers in the school which is relevant! As in other fields of endeavour it is domain knowledge which is critical, not practices of managerialism! As will be seen in other chapters, systems which promote competition between schools, through publication of the rankings of schools based on standardised test scores in a system which provides choice of schools and between teachers through systems of merit pay rather than considered performance evaluation systems to which teachers subscribe, leads to a diminution of cooperation between teachers.

Class size is an issue important to students from less advantaged backgrounds having difficulties with the demands for learning but though that cannot be generalised to all schools, amalgamating classes and schools in pursuit of efficiencies diminishes achievement.

Children from an early age are able to articulate their interests and concerns. Treating them as if they are simply there to be told what they should learn or modifying the standards to be reached in the belief that some students will not cope are strategies doomed to failure. Politicians and all those in the media and business who fail to understand this stand in the way of progress in education.

References

Alexander, R. (2010). Speaking but not listening? Accountable talk in an unaccountable context. *Literacy, 44*, 103–111.
Barbash, S. (2012). *Clear teaching: With direct instruction, Siegfried Engelmann discovered a better way of teaching*. Arlington, VA: Education Consumers Foundation.
Barber, M. & Mourshed, M. (2007). *How the world's best-performing school systems come out on top*. London: McKinsey & Company. Retrieved September 6, 2012 from http://www.mckinsey.com/clientservice/socialsector/resources/pdf/Worlds_School_Systems_Final.pdf
Bazelon, E. (2006, 14 September 14). Forget homework. It's a waste of time for elementary-school students. *Slate*. Retrieved October 12, 2012 from http://www.slate.com/id/2149593/
Biddle, B. J., & Berliner, D. C. (2002). Small class size and its effects. *Education Leadership, 59*(5), 12–24.
Birkett, D. (2001, 5 June). The School we'd like. *The Guardian*.
Bryk, A. S., et al. (2010). *Organizing schools for improvement: Lessons from Chicago*. Chicago: University of Chicago Press.
Cobbold, T. (2008, 26 September). More questions raised about the New York school reporting model. *Save Our Schools*. Retrieved September 6, 2012 from http://www.saveourschools.com.au/media-releases/more-questions-raised-about-the-new-york-school-reporting-model
Cobbold. T. (2010, 1 October). High Farce in New York City. *Save Our Schools*. Retrieved September 6, 2012 from http://www.saveourschools.com.au/league-tables/high-farce-in-new-york
David, J. L. & Talbert, J. E. (2010). *Turning around a high-poverty school district: Learning from Sanger Unified's success*. San Francisco: Cowell Foundation. Accessed 14, 2013 from http://larrycuban.files.wordpress.com/2013/02/sanger-report-2.pdf
Gersten, R. & Keating, T, (1987). Long-term benefits from direct instruction. *Educational Leadership*, 28–31.
Gratton, L., & Ghoshal, S. (2002). Improving the quality of conversations. *Organizational Dynamics, 31*, 209–223.
Johnson, D. (2011, 18 August). Finish that homework! *New York Review of Books*.
Justine Ferrari, J. (2010, April 24). Small classes a costly mistake. *The Australian*.
Leithwood, K., & Jantzi, D. (2009). A review of empirical evidence about school size effects: A policy perspective. *Review of Educational Research, 79*, 464–491.

References

McLester, S. (2012). Professional learning communities at work. *District Administration* September. Retrieved April 11, 2013 from http://www.districtadministration.com/article/rick-and-becky-dufour

Michaels, S., O'Connor, C., & Resnick, L. B. (2008). Deliberative discourse idealized and realized: Accountable talk in the classroom and in civic life. *Studies in Philosophy and Education, 27*, 283–297.

Mulford, B. (2003). *School leaders: Changing roles and impact on teacher and school effectiveness*. Paris: OECD.

OECD. (2010a). *Pisa 2009 results: Executive summary*. Paris: OECD. Retrieved May 10, 2013 from http://www.oecd.org/pisa/pisaproducts/46619703.pdf

OECD. (2010b). *Strong performers and successful reformers in education. Lessons from PISA for the United State*. Paris: OECD. Retrieved September 4, 2012 from http://www.oecd.org/pisa/46623978.pdf

Otterman, S. (2010). *29 July)*. New York Times: Confusion on where city students stand.

Promising Practices Network. (2005). Programs that work direct instruction. Santa Monica CA: Rand Corporation. Retrieved April 13, 2013 from http://www.promisingpractices.net/program.asp?programid=146#overview

Raudenbush, S. W. (2009). The brown legacy and the O'Connor challenge: Transforming schools in the images of children's potential. *Educational Researcher, 38*(3), 169–180.

Ravitch, D. (2009, 9 September). Bloomberg's bogus school report cards destroy real progress. *New York Daily News*.

Ravitch, D. (2010). *The death and life of the American school system—How testing and choice are undermining education*. New York: Basic Books.

Resnick, L. B. (1999). Making America smarter. *Education Week Century Series, 18*(40), 38–40. Retrieved May 8, 2013 from http://www.edweek.org/ew/vol-18/40resnick.h18

Resnick, L. B. (2010). Nested learning systems for the thinking curriculum. The 2009 Wallace foundation distinguished lecture. *Educational Researcher, 39*, 183–197.

Resnick, L. B., & Hall, M. W. (1998). Learning organizations for sustainable education reform. *Daedalus, 127*(4), 89–128.

Rothman, S. & McMillan, J. (2003). Influences on achievement in literacy and achievement in literacy and numeracy. *LSAY Research Reports*. Longitudinal surveys of Australian youth research report 36. Retrieved October 13, 2012 from http://research.acer.edu.au/lsay_research/40

Rowe, K. J. (2003). *The importance of teacher quality as a key determinant of students experiences and outcomes of schooling*. ACER Research Conference 2003 (p. 10). Retrieved September 6, 2012 from http://research.acer.edu.au/research_conference_2003/3/

Schemo, D. J. (2008). Wonder wonk unmasked: How a sociology grad student's anonymous blog tried to throw a lasso of truth around Bloomberg's school-reform hype August 24. Retrieved October 13, 2013 from http://nymag.com/news/intelligencer/49527/index1.html

Sebring, P. B. et al. (2006). *The essential supports for school improvement. Consortium on Chicago school research at the University of Chicago research report. September 2006*. Retrieved January 17, 2009 from http://ccsr.uchicago.edu/content/publications.php?pub_id=86

Wallis, C. (2006, 29 August). The myth about homework. *Time*. Retrieved July 8, 2011 from http://www.time.com/time/magazine/article/0,9171,1376208,00.html

Watkins, C. L. (1995). Follow through why didn't we? *Effective School Practices, 15*(1).

Zyngier, D. (2000). A Review of Alexander, R. J. (2000). *Culture and pedagogy: international comparisons in primary education*. Oxford: Blackwell pp 642 ISBN 0-631-22051-8 Paperback $77. Retrieved May 8, 2013 from http://users.monash.edu.au/~dzyngier/Culture%20and%20Pedagogy%20-%20a%20Review%20Essay.pdf

Zyngier, D. (2004). A tale of two reports or how bad news for Australian education is mediated by the media. *Issues in Educational Research, 14*, 194–211.

Chapter 8
Teacher Pay, Performance and Leadership

8.1 The Call for Accountability

Various groups, including politicians, some economists and some parents groups, from time to time call for greater accountability for teachers by introducing performance or merit pay. The assumptions are that student's performance is principally related to teacher performance and that performance or merit pay will encourage better performance by teachers. There is a very common view that management and leadership mainly involves telling others what to do and sacking those who don't perform. These views are both wrong and destructive.

Whilst there is near universal agreement that teachers are vitally important in the education of children in school, the frequent response in a number of countries is to try to quantify the contribution they make by relating the results of standardised tests to the teacher's performance. Believing that the principal motivator of superior performance is more money, the outcome of the 'assessed' performance is to pay bonuses to the teachers whose students did best. However, the evidence about improved student performance and changed teacher behaviour is a different matter: numerous studies reveal that merit pay, as it is called, is unrelated to students' test scores. Moreover, the procedures for assessing teacher performance are often not adequate and the rewards often not related to the skills and experience attained.

The review of teacher assessment and teachers careers examines motivations, recruitment and promotions policies and practices and the perceived place of teachers in the community. Following that I deal with school leadership.

Performance and pay, employee behaviour, management and leadership are amongst the most intensively studied over the last more than 100 years. The research is not simply anecdotal or confined to a few industries or countries but is vast, covers numerous different industries and economic sectors and activities from war to hospitals, museums to pharmaceutical companies and so on. There can be few areas, in general, where profound intellectual laziness is so common as in views about superior leadership and organisational development: if old myths aren't followed new fads often are.

Many people are still prepared to look no further than their own industry or country, or worse, simply adopt 'prevailing views' or the largely speculative practices of the human resource management school which derives some of its guidance from such questionable approaches as psychological profiling. Often the result is excessive bureaucracy with little gain or even decline in the quality of recruitment, training and development and ultimately productivity and quality of decision making.

In the area of leadership demands for quick decision-making, decisiveness and so on can be promoted without any regard to lessons of history generally. In many cases in knowledge industries such as universities and museums, the practices of leadership and management are held in such low regard by most of the workforce that anything to do with them is considered no more than administration. That indicates a lack of understanding: administration is rule following, the antithesis of leadership. The difference that effective leadership makes is often ignored. An indication of the lack of attention to school leadership in the education debate is that it never gets a mention unless it concerns devolution of authority over hiring of teachers and disposal of the budget. Instead, no stories are told, no role models are mentioned, no research referenced. Yet, as we have seen in reviewing the studies of south Chicago schools, school leadership is the most important support, one upon which and from which everything else flows!

The school environment, and the university environment, differs from that of other enterprises in the nature of the work, the goals, what ought to count as achievement and in the level of qualifications of the staff. But none of that means that whatever could be learned from elsewhere should be ignored. Every organisation comprises people who, it is intended, will behave according to certain rules to achieve certain goals and are more or less controlled by persons who exercise power and authority, whether it is a Roman Catholic Seminary, a Wall St bank, the European Space agency, an airline company or a symphony orchestra.

We know a great deal about people's attitudes to rewards and rules, people's intrinsic motivations, the difficulties of achieving certain goals and the impact of short-term and long-term decisions. One example relevant to education will suffice to show the disjunction between existing knowledge and practice as it concerns achieving success. In the last 2–5 years, as we shall see later, substantial research has been completed covering the medium to long term in different areas including government service and commercial enterprises dealing with the impact of merit pay, the relationship of extra remuneration and performance. The results are clear: a positive and significant relationship does not exist. In other words, paying bonuses to executives, and importantly to teachers, does not have a significant effect on effort or results, of teachers or students. Paying bonuses can justifiably be considered a waste of money!

When bonuses are paid, people try to make comparisons between their remuneration and that of persons whose work they consider roughly similar. However, motivation in high performance situations is mainly intrinsic and the basis of comparison is the individual's previous achievements, not the performance of others. This is the same as the well known cases of athletes, many in the

8.1 The Call for Accountability

performing arts and in science. Comparison with peers is an element of the motivation but monetary reward hardly is. Yet in early 2012 government politicians in Britain decided they would ask education authorities to investigate the institution of merit pay for teachers!

Former Australian school principal and commentator Chris Bonner (2007) said, 'Proposing merit pay is a no-risk strategy for any government: Good teachers are essential and parents are always anxious about their children's learning. It doesn't matter that such messages are unbalanced, poorly researched or even mischievous, and have little to do with day-to-day life in your average school—it all makes good copy. It creates the impression of crisis, helped along by judicious political dog-whistling which ensures that the crisis somehow belongs exclusively to public schools'.

Michael Fullan of the Ontario Institute for Studies in Education (OISE) at the University of Toronto and education adviser to the government of Ontario observed, 'performance-based merit pay is a non-starter… when commonsense tells you it won't work, when no research exists that backs up the claim for merit pay… it is time to give up the ghost'(quoted by Caldwell 2011).

What is important is the belief that one is making a difference through the work being done, a sense of contributing to improvement of the community and/or the group with whom one is working. Teachers, like other professionals and creative people, often spend more time 'working' than they could possibly be paid for because of their commitment to these goals and values.

Any system which recognises performance and provides rewards or sanctions requires clear criteria for assessment and an objective process for their application. The scheme must have salience with those to whom it applies. Systems which seem to reward people with promotion, extra pay or opportunities for reasons other than generally acknowledged superior performance judged by accepted criteria is for the most part demotivating.

Any performance evaluation scheme should lead to adoption of new or improved behaviours which more likely will enhance the value of the contribution. Indicators of performance relevant to that are essential but metrics may not always be appropriate and indeed choosing quantitative indicators because they are quantitative can lead to irrelevance. Assessment of performance is a judgement call, in other words a task of leaders. Extraneous indicators like rewards for achievement not relevant to the principal goals of the person and the organisation divert attention and contribute nothing to the future of the organisation. The mantra that had some favour in recent years that if you can't measure a goal you don't know whether it has been achieved is simply rhetoric!

In many domains performance evaluation is poorly done, uneven, not linked to any clear methodology and therefore regarded with suspicion or cynicism by employees. The nature of the reward may be unrelated to the means of achieving the goals of the organisation. Reputational studies in which good practice is defined by the behaviours of those whom peers consider to be good teachers are of doubtful validity.

Evaluation programs and linked reward schemes should seek to retain those employees—teachers—who are superior. Notwithstanding that, 'career paths and pay systems in schools as in other organisations can be, and need to be, linked to evidence of increasing capacity to promote valued student learning outcomes and, thereby, stronger levers for ensuring professional development and quality learning outcomes for all students' (Ingvarson et al. 2007). Those goals are unequivocally fundamental to the school enterprise.

Performance evaluation is sometimes posed as a way of identifying those whose performance is unsatisfactory and who should therefore be 'let go'. Having in mind that positive reinforcement is a greater motivating factor than negative reinforcement such an approach is hardly effective! Performance management is appropriate when it leads to improved performance, not when it is simply a way of dismissing those whose performance is not presently satisfactory. High standards should be set and people assisted to meet them. That is what happens in successful organisations.

The practice which has become common in some government agencies of employing more senior people on limited term contracts and advertising the position at the expiration of the contract, 'in order to ensure that one always has the best available persons in the position' is destabilising but more importantly flies in the face of best practice in organisations generally: senior people may be engaged for well over a decade. The internationally celebrated Nederlans Dance Company retained Jiri Killian for more than 20 years as Artistic Director; the Art Gallery of New South Wales employed Edmund Capon for 30 years, celebrating his 30th year by purchasing a splendid painting by Cezanne for over US$13 millions funded by public donation!

8.2 Teacher Performance and Evaluation

Schemes to evaluate teachers' performance linked to rewards of any kind need to encompass the full scope of what a teacher is expected to know and what they can show they can do; they require multiple, independent sources of evidence and multiple, independent trained assessors of that evidence as well as have regard to the context in which the teacher is teaching.

Elizabeth Kleinhenz and Lawrence Ingvarson of the Australian Council for Educational Research, Australia (ACER) investigated the processes for teacher assessment (Kleinhenz and Ingvarson 2004). They begin, 'if teaching well is something most teachers can learn to do over time, not just a bundle of personality traits, insightful formative assessment and coaching systems are vital. If experienced and effective teachers are to be kept close to the classroom and provide leadership to other teachers, professionally credible summative assessments systems will be needed that can provide them with the recognition they deserve for evidence of high levels of professional development.' Teachers' real work, however, remains buffered from the kind of professional scrutiny that could contribute to its improvement and genuine leadership is absent. Many teachers are never evaluated.'

Often promotion involves higher pay but then requires tasks not relevant to teaching and for which the appointee lacks training. This 'loose coupling', a term introduced by management expert Karl Weick (1976) describes the gap between the technical core, rewards and actors.. Management of the structures and processes that surround the technical core of education is quite separate from management of the core itself. Although it may seem that educational management is about managing the processes of teaching and learning (the technical core), it is, in reality, nothing of the sort. Instead what are managed are things like student grouping, school organization, timetabling and major school events.

In New South Wales, a review (Ramsey 2000) in 2000 argued 'good teaching does not come about through imposed requirements, but through the individual teacher's commitment to high professional standards. The important changes needed in teaching are those that teachers must make for themselves. They are not changes that governments can mandate or unions can achieve through their industrial activities.'

Kleinhenz and Ingvarson found the Western Australian Level 3 Classroom Teacher position to focus most effectively on the technical core of teaching. Evaluation was summative, criterion-based, and used multiple sources of data to demonstrate attainment of a particular standard of professional knowledge and skill; teachers are assessed by a 'college of specialists'. Evaluation starts with the explication of teachers work in a comprehensive set of professional teaching standards (called competencies), proceeds through processes of assessment that encourages professional learning, and continues into the ongoing work of the successful applicants.

In New South Wales all teachers have to be accredited with the Institute of Teachers. The website states, 'The Framework of Professional Teaching Standards provides a common reference point to describe, celebrate and support the complex and varied nature of teachers work. The Professional Teaching Standards describe what teachers need to know, understand and be able to do as well as providing direction and structure to support the preparation and development of teachers.'

In the US the National Board for Professional Teaching Standards (NBPTS) provides a voluntary certification system for teachers who can demonstrate they have attained its standards for 'highly accomplished' teaching. The process resembles that described for Western Australia. A survey in 2001 found that NBPTS was an excellent professional development experience, had a strong and positive effect on their teaching, had positive effects on students learning and led to positive interactions with teachers, administrators and communities.

A comprehensive consideration of the use of standardised testing in assessment of teachers by a number of leading American researchers (Rothstein et al. 2010) concluded that value-added modelling could add useful information to comprehensive analyses of student progress and could help support stronger inferences about the influences of teachers and programs on student growth. However, they observed 'there is no perfect way to evaluate teachers'. They did note systems for observing teachers' classroom practice based on professional teaching standards grounded in research on teaching and learning. These include 'systematic observation protocols with well-developed, research-based criteria to examine teaching, including observations or videotapes of classroom practice, teacher interviews, and artifacts such as lesson plans, assignments, and samples of student work.'

They also concluded, 'Evaluation by competent supervisors and peers, employing such approaches, should form the foundation of teacher evaluation systems, with a supplemental role played by multiple measures of student learning gains that, where appropriate, should include test scores.' A 'comprehensive system giving teachers guidance and feedback, supportive leadership, and working conditions to improve their performance' is needed. Procedures for removal of ineffective teachers should not end up distorting the entire instructional program 'by imposing a flawed system of standardized quantification of teacher quality'.

In 2011 the Grattan Institute released a report *Better Teaching Appraisal and Feedback* (Jensen and Reichl 2011). The report examines eight methods of teacher appraisal and suggests that schools use at least four of them to effectively appraise teacher's performance through a balanced scorecard approach.

In summary, schemes which unequivocally link implementation to improved student performance are generally lacking. Though there is a strong desire to provide greater recognition to teachers there is no consistent pattern which conforms with the definition of highly accomplished teaching or methods for assessing performance across schools.

8.3 Merit Pay

Teachers operate in a 'social market'. Professor Dan Ariely, James B. Duke Professor of Psychology and Behavioral Economics and founder of the Center for Advanced Hindsight at Duke University in Durham, North Carolina in the US, has with various colleagues, examined the relationship between behaviour and effort and the nature of rewards in money-markets and social-markets. In fact (Heyman and Ariely 2004), '… in social-market relationships (unlike money-market relationships) effort is shaped by altruism, the amount of compensation is irrelevant, and individuals work as hard as they can regardless of payment. Altruism results in a level of performance that is high, constant, and insensitive to payment level…. rewards can decrease motivation and attitudes alter self-perception, increase over justification and turn feelings of competence into feelings of being controlled.'

The Rand Corporation (Stecher et al. 2010) reviewed the progress of Performance-based Assessment Systems (PBASs) in the public service in the US. These were an early response to the increasing size of public and private organisations. They were followed by linking performance to incentives 'in an effort to motivate and direct individual performance and improve organizational outcomes'. While the use of PBASs has spread in the public sector, little is known about whether such programs are having the desired effect: there is currently little evidence concerning the effectiveness of PBASs at achieving their performance goals.

The Education Commission of the States (2010) in the US provides non-partisan information about education policy to help state leaders develop educational systems. In 2010 it summarised what is known about merit pay systems. Five 'enabling conditions' were identified by the Committee for Economic Development as required for a successful merit pay system to foster improvement in student achievement. (The Committee is an independent, non-profit, non-partisan think tank based in Washington, DC comprising some 200 senior corporate executives and university leaders concerned with policy research on major economic and social issues.) These are improved teacher evaluation and development systems, improved data systems, sustainable funding, supportive government policies and wide stakeholder involvement.

Of the many school district merit pay systems, the Commission considered four to be of particular interest and evaluated their effect on student achievement. However, generally there was either insufficient data or a lack of evidence supporting a link with student achievement gains. The Commission concluded, 'Perhaps merit pay does not contribute to student achievement'.

Nevertheless, as SOSs Trevor Cobbold observes, the Teacher Incentive Fund (TIF), introduced by President George W. Bush to help school districts implement merit pay systems, has been dramatically expanded by President Obama in his 'Race to the Top' school funding program.

In July 2011, the Rand Corporation published a report on the New York City Schoolwide Performance Bonus Program (SPBP). Performance bonuses were found to not achieve any of their intended effects, have no positive effects on student achievement at any grade level in schools and no positive effect on how schools performed on annual school progress reports. The scheme was recommended to be not continued: the New York City Education Department did just that.

A survey of over 200 New York City public schools by Roland Fryer (2011) of Harvard University's Department of Economics found no evidence whatsoever that teacher incentives increase student performance, attendance, graduation or teacher behaviour.

In Australia the Productivity Commission (2012) noted very poor evidence to support merit pay related to student test scores. Early results from trials of performance bonuses in a small number of schools, 'together with the long history of mixed results from the US and elsewhere, suggest that an effective and widely-applicable bonus system is unlikely to emerge in the foreseeable future'. The report also noted that the latest Bureau of Statistics data indicated that average real salaries for both teachers and the education and training sector as a whole have increased over the past 15 years but the rate of increase in teacher pay had not been as fast as salaries in other professions. And, not surprisingly, it found that increases in salary were generally related to length of service and that whilst satisfactory performance was a condition for increase in pay, those increases were seldom withheld!

In early 2011, Australian Prime Minister Julia Gillard announced a scheme to offer bonuses to the 'country's best teachers'. An estimated 25,000 teachers, or around one in 10, were to receive incentives under the scheme. The Business Council of Australia endorsed the proposal. Numerous experts on education condemned it. It was later modified. In November 2011, Minister Peter Garrett (2011) proclaimed. 'A new performance and development framework for teachers will also be introduced in schools across Australia from 2013 as part of the implementation of the reward payments scheme.' The scheme will now be tied to the Teacher Standards adopted by Education Ministers.

In May 2012, the OECD Education Directorate, noting the increasing prominence of teachers' pay in the political agendas of many countries, reported on the varying practices in OECD countries (Achiron 2012). It noted considerable variation in practice. 'A look at the overall picture shows no relationship between average student performance in a country and the use of performance-based pay schemes… In countries with comparatively low teacher salaries (less than 15 % above GDP per capita), student performance tends to be better when performance-based pay systems are in place, while in countries where teachers are relatively well-paid (more than 15 % above GDP per capita), the opposite is true.'

8.4 Teacher Certification, Evaluation, Career Paths and Rewards

The wish to reward more effective teachers and have better teachers stay longer in the profession is entirely comparable to the situation in all other areas of employment and of course is to be applauded, not least because recruitment is a very expensive and quite risky process. In Finland and other Scandinavian countries and also Korea (Hong et al. 2010) teachers are highly respected in the community, salaries offered are high and teachers are well qualified: competition to gain entry to the profession is intense. In many other countries such as the US, the UK and Australia teachers are not uniformly well regarded: they are criticised as not knowing enough about the content they teach, for having long holidays, working shorter days than other workers. They are frequently criticised in the media and often it is asserted that failing teachers should be sacked. Noticeable also is the parsimony with which teacher pay claims in the public sector are treated, though this is generally a feature of the way all pay claims are handled.

Rather than dealing with issues such as conditions of work like adequacy of space, access to computers, availability of training and development opportunities and conditions for promotion, bargaining with unions often allows continued pursuit of issues such as teacher/student ratios, that is class sizes, which is not unimportant but not closely related to superior teaching unless we are faced with very large classes or students with special needs.

A report for the Business Council of Australia by Professor Stephen Dinham of Melbourne University's Graduate School of Education (Dinham et al. 2008) carried the commentary of Kleinhenz and Ingvarson further. 'Salary may not be a strong reason why current teachers have chosen to teach, but it is a strong reason why many abler graduates choose not to teach, and this is cause for considerable concern … salary and working conditions are the main reasons why many good teachers leave the profession. Present arrangements in teaching do not encourage, reward or indeed require advanced professional learning.' The report recommended a national scheme for certification of teacher performance.

A recent initiative in Australia has been the introduction of 'Teach for Australia': university graduates are given a short period of intensive training in teaching methods and relevant subjects and then sent into schools. This is based on the program 'Teach for America' (TFA). Linda Darling-Hammond of Stanford University and colleagues (Darling-Hammond 2005a, b) examined that program. They found that 'uncertified TFA recruits are less effective than certified teachers, and perform about as well as other uncertified teachers'. TFA recruits who become certified after 2 or 3 years do about as well as other certified teachers but nearly all of them left within 3 years. 'Teachers' effectiveness appears strongly related to the preparation they have received for teaching.'

The OECD publication, *Education at a Glance* for 2010 compares the salary conditions for teachers throughout the OECD and partner countries. Teachers in countries like Australia, England and New Zealand receive relatively lower salaries and work longer hours than teachers in countries such as Finland whose students perform to very high levels. Teachers in the US are amongst the lowest paid in terms of salaries per unit of time; a lower secondary teacher spends 1,097 h per year compared with an OECD average of 703 h and a European average of 661 h. In Finland only 592 h are taught and 616 h are taught in Korea.

Unions are often blamed for holding back needed reforms. However experience in several countries shows a contrary position (OECD 2010). In Ontario unions played a major role in the introduction of the reforms which have been so successful. Premier McGuinty came into office committed to involving the teachers union and agreed increases in staff for special positions to lead the process of driving higher performance by children of migrant parents whose first language was not English or who were otherwise disadvantaged and also agreed increases in teacher numbers to reduce class sizes. In Germany education reforms have been significantly assisted by the unions.

Union bashing, however, is almost a pastime for some people! Few people stop to recognise that unions as a lobby group exercise a role very similar to lobby groups for other constituents such as the heads of business, collectives of industry and so on such as Business Councils, Grocery Councils and Bankers Associations and so-called think tanks which often lobby on behalf of groups with particular ideological positions.

8.5 School Leadership: Leadership in Education

In the school system the principal is the leader but his or her advice is not often highlighted in the public debate. That schools suffer a principal casualty of recent public sector reform—a de-emphasis on what is termed domain knowledge, understanding and knowledge of the principal discipline which the organisation deploys to meet its objects—is seldom acknowledged. School leadership requires above all an understanding of pedagogy, the nature of teaching practice.

The work of the school principal is as varied as that of any person in a management position (Petersen and Kelley 2001). 'A principal's daily work is characterized by hundreds of short tasks of enormous variety—one minute talking with a teacher about materials, the next coping with a student issue, followed by another dozen questions, issues and problems to be solved.' They are constantly interrupted by a continuous stream of issues, demands and people, as in any management role. Their work, like that of teachers, is not to be considered as occurring only whilst school classes are being held.

Basic ideas of leadership involve ideas of power and access to resources, initiatives in social interpretation, sensemaking or shaping meanings, and the place of individuals among social control options like law, the collective, informal norms, and the person. Despite a great deal of change in many aspects of work and greater knowledge of behaviour and issues, too much attention is still paid to ideas about organisations rooted in the Taylorism of the early twentieth century: closely prescribed procedures, hierarchies of supervision with power concentrated at the top of the organisation, judgements of performance reserved to supervisors with little discussion and so on. The proposition is that employees are unlikely to act in the interest of the organisation unless there is adequate oversight. Managers, especially in part of governments, are being forced into administrative roles making instrumental modifications: they become mere rule followers, seldom exercising their own professional judgement.

Research in a wide variety of situations over the last 30 or so years has advanced beyond the notion of the transactional leader who seeks to achieve change by offering rewards for performance and so on. Transformational leaders can be compared with transactional leaders who operate within the existing system or culture, are risk averse, pay attention to time constraints and efficiency, and generally prefer process over substance to maintain control (Lowe and Kroek 1996). Management by exception is practiced, enforcing rules to avoid mistakes and waiting until problems are brought to their attention. This may be effective in stable, predictable environments: it is still typical of bureaucracies and is encouraged by centralised control and intervention.

8.5.1 Transformational Leadership

Contemporary models of successful organisations reveal not just flatter spans of control or relative freedom from the tyranny of financial imperatives. Instead they are characterised by leaders who support staff rather than command, support ongoing training and development and, in creative organisations, provide opportunities for challenge of ideas rather requiring agreement with those in charge. Trust and positive reinforcement, are typical of high performance organisations.

Recruitment is of very great importance. Freedom to exercise judgement and make mistakes is a significant positive; bureaucratic control destroys creativity. Centralised control is by and large a failure: it does not achieve its ends.

Transformational leaders seek new ways of working, opportunities in the face of risk, prefer effective answers to efficient answers, and are less likely to support the status quo. They do not merely react to environmental circumstances–they attempt to shape and create them. Transformational leaders tend to use symbolism and imagery to solicit increased effort. They accomplishes this by raising the level of intellectual awareness about the importance of valued outcomes, by raising or expanding individual needs and by inducing a belief in transcending self-interest for the sake of the team or organization. Transformational leaders trust people, are principled, maintain high standards, challenge others views but also provide encouragement and intellectual stimulation.

Four behaviours or factors are typical of transformational leadership and especially important:

- 'Idealised influence' involves trust, taking a stand on important issues, emphasising the importance of purpose and commitment and the ethical dimensions of decisions.
- 'Inspirational motivation' involves articulating an appealing vision of the future, maintaining high standards, providing encouragement and meaning for what needs to be done.
- Transformational leaders value 'intellectual stimulations', questioning assumptions and beliefs, stimulating new perspectives and ways of doing things and encourage expression of ideas.
- 'Individualised consideration' means dealing with other people as individuals and considering their needs, furthering their development, giving advice and being a coach.

8.5.2 Transformational Leadership in the School

In successful schools principals are transformational leaders (Hallinger 2007). Three classic studies reveal agreed insights about leadership qualities of effective principals (Reynolds 2001).

- First, [a US review] portrays effective principals as offering stable and appropriate leadership, using formal and informal structures, sharing power and being willing to respond to external-to-the school change. Ineffective principals, by contrast, exhibit unstable, changeable over-time leadership, use formal structures more than informal, don't involve staff and are reluctant to relate either to parents and the community or to the external educational reform agenda.
- Second,… pupil outcomes in secondary schools were better when the head teacher showed both firm leadership and teacher involvement rather than either one or the other.

- Third (a primary school study by Peter Mortimore in the UK) noted that what mattered was 'purposeful' leadership of the staff which occurred when the head understood the schools needs and was actively involved in the school, but was also good at sharing power. 'He or she did not exercise total control but consulted widely, especially on such matters as spending plans and curriculum planning.'

Two major studies by Professor Bill Mulford of the University of Tasmania involving Australia and seven other countries are important. Australian studies which form part of an eight-country exploration reveal successful school principalship as interactive, reciprocal and evolving process involving many players, influenced by context and underpinned by core values and beliefs which inform decisions and actions about individual support and capacity building, school culture and structure (Mulford 2007).

Case studies of Australian schools—quantitative survey evidence from over 2,500 teachers and 3,500 15-year-old Australian high school students (Mulford and Sillins 2003)—show that leadership which makes a difference is both position-based (principal) and distributive (administrative team and teachers) and provides individual, cultural and structural support to staff, captures a vision for the school, communicates high performance expectations and offers intellectual stimulation.

Leadership influences the way students perceive that teachers organise and conduct their instruction and their educational interactions with, and expectations of, their students. 'Students' positive perceptions of teachers' work directly promote their participation in school, academic self-concept and engagement with school. Student participation is directly and student engagement indirectly (through retention) related to academic achievement. School size, socioeconomic status (SES) and, especially, student home educational environment make a difference to these relationships.'

All principals, but particularly those from low SES schools, promoted equity plus social justice through the creation of strong school communities and socially just pedagogical practices and by focusing on the development/reinforcement of a strong learning culture within the school community. Mulford and colleagues found important features of the principals of high-performing schools in high-poverty communities in Tasmania (Mulford et al. 2008). Successful principals were more independent of the system than were principals of low-needs schools, a high sense of purpose, were less concerned about the expectations of employers and better able to mange tensions between ad hoc problem solving and strategic planning. They were also more flexible in their approach to systems and people and had higher levels of awareness, self confidence and capacity to work with others.

In broad terms three major, sequential and aligned elements of practice typify successful school reform. Being innovative is not the first! The first element concerns how people are communicated with and treated. Success is more likely where people are involved in decision making through a transparent, facilitative and supportive structure and are trusted, respected, encouraged and valued. The second element highlights the importance of a professional community with shared norms and values, including valuing difference and diversity, a focus on implementation and continuous enhancement of learning for all students. The final element is a capacity for change, learning and innovation.

The characteristics enumerated for successful principalship conform with the model for transformational leadership outlined above.

If pupils like the way teachers teach, see constant challenge and good organisation and teacher expectations they will do their best work and discuss their work with them. They have good academic self-concept, are confident of their success and satisfied with their learning. Moreover they are satisfied with their relationship with teachers and see schoolwork as useful for future life.

An extraordinarily important point emerging from the research points to the vital importance of getting the social processes right first. 'One needs to first get the personal/interpersonal, distributive leadership, collective teacher efficacy or trusting and collaborative climate 'right'… [then] it can be used to focus on the educational/instructional, including having a shared and monitored mission… Once the educational/instructional is 'right' and there is confidence in what the school is doing and why it is doing it, then the leaders and school can move to development/learning/change, including working with others schools in a 'nested' model.'

Despite differences in systems and government policies, all countries have in common increases in levels of self-management, change, marketisation, accountability and expectations of higher student performance; hardworking, 'can do' principals who engendered trust and respect are a common feature (Gurr et al. 2005). The studies by Mulford and colleagues do not achieve mention in the education debates!

8.6 International Perspectives on School Leadership

School leadership is second only to classroom teaching as an influence on pupil learning and almost all successful leaders draw on the same repertoire of basic leadership practices (Leithwood et al. 2008). Other studies show the same features of successful and support the conclusions of the studies by Mulford and colleagues (Day et al. 2008).

A measure of independence from control by some bureaucratic centre is important to success but often this is ignored. School reform in Chicago revealed factors quite distinct from bureaucratic control as important. The Queensland School Reform Longitudinal Study found alignment between curriculum, pedagogy and assessment to be hindered by inconsistencies between the policies and practices of Education Queensland and the Queensland Studies Authority. In Tasmanian 'high-needs' schools, successful principals were 'more independent of the structures within which they worked and were focused on student outcomes rather than the approval of those higher in the hierarchy'.

The OECD Report on improving school leadership found one of the principal issues affecting school performance to be a tension arising from a lack of clear demarcation of tasks between school board and school principal (OECD 2008). This is a common feature of governance in organisations: 'school leaders can make a difference in school and student performance if they are granted autonomy to make important decisions. However autonomy alone does not automatically lead to improvements unless it is well supported.'

One interesting finding is that the behaviour of principals may depend on the subjects which are being considered. Principals may be more involved in leadership routines such as grade-level meetings and school improvement planning for literacy related subjects than for mathematics or science subjects (Spillane 2005).

Michael Fullan (2010), adviser to the Ontario Premier, asserts that the essence of a principal's power involves six steps to move theory to practice. These include a bias for action including building relationships and communication during implementation, participating as a learner in helping teachers, making instruction a priority, developing others in a way that is integrated into the work of the school and developing a strong two-way partnership with the schools community. Highly effective principals 'consume' research as they go, they 'set out to solve problems and see how research can help them'.

8.7 Teacher Profession and School Leadership

There is no relationship between merit pay and student achievement or teacher behaviour. Career paths and pay systems linked to evidence of increasing capacity to promote valued student learning outcomes become stronger levers for ensuring professional development and quality outcomes for all students. Assessment of teacher achievement must take into account the full range of tasks and expectations, not merely some metric which satisfies the need for quantitative indicators in the false belief that somehow this will allow more accurate choice as to which school will likely produce superior educational outcomes. And it should be kept in mind, as stated elsewhere, that teachers are but one of the influences on student educational outcomes. As David Berliner (2013) points out, 'out-of-school variables account for about 60 % of the variance that can be accounted for in student achievement'. He points to a huge range of out-of-school factors such as neighbourhood collective efficacy, violence rate, level of food insecurity and language spoken at home which total some 60 % of the influence, three times more than the inside-the-school factors. 'So to continue trying to affect student achievement with the most popular contemporary educational policies, mostly oriented toward teachers and schools, while assiduously ignoring the power of the outside-of-school factors, is foolish.'

Superior school systems provide good starting salaries and superior training and development opportunities for teachers and strongly encourage linking students' tests to improvement of teaching *as a routine part of teaching practice,* not as a way of providing information to parents and others to inform their view of relative school success. In superior school systems teachers are respected by the community and the school forges meaningful links with parents and the community. Good teachers know how their students are progressing and use their evaluation to assist progress.

Salary levels of teachers must keep pace with costs of living including housing prices. It is hardly reasonable to expect teaching to be a competitive profession if it is treated just the same as any other and every claim for salary increases is hotly contested. That is not to say, by any means, that every claim must be acceded to! However, governments need to make some choices as to what they consider important. Salary may not be a strong reason why current teachers have chosen to teach, but it is a strong reason why many abler graduates choose not to become teachers. Low salary and poor working conditions are the main reasons why many good teachers leave the profession.

The leadership role exercised by the school principal, and in large schools by head teachers, is critical. That role is enhanced by a situation of relative autonomy. Successful school reform requires people appointed to the position of school principal competent in both pedagogical issues and in exercising genuine leadership skills, including attention to the performance of others, providing moral support, respecting the opinion of others and promoting an atmosphere of cooperation and trust, attending to structures that promote those features and lead to establishing clear shared goals and priorities as well as demanding standards.

Setting high standards and ensuring intellectual stimulation is of very great importance. These are features as true for schools attended by students of economically and socially advantaged children as much as they are for those from less advantaged backgrounds.

It cannot be emphasised too strongly that committed and confident leadership, understanding of and commitment to educational improvement is vitally important, if not central to driving higher standards and higher performance. Simply placing greater responsibility for budget control and staffing is not sufficient and can turn principals into administrators who seldom venture into the classroom.

References

Achiron, M. (2012, May 15). Another perspective on teachers pay. *Educationtoday*.Retrieved 20 August 2012, from http://oecdeducationtoday.blogspot.fr/2012/05/another-perspective-on-teachers-pay.html

Berliner, D. C. (2013, 23 July). Sorting out the effects on inequality and poverty, teachers and schooling on America's Youth. Draft of Chapter 9. In S. L. Nichols (Ed.), *Educational policy and the socialization of youth for the 21st century*. New York: Teachers College Press. In Diane Ravitch's blog, This is your homework: Berliner on Education and Inequality. Retrieved 13 October 2013, from http://dianeravitch.net/2012/07/23/your-homework-berliner-oneducation-and-inequality/

Bonner, C. (2007, 28 February). Education: Fixing what's not broken. *New Matilda*.

Caldwell, B. (2011, 4 May). Reward teachers, by all means, but not in this ham-fisted way. *Sydney Morning Herald*.

Darling-Hammond, L. (2005a). The near impossibility of testing for teacher quality. *Journal of Teacher Education, 56*, 205–214.

Darling-Hammond, L. (2005b). Does teacher preparation matter? Evidence about teacher certification, teach for America, and teacher effectiveness. *Education Policy Analysis Archives* 13. Retrieved 20 August 2012, from http://epaa.asu.edu/ojs/article/view/147

Day, C., Leithwood, K., & Sammons, P. (2008). What we have learned, what we need to know more about'. *School Leadership and Management, 28*, 83–96.

Dinham, S. et al. (2008). Investing in teacher quality: Doing what matters most. *Teaching Talent The Best Teachers for Australia's Classrooms, (pp. 5–52)*. Melbourne: Business Council of Australia.

Education Commission of the States (ECS). (2010). Teacher merit pay: What do we know? *The Progress of Education Reform, 11*(3), 1–4.

Fryer, R. G. (2011). Teacher incentives and student achievement: Evidence from New York City Public Schools. NBER Working Paper 16850. March 2011. Retrieved 20 August 2012, from http://www.nber.org/papers/w16850

Fullan, M. (2010). The awesome power of the principal. *Principal*. National Association of Elementary School Principals.

Garrett, P. (2011). Top teachers to be rewarded. Ministers Media Centre. Retrieved 11 September 2012, from http://ministers.deewr.gov.au/garrett/top-teachers-be-rewarded

Gurr, D. et al. (2005). *The international successful school principalship project (ISSPP): Comparison across country case studies*. Paper Presented at the Australian Council for Educational Leaders National Conference September 2005 and Australian Association for Research in Education National Conference 2005. Retrieved 20 August 2012, from http://www.aare.edu.au/05pap/gur05254.pdf

Hallinger, P. (2007). 'Research on the practice of instructional and transformational leadership: Retrospect and prospect', ACER Research Conference 2007, Retrieved 7 July 2010, from http://research.acer.edu.au/research_conference_2007/7/

Heyman, J., & Ariely, D. (2004). Effort for payment: A tale of two markets. *Psychological Science, 15*, 787–793.

Hong, M. et al. (2010). *Factors mediating the quality of teacher workforce: Finnish and South Korean Cases*. National Association for Research in Science Teaching (NARST) Conference Abstracts 2010.

Ingvarson, L. et al. (2007). Research on performance pay for teachers. Australian Council for Educational Research: 1–151. Retrieved 20 August 2012, from http://research.acer.edu.au/workforce/1/

Jensen, B., & Reichl, J. (2011). *Better teacher appraisal and feedback: Improving performance*. Carlton: Grattan Institute.

Kleinhenz, E., & Ingvarson, L. (2004). Teacher Accountability in Australia: Current policies and practices and their relation to improvement of teaching and learning. *Research Papers in Education, 19*, 31–49.

Leithwood, K. et al. (2008). Seven strong claims about successful school leadership. *School Leadership and Management, 28*(1), 27–42.

Lowe, K. B., & Galen Kroeck, K. (1996). Effectiveness correlates of transformational and transactional leadership: A meta-analytic review of the MLQ literature. *Leadership Quarterly, 7*, 385–426.

Mulford, B. (2007). Quality Australian evidence on leadership for improved learning. *ACER Research Conference 2007—The Leadership Challenge—Improving learning in schools*. Retrieved 20 August 2012, from http://research.acer.edu.au/research_conference_2007/8/

Mulford, B., & Sillins, H. (2003). Leadership for organisational learning and improved student outcomes. *Cambridge Journal of Education, 33*, 175–195.

Mulford, B., et al. (2008). Successful principalship of high-performance schools in high-poverty communities. *Journal of Educational Administration, 46*, 461–480.

OECD (2008). *Improving school leadership*. Paris: OECD Directorate for Education. Retrieved 20 August 2012, from http://www.oecd.org/education/preschoolandschool/improvingschoolleadership-home.htm

OECD. (2010). Strong performers and successful reformers in education: Lessons from PISA for the United State. Paris: OECD. Retrieved September 4, 2012, from http://www.oecd.org/pisa/46623978.pdf

Productivity Commission. (2012). *Schools workforce. Research report.* Canberra: Australian Productivity Commission.

Peterson, K., & Kelley, C. (2001). Transforming school leadership. *Leadership, 30*, 8–12.

Ramsey, G. (2000). *Quality matters revitalising teaching: critical times. Critical choices*. Report of the Review of Teacher Education. Sydney: NSW Department of Education and Training.

Reynolds D. (2001). *Effective school leadership: the contributions of school effectiveness research*. National College for Leadership of Schools and Children.

Rothstein, R. et al. (2010). Problems with the use of student test scores to evaluate teachers. Washington, DC: Economic Policy Institute. Retrieved 13 October 2013, from http://www.epi.org/publication/bp278/

Spillane, J. B. (2005). Primary school leadership practice: how the subject matters. *School Leadership and Management, 25*(4), 383–397.

Stecher, B. M. et al. (2010). *Toward a culture of consequences: Performance-based accountability systems for public services*. Santa Monica CA: RAND Corporation. Retrieved 20 August 2012, from http://www.rand.org/pubs/monographs/MG1019.html

Weick, K. (1976). Educational organizations as loosely coupled systems. *Administrative Science Quarterly, 21*, 1–10.

Chapter 9
Public or Private Schools, Tests and League Tables, Parental Choice and Competition in Australia, the USA and Britain

9.1 The Australian School System

Non-government schools are a feature of many, though not most, countries. The principal argument for their establishment is that parents should be able to choose what school they send their children to. That ability to choose is promoted as a democratic right. In Australia government support for non-government schools followed the Labor Party split in the 1950s and the emergence of the Democratic Labor Party: state aid for Catholic schools was believed likely to gain the Catholic vote in elections and thereby secure government for the Labor Party. A number of different religions now run schools.

In the last 10 years in Australia much greater funds have been provided to independent schools of all kinds supported by the argument that many in the community considered that government schools were not providing education at a suitable standard (Wilkinson et al. 2006). In many countries where there are faith-based schools, there is no government funding. In the US and the UK independent schools have been established to bypass the government funded schools which are considered to be not providing the education which the parents consider appropriate. These charter schools in the US and academies in the UK are often substantially funded by philanthropic foundations and other private sources.

In Australia most of the funding for independent schools comes from the Commonwealth government and most of the funding for government schools from state governments which have the constitutional obligation to fund education. But, as education historian Ian Wilkinson and colleagues point out, 'What has unfolded in Australia over the years differs in quite profound ways to what has occurred in other countries... With the exception of the US, issues that divided Australia for so long, well into the twentieth century, were resolved in these other countries in the early twentieth century.'

The private school sector has expanded to serve a constituency well beyond those seeking faith-based education. The substantial government funding of independent schools in Australia has led to a drifting away from government schools by students from higher socio-economic levels, leaving government schools with the more difficult education tasks of teaching all other children including those from more disadvantaged backgrounds, a task for which they are receiving fewer resources.

The issues are ones of equity—should schools which already receive substantial private support also receive government funding if that diminishes the total funding available to government schools and arguments as to educational performance *and* the way the curriculum is taught. Means testing—determining levels of direct or indirect government funding on the basis of levels of other income—can be anathema.

The availability of various measures of educational achievement in absolute terms and in relation to the inputs of funding can be objectively considered, though all kinds of arguments can be advanced against the conclusions from such considerations.

What is clear is that a large independent school sector increases inequalities through the ability of parents from high socioeconomic backgrounds with higher educational qualifications make more choices than parents from low socioeconomic situations. Well resourced independent schools attract teachers who are more highly qualified and are retained longer on the staff. Their facilities are significantly better than those schools funded solely by government. In the US especially, parents making choices about which school their children might attend are unlikely to choose schools with significant numbers of students from 'minority' backgrounds. Are these developments in the best interests of the community and nation? Parents who send their children to private schools argue that they are being taxed twice because some of their taxes go to support public schools which their children do not attend. However, taxation is not based on whether the taxpayer individually uses government services or not.

9.2 Australia and Government Funding of Independent Schools After 1996

In Australia from 1997 the Howard Government allocated substantial funds to private schools, much to the annoyance of advocates for public schools. With an appeal familiar to Australians, Prime Minister John Howard asserted that one of the reasons for the drift to private schools was that public schools were both 'values-free and too politically correct'.

Parents choosing an independent school do so because of experience with the quality of education and belief about the importance of public education (Beavis 2004; Perry 2007). They believe that they offer a better education, better teachers, smaller classes and so on and espouse traditional values. Those factors are not so important to those who choose a public school.

Australia is the only country to have split the responsibility for public funding of public and private schools unevenly between the federal and state levels of government.

This is a consequence of the adoption of neoliberal policies (Connors 2006). The Government's support for private schools breached the rationale for the introduction of significant state aid to private schools that all children were entitled to a decent standard of resources for learning and that public funding should be provided according to need to assist all schools to reach that standard and to bring about greater equality of educational opportunity.

A subtle but significant change to the rationale for Commonwealth funding to private schools gave a socioeconomic status score to schools according to the area in which the school was situated, not the SES of the student's families. Independent schools draw their students from a wide area so that such a measure was inaccurate. Schools were able to increase their fees without any change to their level of public funding. The policy failed to lower fees and increased the burden on public schools.

Recurrent Commonwealth Government payments to independent schools rose sharply from 1970 through 1982 and again from 1993 through 1999, increasing more rapidly to 2001 and then steadily increasing (Dowling 2007). By early 2005 the Government was spending more on private schools than it was on universities (Jopson and Burke 2005).

In Western Australia in recent years State schools have been allowed to become 'Independent Public Schools'. Under this scheme these schools, in collaboration with their school community 'set their own directions' and have authority for decision-making in respect of selection of staff, management of financial affairs including utility management and staff matters such as leave. They also are able to 'determine the curriculum that best supports the students' needs. Some groups of them work as a cluster 'which enables them to combine ideas and resources to create greater flexibility.' (O'Neill 2013). In the debate in the House of Representatives on the Australian Education Bill, the legislation implementing the Government's policies in response to the Gonski Report (see Sect. 14.11), the virtues of the 'Independent Schools Initiative' were extolled by a Western Australian member. The Coalition indicated in its policy for the 2013 election that it would support the extension of this scheme to all public schools, as appropriate.

A number of evaluations of the outcomes have been made (Cobbold 2013). Trevor Cobbold reported that the Melbourne Graduate School of Education found little evidence of any improvement in student outcomes. '….there was no evidence of substantial differences in outcomes between schools that were selected into IPS and those that were not' and 'in this early phase of the development there little there is little evidence of changes to student outcomes such as enrolment or student achievement'. Most particularly important were the findings, 'Analysis of the secondary data shows that IPS were generally high-performing before transition, and there has been no substantive increase in student achievement after becoming IPS' and 'analysis of available data on student enrolment and behaviour across all public schools showed no change for IPS. There were pre-existing differences in attendance rates between IPS and other public schools which remained unchanged over the 3 years of implementation'.

An expert panel was established by the State School Teachers' Union of Western Australian to examine the Work and Roles of Principals and Deputy-Principals in Western Australian Schools (State School Teachers' Union of Western Australia 2013). The panel was chaired by the former CEO of the ACT Department of Education, Ms Fran Hinton. It received numerous submissions from parents, government agencies and business and was informed by an extensive literature scan. The panel found, '…the biggest risk to the system is that students may fail to achieve desired educational outcomes. It appears that less emphasis is being given to managing risks relating to educational outcomes. The emphasis rather is on other compliance measures, not related to student outcomes, which take school leaders away from the key task of educational leadership. This means there is a risk that desired education outcomes for students may not be achieved' (School Leaders Inquiry 2013).

Cobbold also noted that the Western Australian Auditor General had reported, 'A possible outcome in an open market is that IPSs are more effective in recruiting teachers with experience and specific skills. Other schools may be left with concentrations of inexperienced staff, or a reliance on fixed term staff that causes problems with teacher continuity.'

9.3 Student Socioeconomic Background and School Environment

Social commentator Jane Caro and former Secondary School Principal Chris Bonner have relentlessly attacked the policies of the Australian governments support of independent schools (Bonner and Caro 2007) and so have others including Trevor Cobbold of *Save Our Schools* in numerous articles. Cobbold has also strenuously criticised NAPLAN and drawn attention to the evidence about social and economic advantage and equity and their relationship to education achievement as well as related issues.

The funding system effectively creates a school education market where private schools in receipt of government funding compete with public schools for students. Increased Commonwealth government support for private schools, together with higher fees charged by those schools—they weren't reduced as suggested when government funds were provided—led to drastic reductions in teacher: student ratios, especially in independent (non-Catholic) secondary schools. Government schools felt increased pressure to reach the same educational outcomes as those of private schools (Watson and Ryan 2010).

The critical point about the drift to independent schools is the resulting impact on students by virtue of the influence that the average SES of the school class has on the achievement of the individual student. Laura Perry and Andrew McConney of Murdoch University showed that a student from a low SES background in a high average SES class achieved a significantly higher score than they would in a

9.3 Student Socioeconomic Background and School Environment 157

low SES class and a student from a high SES background scored lower if they were in a low SES class (Perry and McConney 2010; McConney and Perry 2010). The results for reading from PISA 2003 show a difference between the average low SES student in a low SES school and the average high SES student in a similar school of 89 points, or over 2 years of learning.

The association between school SES and student achievement is lower in Canada and Finland than in Australia; both countries outperform Australia on PISA. As those countries show, reducing socioeconomic school segregation and differences among schools promotes higher overall achievement for all students without decreasing the achievement of high-performing students. Poorer students are getting a poorer education!.

Market reforms over the past 25 years have led to the gradual erosion of the size and efficiency of schools serving poorer communities (Tomazin 2007; Teese and Lamb 2002; Teese 2012). 'Self-reliant parents are encouraged to buy their children places in private schools. Student segregation and the residualization of public schools may be a side effect of this assertion of individual interest, but this negative outcome is then excused by deeming it to be a result of market forces….' Segregation is represented as the result of individual's choices when in fact parents' choices have been shaped by deliberate government policies (Vickers 2004).

9.4 The Rudd and Gillard Australian Governments and Independent Schools

The Rudd and Gillard Governments pledged to continue support of independent schools until 2012; yet a Department of Education review uncovered entrenched inequities in the system (Patty 2010). In launching the review of school funding to be chaired by David Gonski the Government made it clear that no school would lose its present level of funding. Thus any increase recognised as necessary for any school would require funds additional to those already allocated and no opportunity would be afforded to address excessive levels of funding!

Infrastructure maintenance at public schools has been neglected. Public schools were 'well below an acceptable standard', with leaking roofs to overflowing toilets, a factor contributing to the exodus of students to private schools (Doherty 2005). Clearly State schools struggle to maintain infrastructure. Or they would have were it not for the extra infrastructure funding as part of the Rudd governments stimulus package—'Building the Education Revolution or BER in response to the GFC of 2008–2009. BER provided funds for buildings at many schools around Australia; the program was heavily criticised in some quarters but the Australian National Audit Office reported that the program was good value for money (Eltham 2010).

If the independent school system is supposed to improve the opportunity for parents to ensure their children receive a quality education, then children at private schools should be achieving better results. However, the most significant characteristic of those schools achieving the highest scores in HSC (Higher School Certificate) or VCE (Victorian Certificate of Education) examinations is the aggregate score required for entry. There is little overlap between (or correlation with) the schools ranked on the basis of number of its alumni mentioned in the *Who's Who in Australia* and the rank according to HSC or VCE score.

9.5 Choice and Competition in the US School System

In the US, over the 25 years from 1980 to 2005 spending per student increased by 73 %, the student-to-teacher ratio in schools declined by 18 % and tens of thousands of initiatives were launched aiming to improve quality of education. However, actual student outcomes stayed almost the same (Barber and Mourshed 2007).

The substantial reforms in the USA since 1980 have emphasised individual responsibility and private enterprise, principal themes of American life: government involvement is considered to only exacerbate problems. So, choice was provided. Vouchers given to students by government to subsidize the cost of the child's schooling were asserted to stimulate emergence of a wide variety of schools to meet the demand, increased competition would mean more flexible public systems and teachers salaries would be responsive to market forces.

Studies of the Milwaukee Parental Choice Program (MPCP), which began in 1990 show no gain! It was long held up by voucher advocates as a beacon for school improvement; results from 2011 confirm earlier studies (Cobbold 2011). Caroline M. Hoxby of Stanford University's Hoover Institute concluded in a 2004 study that charter schools are more likely than public schools to be proficient in reading and math and that this advantage increases with age of the school. Her conclusions are contested.

Charter schools funded by government, run by private entities and able to attract private funding, are claimed by some to be a solution. But a recently published study shows that charter-school students are not outperforming students in traditional public schools (Buckley and Schneider 2007). Charter schools all too often fall short of advocate's claims, something known for some time (Barber and Mourshed 2007).

The most impressive charter schools are the KIPP (Knowledge is Power Program) schools which aim to teach 'academics', self-discipline and good behaviour. They have longer days, some Saturday classes and three weeks of summer school—60 % more time in school than a regular public school. Students, parents and teachers sign a contract agreeing to fulfil certain specific responsibilities. Pedagogy and curriculum are left to individual school leaders. But KIPP schools select their students, regular public schools that must accept everyone who applies, including the students who leave KIPP schools.

The propaganda about public schools being a failure is shown dramatically by the film *Waiting for Superman* (Ravitch 2010). Made by Davis Guggenheim (who made *An Inconvenient Truth*, the film about former US Vice President Al Gore's campaign to educate people about climate change) it tells the story of five children who enter a lottery to win a place in a charter school; four of them seek to escape the public schools, four of them are African American or Hispanic and live in poor neighbourhoods. The film promotes the view that the only way to overcome all the 'problems', is to expand the charter school community. Bad teachers protected from dismissal by unions, difficulty in firing bad teachers and in paying good teachers more all feature as ways in which improving schools, and therefore students' test scores, are prevented. 'It is not globalization or deindustrialization or poverty or our coarse popular culture or predatory financial practices that bear responsibility: it's the public schools, their teachers and their unions.' Amongst the various lies featured by the film is the proposition that doctors and lawyers lose their jobs or are suspended for inappropriate conduct at several thousand times the rate of failing teachers.

The actual inconvenient truth was revealed by research (Haimson 2010). The film used distorted statistics such as 70 % of eighth grade students cannot read at grade level whereas the figure is more properly 25 %. It claimed that it is far more difficult to sack bad teachers than it is to dismiss poorly performing people in other professions when in fact the attrition rate for teachers is much higher than for other professions, in New York City the 4 year attrition rate was over 40 % at the time Haimson was writing and the rate of disbarment of attorneys in Texas was nearly a hundred times smaller than quoted in the film!

The main proposition of the film is plainly absurd. Why would one embrace a lottery system to give students from poor backgrounds an opportunity to attend well-funded schools as a way of raising the education standards of an entire nation?

The reforms in the US address many issues so further commentary is included in other essays including Chap. 12 'International Comparisons'.

9.6 Independent Schools in the UK

Tony Blair's Labour government built on the foundations laid by Margaret Thatcher: it used three new instruments of change in the school system (Hatcher 2005). An office for standards in education (Ofsted) was established to carry out school inspections, a teacher training agency responsible for overseeing the initial and continuing education of teachers was set up and the private sector was brought into run some schools.

Government relied on companies and business entrepreneurs from forprofits and nonprofit organisations to be involved in roles from teaching systems and curriculum to management. Introducing performance-related pay for teachers resulted in contracts awarded to a number of companies to devise criteria for assessing teacher's effectiveness; consultants were hired to train head teachers how to assess their staff.

Services to schools including school meals, maintenance of schools and core education services, many of which used to be provided by local education authorities, were privatised. Setting up specialist schools sponsored by grants was encouraged. Sponsors (on a non-profit basis) were required to pay 20 % of the capital costs of the school and the government provided the rest of the cost of building the school. Ownership of the land and buildings of the existing state school, formerly the property of the local council, was transferred to the new academy.

The new school governing body controlled the school, including appointment and promotion of teachers. Schools deemed by the relevant authority to be failing were required to invite bids from private companies to run them. Faith-based organisations were offered increased opportunity to run academies.

Following the general election in Britain in May 2010, Michael Gove, Education Secretary in the new Government, announced that 500 secondary schools and 1,700 primary schools would be able to achieve academy status by the summer (Wintour and Watt 2010). Gove said they raise standards, promote social justice and can give working-class parents greater choice. Gove has also praised the school system in Alberta. He clearly misunderstood the nature of the changes there; he pledged to adopt the tests used by Shanghai-China, assuming that it was tests which made the difference!

9.7 Market Mechanisms

An OECD study by Sietske Waslander of the University of Tiburg in the Netherlands and colleagues, released October 2010, analysed the empirical research on market mechanisms including voucher programs and charter schools intended to encourage competition and increase parental choice and so improve student achievement (Waslander et al. 2010). The analysis concluded that most effects were small or non-existent.

Choice leads to schools seeking students with a background like the person making the choice. Chris Bonner's recent analysis of schools in the southwestern New South Wales city of Wagga Wagga (Bonner 2011) demonstrates this dramatically! It is claimed that test results help parents choose the best school for their child, a claim particularly advanced by those who embrace a neoliberal view of life. But choice is limited by other factors. Schools are chosen for factors other than simple scores in end of year tests: location of the school, characteristics of the students enrolled, philosophy of the staff and the facilities.

The PISA data reveals that even in countries like Finland and Korea, whose students achieve a relatively high average score, the scores of students from poor backgrounds 'fall far short of their more advantaged counterparts'. However, those disadvantaged students perform better than poor students from the US, reflecting the commitment to education in those countries. The percentage of students living in low economic, cultural and social status (an OECD measure) in the US is more than 2½ times that of Finland and Canada.

A comprehensive review of school choice and equity (Musset 2012) issued January 2012 by the OECD notes, 'In the last 25 years, more than two-thirds of OECD

9.7 Market Mechanisms 161

countries have increased school choice opportunities for parents'. It also notes, 'the evidence shows that more parental choice leads to an increase polarization of students by ability and socioeconomic background'. The report concludes, 'School choice policies are aimed at achieving a number of diverse goals [including] the enhancement of parents' freedom and their right to decide over the education of their children... improve[ment] of student achievement and... equal access to high quality schooling... choice schemes do provide enhanced opportunities for some advantaged parents and students who have a strong achievement orientation, but also harm others, often more disadvantaged and low SES families.' Disadvantaged parents are noted as exercising choice the least because they are not always capable of acquiring the information necessary to make well informed and optimal educational choices for their children.. Also, parents do not necessarily base their decisions on academic aspects but primarily on other factors, such as proximity, peer socioeconomic status, the schools facilities, etc. As a consequence, schools become more and more segregated... Disadvantaged parents and students... are further isolated.

The findings by Waslander and the other studies cited above reinforce the conclusion reached 20 years ago by the study of 'marketisation' in New Zealand (Lauder et al. 1999). Choice and competition reinforce disparities in the community and do nothing to improve student achievement. If overall improvement in educational outcomes is to be achieved then poverty has to be addressed at the same time as additional support is given to schools serving disadvantaged students to ensure that they have at least the same quality of education provision as more advantaged students. The PISA reports make this point time and again. Yet despite that there are still those whose views are quoted in certain media who claim that there is no relation between student performance and socioeconomic background!

9.8 Tests and League Tables: A Democratic Right to Know?

Standardised tests have enjoyed a resurgence in a number of countries. The proposition is that accountability is important, parents wish to know how well their school is doing and how well their children are doing at school and that they way to gain that information is through standardised tests. In some cases this argument has been carried forward to using the results of average test scores for classes as a measure of the competence and performance of teachers, even the entire school. The tests are also considered suitable for use in merit pay schemes.

The question is whether the imposition of standardised tests does lead to improved student achievement. Encouraging good teachers to remain in the education system is of course an important goal. The second question is whether there are any other effects of standardised testing.

The research on standardised or high stakes testing and application of the outcomes is clear: standardised testing narrows the curriculum and focuses teaching on preparation for testing. Advocates for testing often lack understanding of statistical variation and make claims about aggregated scores for schools that simply are not valid. Notions that test scores can be used to judge the quality of teaching are nonsense and such exercises have produced no evidence that either performance of students improves or that behaviour of teachers vary. More than that, there are significant effects on student health and well-being, learning, and, as already noted, teaching and curriculum.

A comprehensive review of international literature by Professor John Polesel of the Melbourne Graduate School of Education at Melbourne University and colleagues (Polesel et al. 2012) for the Whitlam Institute found these negative effects to be such as to question the NAPLAN program introduced in 2007 in Australia. A follow up study found that, in the view of the majority of teachers, these negative effects apply to Australia (Dulfer et al. 2012); Minister Garrett pronounced the study as, amongst other things, not very helpful.

As with all measures there is substantial variation in test scores: the variation is generally greater between classes in the same school than between schools. The variation within the school therefore is such that there is substantial overlap between schools; variation is so great that there is substantial overlap between similar schools. Thus only the very best schools can be distinguished from the very worst which hardly makes it easier for parents to choose the higher performing school. Performance within the school and individual class may be high in some subjects but not in others, good in 1 year but not good several years later. Many teachers and schools over several years contribute to the result in any 1 year.

The late Kenneth Rowe (2000a) observed, 'Measurement of learning outcomes using standardised achievement tests is inherently risky; test scores have low information value about the outlying processes… the majority of such tests assess skills in terms of generalised academic *abilities* and enduring cognitive 'traits' rather than specific learning outcomes arising from classroom instruction.' He concluded, 'Australian politicians and senior bureaucrats currently advocating the publication of such performance information in the form of league tables 'are naively, and in typical fashion, stomping around in an uninformed epistemopathological fog' (Rowe 2000b). Rebecca Hoyle and James C Robinson of the University of Surrey's Department of Mathematics and Statistics found random fluctuations from year to year in test scores can cause large distortions in league-table positions and that value-added tables were no more accurate than raw exam scores (Hoyle and Robinson 2003).

9.9 Evidence is not Always Sufficient!

Educational achievement of any student reflects many influences, most importantly, it reflects the experience before entering school. An individual teacher in any 1 year can hardly claim entire credit or be held wholly accountable for the results of test performance in that year. Tabloid media often pounce upon league tables in a nonsensical manner. One British newspaper *The Independent*, headlined publication of the Chief Inspector of Schools Report on Quality of Education, 'Half of schools failing their pupils'. (Rowe 2000a: footnote ii). There are numerous other examples which show a lack of understanding of basic statistics by many journalists.

The Australian newspaper on 2 December 2008 trumpeted the call to arms (with misinformation), 'Information about school performance must be public… As the federal Governments budget papers pointed out this year, OECD and other research shows that public reporting of student and school results has significant positive impacts on student performance, even after accounting for demographic and socioeconomic backgrounds. This is one reason…, why the Government must… make individual school performance reporting a condition of the new national education agreement to come into effect from 1 January 2009.'

In 2012 *The Australian* published a special wrap around listing schools and their NAPLAN scores! The list was in effect a league table, something the Government had sought to ensure did not result from the publication of NAPLAN scores! *The Australian* continues its campaign against education reform which recognises valid research by, for instance, condemning the New South Wales government for signing on to the Commonwealth Governments Gonski reforms in April 2013.

9.10 No Child Left Behind (NCLB)

No Child Left Behind required each State in the US to develop assessments in basic skills to be given to all students in certain grades in order to receive federal funding for schools. Standardised tests were a central feature of NCLB. Schools that did not demonstrate adequate progress toward the goal of making every student proficient in math and English by 2014 would be subject to 'increasingly onerous standards… In effect states, most of which had vague and meaningless standards, were… asked to grade themselves by creating tests that almost all children could (or should) eventually pass… There was no underlying vision of what education should be or how one might improve schools.' (Ravitch 2010). It is a statistical inevitability that some students will fail in any test so long as there is a cut-off point, no matter what criteria are used. In other words the headline goal of the policy was a nonsense!

The NCLB legislation enacts a belief that setting high standards and establishing measurable goals can improve individual outcomes. NCLB was intended to raise educational achievement and close the racial/ethnic achievement gap—its strategies included focusing schools' attention on raising test scores, mandating better qualified teachers and providing educational choice—these goals have not been achieved. Two of the most prominent educational researchers in the US, Professor Linda Darling-Hammond of Stanford University and Professor David Berliner of the University of Arizona are amongst those, and they are many, who have most strongly criticised standardised testing (Darling-Hammond 2007; Nichols and Berliner 2008).

Darling-Hammond points to the complex requirements of the law which have led to a failure of the program to achieve its goals of raising performance increasing the number of qualified teachers and providing educational choice. Instead there have been unintended negative consequences which frequently harm the students the law is most intended to help. These include a narrowed curriculum, a focus on low-level skills, inappropriate assessment of English language learners and students with special needs; and strong incentives to exclude low-scoring students from school so as to achieve test score targets. The law fails to address the pressing problems of unequal educational resources across schools serving wealthy and poor children and the shortage of well-prepared teachers in high-need schools.

That NCLB failed to achieve its goals is unsurprising since NCLB was introduced on the basis of faked results in Houston, Texas achieved by Superintendent Rod Paige, subsequently appointed by President Bush to be his Secretary of Education (Schemo 2003). In 2002 Houston won a $1 million prize as best urban district in the country, from the Broad Foundation, based in Los Angeles!

The personal experience of Australian teacher Pat Carlton Buoncristiani visiting a school in the US where the strictures of *No Child Left Behind* prevailed is instructive, though it is one person's experience. Buoncristiani (2009) moved from Victoria (Australia) to Virginia in 2000 to take over the leadership of an urban elementary school (grades K-5) with a population 95 % African-American and 60 % living below the poverty line. Test scores were in single digits, the school was dispirited and seen by the community as a failure. Teachers had few strategies for teaching and expectations were low.

Buoncristiani introduced cooperative programs with universities to build teaching skills and worked to improve the image of the school and morale of staff, forwarded good news to the local newspaper and met the school bus each morning to welcome the kids with a smile. The pressures of NCLB were oppressive, teaching subjects not in the test was discouraged.

The pupil of a skilled grade one teacher brought in a worm farm: the whole day was spent looking at worms, their place in garden ecology, singing a song about worms, writing stories about worms. But this prized teaching skill had no place in the tightly mandated nine-week program… At the end of the year when the opportunity arose to take the kids to the swimming pool Buoncristiani's supervisor informed her that she did not approve of that because it would do nothing to raise test scores next year!

Confronting the ongoing criticisms of teachers in the US, one of the major features of the debate, Professor David Berliner gathered the evidence to refute every claim from 'any reasonably smart person can teach through teacher education is out of touch' to 'teachers are borne, not made'. He responded (Berliner 2000) with a list of 12 principles of effective teaching including creating cohesive and caring learning communities, ensuring classroom management systems which maintain engagement with curriculum-related activities, preparing a structure which clarifies intended outcomes, giving opportunities for students to apply what they have learned, encouraging students to work in pairs or small groups, using a variety of formal and informal assessment methods and following through on expectations for learning outcomes. He also emphasized that as in other activities from wrestling to violin playing, practice is vitally important.

'No Child Left Behind' failed because it did not address the factors mainly relating to low educational achievement, namely the economic and social inequality in the community and the impacts they have on the opportunities available as well as the health of the child. Nor did it address the relative re-sourcing of schools determined principally at district level or issues concerning language spoken in the home which may be different from that used at school, factors shown to be important by Johns Hopkins University researchers Doris Entwisle and Karl Alexander (Entwisle and Alexander 1992, 1994).

An outstanding Presidential Address to the Association for Public Policy Analysis and Management in 2011 by Professor Helen F. Ladd of the Sanford School of Public Policy and Duke University shows unequivocally that not only are there large disparities facing the educational achievement of children in poverty but those disparities have been increasing and now greatly exceed the differences between the achievement levels of white and African American children (Ladd 2011).

The National Assessment of Education Progress (NAEP) program is the largest nationally representative and continuing assessment of what Americas students know and can do in various subject areas. Ladd points out that analysis of scores over a 55 year period show significant differences for students of individual states. For instance, differences between Massachusetts and California students are most likely due for the former to 'aggressive and comprehensive education reform' instituted in 1998 and for the latter probably to the continually limited spending by California. Students from many of the southern states such as Mississippi, Alabama, Louisiana, Tennessee and Georgia score poorly compared with students from Maryland, New Hampshire, Minnesota and New Jersey.

A similar situation is revealed by PISA: even in countries such as Finland and Korea whose students achieve a relatively high average score, the scores of students from poor backgrounds 'fall far short of their more advantaged counterparts'. However, the students from disadvantaged backgrounds in those countries perform better than poor students from the US, reflecting the commitment to equity in education in those countries. The percentage of students living in low economic, cultural and social status (an OECD measure) in the US is more than 2 1/2 times that of Finland and Canada.

Another set of studies (Schoon et al. 2011) complement those cited by Ladd. A survey of 18,819 babies born between September 2000 and January 2002 into 18,553 families living in the UK showed persistent poverty as the crucial factor undermining children's cognitive development. The study considered various measures of family stability as well as poverty.

9.11 Standardised Testing in the UK

Standardised tests have come into favour in the UK also. They have been heavily criticised by Emeritus Professor Robin Alexander, editor of the 'Cambridge Primary Review' who observed 'there's always the risk that politics will drag what ought to be a carefully-considered debate about the quality of education into the gutter of electioneering' (Alexander 2010a). Professor Alexander has strongly criticised the way the government of the UK summarily abandoned the Cambridge Primary Review. 'Despite some 250 formal meetings with organisations up and down the country, of which 37 were with ministers or officials of government, House of Commons committees and associated bodies, described as constructive, reasonable and perceptive, a spokesperson for the Department attacked the Review for 'peddling' a collection of recycled, partial or out of date research… I am not going to apologise for delivering what parents want, even if these researchers—often on the basis of out-of-date research—don't like it… Independent is certainly not an apt description of today's report from the self-styled largest review of primary education in 40 years. It is another deeply ideological strike against standards and effective teaching of the 3Rs in our primary schools…' Alexander pointed out that the Primary Review was about reversing the change of the last 20 years and that the government, by dismissing reports from the Review, was sidelining 'the considered written submissions of over 1,000 organisations and individuals, all of whom submitted evidence in the hope that it would make a difference' (Alexander 2010b).

The House of Commons Children, Schools and Families Committee reported in 2009 that a certain amount of national testing at key points in a child's school career was necessary but that teachers creativity in the classroom and children's access to a balanced curriculum had been compromised (House of Commons 2008).

Ken Boston, one time Director-General of Education in South Australia and Director-General of Technical and Further Education in New South Wales, headed the Blair Labour Governments Qualifications and Curriculum Authority (QCA), which had responsibility through the National Testing Authority (NTA) for the national curriculum tests, from 2002 until 2008: he found the personal skills programs designed to overcome problems found by employers led to students being unfit for work: unable to communicate effectively or work in teams, lacking in initiative, the capacity to deal with problems, with no interest in further learning or personal growth; these failings were real, the situation was a crisis (Boston 2009). In Boston's view, 'the primary school curriculum has become a dry husk because the future of the school (not that of your son or daughter) is dependent upon the result [of the tests].'

9.12 Value-Added Tests

In late August 2010, the Los Angeles Times published value-added ratings of some 6,000 Los Angeles elementary school teachers and 470 elementary schools. The *Times* explained, 'A teachers value-added rating is based on his or her students progress on the California Standards Tests for English and math. The difference between a student's expected growth and actual performance is the value a teacher added or subtracted during the year. A schools value-added rating is based on the performance of all students tested there during that period.'

A panel of economists and educators convened by the Economic Policy Institute in Washington DC (Baker et al. 2010) concluded that value-added scores should be only a part of an overall comprehensive evaluation and cautioned against their use in teacher evaluation and compensation decisions to scores on existing...

A group of prominent economists (Cawley et al. 1999) observed some years ago, One current educational reform seeks to reward the value added by teachers and schools based on the average change in pupil test scores over time.... However, the average gain in test scores is an inadequate measure of school performance and current value-added methodology may misdirect school resources.

Success in later life must surely be one of the principal issues driving the search for better schooling. So students who do better at school should go on to get better jobs. Professor James Heckman and his colleagues examined the importance of meritocracy—where ability is more important than privilege. Whereas educational reform seeks to reward the value added by teachers and schools… the data shows no consistent pattern in the relationship between test scores and wages: thus use of a metric such as test scores may misdirect school resources. General intelligence or overall cognitive ability is dominant in explaining test score variance. But the measures of ability are not rewarded equally across race and gender. In fact cognitive ability is only a minor indicator of social performance: it is more important in white collar jobs but much less so in blue collar jobs where many other factors intervene (Cawley et al. 1997). The unequivocal conclusion (Knudsen et al. 2006) is that, the most efficient strategy for strengthening the future workforce, both economically and neurobiologically, and improving its quality of life is to invest in the environments of disadvantaged children during the early childhood years.

9.13 Intrinsic Motivation

There is a further issue: setting of personal goals and seeking to improve on individual past performance is more effective than trying to achieve the goals achieved by someone else or some group of others. Professor Andrew Martin of Sydney University's Education and Social Work Faculty has studied the performance of students who set high personal goals, that is personal bests or PBs

(Martin 2006). Sportspersons frequently set high personal goals rather than relying simply on beating the competition.

Martin reported PBs 'hold implications for motivation and achievement in terms of their facilitating effects for self-efficacy, persistence, educational participation, enjoyment of school, and task interest and engagement'. PBs lead to higher levels of performance, seemingly by reducing the ambiguity about what is to be achieved. From a study of attitudes to goals and self improvement concerning both schoolwork and homework (involving students from years 7 through 12 from various Sydney schools) Martin concluded that PBs were likely an important means to achieve their potential at school. Students are most likely to reach PBs on tasks/goals that are (1) specific, (2) challenging, (3) competitively self-referenced, and (4) focused on self-improvement.

A later study (Martin et al. 2010) reinforced these conclusions. A very large majority of 'low performers' at age 15 years go on to make a successful transition into full-time work or study or a combination of these (Thomson and Hillman 2010).

9.14 Important Issues Missed

The focus on testing ignores health problems that contribute significantly to diminished achievement. Kenneth Rowe (2003) noted that boys exhibit greater externalizing behaviour problems in the classroom and at home, many demonstrate poor achievement progress in literacy and boys make up the vast majority of children identified as at risk in the early years of schooling because of poor progress in literacy. It turns out that boys have a higher prevalence of auditory processing problems: after the age of four boys have less ability to process auditory 'streams' of speech than girls.

Another example is the incidence of chronic suppurative otitis media (CSOM), persistent inflammation of the middle ear, the area between the tympanic membrane and the inner ear including the Eustachian tube, which is best regarded as a disease of poverty. The incidence of this in Australian Aboriginal children is extremely high, higher than in any other country. Berliner (2008) has also noted this as a significant problem in American children. How much of the problem of Aboriginal children at school is due to CSOM?

Programs merely demanding achievement of certain levels of performance without attention to the root causes of the outcomes, the factors which contribute to them and the behaviours and resources which alleviate them, will fail. Provision of early childhood programs, health clinics and social services as well as after school and summer programs will likely make a difference: they do in other countries. Outcome metrics such as standardised test results are lagging indicators: by the time they are received and analysed, the factors leading to them have passed. The results are relevant to remediation only in a stable and relatively homogeneous environment. In the case of student test scores the principal agent is identified as the teacher of that year; other factors are ignored. School is an environment in which children actually spend a relatively short amount of their time!

Schools can be held accountable but only for those things which they have control over such as a safe and supportive school environment which promotes respect amongst students and teachers and for delivering a coherent curriculum. Accountability has greatest meaning within the school itself! And it should be reciprocal: those requiring accountability should be accountable themselves for the provision of necessary resources.

9.15 Effective Student Engagement and Ineffective Standardised Tests

Standardised tests have been designed to deliver accountability and inform choice, both major elements of neoliberal ideology. However they do not accurately measure the ultimate effectiveness of student learning and relating them to teacher effectiveness achieves no change in student behaviour. The principal variation is the class not the school. Class test averages vary with subject and year. Test results are influenced by many factors besides the teacher of the year in which the tests are taken. Relating teacher bonuses to student test results delivers no change in teacher behaviour. Intrinsic motivation is more important in achieving student's engagement and achievement.

Test scores are not leading indicators: by the time the results are available the factors which contributed to the results have likely changed! In many cases the factors which influence the results are not assessed. What on earth is the point of it all? And when all is said and done, the tests are supposed to be representative of general achievement in learning. And that learning is supposed to be indicative of later ability to achieve 'a good job' and be 'a productive member of society'. In fact it is very doubtful that standardised tests are useful in either of these ways. Evidence of the lack of a link between achievement in tests and ability to reason, surely a key outcome, comes from studies of achievement in science tests.

Russell Tytler of Deakin University and Jonathan Osborne of Stanford University, both experts in the study of science learning, examined the links between performance in tests, attitudes to science and scientific reasoning as revealed in previous studies (Tytler and Osborne 2012).They cite the widely referenced ROSE study based in Norway in which students were asked to respond to questions of the kind 'I like school science better than other subjects'. Their responses were scored in a four-point Lickert scale. It turned out that students in more advanced, industrialised countries indicated lower interest in school science and girls had a more negative attitude. All of the samples were opportunistic and not randomly selected, yet in some countries these results were greeted with alarm: the future supply of scientists is a matter of great concern! However, Tytler and Osborne point out that the data can be interpreted as showing that 40 % of boys and 22 % of girls were interested in school science. Is the concern exaggerated they ask.

Again, Tytler and Osborne point to analysis of 1999 data from the Third International Mathematics and Science Study (TIMSS) which found that those countries whose students were most successful offer very traditional science education with an emphasis on learning scientific knowledge but the students in those countries who did well had the most negative attitudes to science. Finally they cite more recent studies comparing the performance of Chinese and American students on tests of conceptual knowledge and scientific reasoning. Those students educated in China perform significantly better in conceptual knowledge but no better in scientific reasoning. Tytler and Osborne ask, 'if the goal is to develop student's ability to think critically, an emphasis on content might have little effect'.

Surely we can conclude that results of tests don't tell us very much about general learning achievement in respect of those factors which will be of most value in later life. And arguably we can extend this generally to the general proposition as to the utility of tests!

Then there is the matter of what tests might tell us about indicators for success in later life. We can incidentally recall that well known experiment conducted by psychologist Walter Mischel, then a professor at Stanford University. A marshmallow was put in front of children aged 4 and they were told that they could eat the marshmallow straight away but if they didn't within 15 min they would get a second marshmallow. Those children who ate the marshmallow right away 20 years later had significantly greater problems with drug addiction and higher incarceration rates. Those kids who waited had better life outcomes including higher college completion rates and higher incomes. *New York Times* columnist David Brooks in his book *The Social Animal: The Hidden Sources of Love, Character, and Achievement* (New York: Random House 2011) points to the common conclusion that the kids who waited the 15 min had learned the consequences of their actions; in any event they generally came from higher socioeconomic backgrounds. The issue is one of self-control.

Research in the last 10 years has shown, in fact that self-control is a better predictor of later academic achievement than IQ (Duckworth and Seligman 2005). A longitudinal study of 140 eighth-grade students was conducted by Angela Duckworth and Martin Seligman of the Positive Psychology Center at the University of Pennsylvania. A composite self-discipline score was created using questionnaire data from students, parents and teachers together with some other data as well as IQ scores. Academic performance data was collected for each student about seven months later. Self-discipline predicted academic performance more robustly than did IQ and also predicted which students would improve their grades whereas IQ did not. Highly self-disciplined eighth graders earned higher achievement-test scores and were more likely to gain admission to a selective high school. As well, they had fewer school absences, spent more time on their homework, watched less television, and started their homework earlier in the day. This research confirmed the results of other studies of self discipline and relationship with academic performance and social functioning.

There is no intrinsic evidence to support the proposition that independent schools achieve better outcomes than public schools. Where differences in educational achievement have been demonstrated they are due very substantially to the higher levels of pre-school education and greater family well being—including a different home environment and greater access to home study resources enjoyed by students who are enrolled at independent schools—as well as factors like lower teacher:student ratios which in turn are influenced by the higher level of resources available to such schools. Independent schools choose who to enrol but public schools are obliged to take whoever is entitled to enrol and end up with the majority of children from disadvantaged backgrounds.

As shown above, James Heckman's research shows no consistent pattern in the relationship between test scores and wages: thus use of a metric such as test scores may misdirect school resources. It is incontestable that many people who have gone on to be successful in later life in various fields did not do well at school and often failed tests, even showing little interest in any subjects including one's related to their later success. These are precisely the points made by Sir Ken Robinson in his consideration of creativity. To the many examples given in the chapter on creativity (Sect. 11.5)—Dick Smith, Richard Feynman, Albert Einstein, Richard Branson, Steve Jobs and Bill Gates—we can add notable Australian Barry Humphries whose portrayals of that uproariously exaggerated parody of Australian suburbia, Dame Edna Everidge and other characters, have made him famous. Humphries is an accomplished landscape painter, an award winning writer; and he has an extraordinary knowledge of music of all kinds. It is true that he did very well in some subjects at school but detested mathematics, spurned sport and claimed conscientious objection to avoid participation in school cadets. How would he have done in NAPLAN tests?

References

Alexander, R. (2010a, 10 March). *The Perils of policy success, amnesia and collateral damage in systemic educational reform*. Miegunyah Distinguished Visiting Fellowship Program 2010 - Public lecture. Retrieved August 29, 2012 from http://www.education.unimelb.edu.au/news/news%20pdfs/Alexander%20Miegunyah%20lecture%20FINAL.pdf

Alexander, R. (2010b). Speaking but not listening? Accountable talk in an unaccountable context. *Literacy, 44*, 103–111.

Baker. E. L. et al. (2010). *Problems with the use of student test scores to evaluate teachers*. EPI Briefing Paper #278. Economic Policy Institute. Washington DC. http://epi.3cdn.net/724cd9a1eb91c40ff0_hwm6iij90.pdf

Barber, M. & Mourshed, M. (2007). How the world's best-performing school systems come out on top. London, McKinsey & Company. Accessed 6 September 2012, from http://www.mckinsey.com/clientservice/socialsector/resources/pdf/Worlds_School_Systems_Final.pdf

Beavis, A. (2004). Why parents choose public or private schools. Research Developments. 12, article 3. Accessed 28 August 2012, from http://research.acer.edu.au/resdev/vol12/iss12/3

Berliner, D. C. (2000). A personal response to those who bash teacher education. *Journal of Teacher Education, 51*, 358–371.

Berliner, D. C. (2008). Letter to the president. *Journal of Teacher Education, 59*, 252–257.

Bonner. C. (2011, May 11). 'My School. PISA and Australia's equity gap'. Inside Story Accessed 29 August 2012, from http://inside.org.au/equity/
Bonner, C. & Caro, J. (2007).The Stupid Country, *How Australia is Dismantling Public Education*. Sydney, UNSW Press.
Boston, K. (2009, 26 April). The Sunday Times: Our early start on making children unfit for work.
Buckley, J. & Schneider, M. (2007). *Charter Schools Hope or Hype*. Princeton NJ,Princeton University Press.
Buoncristiani, P. C. (2009). Been there. done that… it doesn't work. *Dissent* Autumn/Winter, 27–30.
Cawley, J. et al. (1997). Cognitive ability. Wages. and meritocracy. In B. Devlin et al. (Ed.), *Intelligence. Genes, and success: Scientists respond to the bell curve*. New York: Springer.
Cawley, J., Heckman, J. J., & Vytlacil, E. (1999). On policies to reward the value added by educators. *The Review of Economics and Statistics, 81*, 720–727.
Cobbold. T. (2011, March 31). 'Another Nail in the School Voucher Coffin'. *Save Our Schools*. Accessed 28 August 2012, from http://www.saveourschools.com.au/choice-andcompetition/another-nail-in-the-school-voucher-coffin
Cobbold, T. (2013, 13 August). *Reports concede the lack of evidence for school autonomy. save our schools*. Retrieved September 29, 2013 from http://www.saveourschools.com.au/choice-and-competition/reports-concede-the-lack-evidence-for-school-autonomy
Connors, L. (2006). 'Funding'. paper presented at the Cornerstones Conference. NSW Teachers Federation 2006 (ms)
Darling-Hammond, L. (2007). Race, inequality and educational accountability: the irony of no child left behind. *Race, Ethnicity and Education, 10*, 245–260.
Doherty, L. (2005, 19 May). Literacy levels soar as classes shrink. *Sydney Morning Herald*.
Dowling, A. (2007). *Australia's School Funding System*. Melbourne: ACER. Accessed 28 August 2012, from http://www.acer.edu.au/documents/PolicyBriefs_Dowling07.pdf
Duckworth, A. L., & Seligman, M. E. P. (2005). Self-discipline outdoes IQ in predicting academic performance of adolescents. *Psychological Science, 16*, 939–944.
Dulfer, N., Polesel, J. & Rice, S. (2012, November). *The experience of education: The impacts of high stakes testing n school students and their families*. An Educators Perspective. Whitlam Institute. Retrieved December 2, 2012 from http://www.whitlam.org/__data/assets/pdf_file/0010/409735/High_Stakes_Testing_An_Educators_Perspective.pdf
Eltham, B. (2010, May 19). Who Says BER Funding Is A Rort? Building the Education Revolution' *New Matilda*.
Entwisle, D. R., & Alexander, K. L. (1992). Summer setback: Race, poverty, school composition and mathematics achievement in the first 2 years of school. *American Sociological Review, 57*, 72–84.
Entwisle, D. R., & Alexander, K. L. (1994). Winter setback: The racial composition of schools and learning to read. *American Sociological Review, 59*, 446–460.
Haimson, L. (2010, December 29). Fact-checking shows 'Waiting for Superman' lies. Substance News. Accessed 29 August, from 2012, from http://www.substancenews.net/articles.php?page=1875
Hatcher, R. (2005, May). New Labour. Old Britain , the education business. *Le Monde diplomatique*.
House of Commons. (2008). *Children. Schools and families committee*. Testing and Assessment Third Report of Session 2007-08. London: HMSO. Retrieved August 29, 2012 from http://www.publications.parliament.uk/pa/cm200708/cmselect/cmchilsch/169/169.pdf
Hoyle, R., & Robinson, J. (2003). League tables and school effectiveness: A mathematical model. *Proceedings of the Royal Society London B, 2003*(270), 113–119.
Jopson, D. & Burke, K. (2005, May 7). Unis dumb down for foreign cash. *Sydney Morning Herald*.
Knudsen, E. I., et al. (2006). Economic neurobiological and behavioral perspectives on building Americas future workforce. *World Economics, 7*, 10155–10162.

References

Ladd, H. F. (2011). Education and poverty: Confronting the evidence working papers series SAN11-01. Retrieved August 29, 2011 from http://www.sanford.duke.edu/research/papers/SAN11-01.pdf

Lamb, S. (2007). School Reform and Inequality in Urban Australia, A Case of Residualising the Poor. *International Studies In Educational Inequality. Theory And Policy, 10*,1–38.

Lauder, H. et al (1999). *Trading in Futures Why Markets in education don't Work.* Buckingham, Open University Press.

Martin, A. J. (2006). Personal bests (PBs): A proposed multidimensional model and empirical analysis. *British Journal of Educational Psychology, 76*, 803–825.

Martin, A. J., Arief, G., & Liem, D. (2010). Academic personal bests (PBs). Engagement and achievement: A cross-lagged panel analysis. *Learning and Individual Differences, 20*, 265–270.

McConney, A. & Perry. L. (2010). Science and Mathematics Achievement In Australia, The Role Of School Socioeconomic Composition In Educational Equity and Effectiveness'. *International Journal of Science and Mathematics Education, 8*, 429–452.

Musset, P. (2012). School Choice and Equity, Current Policies in OECD Countries and a Literature Review. *OECD Education Working Papers*. No. 66. Paris: OECD. Accessed 29 August 2012, from http://dx.doi.org/10.1787/5k9fq23507vc-en

Nichols, S. L., & Berliner, D. C. (2008). *Collateral damage. How high-stakes testing corrupts Americas schools.* Cambridge, MA: Harvard Education Press.

O'Neill, S. (2013, 9 August). Overview of the Independent Public Schools Initiative. Retrieved October 14, 2013 from http://www.det.wa.edu.au/independentpublicschools/detcms/navigation/information-for-parents-and-communities/overview-of-the-independent-public-schools-initiative/?oid=Category-id-11366864

Patty, A. (2010, May 25). Streamline teacher sackings. say parents. *Sydney Morning Herald*.

Perry, L. B. 2007. School Composition and Student Outcomes, A Review of Emerging Areas of Research. Australian Association for Research in Education Conference. Accessed 28 August 2012, from http://researchrepository.murdoch.edu.au/7280/

Perry, L. & McConney, A. (2010). School socioeconomic composition and student outcomes in Australia, Implications for educational policy. *Australian Journal of Education 54*, 72–85.

Polesel, J., Dulfer, N. & Turnbull, M. (2012). The experience of education: The impacts of high-stakes testing on school students and their families: Literature Review. Whitlam Institute. January. Retrieved December 2, 2012 from http://www.whitlam.org/__data/assets/pdf_file/0008/276191/High_Stakes_Testing_Literature_Review.pdf

Ravitch, D. (2010). *The death and life of the American school system: How testing and choice are undermining education.* New York: Basic Books.

Rowe, K. J. (2000a). Assessment. League tables and school effectiveness: Consider the issues and let's get real! *Journal of Educational Enquiry, 1*, 73–98.

Rowe, K. J. (2000b). *Multilevel structural equation modeling with MLn/MLwiN & LISREL8.30: An integrated course* (4th ed.) The 7th ACSPRI Winter Program in Social Research Methods and Research Technology. The University of Queensland. Camberwell. Vic: The Australian Council for Educational Research: 46.

Rowe, K. J. (2003). 'The Importance of Teacher Quality as a Key Determinant of Students' Experiences and Outcomes of Schooling'. ACER Research Conference 2003,10. Accessed 6 September 2012, from http://research.acer.edu.au/research_conference_2003/3/.

Schemo, D.J. (2003, 11 July). Questions on Data Cloud Luster of Houston Schools. *New York Times*

School Leaders Inquiry. (2013). Documenting the dimensions. Perth: State school teachers' union of Western Australia. Retrieved October 14, 2013 from http://www.schoolleaders.org.au/

Schoon, I. et al. (2011, 20 April). Family hardship, family instability, and cognitive development. *Journal of Epidemiology and Community Health*.

State School Teachers' Union of Western Australia. (2013). Documenting the dimensions: School leaders inquiry. Retrieved October 14, 2013 from http://www.sstuwa.org.au/sstuwa/school-leader-inquiry

Teese, R. (2012, February 15). Gonksi review, tradition or reform for an upside down system?. *The Conversation*. Accessed 12 September 2012, from http://theconversation.edu.au/gonksi-review-tradition-or-reform-for-an-upside-down-system-5307.

Teese, R. & Lamb, S. (2002). Inequality and public policy. Introduction to the special issue. *Australian Journal of Education. 46,* 105–108.

Thomson, S., & Hillman, K. (2010). *Against the odds: Influences on the post-school success of low performers*. Melbourne: National Centre for Vocational Education Research.

Tomazin, F. (2007, May 16). State failing schools in poor areas. *The Age*.

Tytler, R. & Osborne, J. (2012). Student Attitudes and Aspirations Towards Science. In Barry J Fraser et al. (Eds.), *Second international handbook of science education* (Vol. 1, pp. 597–625). Dordrecht: Springer.

Vickers, M. (2004). Education for all Australians, Comprehensiveness. segregation. and social responsibility. Keynote speech presented at the UWS Annual Education Conference. Parramatta. October 9–10. 2004. Retrieved 3 March 2009, from http://www.manningclark.org.au/html/Paper-Vickers_Margaret-Education_for_all_Australians.html

Waslande, S. et al. (2010). 'Markets in Education - An Analytical Review of Empirical Research on Market Mechanisms in Education'. *OECD Education Working Papers 52*. Retrieved 5 January 2011, from http://www.oecd-ilibrary.org/education/markets-in-education_5km4pskmkr27-en.

Watson. L. & Ryan, C. (2010). 'Choosers and Losers, The Impact of Government Subsidies on Australian Secondary Schools'. *Australian Journal of Education 54*, 86–107.

Wilkinson, I. et al. (2006). *A History of State Aid to Non-Government Schools in Australia. Melbourne,* Educational Transformations Pty Ltd.

Wintour, P & Watt, N. (2010, 25 May 25). Coalition's schools plan to create 2.000 more academies. *The Guardian*.

Chapter 10
Curriculum Matters

10.1 What Should Students be Taught?

The questions of what it is that students should be taught and what they should know and be able to do when they emerge from their education are at the heart of the education debate. Every education philosopher has dealt with it. It is arguably among the most important questions.

Speaking about his book on the corrosive effects of high-states testing (Nichols and Berliner 2008) at an American Association for Education Research (AERA) conference, David Berliner pointed out that American 'founding father' and second President John Adams writing to his wife Abigail in 1780 said, 'I must study politics and war, that our sons may have liberty to study mathematics and philosophy. Our sons ought to study mathematics and philosophy, geography, natural history and naval architecture, navigation, commerce and agriculture in order to give their children a right to study painting, poetry, music, architecture, statuary, tapestry and porcelain.' NCLB meant American students would never meet the goals established by Adams.

It is worth recalling that former politicians in many countries from the 1700s on were highly educated, even if they came from working class backgrounds in which case they would attend school in evenings to improve their knowledge; that was the case in Australia's Prime Minister Ben Chifley for instance. This is a matter which has influence on the policies adopted by governments.

The debate over purpose has drawn a distinction between education as improving the mind and education as training. In many countries for many centuries, improving the mind was something which led students to universities whereas developing skills was something one was trained for at technical colleges. At university one gained a degree, at college one received a certificate or a diploma.

This distinction is important: the proposition was that learning depended mainly on instruction which was taken to mean transfer of knowledge as facts. Successful learning was assessed by the student's ability to regurgitate what had been taught, at most 12 months later. More than that, success at learning was considered to depend on innate intelligence. The result for most individuals by the time they reached maturity was little knowledge and little ability to reason and incorporate new knowledge.

It is a matter of the greatest concern that despite increasing educational standards, a major issue remains the extent to which evidence can overcome preconceived views based often on ideology. If this seems unreasonable consider the large number of people who believe evolution does not correctly describe the process by which humans have got to where they are and equally the number of people who deny that burning of carbon fuels over the last several centuries has anything to do with climate change.

As education historian Diane Ravitch (2010) points out in her survey of American education policy, every American child is taught a substantial slab of history about the US post 1608. But whilst they fly the flag, celebrate Thanksgiving and argue about whether the Civil War was about slavery or the intrusion of the Federal Government into the affairs of the states, knowledge of anything more detailed is generally lacking.

Over the last 30 or so years, education as learning skills has become so prominent a goal that the most elementary outcomes are being given emphasis in curricula and judgements of school quality. With the rise of the accountability demands the result has been standardised testing and communication of average student scores in respect of but a few basic areas of knowledge. This has meant little attention to developing understanding. Since the focus is mainly on literacy and numeracy and the funding of education, like most other publicly funded activities, is constrained, the tests are multiple choice which means teachers can mark the results easily or even that the filled responses can be scanned electronically.

What is lost from this is any appreciation of the broader areas of history, science and the arts including music and much more. What is also lost is what Jonathan Osborne of Stanford University refers to in his consideration of science education as argumentation (see Sect. 6.8). The focus on facts has long meant in many subjects an absence of any treatment of the lives, the struggles and the successes of those who contributed to what we now understand or think we know (Osborne 2010, 2012).

Successful education systems are characterised by a broad and strong curriculum after all. These questions all demand thinking rather than parrot-like responses. That is what a strong curriculum is about. Getting it is unfortunately being bogged down in assertions that school leavers can't spell or add up and subtract. There are surveys of that which are far more reliable than the personal anecdotes of media commentators or the personal opinions of respondents to posts on blog sites. Though literacy rates are often reported to be high, comparison with previous times is appropriate. The answer to low literacy is not more force feeding but a curriculum which engages students.

In Finland, whose students consistently achieve amongst the highest scores in international tests for 15 year olds, every student learns music. We also have fairly good evidence that learning music enhances learning in other subjects. We also

10.1 What Should Students be Taught?

know that learning languages other than the dominant one achieves similar outcomes. All European children learn at least two languages, children in Australia, the US and UK mostly learn only English and even teaching kids from central and south America in Spanish is denied in some US states.

What we have then is a narrowed curriculum demanded by those concerned with skills and the needs of the workforce. Demands for evidence of achievement, as if school achievement means later ability, which it doesn't necessarily, has meant an ongoing limited and largely irrelevant school curriculum dominating many years in the life of most people. Many go on to do all kinds of things which have benefited little from schooling. Designing computers or computer software, writing or playing music, sculpting or drawing. Or working in factories doing rather mundane tasks in jobs that they may not hold a few years after they began paid work. Or driving taxis or delivering the mail. Or not working at all! How can we really justify such outcomes as the return on our investment? How can we be satisfied with a response to this that simply criticises teachers?

Additional support is needed for the education of teachers at tertiary level. Yet universities forced to focus on economic entrepreneurship and respond to demands by students have in some cases reduced or even cancelled courses in mathematics and other subjects. Unless there is a concerted focus on training and developing teachers so that they are fully competent to teach the curriculum, curriculum revision is of little or no value.

Political interference in the curriculum reaches its zenith in modern America. The teaching of evolution is the issue that most readily comes to mind because of the famous Scopes Monkey Trial in Tennessee and the more recent case in which eleven parents of students in Pennsylvania sued the Dover Area School District over the requirement that intelligent design be presented as an alternative to evolution as an explanation of the origin of life. The plaintiffs successfully argued that intelligent design is a form of creationism, and that the school board policy thus violated the Establishment Clause of the First Amendment to the US Constitution.

A more recent case is the redefining of the history curriculum in Texas by that State's Board of Education removing mention of conventions, letters and people that they considered not worthy of being included. The role of religion–but not the separation of church and state–receives emphasis throughout (Foner 2010). Conservatives on the board have pushed for downplaying Thomas Jefferson in one high school course, challenging the idea that the Founding Fathers wanted to separate church and state, and that Franklin D. Roosevelt not only did not end the Great Depression but created it. And so on (Thomma 2010).

In the US the nonprofit Common Core (2009) reviewed the education systems in most of those countries in which students consistently performed better than American students in international tests. Lynne Munson, President and CEO of Common Core, in introducing the Report, wrote… 'a strong similarity among these high-performing nations is evident. Each of the nations that consistently outrank the US on the PISA exam provides their students with a comprehensive, content-rich education in the liberal arts and sciences. These nations differ greatly with regard to how they accomplish this goal. Some have a national curriculum and standards but no tests, others have both, and some leave everything up to the states. Interestingly, no state-based nation in our sample currently has a national curriculum or standards, though one is attempting to develop some.'

Australia is not immune from arguments about history curricula based more on what certain politicians consider to be important events and their beliefs about the inculcation of certain values. Nor is the UK. Education Secretary Michael Gove asserted recently that 'survey after survey has revealed disturbing historical ignorance, with one teenager in five believing Winston Churchill was a fictional character while 58 % think Sherlock Holmes was real' (Ball 2013). It turns out that when a retired teacher sought evidence from the Department of Education in a Freedom of Information (FOI) request, the response was that there were not any reliable surveys at all on which Gove could base his assertion. One tweet commenting on this said, When Gove said: 'survey after survey' showed historical ignorance he meant to say: 'I'm making this up'.

As Common Core (2009) found, '…the common ingredient across these varied nations… is not a delivery mechanism or an accountability system that these high-performing nations share: *it is a dedication to educating their children deeply in a wide range of subjects*' (My emphasis).

10.2 A National Curriculum

In all the debate about curricula, about whether there should be a national curriculum in federated states such as Australia, Canada, the US and Germany, the extent to which the semi-autonomous states will adopt any national determined curriculum is a very moot point. The extent to which training in delivering the curriculum will be given to teachers is seldom addressed yet as one commentator observed surgeons don't operate by themselves in their first year out of university, yet teachers very frequently are expected to teach alone, by themselves, in their first year!

Professor Lyn Yates and Dr Cherry Collins of the University of Melbourne, conducting a project on curriculum policies, talk of a fresh approach to the secondary school curriculum to resolve a dilemma that has been the focus of much attention since the 1980s (Yates and Collins 2008; Yates et al. 2011). In a previous time working class boys and girls were encouraged into more skills-based education and futures. To increase retention of students a 'broad equal opportunity frame' which 'disowned' that past was sought. But academic subjects have been a 'stumbling block' to retention. A hierarchy of subjects has developed where those which universities accepted for tertiary entrance ranking purposes have been considered 'infinitely more prestigious'.

They observe, 'Approaching curriculum as Essential Learnings or capabilities is less tied to inherited cultural capital, and is seen as having more opportunity of differentiating approaches for different students without maintaining a tie to an inherited hierarchy of subjects. In following this route, especially in states like

South Australia and Tasmania, Australia has sought a third way that is neither academic in emphasis nor vocational.'

Yates and Collins see three themes of Australian policy-level discourse converging in the 1980s and 1990s: 'a strong utilitarian vision of education, a particular form of Australian egalitarianism, and a focus on the developing child/learner/person as the key agenda. Employer representatives have promoted observable competencies as the form of knowledge that matters, the outcome sought being that the individual is able to 'do things in the world'.'

They also argue (Yates and Collins 2010) that there has been a strong shift in curriculum policy from an emphasis on knowing things to be able to do things. 'Outcomes, politics and management of resources have greater salience in discussions about curriculum than do knowledge or the developing child.' They noted in their discussions with politicians and bureaucrats a 'naive conviction' that knowledge could be treated as fact and that different kinds of knowledge as in English, Mathematics and Science were considered to be the same kinds of knowledge: placing of environmental education in the same KLA [Key Learning Area] as the study of society—mixing up the physical world with the humanly constructed world, domains which require different foundations and approaches—seemed to be of little consequence. 'In the process of the evolving national curriculum, the response to 'unrelenting pressure' from politicians for curriculum accountability and control and a push for centralisation was to move the national curriculum into process concerns and envisaged children not as learners of content or of coherent bodies of knowledge but as cognitive developers moving onwards and upwards in their cognitive processes.'

Globalisation, particularly the globalisation of capital, and the growth of Information and Communication Technology (ICT) is seen as 'the major medium through which work and other communication happen, has revolutionised the economic world in which young people will have to find work. The new workers need to be able to reinvent themselves, to develop new skills, to move between organisations, and above all to develop the meta-cognitive skills to steer themselves and their own lives.' This is Essential Learnings: what should be taught and what children should know based in 'New Knowledge' focused on competitive advantage and continuous improvement. This was advanced by Education Minister John Dawkins in the Hawke Government mimicking Thatcher's Britain: employers' voices are often sought and heard strongly in the frequent reports that are commissioned to produce directions for the purposes of school overall.

When Rupert Murdoch in his Boyer lectures advocated greater involvement in school education, as did the Business Council of Australia, then Minister for Education Julia Gillard agreed! Some businesses claim that the education system does not produce appropriately qualified people and have therefore set up their own education colleges. Corporations are involved in running some of the Academies in England and are active in the politics of education in the US. As has been shown elsewhere (Salancik and Pfeffer 1977) those in power tend to define problems in ways that entrench their power: those terms which give emphasis to authority are those which dominate the discourse.

The Australian Curriculum and Assessment Authority (ACARA) established by the Rudd-Gillard Labor Government in 2008 is charged with developing a uniform national curriculum for Australian schools. Not surprisingly there has been argument over many aspects of the proposed curriculum for each subject area. A reflection of Australia as a federation rather than a nation? Canada, a nation of federated provinces whose students perform slightly better than Australian students in international tests, does not have a national curriculum! Formulation of a national curriculum with its statement of outcomes provides the opportunity for standardised testing of the knowledge supposedly gained from studying the curriculum.

10.3 The History Wars

Amongst the greatest ongoing arguments are those about what should be taught in history. History is something that strongly influences identity. History is generally seen as knowledge of the history of one's ancestors, of the country one lives in. Our history knowledge shapes our attitudes to current events and possible futures and relationships.

Quite often the subjects which politicians demand should be taught are one's which students consider dull and boring and lead them to dismiss the whole subject. Some parents demand that the curriculum to be taught to their children should be the same that they were taught. It is as if there have been no advances in knowledge and understanding over the previous 20 or so years since the parents were at school. The teaching of physics is not expected to make no mention of quantum mechanics (though some expect advances in biology or environmental science to be not taught). Should modern history ignore the collapse of the Soviet Union, the emergence of the European Union or the Middle East conflicts of the last 10 years!

In a supplement to a major report on history in the USA by Roy Rosenzweig of George Mason University and David Thelen of Indiana University, *The Presence of the Past* (Rosenzweig and Thelen 1998) Rosenzweig observed, 'While the history wars have often focused on content–what should be taught in classes or presented in exhibits–our respondents were more interested in talking about the experience and process of engaging the past. They preferred to make their own histories. When they confronted historical accounts constructed by others, they sought to examine them critically and connect them to their own experiences or those of people close to them.' As in other commentaries on teaching of history, and other subjects, respondents pointed out, presentations did not give them credit for their critical abilities. Commercialised histories on television or textbook-driven high school classes failed to engage or influence them.

Given this preference for history as an active and collaborative venture, many respondents to Rosenzweig and Thelen's survey found fault with a school-based history organized around the memorization of facts locked into a prescribed textbook curriculum. They implicitly rejected the recommendations of conservative commentators on history in the schools. For them, the reason students don't know enough 'history' (as defined by standardized tests and textbooks) is the rise of multiculturalism and the decline of a traditional curriculum based on the patriotic story of the American nation—'the very curriculum our respondents described as insulting to their ability as critical thinkers'.

Professor Joyce Appleby, Professor of American History at the University of California (Los Angeles), delivering the American Historical Association Presidential Address in 1997 (Appleby 1997) observed that historians now confront a challenge strikingly different from that of previous times. 'The static in our conversation with the public comes not from an inappropriately positivistic view of history but from its very opposite–confusion about the nature of historical knowledge and the amount of credibility it deserves. Such confusion can well incite indifference, even antagonism. You can't learn what history has to impart if you start with a false idea of what history is and how historians–amateurs and professionals alike–acquire knowledge about the past.' As Appleby pointed out, without genuine understanding people become susceptible to rumours of cultural warfare and academic conspiracies.

Professor Tony Taylor of Monash University completed in 2000 *The Future of the Past*, a Report of the National Inquiry into School History (Taylor 2000) which was followed by a number of other documents (Taylor and Young 2003). Taylor observed, 'school history is most successfully managed in secondary schools if students are given the opportunity to study topics in depth in a manner which allows contemplation of, and response to, evidence, content and issues, in balanced combination.'

Taylor's Inquiry heard that history was often marginalised within 'Studies of Society' and 'the Environment' (SOSE). Proper consultation appeared to have not occurred; implementation appeared to have been hasty, curriculum officials had excessive workloads, little or no background in school history and little or no direct contact with schools. In Primary School, many teachers were inadequately trained.

The Inquiry recommended that a National History Project be established which amongst other things would lead to 'a clearer focus on history as valuable part of lifelong learning which will allow all students to appreciate more fully their heritage and their environment'. A closer collaboration between academic historians, history teachers and professional historians was called for as was 'more effective, locally delivered, sustained professional development specifically aimed at history teachers'.

A comparative study of history teaching in Australia and Canada (Clark 2008) found, again, low levels of knowledge of their country's past by students. Whilst students 'overwhelmingly acknowledge the importance of learning' about their national history in school, many criticised the subject for being dull and boring. Lack of coherence between school or grade levels, repetition of the same material, were frequent complaints. 'Students want a subject that allows them to be critical, to reconcile different points of view, and to use their imagination, rather than recite 'what happened. Teachers report lack of adequate teaching resources and professional development opportunities.'

10.4 Science Education for What?

Enrolments in science are increasingly seen as a problem though the relationship with the declining opportunities for employment in science jobs is seldom explored. Education in science is not just training for those students who intend to become scientists in adult life. And that is the problem! This has been apparent for a very long time and is being strongly addressed within the European community.

At a global level UNESCO in 1993 launched measures to bring about a more thorough infusion of scientific and technological culture into society consistent with the *World Declaration on Education for All*. The need to do this is widely recognised and has been for decades but implementation is a quite different matter (UNESCO 2000). In many countries, including Australia, many politicians and policy makers give support to science only to the extent that it has instrumental relevance, that it contributes to economic growth. The personal experience of the Hon Barry Jones, sometime Minister for Science, was one of continual frustration at the refusal of politicians and bureaucrats alike to grasp the fundamentals of the relevance of this to the growth of society and individuals (Jones 2006, pp. 371–388).

Long time advocate for science teaching, Ruth Dircks, a former President of the Science Teachers Association of Australia (and winner of the 2002 Prime Ministers Prize for Excellence in Science Teaching in Secondary Schools) pointed out a few years ago that 'from time to time the scientific community asks the same question, namely what is wrong with school science? And as a result a report is asked for, often one is produced and then nothing significant happens' (Dircks 2008).

A report commissioned by the Australian Science Teachers Association in 1984 on the place of science in the curriculum drew attention to a lack of community awareness of the role of science, a shortage of trained science teachers and inadequacy of in-service support; there was no national science curriculum outline and many teachers lacked a positive attitude to teaching science. Dircks concluded that what was needed was experts in pedagogy, not in science. When the pedagogy has been sorted out we can finally turn to the scientists.

Peter Aubusson of the University of Technology Sydney has pointed out that 'Governments periodically pay close attention to science education with a view to ensuring it does its work for our society and that we perform in the international contest. This is a mixed blessing, because, while it provides occasional injections of funds, it also brings intrusive scrutiny, criticism and demands for change. Typically there are calls for better science, more scientists and a more scientifically literate society. Consequently, from time to time, ideal outlines for school science are generated for translation into curriculum.' Like many others, Aubusson pointed out that science achievement, at all levels, has become a global competition in which nations want to be seen to triumph (Aubusson 2011).

Aubusson (2013) echoed Dircks' point about periodic concern when he said more recently, 'Every now and then we manufacture a crisis in Australian school

10.4 Science Education for What?

science. People write reports. These recommend change, including curriculum change, and point out the ways in which current patterns of school science education fail. We start by thinking differently about school science, what is taught, how it is taught and what learning about science at school should mean. We imagine better ways of doing things. Then we lose our way and end by doing school science much as we always have.' He observed 'Education is a fundamentally conservative act as each generation seeks to pass on to the next what it needs to know and do. In a world where we no longer can know what we need for a creative and productive future, science education cannot play it safe. It is counter-intuitive but a conservative approach to science education is risky. As a recipe for success, it may deliver failure.'

Claims that students see science as taught to be irrelevant to their lives and the 'response' that too few scientists and engineers are being trained to meet future demands are ongoing. Almost half the university students studying science, maths, technology and engineering do not think their course is relevant to Australian life, a study by Universities Australia late 2011 commissioned by Australia's chief scientist found; students lacked appreciation of the relevance and role of those disciplines in their lives and communities, and of its potential for rewarding career opportunities (Rosenberg 2012).

Students see a disjunction between traditional images of science, particularly as represented in science education and the way contemporary science operates and the abilities required of those working in the field. Working scientists, science graduates working in other areas and year 11 science students interviewed by Russell Tytler and David Symington of Deakin University 'argued for a science education less focused on knowledge structures and more on skills, thinking, preparing for lifelong learning and engagement with science' (Tytler and Symington 2006).

In his foreword to the report *Re-imagining Science Education Engaging students in science for Australia's future* by Tytler (2007), then Australian Chief Scientist Jim Peacock recognised the need to re-energise science, that the way he learned science at school no longer met the needs of today's students (Tytler 2007). Tytler reported on teacher's perception of the science curriculum as rigid, preventing innovation and driven by conservative forces including the cultural conservatism of staff in schools and parents. New approaches are needed for assessment. Academic scientists on panels advocate training undergraduates for narrow discipline knowledge and resist change in the curriculum. The dominant mode of school and tertiary science has somehow got out of kilter with the needs and interests of contemporary society and contemporary youth (Tytler 2007, p. 67).

Peter Fensham, one of Australia's most distinguished researchers in the field of science education, has surveyed the situation in numerous publications. He pointed out that the 'Relevance of Science Education' (ROSE) project of Svein Sjøberg in Oslo surveyed 15–16 year old students in more than 30 countries. Those in industrialised countries, like Australia, are more interested in topics that rarely occur in school science (Fensham 2006).

Whilst most students agree science and technology are important for society they are less likely to agree that science benefits outweigh possible harmful effects and most do not like science compared with other subjects or consider that school science has made them more critical and sceptical and more appreciative of nature. However, positively received approaches to science include presentation of science as a story involving persons, situations and action, real world situations that students can engage with, focal questions that they can engage with and contexts as the source and power of concepts. Moreover, positive responses also attend clearly presented science relating to issues of personal and social significance which are engaging and present problems for investigation.

Fensham refers to the 'humanistic' curriculum developed by Glen Aikenhead, Professor of Curriculum Studies at the University of Saskatchewan. 'Academic science in Australia has been reluctant to endorse changes in science curricula with humanistic characteristics. For academic science, the sciences in schooling were preparatory and prerequisite for science-based study at university. Academic science has exercised control to maintain this situation directly, or indirectly through well socialised disciples among the teaching force. Undergraduate studies [have thus left] graduates for other careers, such as school teaching, deficient in aspects other than foundational conceptual knowledge' (Aikenhead 2006).

As Jonathan Osborne, now at Stanford University, says, 'Science education wrestles with two competing priorities: the need to educate the future citizen about science; and the need to provide the basic knowledge necessary for future scientists. It is argued that the evidence would suggest that it is the latter goal that predominates – a goal which exists at least, in part, in conflict with the needs of the majority who will not continue with science post compulsory education.' (Osborne 2006) He continued, '… sciences dilemma is that it can only function effectively within a tradition where it is taught as received knowledge, knowledge that is unequivocal, uncontested and unquestioned.'

When science is presented to the young student as a body of authoritative knowledge to be accepted and believed the unity and salience of such information is likely apparent to those who hold an overview of the domain but its significance for the young student is arcane: only those who finally enter the inner sanctum of the world of the practising scientist will have any sense of coherence. 'Consequently, only those that ever reach the end get to comprehend the wonder and beauty of the edifice that has been constructed.'

Attitudes toward science are not necessarily scientific attitudes and attitudes toward school science are not necessarily the same as attitudes toward science in general. University academics have substantial influence over the secondary school curriculum in science, as many have said. But they are often not familiar with, indeed may be antagonistic toward, current notions of effective learning such as constructivism. Laboratory work generates positive experiences but school science often fails to generate sufficient experiences of this nature. Aikenhead is also quoted by Tytler and Osborne (2012, p. 608), 'Rote, recitation and expository teaching might provide teachers with a sense of security as they enable to the teacher to remain firmly in control, they make it less likely that the classroom will become a theatre for dealing with awkward, contingent questions which deal with issues of evidence and reasons for belief...'.

Further, instruments for reliably assessing the effectiveness of learning of science do not necessarily lead to an understanding of how knowledge and understanding are developed. The role of argumentation is often not appreciated. Surveys which find that less than 50 % of students have an interest in science cause alarm in some quarters about the future supply of scientists. However, a substantial proportion of respondents do show an interest and as Tytler and Osborne observe the concern may well be exaggerated.

Many prominent scientists issue statements of concern about the low number of students expressing an interest in science but very seldom do they address the kinds of issues which Fensham and Osborne and others have drawn attention to.

On a visit to the famous Exploratorium in San Francisco in its brand new quarters at one of the piers along the eastern side of the city on a Thursday evening in April 2013 the science center was crowded with young adults, mostly couples, actively engaged in experimenting with the exhibits. The Exploratorium is known for its innovative approach to experimentation with phenomena about the natural world: whilst its exhibits have been copied by many science centres and museums around the world, few have gone beyond the copying to the way in which they engage visitors with the exhibits.

The Exploratorium has a very large number of 'explainers' on the floor and visitors can see into the laboratory where new exhibits are being constructed. A visit to the Exploratorium hardly supports the proposition that there is not much interest in science. The Exploratorium is also clear about its business: it presents phenomena. There are no exhibits on climate change or space exploration! The exhibits explore the phenomena relevant to those outcomes and activities.

10.5 Science Education in the European Union

The issues and tensions in the discussion about the science curriculum in Australia are mirrored in the experience of the European Union. Interestingly they are also found in the debate about curriculum reform in China in the last 10 years: the focus on student-centred learning and the constructivist approach to curriculum reform involving the sciences has sparked opposition from prominent academic scientists claiming that the integrity of the discipline has been compromised and the supply of needed scientists for the nation threatened.

The approach adopted by the countries of the European Union to the teaching of science (and technology) makes a very interesting comparison with what is being done in other countries. The European Commission, often criticised in non-European countries for all sorts of reasons is, perhaps surprisingly, able to develop strategies in a more coherent manner than is seen in other countries such as Australia and the US which are federations of states, not distinct nation states.

A 'High Level Group on Science Education' chaired by Michel Rocard, Prime Minister of France under Francois Mitterrand from 1988 to 1991 and a member of the European Parliament, was appointed by the Commission and reported in 2007. The Report (Rocard et al. 2007) observed that, in the light of declining interest in science by young people, Europe's longer term capacity to innovate, and the quality of its research will decline unless more effective action is taken.

The origins of the declining interest among young people in science studies were found by Rocard's group to be due largely to the way science is taught in schools. '… whereas the science education community mostly agrees that pedagogical practices based on inquiry-based methods are more effective, the reality of classroom practice is that in the majority of European countries, these methods are simply not being implemented.' Current initiatives in Europe actively pursue renewal of science education through 'inquiry -based' methods.

Inquiry-based science education (IBSE) had proved its efficacy at both primary and secondary levels in increasing children's and students' interest and attainments levels, the Group found, while at the same time stimulating teacher motivation. '… IBSE pedagogy… creates opportunities for involving firms, scientists, researchers, engineers, universities, local actors such as cities, associations, parents and other kinds of local resources'. Participation of cities and the local community in the renewal of science education was seen as important. Examples are Pollen and Sinus-Transfer.

('Pollen' is a project focused on the creation of 12 'Seed Cities', educational territories that support primary science education through the commitment of the whole community, and is aimed at primary teachers in twelve European countries of the European Union with an emphasis on teaching through inquiry. 'Sinus' and 'Sinus-Transfer' provide secondary school teachers in Germany with tools to change their pedagogical approach to science teaching in secondary school. The focus of these projects has been primarily on pedagogy and not on transforming the content itself.)

10.6 Mathematics: Not Just Skills but a Discipline Requiring Understanding

The issues confronting the teaching of history and science are replicated in other disciplines. Celia Hoyles, Professor of Mathematics at the University of London and adviser to the British Government, emphasises that mathematics is not just numeracy or a set of skills but a discipline requiring understanding (Hoyles 2010).

She talks of the importance of professional development for mathematics teachers, not just a day out at some kind of refresher but serious several day workshops and opportunities for teachers to be connected to a mathematics expert for advice when needed. She also sees as necessary the placing of a mathematics content expert in each primary school, pointing out that simply having an extra assistant in the classroom or the school does not meet the need. England is a country, she observes, where it is fashionable to not like or even understand mathematics and tells of the presentation to her of the OBE by Queen Elizabeth 2, who, when asked if she liked mathematics said in a loud voice, 'Heavens no!'

The inquiry into 'Post-14 Mathematics Education in the UK' by Professor Adrian Smith, distinguished British statistician and former high-level academic, considered it 'as vital that society fully recognises the importance of mathematics: its importance for its own sake, as an intellectual discipline; for the knowledge economy; for science, technology and engineering; for the workplace; and for the individual citizen' (Smith 2004).

'The Inquiry draws attention to possible factors underlying this decline including perceived poor quality of the teaching and learning experience, perceived relative difficulty of the subject, failure of the curriculum to excite interest and the lack of awareness of the importance of mathematical skills for future career options and advancement.'

Very recently Professor Steve Sparks, chairman of the UK Advisory Committee on Mathematics Education, said that maths should be compulsory for all students until 18 or 19—no matter what else they are studying (Bellos 2012). The UK government wants universities to be more involved in the design of A-levels, the examination recognized as the standard for assessing suitability for progression to university; complaints continue that the science exams don't contain enough maths to progress to science degrees! (Burns 2012).

10.7 Curriculum Reform Must Focus on Understanding and Intellectual Development

The editorial introduction for the a special issue of the *European Journal of Education* (Yates and Young 2010) concludes, 'The new curricular principles of competence, capability, and outcomes, and the emphasis on 'doing' rather than 'knowing', however well intentioned, are hardly a recipe for a 'knowledge society for all'. They complained of the emphasis on procedures that were measurable and accountable, rather than subject-based concepts, as a basis for understanding and intellectual development. They saw a new alliance of 'managerial ideals and radical populism' challenging 'the formerly self-evident values of a self-regulating 'big' science'.

The introduction to a National Curriculum Symposium held at Melbourne University in February 2010 asked, 'What is a rich, creative and coherent curriculum for young Australians in the twenty first century?' (Documents referring to this symposium, other than a program listing speakers and topics, are no longer available on the University of Melbourne website.) The recently completed 'Primary Review' in the UK was noted as making 'trenchant criticisms of England's existing national curriculum... and of the UK government's current curriculum reforms.' The finding based on the Review's extensive evidence showed how children's statutory entitlement to curriculum breadth and balance had been severely compromised by a standards agenda of high-stakes testing and prescribed national teaching, and by excessive micro-management of the day-to-day work of schools.

The Review proposed an alternative framework driven by 21st Century aims, grounded in contemporary evidence about childhood, society and the wider world, guaranteeing children's entitlement to breadth, depth and balance, combining national requirements with a protected community curriculum devised locally, and encouraging greater professional creativity and flexibility.

In his book published in 1997 *Is Australia an Asian Country?* (Crows Nest: Allen and Unwin) Stephen Fitzgerald, Australia's first ambassador to China and principle author of a 'National Strategy for Asian Studies', strongly advanced the proposition that Australians needed to gain a greater understanding of Asian communities, to move away from the complacent eurocentred approach to international relations and international business. Whilst Australia does more business with Asia, especially in exporting its raw materials, there has been little change in school curricula.

Towards the end of his term as President of the World Bank in 2005 Australian James Wolfensohn urged government to support sending young people to Asian countries following their education. Though many would gain not very much, many others would benefit substantially. The proposal was not adopted.

Prime Minister Gillard released a White Paper in late 2012 entitled *Australia in the Asian Century*. Amongst other goals the paper called for all school children having continual access to one of five priority Asian languages. The thrust of this policy was referenced in the reforms proposed in response to the Gonski Panel's Review of Funding for Schooling in Australia.

A broad curriculum is one of the elements of all effective education systems. A narrowed curriculum combined at the same time with demands for inclusion of more subjects, often ones which previously were within the responsibility of the parent, leads to increasing superficiality in educational outcomes. Teachers capable of teaching the curriculum, adequate training and ongoing development are all essential. Complaints by politicians, parents and the media about poor outcomes, a focus on inadequate content knowledge but not on pedagogical competence, are wholly unhelpful.

In certain areas such as history and science, political interference has sought to vary curricula to accord with uninformed views as what constitutes history and science. Such efforts ignore the nature of history and historical research and the nature of scientific theory and its development. Great effort can be expended in developing a national curriculum yet the relevance of the fact that in successful school systems in many countries such as Finland and Canada teachers are allowed substantial flexibility in how they teach the curriculum is seldom mentioned.

Too often an emphasis is sought on skill-based education rather than education which would address wider issues including most particularly the need to

10.7 Curriculum Reform Must Focus on Understanding and Intellectual Development

understand issues and develop the ability to ask questions so as to arrive at independent judgement. Students are seldom credited with having sufficient critical ability.

Academic subjects are often seen as a stumbling block. In many cases the curriculum as taught is devoid of context and a human approach disembodied of people, the scientists and their struggles, the ordinary people in history, the failures and successes and the factors that influenced them. The approach to science education in the European Union and its focus on 'inquiry-based' methods of instruction deserve much more attention in countries like Australia.

Narrowing of the curriculum and the teaching of subjects disembodied of argumentation restricts learning and demands by parents and employers as to what should be taught overrides the professionalism of teachers. Focusing on what should be taught rather than how it should be taught ignores decades of research about learning. Requiring certain views to be taught which lack an underpinning in genuine inquiry, such as only one view of history, amounts to indoctrination, not education.

A national curriculum might be helpful but is not the most important aspect of education. Australia should learn from other countries and frame a curriculum which meets the expectations of students without denying the legitimate claims of those knowledgeable about curriculum issues and the current debates. Too often the argument about the content of curricula implies that the Gradgrind imperative of what is learned is far more important than the generation of a genuine interest in the subject and a wish to know more! The aim of education is the stimulation of curiosity and the encouragement of creativity.

References

Aikenhead, G. S. (2006). *Science education for everyday life evidence-based practice*. New York: Teachers College Press, Columbia University.

Appleby, J. (1997). The power of history. AHA Presidential Address 1997. Retrieved October 13, 2012 from http://www.historians.org/info/aha_history/jappleby.htm

Aubusson, P. (2011). An Australian science curriculum: Competition, advances and retreats. *Australian Journal of Education, 55*(3), 229–244.

Aubusson, P. (2013, 12 May). Science in schools: Can we choose a better future? *The Conversation*. Retrieved May 29, 2013 from https://theconversation.com/science-in-schools-can-we-choose-a-better-future-12508

Ball, J. (2013, 13 May). Gove's claims of teenager's ignorance harpooned by retired teacher. *The Guardian*

Bellos, A. (2012, 23 January). How to learn to love maths. *The Guardian*

Burns, J. (2012). A-level sciences lack the maths students need. BBC News 27 April.

Clark, A. (2008). *A comparative study of history teaching in Australian and Canada final report*. Clayton, Victoria: Monash University. Retrieved August 15, 2012 from http://www.historyteacher.org.au/files/200804_HistoryTeachingReport.pdf

Common Core. (2009). *Why were behind: What top nations teach their students but we don't*. Retrieved August 15, 2012 from http://www.giarts.org/article/why-were-behind-report-common-core

Dircks, R. (2008, 22 June). How many reports do we need? ABC Radio National 'Ockham's Razor'. Retrieved August 15, 2012 from http://www.abc.net.au/radionational/programs/ockhamsrazor/how-many-reports-do-we-need/3269176

Fensham, P. J. (2006). *Student interest in science: The problem possible solutions and constraints*. ACER Research Conference 2006:70–73. Retrieved August 15, 2012 from http://acer.edu.au/documents/RC2006_Fensham.pdf

Foner, E. (2010, 5 April).Twisting story in Texas. *The Nation*.

Hoyles, C. (2010). *Rich collaborations: The case of mathematics*. Paper at the Melbourne Graduate School of Education National Curriculum Symposium. University of Melbourne 2–27 February. ms.

Jones, B. (2006). *A thinking reed*. Crows Nest: Allen & Unwin.

Nichols, S. L., & Berliner, D. C. (2008). *Collateral damage. How high-stakes testing corrupts Americas schools*. Cambridge, MA: Harvard Education Press.

Osborne, J. (2006). *Towards a science education for all: The role of ideas. Evidence and argument*. ACER Research Conference 2006 (pp. 2–5). Retrieved August 15, 2012 from http://acer.edu.au/documents/RC2006_Osborne.pdf

Osborne, J. (2010). Arguing to learn in science: The role of collaborative. Critical discourse. *Science, 328*, 463–466.

Osborne, J. (2012). The role of argument: Learning how to learn in school science. In Barry J. Fraser, et al. (Eds.), *Second international handbook of science education 2* (pp. 933–949). Dordrecht: Springer.

Ravitch, D. (2010). *The death and life of the American school system: How testing and choice are undermining education*. New York: Basic Books.

Rocard, M. et al. (2007). *Science education now: A renewed pedagogy for the future of Europe*. Brussels: European Commission Director General for Research. Retrieved August 15, 2012 from http://ec.europa.eu/research/science-society/document_library/pdf_06/report-rocard-on-science-education_en.pdf

Rosenberg, J. (2012, 20 January). Sydney Morning Herald: Students don't see relevance in uni courses.

Rosenzweig, R. & Thelen, D. (1998). *The presence of the past. Popular uses of history in American life*. Columbia University Press. Web site supplement Afterthoughts: Roy Rosenzweig: Everyone a Historian. Retrieved August 15, 2012 from http://chnm.gmu.edu/survey/afterroy.html

Salancik, G. R., & Pfeffer, J. (1977). Who gets power and how they hold on to it: A strategic contingency model of power. *Organisational Dynamics, 5*, 3–21.

Smith, A. (2004). Making Mathematics Count. The Report of Professor Adrian Smith's Inquiry into Post-14 Mathematics Education. London: HMSO. Retrieved August 16, 2012 from http://www.mathsinquiry.org.uk/report/index.html

Taylor, T. (2000). *The future of the past: Final report of the National Inquiry into School History*. Canberra: Department of Education. Training and Youth Affairs.

Taylor, T. & Young, C. (2003). *Making history a guide for the teaching and learning of history in Australian schools*. Canberra: Department of Education Science and Training. Microsoft Word edition (2004). Retrieved August 15, 2012 from http://www.hyperhistory.org/images/assets/pdf/complete.pdf

Thomma, S. (2010, April 1). Not satisfied with U.S. history, some conservatives are rewriting it. Is American history being changed? *McClatchy Newspapers*.

Tytler, R. (2007). *Re-imagining science education. Engaging students in science for Australia's future*. Camberwell: ACER Press.

Tytler, R. & Osborne, J. (2012). Student attitudes and aspirations towards science. In Barry J Fraser et al. (Eds.). *Second international handbook of science education* (Vol. 1, pp. 597–625). Dordrecht: Springer.

Tytler, R. & Symington, D. (2006). *Boosting science learning: What will it take?* ACER Research Conference 2006 (pp. 40–41). Retrieved August 15, 2012 from http://acer.edu.au/documents/RC2006_TytkerandSymington.pdf

UNESCO. (2000). Science for the Twenty-First Century. World Conference on Science: 156 et seq. Retrieved 15 August 2012, from http://www.unesco.org/science/wcs

Yates, L. & Collins, C. (2008). *Australian curriculum 1975–2005: What has been happening to knowledge?* Paper for the Australian Association for Research in Education conference. Brisbane. December. Retrieved August 15, 2012 from http://web.education.unimelb.edu.au/curriculumpoliciesproject/pdf/YAT081051%20AARE2008.pdf

Yates, L., & Collins, C. (2010). The absence of knowledge in Australian Curriculum Reforms. *European Journal of Education, 45*, 89–102.

Yates, L., Collins, C., & O'Connor, K. (2011). *Australia's curriculum dilemmas: State cultures and the big issue*. Melbourne: Melbourne University Press.

Yates, L., & Young, M. (2010). Editorial. Globalisation. Knowledge and the curriculum. *European Journal of Education, 45*(1), 4–10.

Chapter 11
Creativity to Free Choice Learning

11.1 What Creativity is

Creativity, as Wikipedia explains, is most often defined as the creation of novel useful products, in other words both novelty and utility contribute to the understanding of creativity. But as used in this essay it is intended to refer to something more: besides the development of artistic works, it is intended to refer to the association of things that previously have not been associated. In that respect it shares some of the characteristics of innovation which can refer to the realm of ideas, not just inventions, an idea made manifest. One writer has observed that there are over 100 different definitions of creativity in the literature.

Creativity is one of the major issues in education yet it receives hardly any attention in the education debate. As explained in Chap. 10, the focus of much of the debate is instead on what will be 'useful'. That is assumed to be 'knowledge' and, despite all the recent research showing otherwise, teaching is generally perceived as the transmission of that 'knowledge' by 'experts' (the teacher) to 'novices' (the students). As a result, what we end up with is not very useful at all, as is shown by the attitude of the students to the content of their instruction and their actual understanding of it in later years!

Whilst demands for conformity increase through life, thereby diminishing the level of innovation generally calls for innovation are being made all the time. Creativity is not confined to young children or a few adults but finds expression in individual interests and hobbies, in ordinary everyday discoveries. Taking risks and being prepared to be wrong, knowing to how to learn from mistakes, are critical. Stories abound of people who succeed in later life from finding what can be called one's element, that pursuit for which one really has a passion.

Often creativity and innovation find expression in what is called 'free choice learning', visits to museums, botanic gardens and the like. Here people pursue their own special interests. The understanding of the nature of learning in these informal settings has increased dramatically over the last 30 years as these institutions have developed a huge variety of public program offering interaction with their collections and accumulated knowledge.

This essay explores these areas of creativity, innovation and learning outside the formal settings of school.

Professor Tim Jackson from the University of Surrey, until very recently Sustainability Commissioner in Britain, tells the story of installing taping around the windows and doors in his house to keep out the drafts. His 5 years old daughter was helping him '…in the way that 5 year-olds do. And we'd been doing this for a while; when she turned to me very solemnly and said, "Will this really keep out the giraffes?"'

One of the most prominent speakers of creativity and education is Sir Ken Robinson. One-time Professor of Education at Warwick University in England, Robinson now advises the Getty Foundation. He criticizes the education system for failing to change, for not coping with present and future society and its challenges (Robinson and Aronica 2009). The system, he says, was designed and conceived in the context of nineteenth century industrialism based on a certain view of the mind.

He tells numerous stories about young children and creativity to emphasise how creative young children are. His point is that much of what happens in later life drives out creativity. Robinson's numerous talks are full of anecdotes. One concerns his son's appearance in a Nativity play when he was 4 years old. In the part where the three kings come in bearing gifts, bringing gold, frankincense and myrrh, something funny happened. 'Anyway, the three boys came in, 4-year-olds with tea towels on their heads, and they put these boxes down, and the first boy said, "I bring you gold." And the second boy said, "I bring you myrrh". And the third boy said, "Frank sent this." Kids will have a go, they are not frightened of being wrong. If you're not prepared to be wrong, you'll never come up with anything original.'

Another of Robinson's stories is about God. 'I heard a great story recently of a little girl who was in a drawing lesson. She was six and she was at the back, drawing, and the teacher said this little girl hardly ever paid attention, and in this drawing lesson she did. The teacher was fascinated: she went over to her and asked, "What are you drawing?" And the girl replied, "I'm drawing a picture of God." And the teacher said, "But nobody knows what God looks like." The girl assured her, "They will in a minute."'

Young children are extraordinarily capable of coping with diverse situations and interpretations rich in ambiguity, are able to incorporate new situations into their existing experience and come up with new understandings, to continually reinvent their worlds. They tolerate events and statements that most adults would consider silly or even dismiss as just ignorant. We can see it in their games so rich in make-believe, games in which one child might say to another you can be a mummy but you don't have any children.

Artists like Picasso recognised this: 'All children are artists. The problem is how to remain an artist once he grows up.' The easy facility that young children have with new technology from computers to DVD recorders is evidence of this. Very young children happily tap away at computer keyboards, and often tap on any screen that looks like it might react and can't understand why nothing happens.

At a general level measures of creativity are correlated with measures of intelligence. But more specifically it is distinct from intelligence. Creativity is as

11.1 What Creativity is

important as literacy. In the last few decades, in the US and more recently in Australia, the drive to measure everything has led to a narrowly focused view of education which has marginalised even further any attention to creativity. But one cannot say that creativity is not valued.

Tests of creativity are readily available and so are courses on how to administer appropriate ones. The most widely used are the Torrance Tests of Creative Thinking which uses picture-based exercises to assess mental characteristics and creative strengths such as fluency, originality, emotional expressiveness, internal visualisation, richness of imagery, storytelling and fantasy. Creativity Engineering promises to teach people how to 'think outside the box'. In this there is a connection with innovation which indeed depends heavily on creativity.

There continues to be an ongoing debate about creativity and education. One view rejects the proposition that research on creativity should be directed toward unambiguous expressions of talent (Runco 2008). Rather, creative potential should be the primary concern for educators. Children do not need to learn how to have ideas.

Preschool children are fluent and original as soon as they can communicate... teachers often appreciate creativity in a general sense but have little tolerance for the characteristics which are necessary for it (e.g., unconventional thinking, intrinsic motivation).

11.2 Creativity is What Makes us Human

When we are very young most of us are very creative: the stories commencing this essays show that. The games played by young children who often imagine the life of adults learned from watching parents or adults or films. Many of the things very young children say are what they imagine adults like them would say: in the Seven-Up series which followed a number of children from Britain over their lives through late adulthood a 7 years old asked what he read said, 'I read the Financial Times'.

A common view is that by the time we reach early adulthood most of us have lost it.[1] Something happens between those times remembered by most as carefree and innocent and the much more confined and correct times as adults, times we so looked forward to. It is reasonable to assume that schooling has something to do with it. It is *not* reasonable to claim that it is only the education system which is responsible: it is the entire environment in which we grow up. Some research suggests a decline in creativity in US children in the last several decades: though IQ scores are on the rise, scores on the Torrance Tests of Creative Thinking have been declining since 1990 (Merryman 2010). However, other recent research

---

[1] Many people, including Ken Robinson, writing about creativity refer to a story about decline of creativity as assessed by tests used by America's National Aeronautics and Space Administration, NASA, to measure thinking in engineers and scientists. I have been completely unable to find any verification of this including from NASA itself; a reference to a study by a George Land is often given but that does not contain the data or reference the source of the story as alleged!

suggests an increase in the use of imagination by children now even though they play less often than they used to (Case Western Reserve University 2012).

Advances in every area of endeavour are due to creativity, not to doing the same thing over and over, not to behaving in prescribed ways, not to just working hard and not to learning what we are told to learn. But to experimenting, to being creative. Being creative doesn't only mean being artistic, though that is an important area of creativity. More importantly, it means having the courage to try things which are new or unusual, and fail. An important feature is to associate things that do not seem to be connected to each other. Executives in progressive companies and other enterprises value this ability to think laterally and therefore are interested in education programs that develop that.

Many advances are due to what seem accidents or to unexpected coincidences or relationships. Nobel physics prizewinner and genius Richard Feynman found clues to his research that eventually won him the prize for his work on quantum electrodynamics by watching plates wobble as they spun across the Cornell University refectory room. 'As the plate went up in the air I saw it wobble, and I noticed the red medallion of Cornell on the plate going around... I start figuring out the motion of the rotating plate. I went on to work out equations for wobbles. Then I thought about how the electron orbits start to move in relativity... the whole business that I got the Nobel Prize for came from that piddling around with the wobbling plate.' (This is explained on the Wolfram Demonstration Project internet site at http://demonstrations.wolfram.com/FeynmansWobblingPlate/. Accessed Retrieved 21 April 2013)

Marie Attard, a young scientist in Australia, uses the same computer software that engineers use to predict weak points in materials when designing buildings, cars and aircraft wings to find out if the skull of the now extinct Thylacine or Tasmanian Tiger was capable of allowing it to kill sheep, as alleged by graziers in the decades leading to its extinction (Attard 2011).

The solution to the problem of Fermat's Last Theorem was only reached after incorporating the results from branches of mathematics quite different from those where Andrew Wiles had started (Singh 1997). Even without an advanced knowledge of mathematics, reading of how Fermat's theorem was resolved by Wiles through the contribution of many other mathematicians makes fascinating reading as a struggle as great as climbing Mount Everest or winning an Olympic sports event.

Unfortunately government education bureaucracies, bureaucracies within schools, politicians, some parents and some of the media, try to ensure that any attempt to open out teaching through understanding of learning, to take risks through experimentation, is suppressed. Instead, it is back to basics! It is noteworthy that in Finland, teachers have considerable opportunity to experiment. Under Finnish law central government and local authorities have a responsibility to arrange cultural activities. Finnish children learn music from preschool on. There are over 30 symphony, folk music or jazz orchestras funded by the state and by cities.

And the central aspect of this is experience, the issue on which famous American education philosopher John Dewey centred his thesis about constructivism which so

11.2 Creativity is What Makes us Human

fully describes the way people learn. As Randi Pausch, computer scientist, said, 'Experience is what you get when you didn't get what you wanted… Most of what we learn, we learn indirectly' (Pausch 2007). One study concluded that imaginative insights are most likely to come to us when were groggy and unfocused (Paul 2012). Creativity is as important as literacy and numeracy; the assumption that academic ability is the equivalent of intelligence is wrong!

As Robinson says, 'Music, dance, art and poetry along with humanities and history are those things which speak to the nature of what it is to be a human being and the understanding of how to make one's way in the world. Children should have the opportunity to do other things, not as a default, but as an entitlement. More than that since creativity involves bringing lots of different things together to produce something innovative and since any activity of that kind involves a degree of trial and error, making mistakes is a part of life. Unfortunately, schooling and work life eschews mistakes.' Indeed most people and most organisations that achieve success make mistakes as a matter of course.

The highly successful book *In Search of Excellence* by Tom Peters and Robert H. Waterman first published in 1982 pointed out that one of the features of successful companies was that they drilled more holes. In his latest book, *Antifragile The things that gain from Disorder* Penguin, 2012, Nassim Nicholas Taleb, author of *Black Swan,* rails against those who claim to be able to make forecasts and the academics who claim to be experts. The real world is a place of randomness and uncertainty so the task ahead is to learn how to cope with ambiguity. Unfortunately most humans somehow fail to recognise situations outside the context in which they first encountered them. In other words ideas are domain dependent. The consequence is an avoidance of the very situation that will produce innovation. Taleb advocates robustness and redundancy as a counter to trying to accurately predict very rare events.

In an effort to promote learning as something other than simply absorbing lists of people and dates and regurgitating them, many have depicted learning as fun. But Dr Bronwyn Bevan, Associate Director of Program at the Exploratorium in San Francisco, calls for a different word, one that captures the nature of the learning experience more accurately (Bevan, in press). 'Fun doesn't fully encompass the embodied (intellectual, affective) engagement we feel, that can also include inspiration, astonishment, concentration, commitment, and much more.'

Not all learning is pleasurable. Bevan points out that if some other word were found it would be likely that educators would be listened to in new ways.

11.3 The Arts in Schools

Ken Robinson was principal author of *The Arts in Schools: Principles, Practice and Provision*, the report of a national inquiry in 1982 funded by the Calouste Gulbenkian Foundation. This is now established as a key text on arts and education in Britain and internationally. He was editor (with Christopher Ball) of *The Arts and Higher Education, 1984* (Gulbenkian Foundation and the Leverhulme Trust), and principal writer for the Department of Education and Sciences *The Arts in Further Education* published in 1986.

The introduction to the Report, by Peter Brinson (lecturer and writer on dance and director, UK Branch, Calouste Gulbenkian Foundation), particularly expressed the underlying philosophy:

'Underlying our approach is a consciousness of the new world of social relations, of work and non-work, now being brought about by many factors: advances in technology, new forms of communication, the evolution of Britain as a multi-cultural society, economic recession, long-term structural unemployment and so on. Our conviction is that we must develop broader not narrower curricula in our schools, and that the arts have an important place within this broad approach.' This was written 30 years ago! The development of school curricula seems to have taken no notice!

The Report's recommendations pointed out that it was not intended that a special case be made for the arts but to make a general one: that the forms of education now needed to meet the profound changes in British society must take greater account than in the past of the capabilities, values and the processes of teaching and learning that the arts represent in schools… considerable significance should be attached to those activities which are concerned with the life of feeling and the development of creative powers. Brinson pointed out that a pursuit of all kinds of creativity would enable coping with the economic necessities of the world as well as increase the potential for discovery and progress on the many fronts of human interest and activity.

The Report concluded that due account should be taken in the discussions on the school curriculum, of the important contributions of the arts in six areas of educational responsibility including developing the full variety of human intelligence, developing the capacity for creative thought and action, the exploration of values and understanding the changing social culture. An Australian perspective is given by Ewing (2010).

11.4 Reggio Emilia

The environment in the home can lead to high levels of stimulation of the young child which become evident even by the age of 10 months. Some approaches to education and schooling recognise this. One example is the Reggio Emilia movement which has been adopted by many preschool programs around the world. Its foundation is in the view that children should be given some control over their learning: teachers are facilitators of learning rather than instructors.

The principles of the Reggio Emilia philosophy include the notion that learning involves experiences using all the senses—touching, moving, listening, seeing and hearing. Opportunities for exploration of relationships with other children and with the world around them are important. Opportunities for self expressions are emphasized. Multiple points of view are recognised and children are trusted to be interested in things worth knowing about.

Teachers recognise parents as the first teachers: parents are involved in the children's learning. The natural development of children and the relationships children have with the environment including the natural environment are at the centre of the approach. The underlying philosophy recognises the nature of learning, cognitive development and experience as revealed by the studies and views of people such as John Dewey, Frenchman Jean Piaget and Russian Lev Vygotsky.

Distinguished educator and Harvard professor Howard Gardner is known for his exploration of multiple intelligences. He wrote once that he wanted his children to understand the world, but not just because the world is fascinating and the human mind is curious but so that they would be positioned to make it a better place (Smith 2008). Gardner viewed intelligence as 'the capacity to solve problems or to fashion products that are valued in one or more cultural setting'. He recognised people as having a unique blend of intelligences. His initial seven intelligences were linguistic, logical–mathematical, musical, bodily-kinesthetic (the ability to use mental abilities to coordinate bodily movements), spatial (potential to recognise and use patterns of space), interpersonal and intrapersonal (the capacity to understand oneself). He later added two others, naturalist (which enables recognition, categorisation and drawing upon certain features of the environment) and spiritual.

In one of his books Gardner (1999) describes the various activities of young students at the original Reggio Emilia preschool in Italy. The spacious building has open, well lit spaces furnished with inviting chairs and couches, and alcoves. Hundreds of materials from seashells to grains of cereal are stored on shelves and available to the children. The young students explore themes that attract them such as rainbows, the city, poppy fields and an ant city. The children ponder questions and phenomena that arise and end up creating objects, drawings, and photographs and so on representing their exploration of the themes.

11.5 Success and Failure at School

Many stories about people who have become successful reveal that when enthusiasm is encouraged and recognised, education and learning are successful and have personal meaning. But it is not always the education at school which is important or even relevant. Just as importantly, judgments about people early in their life (or even later) are very often wrong.

Australian entrepreneur and adventurer Dick Smith in his early school days could not pronounce his name correctly—it was 'Dick Miff'; when he started to fly planes and helicopters—he has flown to both the North Pole and the South Pole— he had to write out on a sheet of paper the letters of the alphabet and alongside them the Greek letters used for call signs. Richard Branson, creator of Virgin enterprises—some 40 separate companies—was thought pretty hopeless at school; he is dyslexic and cannot distinguish between gross and net in a financial statement and faced with a crossword puzzle he goes blank. Yet in a recent tabloid media poll he was voted the most intelligent man in England.

Richard Feynman, in common with the famous physicists Edward Teller and Albert Einstein, was a late talker; by his third birthday he had yet to utter a single word! The young Feynman was heavily influenced by his father, Melville, who encouraged him to ask questions to challenge orthodox thinking. Apple and Microsoft founders Steve Jobs and Bill Gates both dropped out of college.

11.6 Organisations Encouraging Creativity and Innovation

The major biomedical research institutions whose scientists have won many Nobel and other prizes are typified by leadership which encourages frequent interaction of people from different disciplines, even in one case, requiring presentation of seminars on topics outside their area of expertise (Hollingsworth and Hollingsworth 2000). Effective research and development enterprises ensure as far as possible that they recruit the best possible people and provide a challenging and supportive environment.

An example is the Perimeter Institute for Theoretical Physics near Toronto in Canada funded significantly by Mike Lazaridis, the developer of the Blackberry (Williams 2010). Lazaridis gives great emphasis to creativity. Speaking at the American Association for the Advancement of Science in Vancouver in 2012 he began by asking the audience to identify their prized possession. He answered for himself: 'my education' (Williams 2012).

Acknowledging the present as a technological age, we are surrounded by devices, Lazaridis asked what has value, what has shaped the present. He identified ideas: 'the devices are just ideas made into a form where we can hold them in our hands. It's the ideas themselves that got us this far, and its new ideas that will get us even further… all of us in this room need to let our young people muck about in basements and high school shops and night seminars, we need to let them blow up model rockets and explore the strangest and apparently most useless of ideas.'

Lazaridis concluded, 'all of us in this room need to let our young people muck about in basements and high school shops and night seminars, we need to let them blow up model rockets and explore the strangest and apparently most useless of ideas.'

Innovation after all does not depend principally on one brilliant individual suddenly coming up with some boundary breaking idea. It relies on what Rhodes Scholar and entrepreneur Eric Knight (2011) calls the network theory of success. 'This theory does not diminish individual brilliance but focuses on the tight network of supporters and collaborators gathered around an individual.' Young people developing applications—Apps' for hand held devices—gather in the one room in Silicon Valley exploring their ideas, exchanging information and exploring opportunities with others prepared to invest in innovation.

One of the people driving quite different approaches to education and learning is Professor Stephen Heppell, Chair in New Media Environments at Bournemouth University in the UK Heppell has been involved in the 'Building Schools for the Future' project to which the former Blair Government committed £60 billion to rebuild every secondary school in the country. He has developed a number of new 'ingredients' of learning around the world including superclasses of 90–120 students; vertical learning groups; stage not age; schools within schools or 'Home Bases'; project-based work; exhibition-based assessments; collaborative learning teams; mixed-age mentoring; children as teachers; teachers as learners; and so on. He says, 'Obviously, in a world where every culture, context and community is unique there will be no one-size-fits-all solution, however enlightened that solution might be.' (Le 2010). Heppell observes, 'Schools are full of things that our descendants will look back on and laugh out loud at.'

There are thousands of situations in schools around the world, in developing countries and the developed world where exciting experiments are taking place, where enthusiastic young people are developing a greater understanding of the world around them, of finding their 'element'. Kids designing scientific experiments, studying nature, learning musical instruments, acting in school plays, busting themselves to do better at their chosen sport. And learning how to work the latest technology and social media. In all of these situations it is important to understand the extent to which these modern approaches are genuinely improving the learning opportunities *and* outcomes for the student, that they are being pursued for reasons beyond being just 'modern' or 'new'.

11.7 Free Choice Learning: Learning in Informal Settings

People are attracted to communities where creative opportunities are valued. This is the principal idea behind the organisation Partners for Livable Communities. Amongst other things Partners aims to systematically place cultural assets within the portfolio of community development efforts. Partners believes that 'cultural strategies are not only a major economic force in many communities but contribute tremendously to education, cultural identity, race relations, community pride, quality of life and other, less quantifiable but important, social functions.'

Involvement in learning by the informal sector is far more significant than generally admitted. The 'informal sector' includes museums, science centres, zoos, historic houses, forests and gardens, memorials, streetscapes and even workplaces These are places of memorable experiences. For museums and similar enterprises holding, conserving and interpreting collections, conducting research upon them and developing exhibitions is important but not enough.

In these places individual and group exploration is appropriate. John Falk and Lynn Dierking of Oregon State University and the Institute for Learning Innovation, who with others have studied this area for several decades, calls this free-choice learning (Falk 2009). Visits to museums and similar places are intentional and memories of the visit are long-lasting. Visiting behaviour reflects the person's identity, the match between the way they see themselves and the way they wish to amplify that by their behaviour during their visit. These are interesting, and important and new visions. Spock (2006) of the Minnesota History Center goes as far as suggesting that 'the product museums sell may not be education as much as a self image of intelligence, cultural awareness and curiosity, that is, identity'.

Exploration of the learning experience in museums and other informal settings (as opposed to the formal settings of schools) has dramatically increased in the US and the UK and many museum educators have contributed. Emeritus Professor George Hein of Lesley University in Cambridge (Maryland) and Margaret Alexander of the Maryland Historical Trust presented a good summary of what we know. 'Recent education theory acknowledges, even promotes, the object-based, experiential, thought-provoking, and problem-solving type of learning in which museums excel. The overriding conclusion is that museums offer visitors profound, long-lasting, and even life-changing experiences… Visitors don't equate learning with education or recreation with entertainment.' (Hein and Alexander 1998).

We know now that all learning is contextual (Falk and Dierking 2000). The three contexts—personal, sociocultural and physical—interact *over time* and comprise eight key factors: motivation and expectations, prior knowledge, choice and control, mediation within the group, facilitation by others, advance organizers and orientation, design and reinforcing events and experiences elsewhere. The content—the objects and interpretation of their history and significance—is important but only along with much else about the location, the museum or zoo, how it is organised and designed, what the other experiences at the same location are like.

If visits by school group are to be successful then careful planning, integration of the visit with the curriculum, preparation and follow up at school and opportunities for visiting students to devise their own learning path and work with others are all vital (Griffin and Symington 1997). Family visits are like that: visitors arrive with particular purposes in mind—they don't just arrive because they have nothing else to do—and they focus initially on those things relating to those purposes. But after that they may well take a rather random path through other parts of the museum, garden or zoo.

Listening to what visitors to museums and similar places say during their visit, what they talk about to each other, shows just how they are learning. The meanings of the exhibitions emerge from the discussion just as meaning emerges from the discussions in school classes as was found by numerous researchers including Graham Nuthall and Jonathan Osborne, as recounted in Chap. 6. Research by Paulette McManus (1989) in England, Janette Griffin (Kelly et al. 2005) from the University of Technology in Sydney and by (Leinhardt and Knutson 2004) at the Learning Research and Development Center in Pittsburgh reveal the nature of the learning experience through listening to actual conversations.

As Leinhardt and Knutson say, 'While museum curators and staff examine their own activity and decisions, there is considerably more to visitor learning than just those things that are under curatorial control. But the design of the learning environment is vital. It is, after all, the learning environment that is under the control of the museum. They explore how curators and other museum people can make the most of how they shape that environment, how they provide the meaningful information that addresses issues which answer the visitors' questions.'

Through use of the latest information technology museums' accumulated knowledge has become more accessible to visitors and general public alike. With personal digital electronic devices the visitor can download images and text from websites or within the museum itself. Interactive technology has greatly enhanced some exhibitions, especially in science centres (Friedman 2007). Social media has generated an explosion in the way museums interact with their visitors and vice versa.

YouthALIVE, a major initiative in 56 cities in the US, brought together over 7,000 young people and 72 museums of all kinds in educational enrichment and work-based learning programs between 1991 and 1999 (Baum et al. 2000). It involves youth in a range of activities including after school activities, working as guides and explainers, workshops, and working in various departments. More than 70 % of the participating adolescents were from low-income communities and 63 % were African American or Latino. Those participating reported increased awareness of issues, useful knowledge and skills, social awareness, and confidence in themselves and their relationships with others: the program's success benefited from included flexibility in the learning environment. 'Ordinary people, given opportunities, will display extraordinary talents.' The program was supported by DeWitt Wallace-Readers Digest funds and administered by the Association of Science-Technology Centres. ('YouthALIVE' should not be confused with the 'Youth Alive' programs run by a variety of church groups in various cities.)

Special programs engage younger people especially who are at risk, such as people struggling with drug dependency, economically and socially disadvantaged youth including those who are long-term unemployed or homeless in ways that expand their understandings and recognition of their own capabilities. Some of those programs include drama and dance; some involve taking responsibility for care of animals. Many of these are after-school programs. Shirley Brice Heath, formerly of Stanford University, has been among the people researching such programs (Heath 2000; Heath and McLaughlin 1994).

Creative Partnerships is the flagship creative learning program delivered by the English organisation 'Creativity Culture Education' headed by Paul Collard, brought to Western Australia by the WA Government's Commissioner for Youth and Young People in late 2011 as 'Thinker in Residence'. Creative Partnerships is designed to develop the skills of young people across England, raising their aspirations and achievements, and opening up more opportunities for their futures. It has supported thousands of innovative, long-term partnerships between schools and creative professionals including artists, performers, architects, multimedia developers and scientists delivered through a range of organisations that administered the programs locally. The program commenced in 2002 and has worked with over 2,700 schools across England.

The Cameron coalition government in Britain in 2011 cancelled support for Creative Partnerships and Find Your Talent, also managed by Creativity Culture Education; funding for ACE, a program which distributes funding to arts venues, galleries, theatre groups and other arts organisations was cut by 30 % (Murray 2010).

The UK Governments Office of Education Standards, Ofsted, has recognised the benefits of Creative Partnerships in several of its reports. Schools in challenging circumstances show the greatest improvements in pupils' ability across a range of key areas. This was confirmed by considering inspection reports from 180 more schools: creative learning practices in schools are improving standards and pupils personal development

11.8 Lifelong Learning and Public Broadcasting

Huge numbers of adults are engaged in all kinds of learning activities, in addition to visiting places such as museums, zoos and libraries. These range from courses of various kinds run by societies, friends and support groups associated with places such as museums and zoos as well as special interest groups involved in activities such as gardening and so on.

Public broadcasting in many countries, such as the ABC, BBC and the Public Broadcasting Service (PBS) in the US feature, in addition to entertainment offerings, programs with substantial content in all fields from religion and philosophy to science, history and current affairs as well as music, drama and other art forms at a standard which rivals the offerings of advanced secondary school through undergraduate university. And they are presented by people with significant knowledge and communication ability. Many feature the experts in the field.

If governments were seriously concerned about education and its contribution to a well-informed citizenry, there would be frequent advocacy for these enterprises with clear mention of the value of their contribution. Public media like the ABC and the BBC are major contributors to an informed public, a prerequisite for a democratic society. All of this seems irrelevant to the politicians 'hell bent' on achieving efficiency, no matter the cost, on minimising the costs to the taxpayers. Then there are those constantly asserting that these public media are havens of left-wingers peddling distorted views of everything from history to science.

11.9 Education Means Creativity Means much more than School

Creativity is of the most fundamental significance to the future of every nation and every community. And indeed every person. That is demonstrated far more widely every day in the development of new ways of doing things, new applications and new contraptions. Consider social media, the ways in which small and large devices are evolving in response to the looming challenge of climate change and energy production. Consider the ways in which myriad challenges were overcome in the transport of the mirrors made in Europe for the European Space Observatory in Paranal in Chile along difficult roads to their site near the summit, the eventual landing of the Curiosity rover on Mars and the previous triumph of the Cassini-Huygens probe to Saturn. These contrast with the fiascos of Britain's submarines (Hopkins 2012) and the new Dreamliner aeroplane (Surowiecki 2013) dogged by adherence to drives for efficiencies through silly notions about outsourcing and more.

More stories of creativity need to be promoted. Richard Feynman went to biology classes after he was appointed to Cornell University. He was curious as to what the substance lecithin, the brownish fatty substances occurring in animal and plant tissues, was. He pestered the professor teaching the course until the professor admitted that he didn't know. The doctor who keeps asking questions because the answers about the patient's condition don't seem quite right is using the same creative abilities.

Exploiting opportunities and responding to challenges do not involve simply doing better what was done in the past but in finding new connections between processes and events which once were seen to be not related to each other. Creativity and its encouragement is an essential component of all successful education systems.

Encouraging creativity means recognising the importance of inspiration and risk-taking, access to different experiences and sources of knowledge. And it means persistence. It inherently results in many failures. That means allowing failure and seeing it as part of the learning and creative process. It means providing maximum opportunity for students to find and explore their own interests. That does not mean that such a level of flexibility and choice might prevail so that effective instruction is ignored or students end up gaining next to nothing. Having the opportunity to pursue those discoveries requires the high risk strategy of betting that they will produce something of value. Often the gain will only become apparent a long time ahead.

Continuation of a regimented approach to schooling with its hierarchy of subjects, its curriculum determined in detail by people outside the system concerned to ensure that only what is right is taught, its focus on what will be useful in work life rather than in a life lived, risks consequences of the kind envisaged by Ivan Illich (1926–2002), Austrian philosopher, Roman Catholic priest and critic of the institutions of contemporary western culture, the school as no more than an instrument of state power.

Students should be given opportunities to interact with people such as artists and scientists, exposed to the personal journeys of those who have made important discoveries and advanced understanding. They should have a degree of control over their learning journey and be given the opportunity to cooperate with others in learning.

Learning outside the classroom, in museums, botanic gardens, national parks and so on, provides significant opportunities for learning which engages many senses and enhances many skills. Successful use of visit opportunities requires planning and integration with the school curriculum. Most young people spend more time in these informal learning environments than in the formal environment of school classes.

There should be greater encouragement of use of the rich array of learning opportunities provided by public broadcasting through radio and television now delivered through a variety of platforms. The media can and do play a far more important role than is realised: it is not all mere entertainment. Consider the radio and television programs of the BBC, ABC and PBS and indeed the radio stations of many European countries such as Radio Netherlands.

Last, can't there be a stop to this arid argument about whether innovation is something that only happens in the private sector? The fact is that most of the basic research which provides the basis for later applications is undertaken not mainly in the private sector but in enterprises principally or entirely funded by government: basic research is simply too risky. At the same time there could be a realisation that there are organisational models for successful pursuit of innovation and creativity, they aren't based on neoclassical models of competition and financial rewards for 'the best' and they aren't typified by industries like the companies in 'Big Pharma', huge pharmaceutical companies promoting the myth that the high price of drugs shows how worthwhile they are or that they need to charge high prices because their research and development costs are so high! (Anglell 2004).

References

Anglell, M. (2004, 15 July). The truth about drug companies. *New York Review of Books*.
Attard, M. (2011, 17 December). What killed the Tasmanian tiger? *ABC RN 'The Science Show'*. Retrieved December 20, 2011, from http://www.abc.net.au/radionational/programs/scienceshow/what-killed-the-tasmanian-tiger3f/3735644
Baum, L., Hein, G. E., & Solvay, M. (2000). In their own words: voices of teens in museums. *Journal of Museum Education, 25*(3), 9–14.
Bevan, B. (In press). What makes learning fun? Deborah Perry. In *Visitor Studies*. Walnut Creek: AltaMira Press.
Case Western Reserve University. (2012, May 30). Despite less play. children's use of imagination increases over two decades. *ScienceDaily*. Retrieved August 22. 2012 from http://www.sciencedaily.com/releases/2012/05/120530133720.htm
Ewing, R. (2010). The Arts and Australian Education: Realising potential. Australian Education Review 58. Retrieved 22 August 2012, from http://www.acer.edu.au/documents/AER-58.pdf
Falk, J. H., & Dierking, L. D. (2000). *Learning from museums: Visitor experiences and the making of meaning*. Walnut Creek: Altamira Press.
Falk, J. H. (2009). *Identity and the museum visitor experience*. Walnut Creek: Left Coast Press.
Friedman, A. J. (2007). The extraordinary growth of the science-technology museum. *Curator the Museum Journal, 50*, 63–76.
Gardner, H. (1999). *The disciplined mind. What all students should understand*. New York: Simon and Schuster.

References

Griffin, J. M., & Symington, D. J. (1997). Moving from task-oriented to learning-oriented strategies on school excursions to museums. *Science Education, 81*, 763–779.

Heath, S. B. (2000). Making learning work. *After School Matters, 1*, 33–45.

Heath, S. B., & McLaughlin, M. (1994). The best of both worlds: Connecting schools and community youth organisations for all-day, all-year learning. *Educational Administration Quarterly, 30*, 278–300.

Hein, G. E., & Alexander, M. (1998). *Museums: Places of learning.* Washington DC: American Association of Museums.

Hollingsworth, R., & Hollingsworth, J. (2000). *Major discoveries and biomedical research organizations: Perspectives on interdisciplinarity. Nurturing leadership and integrated structure and cultures.* Symposium presentation. Retrieved August 22, 2012, from http://www8.umu.se/inforsk/universitetsligan/hollingsworth.html

Hopkins, N. (2012, November 15). Slow, leaky, rusty: Britain's £10bn submarine beset by design flaws. *The Guardian.*

Kelly, L. et al. (2005). Museums actively researching visitor experiences and learning (MARVEL): A methodological study. *Open Museum Journal, 7*, 1–19. Retrieved August 28, 2012, from http://epress.lib.uts.edu.au/research/handle/10453/6061

Knight, E. (2011, June). The Sun King: Shi Zhengrong. *The Monthly.*

Le, T. (2010, September 23). The end of education Is the dawn of Learning. *Fast Company.* Retrieved August 22, 2012, from http://www.fastcodesign.com/1662358/the-end-of-education-the-dawn-of-learning-a-conversation-with-stephen-heppell

Leinhardt, G., & Knutson, K. (2004). *Listening in on Museum conversations.* Walnut Creek: Alta Mira Press.

McManus, P. M. (1989). Oh. Yes. They Do: How Museum Visitors Read Labels and Interact with Exhibit Texts. *Curator, The Museum Journal 32*, 174–189.

Merryman, A. (2010, July 10). The creativity crisis. *Newsweek.*

Murray, J. (2010, November 2). School arts to be hit by cuts. *The Guardian.*

Paul, A. M. (2012, February 1). Why morning routines are creativity killers. *Time.* Retrieved April 19, 2013, from http://ideas.time.com/2012/02/01/why-morning-routines-are-creativity-killers/

Pausch, R. (2007). *The last lecture.* Retrieved August 22, 2012, from http://www.cmu.edu/randyslecture/

Robinson, K., & Aronica, L. (2009). *The element: How finding your passion changes everything.* London: Penguin.

Runco, M. A. (2008). Creativity and education. *New Horizons in Education, 56*, 96–104.

Singh, S. (1997). *Fermat's last theorem.* London: Fourth Estate.

Smith, M. K. (2008). Howard gardner and multiple intelligences. In *The encyclopedia of informal education.* Retrieved August 22, 2012, from http://www.infed.org/thinkers/gardner.htm

Spock, D. (2006). The puzzle of museum educational practice: A comment on rounds and falk. *Curator the Museum Journal, 49*, 167–180.

Surowiecki, J. (2013, February 4). Requiem for a dreamliner? *New Yorker.*

Williams, R. (presenter). (2010, April 10). Canada's perimeter institute for theoretical physics. *ABC RN 'The Science Show'.* Retrieved August 22, 2012, from http://www.abc.net.au/radionational/programs/scienceshow/canadas-perimeter-institute-for-theoretical-physics/3109998

Williams, R. (presenter). (2012, June 5). Mike lazaridis: The power of ideas. *ABC RN 'The Science Show'.* Retrieved August 22, 2012, from http://www.abc.net.au/radionational/programs/scienceshow/mike-lazaridis—the-power-of-ideas/4053180

Chapter 12
International Comparisons

'In the most successful education systems, the political and social leaders have persuaded their citizens to make the choices needed to show that they value education more than other things. … the best-performing education systems embrace the diversity in student's capacities, interests and social background with individualised approaches to learning.

Second, high-performing education systems stand out with clear and ambitious standards that are shared across the system, focus on the acquisition of complex, higher-order thinking skills, and are aligned with high stakes gateways and instructional systems. In these education systems, everyone knows what is required to get a given qualification, in terms both of the content studied and the level of performance that has to be demonstrated to earn it. …

Third, the quality of an education system cannot exceed the quality of its teachers and principals, since student learning is ultimately the product of what goes on in classrooms…'

OECD, PISA 2009 Results: What Makes a School Successful? Resources, Policies and Practices, volume IV.

12.1 Misinformation and Urban Mythologies

Education systems, especially school systems, have been the subject of numerous studies, many of them extremely careful. Conclusions which might be drawn from comparisons with countries with successful systems have not always been translated to formulating reforms in other countries. That is despite the fact that economic and social differences between children are remarkably similar across countries though of course there are cultural influences which must be taken into account. Comparisons are often muddied by misinformation or urban mythologies, especially when it comes to European and Asian countries.

The United Nations Human Development Reports (United Nations 2010, 2013) provide background against which considerations of development or lack of it can be assessed in particular countries. Over the 40 years from 1970 to 2010 the average increase in school enrolment was almost the same in countries whether growth was negative or positive (2013).

The OECD has conducted regular tests of students every 3 years since 2000 through the program known as PISA. PISA assesses reading, mathematical and scientific literacy and gathers a vast amount of other data. 'Literacy' is taken to mean the competencies gained through their life expected to equip young people to cope effectively with adult life in a rapidly changing society and how knowledge can be applied to real-life problems. The assessment involves a sample of 15 year old students, a time when they are approaching the end of compulsory schooling; PISA therefore gives some measure of the knowledge, skills and attitudes accumulated over approximately 10 years of education in school and outside (OECD 2006). The latest survey reports results for 2009 (OECD 2010a, b, c).

The OECD also publishes *Education at Glance* every year. The PISA 2009 reports are of special interest because they examine the systems of a number of successful countries and compare the practices there with those in the US. They are not simply a tabulation of test results but analyse and comment upon the factors contributing to the results.

The PISA survey for 2007 was the basis for an analysis of the characteristics of successful school systems by the McKinsey Company's Michael Barber and Mona Mourshed (Barber and Mourshed 2007); Barber was the first Secretary of State for School Standards in the Government of Tony Blair in Britain. They reviewed 25 of the world's best school systems in 2007 using the same criteria as were used by the PISA program. Wide variations in the quality of education were noted. Generally school systems were observed to have barely improved over several decades despite substantial expenditures and many reforms. For instance, despite various reforms in England over 50 years there was no measurable improvement in standards of literacy and numeracy in primary schools.

The report (unsurprisingly) observed 'changing what happens in the hearts and minds of children … is no simple task.

High-performing school systems were consistently found to do three things well'. These they termed drivers:

- They get the right people to become teachers;
- They develop these people into effective instructors (the only way to improve outcomes is to improve instruction); and
- They put in place systems and targeted support to ensure that every child is able to benefit from excellent instruction (the only way for the system to reach the highest performance is to raise the standard of every student).

Achieving these requires rigorous standards and assessments, clear expectations, differentiated support for teachers and students, and sufficient funding, facilities and other core resources ranging from funding structures to governance and incentives. But '… reform efforts which fail to address these drivers are unlikely to deliver the improvements in outcomes that system leaders are striving to achieve'. These conclusions prevailed 'irrespective of the culture in which they were applied'.

McKinsey & Co's second report published in late 2010 described how better school systems kept getting better (Mourshed et al. 2010). Twenty systems around the world were analysed; more than 200 interviews with system stakeholders were held and analysis of some 600 interventions was completed.

The appropriateness of interventions to achieve change depends on which stage the system is at. To move from poor to fair requires support for students in achieving literacy and math basics and providing 'scaffolding' support for low-skill teachers. To move to good requires high quality performance data, teachers and school accountability, appropriate financing and organisation structure and pedagogy models. Further advances—from good to great—require teaching and school leadership and appropriate career structures like those in medicine and law. Last, in achieving excellence the focus is on peer-based learning, system-wide interaction, innovation and experimentation.

The existence of a mediating layer between the central administration and the school and continuity of the systems leadership are important features of improvement. Injection of new leadership appeared to be the most important. New leaders have staying power: tenure is generally from 6 to 7 years (We can note that average tenure of urban school districts in the US is nearly 3 years and of education secretaries in England 2 years).

Time spent at school, recruitment of teachers, salary levels, attention to professional development—important in influencing quality of instruction—status of the profession within the community and school leadership significantly determine the differences in outcomes. These are critical issues for Australia! In the best systems student tests are used by teachers to improve their performance, not as the basis for parent's choice of schools!

Singaporean students achieve to a high level despite expenditure per student being less than that of almost every other developed country. In Finland students do not start school until they are 7 years old and attend classes for only 4 or 5 hours each day during their first 2 years of schooling: their PISA scores are a full 50 points ahead of their peers in Norway.

The best-performing systems recruit their teachers from the top levels of the school system; the lower performing school systems in the US recruit from the bottom third of high-school students. (Something similar occurs in Australia.) The US also spends much more per head than the OECD average and teachers work longer hours but student achievement is generally average.

In the best systems, entry to the teaching profession is very competitive, the quality of teachers being lifted by relatively little salary variation. Countries with high-performing systems pay starting salaries above the OECD average of 95 % of GDP per capita; in the US the starting salary is 81 % of GDP per capita. Most school systems wait until after graduation before selecting recruits. The best performing systems delay permanent appointment until some time after initial employment. The ultimate salary may not be large. Though some teachers will claim they do not enter the profession for the money it is also clear that 'unless school systems offer salaries which are in-line with other graduate starting salaries, these same people do not enter teaching'.

The ability of a school to attract the right people is closely linked to the status of the profession: countries seemingly as widely different as Finland and Korea agree in this! In both countries opinion polls show that the general public believe that teachers make a greater contribution to society than any other profession. Once teaching becomes a high status profession more talented people become teachers. If the profession has a low status, obviously the calibre of the people attracted to it declines. Making teaching the preferred career choice depends less on high salaries or culture than it does on a small set of simple but critical policy choices concerning selection and training, starting compensation and managing the status of the profession.

Quality of instruction is achieved by building practical skills during initial training, placing coaches in schools to support teachers, selecting and developing effective instructional leaders and enabling teachers to learn from each other. Overcoming weaknesses is advanced by reference to best practices and motivation to improve. Enabling teachers to learn from each other is helpful.

School leadership is second only to classroom teaching as an influence on learning. That means getting the right teachers to become principals, developing their instructional leadership skills and having them focus on that. Setting high expectations at the level of the individual student and intervening if there is declining performance is also a feature of high performing systems (We might recall that at Sect. 7.3 about the South Side of Chicago we learned that leadership was the critical 'support' in driving schools to be successful; other studies of the importance of school leadership are summarised at Sect. 8.5).

Last, setting out to be transparent by publishing inspection or examination data 'seldom leads to improvement for this reason alone … and indeed … is perceived as an obstacle rather than an aid to improvement'. The best systems take monitoring through examinations and inspections inside schools 'seriously, constantly evaluating student performance and constructing interventions to assist individual students in order to prevent them from falling behind' (Barber and Mourshed 2007, p 38).

12.2 Successful Schools

One of the PISA 2009 survey reports drew from successful education systems a set of lessons for the US (OECD 2010c). Selected OECD countries and partner countries were covered. This essay summarises that report and deals with OECD countries Korea, Japan, Canada (Province of Ontario) which are reported on for PISA 2009 and Finland and New Zealand (based on the PISA 2009 data and other studies) and 'partner countries' Singapore and two Chinese cities Shanghai and Hong Kong.

PISAs conception of reading literacy encompasses the range of situations in which people read, the different ways written texts are presented, and the variety of ways that readers approach and use texts, from the functional and finite, such as finding a particular piece of practical information, to the deep and far-reaching, such as understanding other ways of doing, thinking and being. These kinds of reading literacy skills are more reliable predictors of economic and social well-being than the number of years spent in school or in post-formal education: countries of similar prosperity can produce very different educational results.

Successful schools, those delivering high-quality education to all students, also provide access to more teachers by disadvantaged students; they provide equity in learning opportunities. What happens in school has a direct impact on learning. In turn, what happens in school is influenced by the resources, policies and practices approved at higher administrative levels in a country's education system. Whilst most successful school systems grant greater autonomy to individual schools to design curricula and establish assessment policies, these same school systems do not necessarily allow schools to compete for enrolment. Teachers' pay tends to be prioritised over class size. Schools with better disciplinary climates, more positive behaviour among teachers and better teacher-student relations tend to achieve higher scores in reading. The nature of the school systems in each country and the particular features of recent reforms are now outlined.

The Grattan Institute in Australia also based a widely quoted review of Australia's achievement on the PISA 2009 results and focused on comparison with Asian countries (Jensen et al. 2012; Thomson et al. 2010).

12.2.1 Finland

Education in Finland, according to the Finish National Board of Education, is a basic right set out in the constitution. Finland has been cited as a leader educationally for several years. Its reforms were triggered by financial crises in the early 1990s, collapse of the Soviet Union and entry to the European Union in 1995. 'Public authorities must secure equal opportunities for every resident in Finland to get education also after compulsory education and to develop themselves, irrespective of their financial standing. Municipalities are responsible for the provision of education and implementation. Finland's education system builds on the equality of opportunity, competent teachers, support for welfare and learning of students including for those with special needs, supportive assessment and evaluation, cooperation between education authorities and relevant organisations'.

The organisation of schoolwork and education focuses on student's activity and interaction with the teacher, other students and the learning environment. There are no national tests or ranking and no streaming of students. 'Finnish educators believe that if schools focus on early diagnosis and intervention, most students can be helped to achieve success in regular classrooms. Its principal mechanism for supporting struggling students in a timely fashion is the 'special teacher', a specially trained teacher assigned to each school' (OECD 2010c). Schools are full-service schools: they serve a hot meal every day for students, they provide health services as well as a wide range of mental health and other services for families in need without means testing.

Pasi Sahlberg, former senior Education Specialist at the World Bank and now heading up education in Finland, has provided one of the best summaries of the education system in Finland (Sahlberg 2007, 2012). 'Finland is an example of a nation that has developed from a remote agrarian/industrial state in the 1950s to a model knowledge economy, using education as the key to economic and social development'.

Sahlberg points out that the legislation which changed teacher education and upgraded the profession in Finland was passed by the Finnish Parliament in 1978 and implemented in 1979 (Quince 2012). The main goal of the comprehensive education system was to create equally good schools irrespective of location and family background: schools were given equal resources and equally good teachers. The response to increasing difference has been to give more resources to those schools not performing well or under-resourced. Oversight of schools was devolved from the central government to local government in the 1980s. The initial resistance to the reforms dissipated after the results of the second round of PISA evaluations for 2003 showed Finnish students to be achieving above other OECD countries; the excellent PISA 2000 results were not sufficiently convincing.

12.2.2 New Zealand

New Zealand is amongst the highest performing countries educationally: many of the features of the system in that country are shared with others of the highest performing countries including Finland though there are substantial differences in cultural diversity. In New Zealand there is substantial variation in achievement within schools but little between schools. The student population is very diverse with large enrolments of Maori and Pacific Islander children in some schools. 'The central professional challenge for teachers is to manage simultaneously the complexity of learning needs of diverse students' Alton-Lee (2003). The New Zealand studies provide a useful comparison with the practices in Finland with its relatively ethnically homogenous population whose students are highly successful in international tests.

New Zealand has a level of tertiary educated people well above the OECD: almost 50 % of 25–34 year olds are tertiary educated compared with just over 30 % of 55–64 year olds; children of tertiary educated parents are very likely to become tertiary educated themselves (OECD 2012). There is a high level of employment of graduates, just above the OECD average.

In 1989 the New Zealand Government abolished the Government Department of Education, replaced it with a much smaller Ministry, an Education Review Office, a Qualifications Authority and some other smaller agencies (Fiske and Ladd 2000; Wylie 2012). Control of its more than 2,700 primary and secondary schools were turned over to locally elected boards of trustees, parents and some education professionals in some cases. Virtually overnight, one of the world's most tightly controlled public education systems became one of the most decentralized.

The changes were largely driven by a Government Treasury resolved to address fiscal deficit issues and restructure the economy: 'fundamental to this analysis was the premise that human behaviour is primarily self-interested' (Wylie 2012, p. 77). The changes followed a review by a business man who found schools were not responding to parents' needs and concerns and the overall system was inadequately managed (Fiske and Ladd 2000) 'Each school should be able to manage its own resources', he said.

Two years later, in 1991, following a change of government, further reforms were enacted which involved full parental choice of schools and encouraged the development of a competitive culture in the state education system. Of course, not all parents were able to exercise that choice. As pointed out elsewhere availability of such an option can lead to increased socioeconomic stratification.

Systems for evaluating student achievement were not put in place. However, schools were subject to evaluation mainly through managerial criteria. School principals and teachers became less prepared to share knowledge. Schools in some areas and those serving minorities had difficulties coping with the changes and the need to assemble a governing board. On the other hand the abolition of the large central bureaucracy was generally welcomed. Self management drove principals to be managers of budgets and staff and student recruitment, not leaders in learning!

Cathie Wylie, chief researcher at the Council for Education Research, one of several writers about these reforms, found reactions of amazement to these reforms from some overseas colleagues. The principal of an award-winning Canadian school observed that they had tried these kinds of reforms 20 years previously but found the competition between schools to be too costly.

Wylie observed that while innovation was able to be fostered, no system of support for schools in building change was developed, networks for sharing pedagogy were not built and so development of an understanding of how learning motivates and really engages students was missing. Such sharing of knowledge and cooperation are clearly characteristic of many successful reforms in many other domains, as mentioned elsewhere. Inservice training was reduced, funding for implementing new curricula was reduced.

Though there were some gains from these reforms some features essential to effective school reform and improvement of student learning were entirely absent. These can be summarised as a failure of schools to build and sustain strong school cultures to achieve those goals. That was especially so of schools serving minorities such as Maori. Wylie concludes that a national system focused on continuing learning within national policy frameworks well grounded in strong evidence is required together with more support at the local level.

Alton-Lee (2003) at the ACER Conference in 2003 identified ten features characterising quality teaching. These included a focus on student achievement and on raising achievements in learning and social outcomes, pedagogical practices which enable classes and other learning groupings to work as caring, inclusive, and cohesive learning communities, effective links between school and other cultural contexts in which learning occurs, effective and sufficient teaching in class management rather than control ensuring compliant behaviour, complementary combinations of teacher-directed and other groupings including structured peer interaction, feedback on student task engagement, promotion of student self-regulation and critical thinking and constructive engagement of teacher and student in goal oriented assessment.

12.2.3 China

China has made huge strides in educating its population. There is popular support for expanding education to reach more people. It is less than three decades since educated people including teachers were sent to rural areas to work as part of the Cultural Revolution. There is substantial commitment to education for all with attention being paid to schools in disadvantaged areas and poorly performing schools together with the strong commitment by families to education. This has resulted in superior performance by students. A common theme of the system in China, as in Japan and Korea, is that achieving high scores is paramount and motivation is basically driven by family or other social expectations: intrinsic motivation or genuine interest in the subject matter per se, are not the driving factors.

Reform of the system was launched in 1998, expansion of universal basic education having begun in the 1980s. The system includes private for-profit enterprises and allows non-government financing of schools. Plans involve thousands of professionals and experts and seminars as well as over 2 million submissions from all walks of society. The blueprint for 2020 was chaired by Prime Minister Wen Jiabao.

A major document issued in 2001 called for a move away from knowledge transmission towards fostering learning attitudes and values, more comprehensive and balanced learning experiences, improved relevance and content interest, student participation and ability to analyse and solve problems. 'To every question there should be more than a single answer' poses a challenge to the orthodoxy and authority of teachers over the information they teach.

The reform discourse of student learning, underpinned by constructivist theory was opposed by leading academic scientists who maintained that it damaged the integrity of the discipline and hindered production of new scientists; these and other objections are being gradually overcome. *Learning to Learn*, published 2002, acknowledges that learning is the active construction of knowledge by the learner and a process achieved through learning experiences which may lead to construction of different kinds of knowledge.

Examination pressure has been a major concern to educators, parents and policy makers: 'there is a general belief that emphasis on examinations jeopardises the genuine development of young people and is detrimental to the entire national population'. The 2020 plan calls for a reduction in student workload, school-based curricula and a credit system at the senior secondary level to make learning more individualised and flexible.

Teachers meet in study groups at scheduled times, together with related personnel, to draw up detailed lesson plans which also serve as documentation of the teacher's professional performance. The study groups are supervised by teaching-study office and in turn by an officer from the Education Department. Teachers are observed by others including new teachers (in order to learn) and senior teachers (for mentoring). PISA 2009 reports that students are considered still to not have much autonomy in their study, outstanding schools are still rare and examination pressure still prevails.

In Shanghai teachers must be highly qualified—secondary teachers must have a degree and professional certification. Every teacher is expected to engage in 240 h of professional development within the first 5 years. Integration across disciplinary boundaries and test abilities to apply knowledge to real-life problems are a feature of the reformed curriculum.

As part of reform museums and similar places became crucial to the new curriculum. A 'supplementary system' of institutions or programmes outside schools in the arts and all kinds of subjects not offered by schools exist, and are supported by parents.

Shanghai-China, a principal recipient of migrant workers, was the first jurisdiction in China to introduce neighbourhood attendance at primary and junior secondary levels, requiring students to attend their local schools. Converting 'weaker' schools to 'stronger' schools has involved upgrading buildings, financial transfer payments, pairing better schools with weaker one's so that the principal of the stronger school becomes also the head of the weaker school and sending experienced, including retired, teachers to the weaker schools to mentor the teachers there. 'It is believed that the ethos, management style and teaching methods of the good schools can in this way be transferred to the poorer school'.

In Shanghai, class sizes have been reduced, all teachers have mentors, teachers are organised into research groups and lesson preparation groups. Classroom observation and feedback are frequent and there are professional learning communities at district level (Williss 2012).

In the Zhabei district of Shanghai, characterised by high crime and poor education, teachers are encouraged to instil low-performing pupils with greater confidence in their abilities to become potential achievers: now 80 % of secondary graduates proceed to university compared with the municipal average of 56 %.

12.2.4 Singapore

Singapore has transformed itself from a developing country to a modern industrial economy in the space of one generation. Education has always been seen as central to the development of the country both economically and culturally. Persistent political leadership has driven ambitious standards and a culture of continuous improvement. Students from Singapore consistently perform extremely well in all international tests. There is a demonstrated commitment to equity and meritocracy. Singapore's housing policies provide for government-built but self-owned apartments and communities are mixed ethnically.

Singapore's first Prime Minister Lee Kuan Yew set two overarching goals: to build a modern economy and create a sense of national identity (OECD 2010c, p. 160) As in China before the recent reforms, in pre-independence Singapore only the affluent were educated. Lee Kuan Yew recruited 'the best and brightest people' into his government. 'From the mid-1990s on, Singapore has sought to become a player in the global knowledge economy, encouraging more research- and innovation-intensive industry and seeking to attract scientists and scientific companies from around the globe'.

A single education system was established and universal primary and lower secondary education were attained by the early 1970s though the standard was not very high. In the 1980s, schooling was varied to enable multiple pathways for students so as to reduce the drop-out rate and improve quality to produce a more technically qualified labour force. Heavy investment occurred in post secondary technical education. Industry focus is on a knowledge- and skill-intensive industry requiring high quality education in order to make Singapore globally competitive economically.

Singapore makes extensive use of international benchmarking as a way of continually improving the system: staff of the ministry, National Institute of Education (NIE) and schools all visits other systems to explore their practices.

Teachers are recruited from the top third of the secondary school graduating class by special panels. All training is undertaken at NIE: programs are designed in consultation with academics with the teacher in mind and thus there is a strong pedagogical component.

The education system has changed from a knowledge-transmission education model to a one emphasising creativity and self-directed learning advanced through Ministry of Education policy directives, regular meetings and professional development opportunities. Local councils provide support to families in need of financial help. Children who require special support in learning to read and in mathematics are provided with systematic intervention by teachers in small groups. Though preschools are privately funded government provides low-income students with financial support.

In recent years streaming has been replaced by subject matter banding, movement between streams has been made more flexible, and special attention is given to weaker performers.

12.2.5 Japan

*Japan*s education system is grounded in a deep and enduring commitment to children and is typified by a clear goal of 'fostering a deep conceptual understanding'. There is strong support at home for children in their education. Strong incentives are provided to take tough courses and study hard. There is a shared belief that effort makes the difference. 'Individuals gain esteem by doing things that the group values... [This cultural factor] lies behind the good educational performance'. A shared belief that education is the key to the country's future, continuous international benchmarking, incentives for teachers and especially students, a coherent and focused curriculum and careful attention to financial allocations are all important features of the system.

Though classes are heterogeneous, expected outcomes are set 'at the top of the range of possible outcomes worldwide'. High achieving students help lower-achieving students within the group, the classroom and the school. Teachers and principals are often reassigned amongst schools to ensure distribution of the most capable teachers amongst schools is fair and equitable.

The only tests now are entrance exams for high school and university; results are published by newspapers so everyone knows the rankings of schools and their success in getting students into the right high schools and universities: 'stories are written about students who succeeded against all odds in the exams and others who did not'.

Japanese teachers have a high degree of autonomy. There is substantial accountability to parents, peers and others but is not based on student assessment. Teachers spend a great deal of time thinking about their lesson planning. Communication with parents is maintained by means of notebooks shuttled between home and school by the student.

Students are attracted to the teaching profession by the high regard in which teachers are held. Prefectures are prepared to provide the training in the necessary job skills: induction lasts a full year. 10 years after teachers commence their teaching they are required by law to undertake additional training.

University professors and education ministry staff are the 'key figures' in setting the curriculum which is detailed, demanding and closely followed by each prefecture. There is an emphasis on student engagement. Classes are large and most instruction is for the whole class, features which the writers of the PISA report observe at first glance violate the most common sense principles.

Students are not held back if they are having difficulty and those requiring special education are assigned to heterogeneous regular classrooms. Teachers meet frequently to discuss students having difficulty: such students may get special instruction after school. There is a high degree of cooperation among students in the learning process.

12.2.6 Canada

Canada does not have a national education policy: the provinces are responsible for their own systems. Students from Ontario and Alberta perform to a very high level. School boards, which employ staff and appoint principals, are made up of elected people as in the US; there has been a significant reduction in the number of boards. In Ontario earlier approaches to education based on more neoclassical economic views which marginalised teachers unions and favoured certain sections of the population have been overturned.

Reforms in Ontario were driven by Premier Dalton McGuinty, elected in 2003. Prescription from the top and an anti-union stance were jettisoned: in cooperation with the union additional teaching positions were created including a special teacher in each school who works with a team of teachers to focus on students experiencing difficulty! McGuinty was advised by Professor Michael Fullan from the Ontario Institute for Studies in Education (OISE) at the University of Toronto.

Present policies are grounded in a 'centrally-driven pressure for higher results, combined with extensive capacity building and a climate of relative trust and mutual respect'. Though classes are heterogeneous, particular attention is given to children of migrant families: the culturally diverse population is seen a contributing to richness and representing a challenge. In secondary school students are placed into tracks or streams based on perceived ability levels: these practices have been criticised for not sufficiently challenging students in the lower tracks.

Seven 'Big Ideas for Whole System Reform' formed the basis of the McGuinty and Fullan reforms (Fullan 2010). These were:

- All children can learn.
- A small number of key priorities.
- Resolute leadership/stay on message.
- Collective capacity.
- Strategies with precision.
- Intelligent accountability.
- All means all.

Fullan observes that the breakthrough comes when children actually achieve gains that hitherto many did not think possible; significant results can be obtained when specific strategies are applied. It is the actual experience and corresponding results that convince teachers that it can be done, not moral exhortation or mounds of evidence from other situations. The best energizer is actually accomplishing something significant and then building on it.

The reforms rested heavily on the confidence that the government had in the quality of the Provinces teachers. Special attention was paid to leadership development, especially for school principals and in 2008 government initiated the Ontario Leadership Strategy spelling out skills, knowledge and attributes of effective leaders: a new province-wide appraisal program has been developed for school leaders. Professional rather than administrative accountability is the focus.

Teachers are recruited from the top end of the talent pool and it is difficult to get into a teachers college.

12.2.7 Korea

Two generations ago, South Korea had an economic output equivalent to that of Afghanistan today and was 23rd among current OECD countries in terms of educational output. Today South Korea is one of the top performers in terms of the proportion of successful school leavers, with 94 % of children obtaining a high school diploma. Korea's average performance was already high in 2000, but policy makers were concerned that only a narrow elite achieved levels of excellence in PISA. Within less than a decade, Korea was able to virtually double the share of students demonstrating excellence in reading literacy.

Like Japan, Korea pays its teachers comparatively well and provides them with ample time for other work than teaching, which drives costs upwards, while paying for this with comparatively large class sizes. Like Hong Kong-China and Shanghai-China, the share of disadvantaged students in Korea who excel at school despite their disadvantaged background is about twice as high as in the US.

As in Finland, social advantage in Korea is associated with less variation in educational achievement than in the OECD as a whole. Students differ in achievement but not in a way that is so substantially related to their social background.

Korea makes frequent use of assessment or achievement data—standardised tests—for the purpose of benchmarking and information about curriculum and teacher practices. More than 80 % of students attend schools that provide parents with information about students achievement relative to other students; in this respect Korea resembles Sweden, the US and Norway amongst others but is unlike many other countries including Finland.

Expenditure on primary, secondary and post-secondary non-tertiary education increased significantly between 2000 and 2009, much of that increase being absorbed in reducing class size (OECD 2012). Private funding for primary and lower secondary school education is substantial; private funding of universities is also very high at 75 % compared with an OECD average of 27 % (OECD 2008).

In 2010 98 % of 25–34 year olds had attained an upper secondary education, the highest proportion of any OECD country. The proportion of tertiary-educated Koreans has increased dramatically in the last 14 years, doubling to 40 %, the largest percentage increase among all OECD countries; of 25–34 year-olds 65 % now are tertiary educated, again the highest proportion of any OECD country. Males are much more likely to be tertiary educated than women, and this is reflected in employment rates, but almost all 25–34 year old women now obtain tertiary qualifications.

12.2.8 Sweden

Before proceeding to consider the important differences between these countries whose students perform to a very high level it is worth considering Sweden where some reforms have taken place in recent years. Sweden has generally performed well in international tests such as PISA.

Significant changes have taken place in the Swedish education system over the last 20 years; some of them are similar to those which have occurred in the US and UK Financial responsibility was transferred from the state to municipalities, pupils could choose which school within the municipality to go to and no longer had to attend the nearest school and municipalities had to provide private schools with a grant equal to the average expenditure per pupil in the public school system. Private schools cannot charge fees (Böhlmark and Lindahl 2008).

There have been short-term effects of the reforms but they are too small to have any lasting positive effect. The school voucher reform from 1992 opened up the Swedish school system to private providers and had an immense impact on municipal schools (Wiborg 2010). Competition for funds, together with parental choice, led to segregation within the public education sector: popular schools have increased their enrolment and less popular schools have lost pupils and therefore also funding: some schools have become elitist and others developed a poor reputation. Parent's choice of schools has reinforced the existing segregation related to housing (Residential segregation has also increased over the same period).

Swedish schools have become more homogeneous (Skolverket 2010). Streaming has evolved as an organisational principle within the unified compulsory school. Commonly, pupils are separated into different classroom groups based on special support needs or attainment levels. Stigmatising effects often arise, leaving a negative impact on pupil's self-image and motivation.

However, Swedish schools are far from identical to schools in the UK and operate in a different context: this means that policy-makers and the press are wrong in drawing parallels with the free-school type reforms proposed for the UK. The Swedish experiment has proved expensive, it has not led to significant learning gains overall and has increased inequality. Recently test scores of Swedish students have declined and Sweden has fallen down the rankings somewhat.

In Sweden almost 82 % of educated people are employed, the highest level of all OECD countries after Iceland and the average difference in employment between tertiary educated and upper secondary educated is relatively small. Some 7.3 % of Sweden's GDP was spent on education compared with the OECD average of 5.8 %. Annual income for teachers at the end of their career is less than the OECD average.

UK Education Secretary Michael Gove, shortly before coming to office, claimed on BBC4 that academic studies show that 'free schools'—which are privately run but funded by government—lead to raised standards (In October 2013 it was announced that a 27 year old woman who had no teaching qualifications had resigned from the position of principal of Pimlico Academy, a free school (with 60 pupils) established by a charity set up by Lord Nash, a junior schools minister and one of Michael Gove's closest allies (Syal 2013). Education Secretary Gove has claimed that removing the requirement for staff to have qualified teacher status would replicate the 'dynamism' that he believes is found in private schools and has extended this freedom to free schools).

The socioeconomic composition of schools, according to the latest OECD (2012) report, poses significant challenges for disadvantaged students and those with an immigrant background, most of them enrolled in disadvantaged schools. A large proportion of 4 year olds are enrolled in pre-school but annual expenditure is low. Whilst spending on tertiary education increased by a greater amount in the last 14 years than in any other OECD country, most of the spending was privately funded.

On her blog of March 26 2013 Diane Ravitch reported comments by Professor Henry M. Levin, director of the National Center for the Study of Privatization in Education at Teachers College, Columbia University at a conference in Sweden convened by the Royal Swedish Academy of Sciences to review evidence about the education reforms in Sweden (Ravitch 2013b). Levin observed that *Forbes Magazine* recommended for the US that: '…we can learn something about when choice works by looking at Sweden's move to vouchers.'

Levin pointed to the 'dramatic' rise in private school enrolments and a 'fairly precipitous decline' on international test scores in reading, science and mathematics. He evaluated the Swedish reforms, based on published studies, on four criteria. In respect of Freedom of Choice he found the reforms to have been highly successful, in respect of productive efficiency he found virtually no difference in achievement between public and independent schools for comparable students.

As to equity Levin pointed out that a 'comprehensive, national study sponsored by the government' had found that socioeconomic stratification has increased as well as ethnic and immigrant segregation: better qualified educators were drawn to schools whose students had higher socioeconomic status and were Swedish born; international testing revealed rising variance in test scores among schools. There was no direct assessment of the effect of the reforms on social cohesion though Levin surmised that increasing stratification represented an obstacle to that.

These outcomes are similar to what has been found in other countries where 'marketisation' and choice have been introduced such as New Zealand. Levin pointed to similar outcomes in Chile and the Netherlands.

12.3 Lessons from PISA 2009 for the US (and Other Countries)

In drawing lessons from these examples and others, the PISA 2009 Report comments on the system in the US and makes some important and telling points. Attention was specially drawn to the gross inequities in funding which characterise the US system. 'The relationship between the total amount spent, without respect to how it is distributed, and the results obtained for what is spent, may be the single most important factor for the US'.

In the US teachers are often recruited from lower performing segments of high school graduates in low status education institutions. High performing education systems, on the other hand, recruit from the highest levels of graduates. A substantial proportion of teachers leave within the first 5 years of their employment. The seemingly low-cost solution to teacher employment actually costs more in extra specialists and managers. In the US socioeconomically disadvantaged schools have less financial resources than advantaged schools. This is a radical difference from high performing systems in all the countries mentioned earlier including Finland, China and Ontario Canada. An additional factor concerns the manner in which socioeconomically disadvantaged schools are treated. High performing systems are notable for the way in which they treat this issue, as already noted.

'[The] system of school finance in the US ... allows wealthy people to form a school taxing district with other wealthy people who, collectively, are able to pay very low tax rates and produce very large tax revenues, enabling these wealthy people to hire the best teachers in the state for their children and to surround their children with other children from other wealthy families, thereby creating overwhelming educational advantages for their children. At the other end of the spectrum, poor families, who cannot afford the homes that are available in the communities that are home to wealthy people, end up paying very high tax rates but raising very little revenue'.

Unfortunately responses of US authorities to the results of PISA and other international tests fail to understand the lessons. PISA questions have been asserted to contain an ideological bias (Loveless 2009). China's image was asserted to be the main driver (Dillon 2010). The recent book *Battle Hymn of the Tiger Mother* by Yale University law professor Amy Chua asserted that American parents have let their children down by not insisting that their grades be the best and that they work hard at their schoolwork (Johnson 2011).

It is true that in some Asian countries, private tutoring of students after school is a major issue. Indeed some reports suggest that rather than being about remedial help it is more about competition. The Asian Development Bank (2012) notes that 'shadow education' is expanding at an alarming rate with household income being diverted into an unregulated industry creating inefficiencies in the country's education systems. The pressure on the individual student can be extreme as pointed out by Mark Bray of the Comparative Education Research Centre, University of Hong Kong (Radio Australia 2012). Asian society values education very highly but to attribute the performance of all Asian students simply to out of school tutoring would be to ignore all the other evidence about teacher training and support and school curricula revealed by the OECD in its studies for PISA.

Ravitch (2010, 2011) observed after summarising the outcomes of the PISA study, 'The lesson of PISA is this: Neither of the world's highest-performing nations (referring to China and Finland) do what our 'reformers' want to do. How long will it take before our political leaders begin to listen to educators? How long will it take before they realize that their strategies have not worked anywhere? How long will it be before they stop inflicting their bad ideas on our schools, our students, our teachers, and American education?' Others have said the same thing (Ripley 2010, Horin 2011).

A very recent example of the seeming inability of US authorities to understand the issues is the demand by Rahm Emanuel that Chicago teachers sign a new contract involving longer school days: in the US teachers already spend between 1,050 and 1,100 h a year teaching, much more than in almost every country. Long teaching hours are not a significant indicator of student educational achievement.

Ravitch repeated these views in her review of Finnish Director-General of Education Pasi Sahlberg's book, *Finnish Lessons: What Can the World Learn from Educational Change in Finland?* (Sahlberg 2012). And in reviewing other assertions about school reform (Ravitch 2012a): 'Schools are crucial institutions in our society and teachers can make a huge difference in changing children's lives, but schools and teachers alone cannot cure the ills of an unequal and stratified society. … Children need better schools, and they also need health clinics, high-quality early childhood education, arts programs, after-school activities, safe neighborhoods, and basic economic security. To the extent that we reduce poverty, we will improve student achievement'.

12.4 Successful Systems Share Common Feature: All Children Can Learn

Those systems where student performance is superior share common features notwithstanding local differences. A number of countries including Finland and Korea have shown substantial improvement over the last 20 or so years: policies at the leadership level of government have been largely responsible though these have been possible because of strong community support for significant investment.

Education is an essential element of long-term community development. Capacity at the level of local school management combined with a degree of devolution of authority in relevant areas creates significant incentives for teacher performance.

International reports emphasise that teachers make a significant positive contribution to student achievement when they are able to deliver quality instruction within a broad curriculum, have high status in the community and their school has competent leadership. The importance of leadership in encouraging professional development and setting high standards for student achievement as well as building strong connections with the community has been emphasised elsewhere (Sect. 7.2) and is especially evident in the studies of schools in the south side of Chicago.

What is also evident is that successful systems vigorously pursue the proposition that all children can learn and pay particular attention to those students having difficulties, whether it is for reasons of language or other factors. Just one example is the experience of the DuFours in Illinois and the application of their approaches in California (Sect. 7.4). Premier McGuinty's initiatives on coming to office in Ontario are noteworthy. The involvement of retired teachers to assist in classes in poorer parts of Shanghai China must also be mentioned. And successful school systems are mostly in countries where preschool attendance is very high and subsidised if necessary as in the case of Singapore. It is not irrelevant that the

Australian Capital Territory and Western Australia have high levels of participation in preschool and high school student achievement levels.

The argument has been advanced by some that the high achievements of students in Asian countries, evident especially in the PISA 2009 results and much commented on in Australia and the US, are due significantly to high levels of participation in out of school coaching in those countries. The rhetorical question is then posed why do we want that here? This argument must surely fall for two reasons. First, those participating in high levels of coaching are mostly from higher SES levels of the community, yet the high average student achievement levels typically involve attention to lower SES levels of the community. Secondly, as mentioned, all the countries, including these successful Asian countries where students achieve to a high level share a number of common features. And, as Diane Ravitch has pointed out very strongly, as has David Berliner, those features are not found in the vast majority of school systems in the US.

There is no good reason to adopt reforms along the same lines as those in the US: countries with successful education programs share few if any features of the US system. In Australia the additional financial support given by the Howard Government to independent schools is part of such approaches. Equity, the gap between socioeconomically advantaged and disadvantaged students, is a major issue and has been increased in Australia in the last decade. Students in Australia from disadvantaged backgrounds are doing much worse than in most other top performing countries. Comparisons of the high performing countries with others show how strongly policies which do not incorporate neoliberal notions and neoclassical economics contribute to the high achievement.

The survey of school systems shows that a major failing of education reform is the lack of connection which governments and others make between education and other policy prescriptions relating to poverty and inequality, indigeneity, health and even provision of services like libraries and museums.

A final point should be made with particular reference to international comparisons of international achievement. Much has been made of what are asserted to be falling standards of achievement by students in the US and Australia. To an extent there is a serious misuse of statistics involved. The achievement levels of US students are at higher levels than for many decades; importantly, other countries, notably Finland and Korea and some Asian countries, have put much more effort into reforms, and reforms which have made a difference, than has been the case in the US. It should be noted, as commented by Parsi Sahlberg, that Finland didn't start out trying to have the most successful education system in the world. They embarked on their reforms in order to achieve high levels of equality. That is something to which the US subscribes rhetorically but not in fact!

In the case of Australia, though in a simple tabulation Australia would seem to have slipped down the rankings, Australian students are still equal second or third in the world when statistical significance is considered, as it should be. Australian students significantly and consistently outperform students in the UK and the US as well as many European countries whose achievement are above or near the OECD average including Norway, Sweden, Denmark, France, Switzerland,

Iceland and Ireland in all subjects assessed by the OECD in PISA 2009. In reading Australian students also outperformed students in Belgium, Estonia, Poland and Germany. In mathematics literacy Australian students outperform students in Austria and Slovenia. And in science literacy students from Belgium, as well as those mentioned already, all achieve to a significantly lower level than Australian students. These are facts almost never mentioned in the vociferous claims about falling standards in Australia.

That the achievement of Australian students has declined slightly and that the gains made by other countries has outstripped those in Australia are issues which must be addressed. As we will see in the next chapter, the Australian school system has a high level of inequity and an extremely confused and incoherent funding environment. Considering that there have been significant though slight declines in the achievement levels of the better students surely suggests a need to examine the additional government support for independent schools in Australia, justified as it has been as in the US on the proposition that government schools are failing!

References

Alton-Lee, A. (2003). *Building teacher quality: What does the research tell us?* Paper presented at the ACER Research Conference 2003. Retrieved September 4, 2012, from http://www.acer.edu.au/documents/RC2003_Proceedings.pdf

Asian Development Bank. (2012, July 4). *ADB study highlights dark side of shadow education.* Retrieved September 5, 2012, from http://www.adb.org/news/adb-study-highlights-dark-side-shadow-education

Barber, M., & Mourshed, M. (2007). *How the world's best-performing school systems come out on top.* London, England: McKinsey & Company. Retrieved September 6, 2012, from http://www.mckinsey.com/clientservice/socialsector/resources/pdf/Worlds_School_Systems_Final.pdf

Böhlmark, A. & Lindahl, M. (2008, September). Does School Privatization Improve Educational Achievement? Evidence from Sweden's Voucher Reform'. Discussion Paper No. 3691 for Iza Institute for Study of Labor in Bonn. Germany.

Dillon, S. (2010, December 7). Top test scores from Shanghai Stun Educators. *New York Times.*

Fiske, E. B., & Ladd, H. F. (2000). *When schools compete: A cautionary tale.* Washington: The Brookings Institution.

Fullan, M. (2010). The big ideas behind whole system reform. *Education Canada, 50*(3), 24–27.

Horin, A. (2011, January 1). Where true school reform occurs. *Sydney Morning Herald.*

Jensen, B. et al. (2012). *Catching up: Learning from the best school systems in East Asia.* Carlton: Grattan Institute.

Johnson, D. (2011, August 18). Finish that homework! *New York Review of Books.*

Loveless, T. (2009, February 25). *The 2008 brown center report on American education: How well are American students learning?* Washington: The Brookings Institution. Retrieved September 5, 2012, from http://www.brookings.edu/reports/2009/0225_education_loveless.aspx

Mourshed, M., Chijioke, C., & Barber, M. (2010). *How the world's most improved schools systems keep getting better.* London: McKinsey & Company.

OECD. (2006). *Assessing Scientific, Reading and Mathematical Literacy A framework for PISA 2006.* Paris: OECD. Retrieved October 19, 2012, from http://www.oecd.org/pisa/pisaproducts/pisa2006/37464175.pdf

OECD. (2008). *Education at a Glance: OECD indicators*. Paris: OECD. Retrieved September 10, 2008, from http://www.oecd.org/education/skills-beyond-school/41284038.pdf

OECD. (2010a). *PISA 2009 results: What students know and can do: Student performance in reading, mathematics and science I*. Paris: OECD.

OECD. (2010b). *PISA 2009 results: What makes a school successful? Resources, policies and practices IV*. Paris: OECD.

OECD. (2010c). *Strong performers and successful reformers in education: Lessons from PISA for the United State*. Paris: OECD. Retrieved September 4, 2012, from http://www.oecd.org/pisa/46623978.pdf

OECD. (2012). *Education at a Glance 2012 OECD Indicators. Chapter C How do early childhood education systems differ around the world?* Paris: OECD. Retrieved September 13, 2012, from http://dx.doi.org/10.1787/eag-2012-en

Quince, A. (presenter). (2012, September 2). Finland: The real education revolution. *ABC RN 'Rear Vision'*. Retrieved September 3, 2012, from http://www.abc.net.au/radionational/programs/rearvision/finland-the-real-education-revolution/4228418

Radio Australia. (2012, July 6). *Asia spending billions on private tuition for kids*. Retrieved September 5, 2012, from http://www.radioaustralia.net.au/international/radio/program/connect-asia/asia-spending-billions-on-private-tuition-for-kids/974298

Ravitch, D. (2010, December 14). The real lessons of PISA. *Edweekblog*. Retrieved September 5, 2012, from http://blogs.edweek.org/edweek/Bridging-Differences/2010/12/the_real_lessons_of_pisa.html

Ravitch, D. (2011, December 29). School reform: A failing grade. *New York Review of Books*.

Ravitch, D. (2012a, March 8). Schools we can envy. *New York Review of Books*.

Ravitch, D. (2013b, March 26). *Vouchers in Sweden: Scores fall, inequality grows*. Retrieved April 18, 2013, from http://dianeravitch.net/2013/03/26/the-swedish-voucher-system-an-appraisal/

Ripley, A. (2010, December). Your child left behind. *The Atlantic*. Retrieved September 5, 2012, from http://www.theatlantic.com/magazine/archive/2010/12/your-child-left-behind/8310/

Sahlberg, P. (2007). Education policies for raising student learning: The finnish approach. *Journal of Education Policy, 22*, 147–171.

Sahlberg, P. (2012). *Finnish lessons: What can the world learn from educational change in Finland?*. New York: Teachers College Press.

Skolverket. (2010). *What influences educational achievement in Swedish schools?* Stockholm: Skolverket.

Syal, R. (2013, October 10). Free school head with no teaching qualifications quits after six months. *The Guardian*.

Thomson. S. et al. (2010). *PISA in Brief Highlights from the full Australian report: Challenges for Australian Education: Results from PISA 2009*. Melbourne: ACER. Retrieved 22 October 2012, from http://www.acer.edu.au/documents/PISA-2009-In-Brief.pdf

United Nations. (2010). *United Nations Human Development Report 2010—20th Anniversary Edition. The Real Wealth of Nations: Pathways to Human Development. Chapter 3*. New York: United Nations. Retrieved September 7, 2012, from http://hdr.undp.org/en/reports/global/hdr2010/

United Nations. (2013). Human development report 2013. The rise of the south: human progress in a diverse world. New York: UNDP. Retrieved June 9, 2013 from http://www.undp.org/content/undp/en/home/librarypage/hdr/human-development-report-2013/

Wiborg, S. (2010). Swedish free schools: Do they work? *LLAKES Centre for Learning and Life Chances in Knowledge Economies and Societies*. Retrieved September 5, 2012, from http://www.llakes.org/wp-content/uploads/2010/09/Wiborg-online.pdf

Williss, M. (2012, May 8). Australian teacher performance and development framework. *On Line Opinion*. Retrieved May 14, 2012, from http://www.onlineopinion.com.au/view.asp?article=13591

Wylie, C. (2012). *Vital connections: Why we need more than self-managed schools*. Wellington: NZCER Press.

Chapter 13
Universities and Tertiary Education

13.1 Universities and Society

The contribution of universities to education is critical in a number of ways. Obviously, through their scholarship they contribute knowledge and understanding. Through their research in the education field specifically and in the involvement of postgraduate students in that research, they make important contributions to the economy and many other areas. University academics play a part in influencing and in some cases determining, the content of syllabi and examinations at secondary school level. This can have a great influence on the uptake of the subject and how people come to view the importance of the subject in later life: the nature and importance of history and historical research is a case in point as are science and scientific knowledge. Thirdly, universities play a role in training teachers.

Much of the debate about universities focuses on the research rather than on the teaching and learning. Almost universally appointments of academic staff are made on the basis of research competence rather than teaching ability. And the advancement of academic staff similarly privileges research. Because of that many academic staff offload their tutorial responsibilities to graduate students. Many students don't bother to attend lectures but decide to crib notes from other students or simply study the textbook. And tutorials are of marginal benefit. Even the top universities in the UK have suffered. The practice at All Souls College, Oxford of requiring prospective entrants to write an essay addressing one word, such as death or water, is gone (Lyall 2010).

In the last few decades of the debate about universities generally the focus has tended to be on the phasing out of certain subject areas, in the arts and humanities in particular, and the increasing attention given to economics and commercial subjects such as business administration. The ethics of involvement of faculty in research for companies and government concerned with pharmaceuticals, military weaponry also attracts debate.

Typically universities offer defined subjects at undergraduate level and gaining a degree requires successful completion of those subjects. A different approach is taken by Roskilde University in Denmark established in 1972. An inter-disciplinary approach to the identification and solving of problems has replaced the traditional division of study into narrow academic disciplines. Students are encouraged to demonstrate the relevance of different theoretical perspectives to their chosen subject. And in project work students are trained to organise and write major project reports based on the results they have obtained during research and analysis. Research staff are assigned as tutors to the project groups and interact with the group as advisor and discussion partner.

Access is particularly difficult in some countries and to some universities. In the UK for instance a few universities are overwhelmingly the source of recruits to highly paid positions in law and commerce. Increased fees have made access more difficult. In Australia the impact of fees and patterns of individual expenditure have led to the majority of undergraduate students being employed for over 20 h a week. They attend tutorials mainly because their presence or absence is taken into account in awarding degrees. They may arrive at the tutorials without having attended lectures or read the selected course readings. Exams have been replaced by assignment essays so that students may pass merely by choosing a limited range of topics to study.

13.2 Issues for Universities

The important issues for universities, in addition to teaching effectiveness, include their place in the future intellectual space of society and the role staff play as 'public intellectuals'; access by students on merit criteria before any other consideration such as socioeconomic status, disability, language difficulty or in some countries including Australia, indigeneity. The extent to which course structure reflects what is important and not just what students are prepared to pay for and their functioning as organisations is increasingly an issue as governments urge universities to be more entrepreneurial and seek more of their funds from non-traditional sources.

The drive to gain more non government funding has involved the appropriation of what have been seen as good business practices. In reality this has meant little more than increasing the number of people in marketing and revenue generation and an increase in reporting information in order to comply with what is seen as accountability. This has meant less concern with academic matters including scholarship and less influence of academic staff. In some universities, corporate culture has gone as far as hiring brand consultants whose reports recommend how academics should speak in public! These issues are taken up later in this essay.

Participation in society as a 'public intellectual' is most often asserted to be the principal reason for according academics tenured status. More often academic staff devote themselves to their own research, avoid the media and administrative work or only participate in routine tasks of administration including attending meetings.

13.2 Issues for Universities

Or being a public intellectual is narrowly defined as speaking at conferences of their discipline. What is needed is active engagement! And support for that.

The propositions are that academics should not speak publicly outside their field and that involvement in popularisation activities such as contributing to media presentations leads to oversimplification of knowledge, and therefore is to be discouraged, pushed to the margin. That is especially so when it comes to exercises such as consideration for promotion and recognition through awards and membership of societies. The analytical ability gained by most scholars is such as to enhance analysis of public policy notwithstanding that they are unlikely to adjust to the political need for compromise in many situations. Comparison with minor political parties and their obsession with control is not entirely inappropriate.

An example of the engagement of academics in public policy is the involvement of many scholars around the world in the elucidation of the impacts of rising carbon emissions on global climate. The attempted marginalisation, sometimes engaged in, of people not climatologists as not entitled to comment misses the point: the issue is whether the views expressed represent an honest response to the data uninfluenced by one's affiliations and the simultaneous declaration of such affiliations. It is as wrong for scientists to discount conclusions about climate change without revealing that they receive financial support for their research from energy companies as it is, for example, for economists engaged by the Iceland Chamber of Commerce to not reveal their affiliation in reporting favourably on the economic situation of that country, as was demonstrated in a recent film on the 2008 financial crisis. Discounting the engagement in popularisation and public policy is an engagement in elitism, comparable to the closed door conspiracies of business cartels.

In Australia in recent years academic staff have increasingly contributed to public debate and a new website The *Conversation* has been created and contributions to it are frequently reprinted on other sites. A former head of the Department of Prime Minister and Cabinet (and his successor), however, had harsh words for academics and their participation in public policy formulation. Peter Shergold (now an academic at the University of New South Wales) observed 'there remains a chasm between research and influence and between the policy intellectual and the policy practitioner. The potential of academics to act as knowledge brokers in the development of public policy remains largely unfulfilled' (Shergold 2011). Would it be accurate to say that many within government involved in public policy become infatuated with the importance of their own contribution and seek to magnify that by marginalising the contribution of others whose contribution may sometimes be couched in rather obscure language?

13.2.1 Issues of Access

The GFC hit US university endowments seriously. It threatens the extent to which scholarships are provided to less well-off families: State governments offered scholarships more often on merit—meaning high achievement—rather than need (Delbanco 2009). The problems are exacerbated by declines in tuition revenue and state grants. Literary critic and Columbia University professor Anthony Delbanco claims America can no longer claim to be a nation of equal opportunity where talent and effort can overcome poverty and prejudice. Yet too many students who can continue their education beyond secondary school find themselves in underfunded and overcrowded colleges. The US system is a highly stratified one in which merit is the ubiquitous slogan but disparity of opportunity is often the reality. Though today's students at US universities are richer on average than their predecessors, universities offer students neither a coherent view of the point of college education nor any guidance on how they might discover for themselves some larger purpose in life.

Further cuts in funding to universities by the UK government in early 2010 before the general election brought the response from the Russell Group of 20 leading universities that they would be brought to their knees: 800 years of higher education was being jeopardised (Shepherd 2010). Increased numbers of graduates face a greater scramble as the number of applicants for each job increases to 70 and available positions are predicted to decrease (Vasagar 2010).

Anthony Grafton (2011) of Princeton University provides some stark realities of the student experience. Much of his commentary applies generally at least to universities in the developed world: the relentless drive for accountability and efficiency, the belief that the courses offered should be only those in demand, the resulting downsizing of many faculties.

Many universities in the US offer faculty salaries and working conditions that few others can match, spending more on their staff and students than peers overseas. Many offer generous aid for undergraduates and pay full fees for doctoral students.

But Grafton also points to 'ferocious criticism' and 'festering sores': professors at the most prestigious universities publishing the work of 'paid flacks for pharmaceutical companies under their own names' and 'head football and basketball coaches earn millions and their assistants hundreds of thousands for running semiprofessional teams. Few of the sports teams earn much money for the universities that sponsor them and so on'. Too many professors entrust the face-to-face teaching of actual students to underpaid graduate students.

One study by Richard Arum and Josipa Roksa, quoted by Grafton, analysed data from the Collegiate Learning Assessment (CLA) administered to university students in their first semester at university and again at the end of their second year and data from the National Survey of Student Engagement. It revealed that some 45 % of students effectively had made no progress in critical thinking, complex reasoning, and writing in their first two years. Most students spent only about 12 h a week studying, half that of 40 years earlier. Half had taken courses that required no more than 20 pages of writing in the previous semester.

'… vast numbers of students come to university with no particular interest in their courses and no sense of how these might prepare them for future careers.'

Most students consider that what the university offers is not skills or knowledge but credentials: a diploma that signals employability and basic work discipline. Those who do manage to learn often come from highly educated families and attend highly selective colleges and universities.

Now families and students pay a much greater share of the costs of enrolment: borrowings have to supplement family savings, student earnings, and scholarship. Debt per student, on average, is now twice as it was 10 years ago. Student debt exceeds total credit card debt! Poor students borrow more.

Those students that dropout still carry the debt no matter whether they gain employment or not. Unemployment among graduates has risen and so have rates of student loan default.

At some universities academic salaries have been capped, desk telephone's removed, repairs of classrooms, now used from early morning till late at night, postponed but millions of dollars are spent on competitive sports! (It is not very different from the situation depicted in the TV series *The Wire* about Baltimore in which savings in expenditure on policing is sought by the city's treasury officials by such devices as refusing permission for officers to take police cars home at night! Or removal of pot plants from New South Wales government offices in the 1980 s.).

13.2.2 Corporatisation, Managerialism and Leadership in Universities

Corporatisation, adherence to business practices concerning organisational structure and corporate planning, employment of people in marketing and fundraising and the appointment to governing bodies of business people has had substantial impact in universities throughout Europe, the UK and Australia and New Zealand. As already pointed out, this has mean academics having less influence (Carney 2008).

There are issues of leadership at many levels in universities. Rather than appointment by merit, there is a kind of last man standing operating at Faculty level where those prepared to take the job get it. Those who could make a much greater contribution decline: the tasks are often administrative and mundane, and as such 'loosely coupled'. University presidents and vice chancellors may fail to join in alliances with their counterparts in other universities, preferring to independently advocate for their own institution or join with only a few others in marginalising other universities. Advocacy of performance indicators by some groups of long-established universities can be seen sometimes as a device to marginalise other universities in the hope of gaining more funding for themselves. This can happen also in certain disciplines where certain approaches are denigrated and others promoted by those who perceive they have the power.

The academy is an example of what distinguished management writer Henry Mintzberg (1983) calls 'professional bureaucracies': they seek control over groups outside the academic area whilst at the same time resisting outside interference. The structure of most universities is increasingly highly pyramidal.

There have been few studies of contemporary models of leadership in universities (Pounder 2001). Leadership expert Mumford (2003) observed a few years ago that creative people require leaders who don't just have technical skills. 'Leaders of creative efforts… must have the social and organizational skills needed to sell people and projects. Inspirational motivation is less important in motivating creative people than engagement of people in a mission where they can make a unique autonomous contribution… Leaders of creative efforts have to devote as much effort to managing the context surrounding the work as to managing the work itself. Autonomy in people's work must be accompanied by a structure that will support autonomous efforts.'

The practices found to be successful in research and development enterprises, particularly research centres which have been responsible for major breakthroughs in biomedical research, have emphasised leadership by scholars and researchers expert in relevant domains of knowledge as well as rigorous attention to hiring high quality staff, an environment of constant challenge to ideas and encouragement of interdisciplinarity and of innovation. Examples are Columbia University, California Institute of Technology (CalTech) and two colleges at the Universities of Cambridge and Oxford in the UK (Hollingsworth and Hollingsworth 2000). These features also are found more generally in successful centres of innovation, creativity and research and development (Quinn et al. 1996; Elkins and Keller 2003).

In a scathing analysis of public management in Britain Ron Amann (2003), onetime Professor of Comparative Politics at the University of Birmingham and later founding Director-General (Permanent Secretary) of the Centre for Management and Policy Studies in the British Cabinet Office, compared the practices imposed by the UK government, particularly in the higher education sector, to those which applied in the highly centralised and inefficient system of the Soviet Union. 'The periphery knew that the centre didn't know and the centre knew that they knew. Around this fundamental core of dishonesty grew a series of ever more elaborate controls and stratagems which brought an entire social system to its knees.'

One of the features of the drive to corporatisation is the talking up of the importance of 'accountability' which has generated a drive for metrics which characterise quality. In the UK 'Research Assessment Exercises' (RAEs) have been in place since 1985. These have revealed comparatively high quality research at some of the newer universities which had not previously been funded significantly. Under the new government in the UK RAEs are to be replaced by the 'Research Excellence Framework'. This will be 'a process of expert review, informed by indicators where appropriate. It is to be undertaken by the four higher education UK funding bodies and managed by a team overseen by the REF Steering Group' (REF 2014).

In Australia, these exercises aimed at identifying research quality have been embraced with some enthusiasm by government bureaucrats and sometimes those in universities. This has led to an exercise in collecting and analysing a vast amount of data, judgements about the relative merit of certain kinds of contributions and the scholarly impact of various journals and other publications. This has been undertaken, by all accounts, with greater fervour than in some other countries but produced little gain to the quality of scholarship whilst absorbing a great deal of time and financial resources. It amounts to little more than arranging deckchairs. Like restructures everywhere and mergers and acquisitions in the corporate world it provides gains to those involved in the process and very little indeed to those subject to the outcomes.

Lost in the exercise has been a genuine recognition of the critical importance and nature of research leadership and the importance of critical judgement in identifying directions in research. The comments made already in respect of creativity are relevant. Unfortunately the armies of bureaucrats seldom engage in exploring these issues. It is fair to say that very often scholars do not either, being content to fall back on established beliefs.

The competitive 'spirit' is common in major areas of research such as the biomedical area where being the first to discover the molecular structure of a protein or synthesise a naturally occurring compound attracts considerable publicity and grant funds. However, as interviews with Nobel prize-winners reveal, cooperation is extremely important to success and acknowledgement of the contribution others is a common feature of research leaders.

The dependence on major grants of some research centres in American universities and in some other countries has also led to appointments of star researchers through processes which bypass normal recruitment. Overheads attached to grants are charged by the universities so hiring staff who attract grants likely helps the university's budget.

That some of the world's past leading scholars would have failed to get funding for their research through systems such as research assessments and quality frameworks is only occasionally acknowledged. That there are very good processes already identified to achieve the same ends, not least the use of peer review (together with other forms of evaluation and with all its faults) is mostly ignored though an element of peer review is used in research assessments.

Simon Head, Associate Fellow at the Rothermere American Institute at Oxford and a Scholar at the Institute for Public Knowledge at New York University, is one of many who have drawn attention to the significant move by universities towards corporate structures and corporate behaviour, increasing prominence of grant funding from business enterprises in determining the directions of research and adoption by governments of practices mostly American in origin, conceived in American business schools and management consulting firms (Head 2007, 2011).

Head asserts that 'these intensive management systems... make use of information technology (IT), [are] marketed by corporations such as IBM, Oracle, and SAP [and] then sold to clients such as the UK government and its bureaucracies, including the universities. This alliance between the public and private sector has become a threat to academic freedom in the UK, and a warning to the American academy about how its own freedoms can be threatened.'

The management systems which now dominate in the UK reached universities in the 1990s through government by way of major consulting firms. Emphasis is given to financial and other quantitative performance indicators. They increase the pressure on courses to be self-funding and on the university generally to raise more of its own funding, in other words increasing reliance on student fees.

One of the outcomes of the 'reforms' at UK universities has been attention to indicators of innovation and learning. Government has sought increased attention to research which has a more general impact beyond the academy, on the end users of research such as businesses, the public service and so on. It is this which has led to involvement in contract research. Head also points out that the 'Key Performance Indicators' (or KPIs) developed as part of this exercise have varied at the whim of successive UK governments.

In the US the trend over recent decades to gaining more non-government funding has led some commentators to decry the subversion of the purpose of universities by defence and pharmaceutical industries. Science writer and commentator Dan Greenberg (2001, 2010), who once likened the demand for accountability in universities to trying to capture and weigh a fog, draws attention to how government and business funding of universities has subverted their purposes. His satirical novel *Tech Transfer* charts the events at a university overtaken by corporate interests.

Christopher Newfield, professor of literature at the University of California Santa Barbara, has coined the term *cognotariat* to connote a small 'creative class' which achieves the creativity and freedom attributed by stereotype to all knowledge workers (Newfield 2010). 'In the American university system', he writes, 'which has parallels in Europe, recipients of higher education are increasingly prepared for a working life in a knowledge economy where independence and social protections have been eroded'. His scathing criticism traverses several issues amongst which are the substantial decrease in employment conditions for academic staff, the relationship of graduate students produced and numbers of positions in the workforce requiring graduates and the way in which industry makes use of universities.

Levels of funding of universities differ as to the different types of education: professional schools receive about three times more funding per student than do undergraduates and medical students receive 10 times more funding. Now, only those academics who contribute directly to the university's proprietary knowledge gain the level of support once enjoyed by all. The share of instructors lacking full-time and/or permanent contracts has doubled over the last 30 years: teaching staffs are now 70 % temporary, people who have no say in university governance even at department level.

Open innovation strategy has led to intellectual property no longer being viewed as shoring up competitive advantage but as 'a bridge to collaboration with other firms that would enable companies to acquire the technologies and competencies they needed to compete successfully'. Access to the intellectual capabilities of universities allows firms such as Intel to fund projects at far less cost than would be incurred were they to undertake the R&D themselves. The funding brings money the university would not otherwise have, together with state-of-the-art equipment and excellent scientific input from the firm's staff.

In exchange the firm gets access to research results, often exclusively for a set period, and first pick of inventions that may turn into useful intellectual property. The university publicises the alliance with a prestigious firm and trumpets the interim research results. 'The strategy works because it can absorb other people's inventions, turning them into its own IP at a discounted cost.'

A recent survey of the status of university staff in English-speaking countries has noted severe declines in funding by governments over the last 10 years, an increasing trend towards user-pay financing and an increase in bureaucratic control which facilitates external influence over changes in teaching and research (Robinson 2006). Salaries of academic staff have experienced a real long-term decline in most countries.

In Australia, as we enter the second decade of this century two universities are moving to restructure their programs to focus more on postgraduate students who will be paying larger fees (Simons 2010). Competition between the older established universities on the one hand and the others can be intense.

13.2.3 What do University Students Know?

Whilst many perceive problems with young adolescents dropping out of school and of those who do finish school being nevertheless not sufficiently prepared for work, there would be a general perception that university graduates, certainly those from the more prestigious universities, would be both intelligent and knowledgeable. Professor James Wilkinson, Director of the Derek Bok Centre for Teaching and Learning, Harvard University in his 'Menzies Oration' a few years ago challenged that (Wilkinson 2006).

Wilkinson dealt with the issue which most particularly defines universities, teaching and learning, what he called the 'what' and the 'how' of undergraduate education. The most important thing [students] can learn is the process of inquiry itself, modeled by the faculty in the course of their teaching. Thus how a subject is taught is crucial. Yet it is a curious fact that most discussions about undergraduate curricula focus almost exclusively on content: discussion about pedagogy is lost. 'The assumption seems to be that if we can just get the content right, the teaching and learning will take care of themselves. That is an assumption with which I could not possibly disagree more strongly.'

The point is that choosing appropriate content is necessary but not sufficient to get anyone to learn anything: it needs to be taught well. Wilkinson explains that by taught well he means taught so that they are capable of understanding and applying what they claim to know.

'For many students, particularly those studying a specialist curriculum, what the university offers is a series of answers to questions they have never learned to ask, generated by a research process they have never been encouraged to understand... The skill that would be of most practical value to our undergraduate students... is the ability to ask good questions and to work at seeking answers based on evidence.'

The research by Richard Arum and Josipa Roksa quoted above is relevant.

13.3 Tertiary Education Reform in Australia

Australia is a federation in which the States have constitutional responsibility for education. Therefore universities are established under State or Territory legislation. Major changes in universities have occurred over the last 30 years. The Whitlam Government of 1972–1975 assumed the entire responsibility for funding tertiary education institutions: in 1974 the states gave up responsibility for funding higher education. In the 1980s John Dawkins, education minister in the Hawke government, amalgamated colleges of advanced education and institutes of technology which were intended to be concerned with vocational training with existing academic universities concerned with education and research. The mergers and acquisitions meant 76 organisations became 36 [new] universities which grew to 44 by 2002.

The majority of students contribute to the cost of tuition through a 'Higher Education Contribution Scheme' (HECS) under which government funds the fee, allowing deferral of payment until their remuneration from employment reaching a certain level. The fee represents the difference between the government subsidy per place and the price the government sets per place. HECS was introduced by the Hawke Government in 1989 and modified by the Howard Government in 1996. The number of students enrolled increased dramatically.

In 2002, Brendan Nelson (Education Minister in the Howard Government from 2001 through 2005) issued a number of Discussion Papers on the Higher Education sector. The preface to the first of the papers, 'Higher Education at the Crossroads' (Nelson 2002a) said, 'The kind of Australia in which the next generation will live, to a large extent will depend on Australia's institutions of higher learning—universities. That which will most influence and inform our future, is not what we know—but what we don't. It is now time for us as a nation to have the maturity to recognise that there is a need to meaningfully consider and conduct a debate of the policy options that lie before us in relation to reform to the way we administer, fund and support Australian universities'.

The Australian Universities Commission (AUC) was established in 1959. The Tertiary Education Commission (TEC) was established in 1977 but abolished in 1988 when the Minister became wholly responsible for advanced education policy. Nevertheless, Australian universities have a high degree of autonomy relative to the situation in other countries, governance being vested in a Council or Senate; they are self-accrediting. The majority of funds are provided by government though non-government funding is increasingly significant.

Governance is an issue in the sector as it is elsewhere! In one of the reports issued by Minister Nelson which dealt with the challenges of governance and management (Nelson 2002b) it was observed that 'too often members of governing boards see themselves as representatives, rather than as contributing skills necessary for an effective governing body'. That is despite the fact that it is clearly established that members of boards owe their first responsibility to the organisation and not any body that might have contributed to their membership of the board.

Ministers, especially John Dawkins and later Brendan Nelson, did want to tell academics how to go about their jobs and become more productive. As staff student-ratios increased, fewer staff had to cope with more students; productivity was indeed seen to be achieved. A formula for increasing funding each year was adopted but did not reflect the rate of increase in salaries and additional funds were no longer provided to meet the increased salaries, something many governments did in recent decades. Enterprise bargaining was introduced allowing negotiation of salaries with the relevant trade union. Universities were urged to gain more funds through research and consultancy services; more staff were hired in areas like marketing and corporate management in pursuit of what was seen as the 'business model'.

The rational or market economic ideology applied to universities has certainly generated concern. Distinguished economist Max Cordon, professorial fellow at the University of Melbourne and Emeritus Professor of International Economics at Johns Hopkins University, reviewed what in essence has become a highly interventionist policy where 'performance' is monitored and being business-like is advocated (Corden 2005). This pervasive accountability and transparency mantra has been criticised by many people: 'managing places of learning and culture by statistical control, as if they were a factory, is abhorrent and destructive' (Dodgson 2012). Nevertheless, huge resources have been devoted to determining metrics by which the quality of research can be assessed.

Responding in 2003 to the Discussion Papers released by Minister Nelson distinguished academic Professor Peter Karmel (2003) asserted that Minister Nelson had adopted 'a big brother knows best' philosophy which contrasted with the 'free market' emphasis Government was giving to the economic world in which 'central planning has lost all credibility'. In Karmel's view each university ought to be able to determine its own priorities in the light of its circumstances, national priorities expressed by government and its assessment of current and future environments.

13.4 The Bradley Review in Australia

In March 2008, the Australian Government initiated a Review of Higher Education to examine the future direction of the higher education sector, its fitness in meeting the needs of the Australian community and economy, and the options for ongoing reform. The Review was conducted by an independent expert Committee, led by Emeritus Professor Denise Bradley AC, former Vice Chancellor of the University of South Australia.

The Committee pointed to future needs for highly skilled people able to adapt to the uncertainties of a rapidly changing future, emphasised the imperative of the rights of all citizens to share in its benefits (Bradley et al. 2008). 'Higher education will continue to be a cornerstone of our legal, economic, social and cultural institutions and it lies at the heart of Australia's research and innovation system.' The panel concluded, 'while the system has great strengths, it faces significant, emerging threats which require decisive action'.

Bradley noted that developed and developing countries alike accepted that there were strong links between productivity and the proportion of the population with high-level skills. Accordingly they had invested in both the number and quality of graduates; the committee asserted that Australia was falling behind other countries in investment in higher education. '… government provision of funds for underlying infrastructure to support research in universities is very significantly below the real costs. This is leading to a pattern of quite unacceptable levels of cross-subsidy from funds for teaching, adversely affecting the quality of the student experience.'

A major thrust of the report was the recommendation that an increase in the proportion of the population attaining higher education qualifications be pursued: the benefits of higher education should be genuinely available to all. Australia was ninth out of 30 OECD countries in the proportion of the population aged 25–34 years with university qualifications, down from seventh a decade previously. Twenty nine percent of Australian 25–34 year-olds had degree-level qualifications but in other OECD countries targets of up to 50 % had already been set. 'Australia is at a great competitive disadvantage.'

Amongst other things the Committee recommended performance be benchmarked against other OECD countries, institutions be free to enrol as many students as they wished, criteria for awarding of higher degrees be tightened and funds for research increased to more fairly reflect costs. The Australian Government should assume primary funding responsibility and overall regulatory responsibility for universities and establish an independent national tertiary education body.

The committee also recommended that funding for teaching be increased and significant increases be provided for students from low socioeconomic backgrounds and from regional and rural areas. As to a national framework the Committee urged simplification and streamlining so that each university could play to its strengths. Universities supported the reviews recommendations!

In response the Government reiterated its commitment to 'making Australia one of the most educated and highly skilled workforces in the world in order to secure national long term economic prosperity'. It spoke of 'an unprecedented investment in universities and tertiary education system to drive comprehensive reform across the ... sector' (DEEWR 2009). The vision was to boost Australia's share of high skilled jobs to drive productivity growth, and increase equitable access to a diverse sector so as to take advantage of future opportunities. 'Self-fulfilment, personal development and the pursuit of knowledge as an end in itself; the provision of skills of critical analysis and independent thought to support full participation in a civil society; the preparation of leaders for diverse, global environments; and support for a highly productive and professional labour force should be key features of Australian higher education.'

As part of the 2009 Budget, the Government announced it would provide an additional $5.4 billion to support higher education and research over the next 4 years in 'a comprehensive response to the Review'. In future universities would be funded for student places on the basis of demand. New indexation arrangements would replace the current minimum wage-based arrangements for the salary component with a measure that better reflects professional salary movements; productivity improvements will still be required to contribute to wage increases.

An Office of Teaching and Learning was established in late 2011 following a review by Alison Johns from the Higher Education Funding Council of England (Johns 2011). The Office provides grants to 'academics and professional staff' to 'explore, develop and implement innovations in learning and teaching and to develop leadership capabilities, commissions research of 'strategic significance' to develop policy in relation to teaching and learning in the higher education sector and provides awards, fellowships and secondments to encourage innovation in teaching and learning in that sector.

In 2011 the Commonwealth Government launched the Higher Education Participation and Partnerships Program. It aims to ensure that Australians from low SES backgrounds who have the ability to study at university get the opportunity to do so. Universities will be assisted to undertake activities and implement strategies that improve access to undergraduate courses for people from low SES backgrounds, as well as improving the retention and completion rates of those students. In addition, the scheme supports the goal to have 20 % of domestic undergraduate students from low SES backgrounds by 2020. The program provides a total of $736 million over the four years to 2015. A grant of $21 millions to universities in Sydney as part of the partnerships program was announced in August 2013.

When the finishing touches were being put to strategies for funding the Gonski Panel's recommendations on Funding for Schooling, the Australian government withdrew further funding from universities claiming that there was strong growth in the sector which in the view of the minister meant that universities could absorb the loss. Of course that was strongly disputed. What was just as unfortunate was that in the debate and media reporting it distracted significantly from the decisions about the increased funding of schools. The profound changes in university life wrought since the Dawkins reforms seem to be not apparent yet to those charged with determining resources for universities. Australia's Nobel Prizewinner Peter Doherty said as much in his condemnation of the funding reduction.

13.5 Assessing the Value of Universities

Governments of both political persuasions, since the mid 1990s, have concerned themselves with the evaluation of research and more recently with evaluation of teaching and learning. Use of a formula encapsulating performance measures were introduced in the 1990s as part of the Research Quantum (RQ) exercise (Butler et al. 2005). Various schemes of assessment replaced the RQ; the latest scheme is 'Excellence in Research for Australia' (ERA), a research management initiative of the Rudd Government developed by the Australian Research Council (ARC). It replaced the Research Quality Framework developed by the Howard Government. In addition the 'Higher Education Research Data Collection' collects statistics about research in Australia. The 'Group of Eight' (the larger established universities in capital cities), favour research assessments as a way of showing they are more deserving of support than smaller universities.

In late 2011 the Commonwealth Government (DEEWR 2011) published *Advancing Quality in Higher Education* proclaiming a commitment to 'ensuring that growth in university enrolments is underpinned by a focus on quality'. The Tertiary Education Quality and Standards Agency TEQSA (incorporating the Australian Universities Quality Agency founded in 2000), was established in July 2011 as a result of the Bradley Review, will carry out 'regulatory activities' from January 2012. Universities will be rewarded for delivering outcomes through the 'performance funding' arrangements which translates to agreement on strategies to achieve the teaching and learning mission and additional funds will be provided for universities that meet their agreed performance targets relating to national participation objectives.

TEQSA will 'regulate higher education using a standards-based quality framework and principles relating to regulatory, necessity, risk and proportionality, protect and enhance Australia's reputation for and international competitiveness in higher education, as well as excellence, diversity and innovation in higher education in Australia, encourage and promote a higher education system that is appropriate to meet Australia's social and economic needs for a highly educated and skilled population, protect students undertaking, or proposing to undertake higher education by requiring the provision of quality higher education and ensure that students have access to information relating to higher education in Australia.'

A new website, MyUniversity, was developed to support the move to a new more student-centred higher education system and improve transparency. A structural Adjustment Fund was established to assist universities to improve the quality of teaching and learning… A new package of initiatives including two new performance measurement tools, the University Experience Survey and the Australian version of the CLA will be used.

Some Vice Chancellors don't seem to have understood the increased government interest in learning and teaching in the Higher Education Sector! In late 2011 the Vice Chancellor of the University of Sydney informed academic staff that the university would not meet its fee income targets: Dr Spence told the university

13.5 Assessing the Value of Universities

stringent measures would be needed as a result. Staff not 'pulling their weight' could no longer be 'carried'. Sydney University Academics (2011) estimated that up to 150 academic and 190 general staff jobs were under threat.

Whilst Spence referred to both teaching and research the outcome would appear to be that the only way a staff member can avoid being 'considered for possible redundancy or alternative arrangements' is by having four publications to their name in that period. Later commentary described a bureaucratic environment of unbelievable proportion (Rees 2012a).

The Commonwealth Government commissioned a review of 'base funding' of universities (Lomax-Smith et al. 2011) and the Report was delivered to the Minister in October 2011. The report in particular recommended that more students who commence study should be better supported. In receiving the report Senator Evans noted that investment in higher education had increased from $8 billion in 2007 to more than $12 billion in 2011. Further consultation was planned.

There is an ongoing argument about the value to society of university attendance, the assertion that the principal value is to the individual. It would follow that those attending university should bear the full cost of their attendance. A report from the Grattan Institute in Sydney (Norton 2012) argued that public benefits such as volunteering and civic behaviour would in almost all cases accrue to the community anyway: graduates are such big winners that they would study even without subsidies. A comparison was drawn with newspapers and supermarkets as providing substantial private benefits without government subsidy because there are 'ample private incentives'. The assertion was also made that fairness did not justify tuition subsidies because with HELP schemes in place, tuition charges do not seem to deter people from lower socioeconomic backgrounds from higher education. The estimate was that cuts to tuition subsidies could yield savings of around $3 billion in a year.

Professor Bruce Chapman of the Australian National University (in Palmer 2012), architect of the HECS, pointed to the difficulty of putting an accurate figure on externalities from higher education. Universities Australia's chief executive Belinda Robinson (in Palmer 2012) asserted that the Report applied a very narrow and theoretical definition of public benefit. Other critics of the Report (Rees 2012b) saw it as an example of the application of economic rationalism and pointed out that Australia spends only 0.7 % of GDP on higher education. Senator Evans, quoted in various reports, stated that implementation of the Report would impact on poorer families and lead to higher debts. Vice Chancellor of the University of New South Wales Professor Fred Hilmer, speaking on behalf of the 'Group of Eight' institutions, said universities must be allowed to set their own fees or they would go into the red, class sizes would increase and so on (Rosenberg 2012).

Two points need to be made. In the US serious failings in education such as tuition costs have been identified as a major contributor to the 'Great Divergence', the huge gap which has opened up between the very rich and the poor since 1980

(Noah 2012). High school graduates aren't receiving a significantly better education, on average, than their parents did.

Secondly, as the OECDs *Education at a Glance* 2012 points out, substantial economic benefits to the state are generated through the income taxes, social contributions and lifestyle behaviour of graduates. The return to the community from investment in higher education far outweighs the public cost of their education. In the US overall, the net public return amounts to USD 2,32,779 for each tertiary-educated man (higher than in any other country), and USD 84,313 for each woman (OECD 2012). In the UK, tertiary graduates generate USD 87,000 (GBP 55,000) through income tax and social contributions. And there is the student debt.

One would have to conclude that the notion of asking students to pay higher fees appears easier than a much more sensible idea: raising taxes on higher earning citizens. But the return to the public is sufficiently high surely to justify encouraging more people to enter university and complete a degree.

That the Grattan Report's assertions are surprising is an understatement. In one of the reports issued by Minister Brendan Nelson (2002c) it is reported, 'The national benefits of higher education are significant. Its total economic impact annually has been estimated to be $22 billion. The average rate of return to the Government on its investment in higher education has been estimated at about 11 %. However, the greatest national benefits are those more difficult to measure and include the impact of graduates on productivity in the workplace, the impact of research outcomes on productivity and innovation and the social impacts of a more highly educated population. The private benefits are also significant. Studies over the past decade have indicated that average private returns to higher education are between 9 and 15 %.'

At the time that was written operating expenditure of universities totalled $9.006 billion and revenue amounted to $9.3 billion of which the Commonwealth government contributed about half ($4.5 billion and HECS funding represented an additional $1.68 billion, an increase of 162 % on 1991 HECS revenue).

13.6 Universities and Research: Why Can't We Have a Silicon Valley in Australia?

The development of centres of significant innovation of the kind for which Silicon Valley has become famous, is an issue relevant to universities, as well as to other major research enterprises, public and private. Professor Jane Marceau, formerly of the OECD and more recently Professor at a number of universities in Australia, reviewed a survey of the characteristics of places like Silicon Valley and drew conclusions about the Australian situation (Marceau 2005). To be successful such developments need lots of money, a powerful university at the centre and control over surrounding land. In the US very substantial Federal Government grants to certain universities were followed by very large venture capital infusions. The powerful universities had the ability to attract public and private funds and gain significant political support. Their control over surrounding land allowed the creation of suitable residential suburbs which would attract superior research staff.

In Australia much debate continues about the contribution of the research enterprise to innovation and commercially beneficial products and processes. However, governments have been reluctant to provide the necessary core funding and demanded results in the short term. They have tried to do it on the cheap and been overly prepared to acquiesce to the demands of business enterprises, many of which are multinationals and more likely seek results from their home country anyway. In some cases it has to be said those most vocal have not necessarily been the best informed. The result has been a limited number of developments.

The major Commonwealth Government research enterprise, CSIRO, has been increasingly driven to targeted priorities closely related to goals identified by commercial business as useful! Relevance has become an important criterion without any clear agreement on what that might mean, or most importantly examination of the consequences of such a specification. Having in mind the history of research which ends up winning Nobel Prizes and achieving similar significance and the nature of the environment which encourages innovation, narrow specifications would seem problematic to say the least. Such demands tend to typify conservative governments keen to please business and its more immediate demands based on the proposition that government is useful only to the extent that it can support commercial business.

13.7 Universities and Skills Training

Tertiary and Further Education colleges (TAFEs) vocational and education training sector (universally abbreviated by those in the sector as 'VET') are funded mainly by the States. In 2012 they suffered substantial cuts in funding, especially in Victoria and New South Wales. Staff were retrenched and some campuses closed. Processes to assess quality of the courses offered were not available. In Victoria the Brumby Government (2007–2010) introduced a voucher system under which private providers could compete with TAFEs for funding (Eltham 2012). Supposedly, more choice would be provided to students. Enrolments at private courses grew by over 300 % between 2008 and 2011 whilst TAFE enrolments increased by only 4 %. Government spending therefore increased by $475 millions beyond budget. With no cap on places eligible for funding and aggressive recruiting including offers of attractive incentives, over-enrolment by private providers was rampant. Regulation which might check quality of the courses offered was non-existent because the Registration and Qualifications Authority lacked the resources. As with the expansion of private providers of tertiary educational courses in which overseas students enrolled in substantial numbers in the expectation of gaining preference in their residence visa applications, the outcome was a disaster.

13.8 Teacher Training

Because there is such a strong focus on the teacher as the critical ingredient in learning at school, attention is paid to the instruction and training of teachers at universities (and colleges) (The best school systems, such as Finland, recruit their teachers from amongst the best graduates; many other countries, including the US do not).

Central governments concern with the nature and quality of teacher training can be such that a government agency acquires the authority to approve, or not, the specific teacher training courses offered at university. In New South Wales, the Government established the Institute of Teachers. A major responsibility of the Institute is 'to assure both the profession and the community of the quality of teacher education programs. This is achieved through approval of programs offered by providers of initial teacher education'. Courses ('programs') are approved for a maximum of five years and any variation has to be notified to the Institute and if the change is significant, the program may require re-approval.

The Australian Prime Minister's response to the Gonski Report, as mentioned in the essay on Australian policy, includes a commitment to upgrade the quality of entrants to teacher training. Perhaps predictably some universities complained, again, of interference in their standards. The reductions followed earlier reductions of funding in programs to encourage improvements of teaching within universities.

Despite the evidence from inquiries that the level of government support for universities had declined in Australia over the decade to 2006, alone amongst OECD countries, little was done to redress the situation, including addressing the indexation arrangements for recurrent funding. Now that universities are able to enter into their own salary and wage agreements with staff that aspect of the issue becomes one for them. The result of ongoing declines in funding, resulting to no insignificant an extent to failed ventures into overseas countries and dependence on overseas full fee paying students, has been ongoing reductions in numbers of staff and increased hiring of casual staff.

13.9 The Importance of Government Investment in Tertiary Education

Corporatisation and managerialism have well and truly invaded universities but achieved no great gain in any area fundamental to their purpose. Major issues of teaching and learning remain unaddressed and relatively pointless exercises in quality assurance take huge amounts of time. Leadership of research has often failed to learn from the best examples in the most successful research enterprises. Too often bureaucratic intrusions are allowed, mythological attitudes amounting to elitism pervade daily functioning and decision-making and proper participation in the intellectual life of the community are sidelined and discounted.

That participation in enhancing leadership is not an exercise in administration, that allowing unproductive exercises in evaluation of quality means bypassing the judgement that should accrue to scholars of integrity and that accepting the replacement of public funds by corporate contributions too often means a sacrifice of intellectual objectivity all need far more attention. Brendan Nelson's reports on the Australian Higher Education sector observed at one point that the reporting arrangements of universities were excessive: the arrangements represented a considerable impost on universities: they simply address accountability but provide no information on outputs or outcomes.

Far too much of the intervention by governments into the sector are based on the proposition that, like opera or art museums, the principal beneficiaries are the elite who ought to be able to pay much more of the cost themselves. Further, the intervention is often prescriptive, as it is with research agencies, as if demanding strategic plans and metrics of quality will produce quality. Innovation comes from an environment of high risk in which the mistakes are many and the wrong paths are too often travelled. We do know a great deal about the kinds of environments that produce good research outcomes. And they aren't ones dominated by 'central casting'. It is not that the refugees from the centralised economies of Europe post World War 1 were wrong to object to centralised planning, it is that the failures of the market have been vastly underestimated and centralised control has prevailed at the same time as freedom was proclaimed. One of the most ridiculous and very likely most costly outcomes of the present economic and political regime is the vocal questioning of the worth of universities which is becoming evident in the US.

Many students are poorly taught and not strongly motivated. For instance, first-year university students in Australia report that they lack appreciation of the relevance and role of those disciplines in their lives and communities, and of their potential for rewarding career opportunities. They have incurred substantial debt and many of them are unlikely to be able to repay that debt. Unemployment amongst graduates is far higher than one would anticipate considering the oft heard rhetoric about the future need for graduates and is particularly high in countries severely affected by the GFC.

Funding of universities in most countries has shrunk, staff salaries have declined, fewer academics now gain tenure whilst at the same time commercial firms and governments make increasing use of universities for research and development to increase their intellectual capital.

The assertion that the benefits from tertiary education accrue principally to the individual and that the state should contribute only a minimal amount simply cannot be supported! If we wanted to advance the economy we should look to education. Not only will investment in schooling bring substantial gains but the two other areas of education, pre-school and post-school, are one's where the returns are substantially in advance of the return from equities over the longer term and produce great social benefits as well. Academics should be far more active in promoting that!

The politicians fronting successive governments in Australia and other countries promote the importance of tertiary education in the contribution it will make to the future of the nation. Brendan Nelson, Minister in Australia's Howard Government, wrote, 'our success in no small way will determine the kind of country in which Australians will be living 25 years from now' (Nelson 2002a). Similar sentiments were expressed when the Bradley Review was presented to the Australian government in 2008. The actual policies implemented have not matched that high blown rhetoric!

References

Amann, R. (2003). A sovietological view of modern Britain. *Politics, 74*, 287–301.
Bradley, D., et al. (2008). *Australian Higher Education. Final Report.* Canberra: Department of Education, Employment and Workplace Relations. Retrieved March 8, 2009 and May 14, 2013, from http://www.innovation.gov.au/HigherEducation/ResourcesAndPublications/ReviewOfAustralianHigherEducation/Pages/ReviewOfAustralianHigherEducationReport.aspx
Butler, L., et al. (2005). *Strategic assessment of research performance indicators—an ARC Linkage Project*. Retrieved August 31, 2012, from http://cpi.anu.edu.au/repp/2005_linkage_grant.html
Carney, S. (2008). In negotiating policy in an age of globalization: Exploring educational "Policyscapes" in Denmark, Nepal, and China. *Comparative Education Review, 53*(1), 22
Corden, W. M. (2005). Australian Universities: Moscow on the Molonglo. *Quadrant, 49*(11), 7–20.
DEEWR. (2009). *Transforming Australia's higher education sector*. Retrieved October 7, 2012 and May 14, 2013, from http://www.innovation.gov.au/HigherEducation/Documents/TransformingAusHigherED.pdf
DEEWR. (2011). *Advancing quality in higher education*. Retrieved August 31, 2012 and May 14, 2013, from http://www.innovation.gov.au/HigherEducation/Policy/Pages/AdvancingQualityInHigherEducation.aspx
Delbanco, A. (2009, May 14). The Universities in trouble. *New York, Review of books.*
Dodgson, M. (2012, January 22). Measures of Leadership: Reflections on Robert S. Mcnamara. ABC RN Ockhams Razor. Retrieved 31 August 2012, from http://www.abc.net.au/radionational/programs/ockhamsrazor/ockham27s-razor-22-january-2012/3732754.
Elkins, T., & Keller, R. T. (2003). Leadership in research and development organizations: A literature review and conceptual framework. *The Leadership Quarterly, 14*, 587–606.
Eltham, B. (2012, August 16). Bailleu takes the axe to TAFE. *New Matilda*. Retrieved September 1, 2012, from https://newmatilda.com/2012/08/16/bailleu-takes-axe-tafe
Grafton, A. (2011, November 24). Our Universities: Why are they failing? *New York Review of Books.*
Greenberg, D. S. (2001). *Science, money, and politics*. Chicago: University of Chicago Press.
Greenberg, D. S. (2010). *Tech transfer: Science, money, love and the ivory tower*. Washington DC: Kanawa Press.
Head, S. (2007, August 16). They're micromanaging your every move. *New York Review of Books*
Head, S. (2011, January 13). The grim threat to British Universities. *New York Review of Books.*
Hollingsworth, R., & Hollingsworth, J. (2000). *Major discoveries and biomedical research organizations: Perspectives on interdisciplinarity*. Nurturing leadership and integrated structure and cultures symposium presentation. Retrieved August 22, 2012, from http://www8.umu.se/inforsk/universitetsligan/hollingsworth.html

References

Johns, A. (2011). *Higher education learning and teaching review*. Canberra: Office of Learning and Teaching.

Karmel, P. (2003). Higher education at the crossroads: Response to an Australian ministerial discussion paper. *Higher Education, 45*, 1–18.

Lomax-Smith, J. et al. (2011). *Higher education base funding review final report*. Retrieved September 23, 2012 and October 8, 2013, from http://www.innovation.gov.au/highereducation/Policy/BaseFundingReview/Pages/Library%20Card/HigherEd_FundingReviewReport.aspx

Lyall, S. (2010, May 27). Oxford tradition comes to this: Death (Expound). *New York Times*

Marceau, J. (2005, December 12). Why can't we all have a Silicon Valley? *Australian Review of Public Affairs*

Mintzberg, H. (1983). *The professional bureaucracy. In Structure in fives*. New York: Prentice Hall.

Mumford, M. D. (2003). Editorial: Introduction to special issue on leading for innovation. *The Leadership Quarterly, 14*, 385–387.

Nelson, B. (2002a). *Higher education at the crossroads. An overview paper*. Canberra: Department of Education, Science and Training.

Nelson, B. (2002b). *Meeting the challenges. The governance and management of universities*. Canberra: Department of Education, Science and Training.

Nelson, B. (2002c). *Setting firm foundations. Financing Australian higher education*. Canberra: Department of Education, Science and Training.

Newfield, C. (2010). The structure and silence of the cognotariat. *Eurozine*. Retrieved August 16, 2012, from http://www.eurozine.com/articles/2010-02-05-newfield-en.html

Noah, T. (2012). *The great divergence*. New York: Bloomsberry Press (First published in 10 parts in the online magazine *Slate* in 2010).

Norton, A. (2012). *Graduate winners: Assessing the public and private benefits of higher education*. Carlton: Grattan Institute.

OECD. (2012). *Education at a glance 2012 indicators*. Chapter C *How do early childhood education systems differ around the world?*. Paris: OECD. Retrieved September 13, 2012, from http://dx.doi.org/10.1787/eag-2012-en

Palmer, C. (2012). HECS architect says Grattan Institute fee proposal will be seen as unfair. *The Conversation* 6 August. Retrieved August 30, 2012, from http://theconversation.com/hecs-architect-says-grattan-institute-fee-proposal-will-be-seen-as-unfair-8666

Pounder, J. S. (2001). "New leadership" and university organisational effectiveness: Exploring the relationship. *Leadership and Organization Development Journal, 22*, 281–290.

Quinn, J. B., Anderson, P., & Finkelstein, S. (1996). Managing professional intellect: Making the most of the best. *Harvard Business Review, 74*(2), 71–80.

Rees, S. (2012a, April 23). What's ailing sydney University. *New Matilda*.

Rees, S. (2012b, August 13). Grattan report a win for uni bullies. *New Matilda*.

REF. (2014). *Research Excellence Framework*. Retrieved August 30, 2012, from http://www.hefce.ac.uk/research/ref/

Robinson, D. (2006). The Status of Higher Education Teaching Personnel in Australia. Canada, New Zealand, the UK. and the US. Report for Education International March 2006. Retrieved August 31, 2012, from http://www.caut.ca/uploads/ei_study_final.pdf

Rosenberg, J. (2012, August 7). Unis must be allowed to set own fees, says Hilmer. *Sydney Morning Herald*.

Shepherd, J. (2010, January 11). Universities tell Gordon Brown: Cuts will bring us to our knees. *The Guardian*.

Shergold, P. (2011, May 4). Seen but not heard. *Australian Literary Review: The Australian*.

Simons, M. (2010, March). Dangerous precedent: The Melbourne model. *The Monthly*.

Sydney University Academics. (2011, December 5). Sydney University academics speak out. *New Matilda*.

Vasagar, J. (2010, July 6). Graduates warned of record 70 applicants for every job. *The Guardian*.

Wilkinson, J. (2006). *Undergraduate education: What good is it? An International Perspective*. Menzies oration on higher education. Melbourne University. Retrieved August 31, 2012, from http://www.unimelb.edu.au/speeches/transcripts/84JWilkinson20060711.doc

Chapter 14
Policy Development in Education and Schooling in Australia

14.1 Public Policy and the Education Debate

Public policy debate about education in Australia is largely centred on the relative merit of public and private (Catholic or independent) schools, how well Australian students do in tests, both national and international, and on the nature of the curriculum and the need for a 'National Curriculum'. That is certainly so of the last 20 years. There is almost no mention of early childhood though Ministers for Education in the Commonwealth and some states are also responsible for early childhood and sometimes 'youth'. Ministerial responsibility for tertiary education is usually a responsibility separate from schools.

From 1997 the education landscape in Australia has been dominated by issues of funding and equity. Debate became more shrill following the commissioning of the Review of Funding for Schooling (see below). A major feature of the commentary was reference to Australian students 'declining achievement' in international tests, usually depicted as 'Australia is falling behind its Asian neighbours'. The distortions inherent in this depiction will be taken up later. Arguments about funding continued through 2012, especially following the announcement of the Governments response to the Gonski Report. Indeed it seemed that no policy was valid without precise information as to how it would be funded!

Reviewing the school funding system in Australia recently Dowling (2007) of ACER observed that in Australia, colonial railways were built to three different gauges, a problem in pre-Federation days once the railway lines of different systems met. So called 'rail gauge' issues are particularly evident in school funding, 'an area of education that should be most amenable to quantification and measurement': instead 'it is plagued by inconsistency which arguably… has a broader impact, as all other aspects of education are dependent on the primary issue of funding.' He quotes Professor Max Angus of Edith Cowan University as believing that no political party has any motivation to fix this because 'maximum flexibility comes from maximum obscurity, which appeals to politicians seeking maximum freedom to do as they will.'

There has been a history of discrimination against Indigenous peoples including denial of educational opportunities and dislocation of families. [Indigenous] *lan-*

guage, the speaking of which was forbidden almost everywhere in the early centuries of European occupation, is essential to identity but literacy is mostly judged only in terms of facility with the English language. Before 1788 many Aboriginal people could speak three or more languages. Few non-Indigenous Australians are literate in more than one.

There is a general failure to link educational achievement to children's wellbeing: childcare—so important in future educational outcomes—is marginalised as pointed out in the separate essay on early childhood (see Chap. 5).

As the Rudd Labor Government elected in 2007 took office considerable debate continued about the extensive support by Howard Government of independent schools. Social commentator Jane Caro and former school principal Chris Bonner (Bonner and Caro 2007) in their book, *The Stupid Country* asserted that through the 'wide spread neglect of public education and a gap between its best and worst performing school students' Australia was well on its way to becoming the stupid country. The Howard Government reforms were seen by some as media-manufactured education crises as in the US (Beder et al. 2009). Educational funding shifted from being an investment in the nation's future to an expense that needed to be justified, rationalised and reduced.

14.2 Australian Students Educational Achievement

Australian students do well to very well in the international tests, PISA and TIMSS though there have been declines in some areas over the last several years. This is taken up in the essay on International Developments (Chap. 12). Since there is much commentary to the effect that Australian student's performance is declining it is important to make a few points.

The reaction of the media is a different matter, a feature of reportage to the present day as we will see. Zyngier (2004) has pointed out that much of the media commentary on significant reports on education, whether international or about Australia only, tends to focus on existing agendas rather than the findings of the reports. He reviewed several reports issued 2002. OECD and other reports on public schools criticise Australia's lack of attention to issues of equality and equity. However, media reports deal mainly with government and private spending on education and only one article dealt with social issues. Research on education and schooling sometimes promotes a deficit model of education in which the benefit of education is the eventual improvement in social and economic terms of children from disadvantaged backgrounds. That is an instrumental matter: the principal purpose of education should be characterised using quite different criteria!

The results of PISA tests reveal, in broad terms Australian students as doing very well. Considering the statistical variation, Australian students are equal second in all three areas of assessment. In the commentary the fact that Shanghai–China and Singapore participated in PISA for the first time in 2009 is often forgotten or glossed over. That affects Australia's rank but not its score! In reading

Australian students were ninth. Two of the eight countries ahead of Australia were Shanghai and Singapore. Another was Hong Kong (not a country). However, considering the statistical variation Australian students came in equal second after six other countries including Finland, Korea and Canada) along with New Zealand, Japan and the Netherlands.

Applying the same approach to mathematics we can note that although Australian students came in at number 15, again it was equal second along with New Zealand, Belgium and Germany. Twelve countries were in the top group, again including Finland and Korea and Shanghai, Singapore, Hong Kong and Macao (not a country).

And in science, Australian students Australia ranked 10th but again were equal second, this time with seven other countries; six countries were equal first. In considering the achievements of students in other countries, New Zealand and Canada might be paid special attention.

There was a strong connection between socioeconomic status (SES) and student achievement in Australia, between parent education background and student results, between home educational resources and student results and between the socioeconomic composition of schools and school results as noted by Cobbold (2012a).

That Australian students do better in the PISA international assessments than Germany (in the same group as Australia in math and science), the UK, France, Denmark, Norway and Sweden, and notably the US, is very seldom mentioned in debate either. As pointed out in the essay International Comparisons, there is considerable commentary to the effect that in the Asian countries, which Australia is falling behind, students spend considerable time in out of school tutoring and swotting. The relatively strong performance of students from the UK, US and Eastern Europe and the Russian Federation in TIMSS and PIRLS contrasts with the results of PISA tests!

Commentators engaged in education research generally see room for improvement and note the widening gap between the performance of Indigenous and non-Indigenous students. Frequently the increasingly competitive global economy is highlighted as requiring Australia to do better educationally: average is considered simply not good enough.

Several newspapers were quick to condemn Australian students' performance in the international mathematics and science study, TIMSS, 2007 with comments such as, Doesn't add up: 'Borat kids beat Aussies referring to the good results of children from Kazakhstan (Ferrari 2008). These comments are inconsistent with a statistically valid interpretation of the results and border on inflammatory. They are instead part of an agenda favouring support for independent schools because government schools are failing! Similar comments are often made in the media of other countries about the results of international tests.

Sue Thomson and colleagues at ACER provided another comprehensive set of reports on the results of the TIMSS and PIRLS (the international reading study conducted by the same organisation) tests conducted in 2011 (Thomson et al. 2011, 2012). The cycles for the two tests coincided for the first time in 2011. The surveys included questionnaires which examined a range of issues related to qualifications, pedagogical practices, use of technology, assessment and assignment of homework as well as seeking responses from school principals about institutional practices such as teacher recruitment, teacher morale, school and teacher autonomy and other practices. Both tests have a focus comparing intended and presented curricula, as distinct from PISA which has a literacy focus. Both relied on samples of students and schools, in the 2011 program almost 300 schools and between 6,000 (year 4) and 7,500 students (year 8).

In math and science at year 4 Australian students scored higher than did students from 23 to 27 other countries but lower than students from 17 to 18 countries. In math the 2011 score was similar to that for 2007 and was an improvement from 1995. In science the score was the same as in 1995 but a decline from 2007. By year 8 Australian students scores were below those of six to nine other countries and higher than 26 or 27 countries; no change from 1995 results were evident. In year four reading Australian student scores were significantly lower than those for 21 other countries and higher than for 18 other countries. In all cases ACT students scored higher than students from other states territories and the Northern Territory students consistently had the lowest scores.

Thomson and colleagues point to the substantial 'tail of underachievement' in Australia in math and science. 'For such a highly developed country, this level of underperformance is not acceptable and its minimisation should become a priority, particularly if the aim for Australian education is to be one of the top five education systems in the world.' They also say 'It is evident that student motivation and self-confidence are also important factors within Australia'. Similarly, teacher's job satisfaction is important, as is the provision of a supportive, ambitious school climate.

Australian media predictably greeted the TIMSS and PIRLS results with the usual headlines connoting failure by Australian students. The *Australian Financial Review* headlined their response as 'Australian students get C on global report card' (Dodd and Mather 2012), *The Age* as 'Australia's disaster in education' (Topsfield 2012) and the *Sydney Morning Herald* as 'Australian students could do better' (Tovey 2012). No comment whatsoever was made in the media in respect of the practices of other countries despite considerable commentary in the reports!

Schools Minister Garrett was quoted as criticising budget cuts to education by eastern State governments and urging all States and Territories to sign up to the National Plan. ACER CEO Geoff Masters expressed surprise at the results and observed that Australia had stagnated whilst other countries had advanced.

Professor Emeritus of Education at the University of South Australia Alan Reid (2012) pointed out that much of the 'wave of commentary unleashed' in response to the 2011 TIMSS (math and science at years 4 and 8) and PIRLS (reading at year 4) amounted to hyperbole and misinformation that distorted the results and dumbed down the public discussion. Opportunities to use the information to refine thinking about teaching and learning were missed. Reading, math and science reveal nothing about a whole range of other subjects from arts through civics to health or critical domains like problem solving, creativity and inter-cultural understanding. The test results were taken at face value with no attempt to question the nature of the tests.

14.3 The Rudd and Gillard Education Revolution

In the campaign for the 2007 Australian Federal election then Opposition leader Kevin Rudd made an education revolution a major plank of his platform. 'As a growing body of evidence shows, long-term social and economic outcomes are significantly influenced by the investment that nations make in the education and training of their people. On measures of pre-school, school, vocational and tertiary education and research, Australia has fallen well behind its competitors. Labor believes we need an education revolution… a new national vision—for Australia to become the most educated country, the most skilled economy and the best trained workforce in the world.'

The right of all children to quality education was proclaimed and the responsibility of government to invest in raising standards at all levels, ensure fairness in allocation of resources, monitor outcomes to identify where action to improve opportunities and guard against unjustifiable inequality and discrimination, especially in respect of Indigenous children was acknowledged.

Speaking to the National Press Club on 27 August 2009 Prime Minister Rudd devoted considerable time to the Education Revolution, emphasising accountability through performance measures, though not league tables, and advocating replacing principals and teachers if they did not lift their performance and schools reorganised or merged. Unions representing teachers not surprisingly responded strongly to these statements.

14.4 The State and Territory Ministerial Declarations

State, Territory and Australian Government Ministers, meeting as the Australian Education Ministers Council, have adopted a number of frameworks over the years referred to as the Hobart, Adelaide and Melbourne Declarations. They constitute a commitment to collaboration to improve Australian schooling, broad directions to guide schools and education authorities in securing particular outcomes for students. (Similar commitments have been entered into in respect of early childhood education.)

The common threads of all the Declarations acknowledge the paramount contribution of quality teachers to advances in education; much of the debate revolves around the different practices of countries like Finland and others like the USA and the UK. But the issues are very much accountability and measurement, how to achieve superior performance, what is to be done in the face of poor performance and seek involvement of government departments, of parents, of teachers (and teacher unions).

The Melbourne Declaration, the latest, commits Ministers to working together to ensure high-quality schooling for all young Australians (MCEECDYA 2008). It acknowledged major changes in the world that are placing new demands on Australian education. The goals included promoting equity and excellence in schooling, supporting young Australians to become successful learners, confident, creative and active and informed citizens. Early childhood was recognised as being the foundation for later development. World class curriculum and assessment was to be designed through cooperation amongst all governments. The needs of indigenous children and those from low socioeconomic backgrounds were to receive attention. The Melbourne Declaration was asserted by the NSW Secondary Principals Council (McAlpine 2008) to lack the level of commitment to equity of the Adelaide Declaration of 1999 and was subject to a damning criticism.

14.5 Australian Business

The Business Council of Australia (BCA) has been a major advocate of reform in schools, especially supporting performance pay for teachers, greater authority for school principals to recruit to the their teaching staff and more recently testing of teachers. Professor Geoff Masters of ACER completed a report for the Council in mid 2007 (Business Council of Australia 2007). The Report claimed that the greatest return will come from additional investment in:

- more autonomy and improved training for school principals;
- a standard national, competency-based teacher certification program;
- some form of variable compensation for the highest performing teachers;
- more engagement between business and secondary schools aimed at helping to make students job-ready;
- a standardised national curriculum; and
- early childhood development and early school education.

The Report identified five issues: early intervention, customisation (making education and training more responsive to the needs of individual learners, interests and aspirations), professionalisation of teaching, increased investment and improved governance.

The BCA adopted these recommendations. But media interviews with BCA Chairman Michael Chaney, for instance with radio station 2UE's John Laws about the Report descended into the usual rhetoric about quality crises, schools being stuck in the 1960s and students performing poorly compared with those in some other countries, too many students dropping out of school not fit to play an appropriate role in the economy and so on. The Masters' report didn't say anything about a 'quality crisis' or being 'stuck in any decade'!

14.6 Australian Literacy and Numeracy

In January 2008 the Australian Bureau of Statistics released the 2006 Adult Literacy and Life Skills Survey of Australians aged 15–74 years (Australian Bureau of Statistics 2008). The Survey assessed prose literacy (e.g. ability to read newspapers), document literacy (e.g. ability to use bus schedules) as well as numeracy and problem solving skills, and the ability to understand health related information (e.g. first aid advice). Fewer Australians had literacy assessed as being in the lowest category than a decade previously.

People with jobs and those with higher incomes and those who had completed a qualification were more likely to gain higher assessments, a result agreeing with assessments in other countries. Literacy levels tended to decrease with age. The exception to this was the 15–19 years age group, which had lower levels of literacy than the 20–24 year age group. The same survey was undertaken by a small number of other countries. Australia's assessments were similar to those for Canadian people and for the highest levels were 4–5 % better than for US assessments.

In April 2011 the Community Services and Health Industry Skills Council reported, Approximately 53 % of working age Australians have difficulty with numeracy skills; 46 % of Australian adults have difficulty with reading skills, and 13 % are classified in the lowest literacy category 'As a result, between 7 and 8 million Australians are in danger of being confined to low-wage jobs with little prospect of improvement. The Council called on the Government to put in place a 10-year plan to improve adult education and the quality of training in high schools (Community Services and Health Industry Skills Council 2011). Without massive improvement in the literacy and numeracy skills of Australian adults, Australian industry will not remain internationally competitive.'

The report did not mention that Australia's skills levels were similar to Canada's or that young adults have higher skill levels than older people, nor that there had been declines in the proportions of people assessed as having low skills than a decade ago. It is difficult to find the sources for the claims about the levels of language, literacy and numeracy in the report and some of the claims are alarmist.

14.7 Testing Australian Students: NAPLAN and My School

The Rudd Government established the Australian Curriculum Assessment and Reporting Authority (ACARA) which became operational in 2009. It is governed by a board comprising executives from State Government Education Departments and relevant commercial businesses. It is subject to Ministerial direction. It is responsible for establishing a national curriculum from Kindergarten to year 12 in specified learning areas, a national assessment program aligned to the curriculum and relevant data collection, analysis, evaluation, research and reporting.

A special website—My School—was established by ACARA containing data on schools and students. Results of specific tests under the NAPLAN scheme are included for each school along with data on socioeconomic and educational background of the families of the students and financial data about the schools including the amounts provided by Commonwealth and State governments to each school.

The results of NAPLAN tests which assess performance by all students in Australian schools in four separate alternate years from year 3 through 9 in reading, writing, language conventions (spelling, grammar and punctuation) and numeracy were placed on the My School website. The tests are developed collaboratively by States and Territories and government and non-government sectors with technical advice from experts in assessment and educational measurement. The National Assessment Program is run at the direction of MCEECDYA. ACARA is responsible for the overall management of the scheme, in collaboration with representatives from all states and territories and non-government school sectors.

Students in remote areas do significantly less well than others and Indigenous students achieve significantly lower scores than non-Indigenous students. Greeting the NAPLAN 2008 results Education Minister Gillard said, '[These results] will enable teachers in classrooms around Australia to identify the children who are going well, but also very importantly the children who need an extra helping hand to reach the minimum standards required'. (One could ask don't teachers already know which children are doing well and who aren't?)

With one exception the NAPLAN results for 2011 show no significant change for disadvantaged students or in the large gaps between scores for disadvantaged and advantaged students (Cobbold 2012a). Average results have not improved since 2008 for most year levels. The only statistically significant improvement was in year 3 reading and year 5 numeracy. As expected students whose parents have completed advanced education levels and are employed in professional jobs scored highest. Students from the ACT score highest on average and those from the Northern Territory lowest. There is little statistically significant difference between the student scores of other states.

Disadvantaged students such as year 9 students whose parents had not completed year 12 are the equivalent of 3–4 years of schooling behind the most advantaged students, those whose parents had completed a university degree. The average reading and numeracy results of those students have not improved since 2008, except for year 5 numeracy. Indigenous students in year 9 are just over 3 years of behind non-Indigenous students. There has been no improvement in this gap since 2008. Indigenous students scores have mostly not improved, though there have been improvements for years 3 and 7 reading and year 5 numeracy. Remote area year 9 students are about 2 years of schooling behind other students.

The results for 2012 are similar to those for other years: ACT students achieve higher scores on most occasions in most tests and Northern Territory students achieve lowest scores. If anything, there have been small though significant declines in most states in most subjects with one or two improvements, again small from 2008 to 2012.

So whilst the gap between advantaged and disadvantaged student scores has increased in recent years and there has been no improvement in overall scores in NAPLAN, there has also been no significant decline! What do these results tell us?

The use of NAPLAN tests to assess school performance has generated considerable controversy. There have been accusations of cheating, teachers altering the student's answers, students sharing information in the break between tests or restricting certain students, such as children likely to do poorly, from sitting the tests (Perkins 2010). Trevor Cobbold of *Save Our Schools* has commented frequently on this issue.

Following numerous submissions to the Senate Education Committee inquiry into reporting school literacy and numeracy tests, which criticised the use of NAPLAN and of the social indices, Minister Gillard provided an extra $11 million in funding to 110 disadvantaged schools in addition to the governments $2.5 billion national partnership package with the states to assist disadvantaged schools.

In July 2010, the Australian Education Union (AEU), the Australian Government Primary Principals Association (AGPPA) and the Australian Secondary Principals Association (ASPA) hosted a National Symposium in Sydney intended to give advice for Ministers and ACARA on NAPLAN, the use of Student Data, My School and League Tables (Australian Education Union 2010). A number of prominent researchers presented their views. They were of one mind in expressing the greatest concern about the use to which NAPLAN scores were being put.

Emeritus Professor Alan Reid of the University of South Australia asserted that the Rudd/Gillard government had mainly focused on the economic purposes of education, with the major priority being the preparation of human capital for the labour market.

Brian J. Caldwell, Managing Director and Principal Consultant at Educational Transformations and Professorial Fellow at the University of Melbourne, said 'the dysfunctional effects of current policy would inhibit passion in learning as well as innovation and creativity…'

Melbourne University statistician Margaret Wu pointed out that the My School website was a league table and that NAPLAN results were not suitable for measuring student achievement level, student progress, and teacher or school performance.

Professor Alan Luke and colleagues from the Queensland Institute of Technology who had been studying 44 greater Brisbane metropolitan area schools over the past several years had surveyed and interviewed a random stratified sample of 106 year 1 teachers/classrooms, with achievement data on 650 of their students. The three-year study examined social class and home literacy resources of families, teacher-self reported curriculum emphases in early literacy, and results on three outcome measures: standardized reading achievement test results, a best exemplar narrative or descriptive writing sample, and teacher moderated judgments on a language/literacy developmental continuum.

Preliminary results showed a strong emphasis on basic skills and a focus on specific skill-acquisition goals but little direct engagement with matters of intellectual and cultural substance. In the US, Luke said, testing had led to a virtual industry of student measures… tests have become the de facto curriculum which inflated attention to the end-of-year results and exaggerate basics skills.

Economist Gruen (2010), former Associate Commissioner of the Australian Productivity Commission, said of the Australian situation, 'Education is a demoralised, underpaid, over bureaucratised sector and so the great teachers who stay in the system do so out of love, altruism and/or desperation and risk aversion. It's all not good. Not good at all.'

Low educational achievement mainly concerns children from disadvantaged backgrounds defined by ethnicity and indigeneity, geographic remoteness and location in high density urban areas on the geographic and economic fringes of cities. To paraphrase consultant Margaret Preston, people already in or aspiring to be in high SES strata of society are articulate and politically powerful and their advocacy drives the government funding of independent schools through market driven strategies aimed at school improvement such as testing and performance pay for teachers.

In February 2011, a revised version of the My School website was launched with additional features including a profile page for each school, financial information for each school, an indication of students' literacy and numeracy achievement as they progress through school and NAPLAN performance over a number of years. Financial information was presented in a format devised as a result of advice from an independent accounting firm to meet the requirement of the Minister that recurrent income and capital expenditure be comparable nationally. Explanations about interpretation of various statistics and guides to understanding were included on the site. The index of social and educational community advantage (ICSEA) was revised—based on statistics from the student's family—and explained. Nevertheless some schools complained. The executive officer of the Independent Schools Association in Queensland asserted that the presentation was like comparing apples and oranges!

The challenge for the My School website still remains the encouragement of best practice in teaching accompanied by changes in recruitment and career structure of teachers and dependent upon achieving of greater trust by the community in schools and teachers without compromising ongoing setting of high standards. The development of a broad and demanding curriculum is critical. These issues flow from strong leadership at government level.

Recent research by the Whitlam Institute, as already mentioned (Chap. 9), found negative impacts of NAPLAN on students and their families. There appears to be a move by a number of parents to have their children not take NAPLAN tests, as reported by Cobbold (2013b). A new coalition has been set up to organise support for a boycott of the NAPLAN tests. The Boycott Naplan Coalition was founded by 'The Popular Education Network Australia' (PENA), 'The Teacher and Education Support Staff Alliance' (TESA) and the 'Say No To NAPLAN Group'.

14.8 Improving Australian Teaching Standards

The Commonwealth Government in 2010 established the Australian Institute for Teaching and School Leadership (AITSL) as a company limited by guarantee. It is wholly funded by the Commonwealth Government and operates under its own constitution and is governed by an independent board of directors drawn from state government departments, schools and teachers organisations. Its goal is to promote excellence in the profession of teaching and school leadership.

The National Professional Standards for Teachers in Australia were announced by AITSL in February 2011 and are intended to form the basis for registration and certification of teachers. The Standards are endorsed by Education Ministers (the Ministerial Council for Education, Early Childhood Development and Youth Affairs or MCEECDYA) and support the Melbourne Declaration of the Ministerial Council. They are promoted as describing the key elements of quality teaching and articulate what teachers are expected to know and be able to do at four career stages: Graduate, Proficient, Highly Accomplished and Lead. The Standards are grouped into three domains: Professional Knowledge, Professional Practice and Professional Engagement. The Standards and their descriptors represent an analysis of effective, contemporary practice by teachers throughout Australia and are a public statement of what constitutes teacher quality.

The seven Standards are (1) Know students and how they learn; (2) Know the content and how to teach it; (3) Plan for and implement effective teaching and learning; (4) Create and maintain supportive and safe learning environments; (5) Assess, provide feedback and report on student learning; (6) Engage in professional learning; and (7) Engage professionally with colleagues, parents/carers and the community.

As of early 2012 further work was to be undertaken on the implementation of the Standards as a basis for teacher evaluation and career progression. In April 2012 an Australian Teacher Performance and Development Framework Consultation proposal was released by AITSL. Principles guiding the implementation of the framework include a focus on student outcomes, a clear understanding of what effective teaching is—reference is made to the Professional Standards for Teachers, support for teachers and school leaders, access to quality development opportunities and monitoring and evaluation of implementation. The document sets out a process for performance development and evaluation.

Neither the Professional Standards nor the Performance and Development Framework referenced the studies undertaken by Elizabeth Kleinhenz, Lawrence Ingvarson and colleagues from the Australian Council for Educational Research, Australia (ACER) outlined in the essay on Pay and Performance! In November 2011 School Education Minister Garrett announced that the reward payment scheme for teachers was to be linked to the National Standards for Teachers, not student's NAPLAN results (Garrett 2011).

14.9 The Gonski Review

On 15 April 2010, Julia Gillard, then Minister for Education, initiated a review of funding arrangements for schooling to develop a funding system which is transparent, fair, financially sustainable and effective in promoting excellent educational outcomes for all Australian students. A review panel was established to be chaired by businessman David Gonski AC. The Panel included Ken Boston, distinguished educator and a number of prominent citizens including Katherine Greiner, former Lord Mayor of Sydney and the Hon Carmen Lawrence, former Premier of Western Australia and member of the Australian Parliament.

Advocates for ongoing funding for independent schools loudly proclaimed the appropriateness of continuing the arrangements which had been put in place by the Howard Government. In early 2011 however, a number of capital city daily newspapers called for an end to the arrangements which gave undue preference to independent schools (Cobbold 2011). Comments ranged from 'Elite private schools do not deserve to continue to receive generous federal taxpayer handouts' *to* 'It's time to fund need rather than greed' (*Herald Sun*, Melbourne), to '[the present system is] a brazen case of resources greed, not education need—evidence that the education class divide is widening, with the help of governments' (*Daily Telegraph*, Sydney) to 'The great divide between what Australia's richest and poorest schools spend on educating their students has now been revealed' (*Courier Mail*, Brisbane). *The Age* of Melbourne criticised public subsidies for schools as constituting 'chauffeur-driven limousine standards'. Claims were made by spokespersons for continuing funding of independent schools: they could be considered as simply wanting 'another arrangement to guarantee their privileged funding'. (Cobbold 2011).

In the lead up to the presentation of the Gonski Panels Report a number of studies and programs about education attracted attention. The Grattan Institute released a report *Catching up: Learning from the best school systems in East Asia* highlighting the achievement of four of the world's five highest performing education systems—Shanghai, Hong Kong, Korea and Singapore (Jensen et al. 2012). Author Ben Jensen observed, 'As the world's economic centre is shifting to the East, we can learn from its most effective school systems about reforms to improve our children's lives.' He asserted spending more money, cultural differences or rote learning were not the cause of the results. The results were a consequence of recognition of the importance of high quality teachers, improvement in pedagogy, school-based research and openness to new ideas.

Much has been made of this difference between Australian student's results and those of Asian students. Often, it is asserted that Australia is falling behind Asia educationally. That several of the Asian countries in PISA 2009 were participating for the first time and that some of those countries such as Shanghai, Hong Kong and Singapore were in fact cities, not countries, were ignored. Nevertheless the attention in those countries to less advantaged students, a feature of the best schools systems as mentioned many times in these essays, was also ignored. The ABC's flagship TV current affairs program *Four Corners* explored progress at three schools, highlighting engagement by principals and teachers with students and positive outcomes. Several commentaries repeated the findings that Australian student's achievement was declining.

Zyngier (2011) summarised the education landscape in Australia to be addressed by the Gonski Panel thus: 'Most of the so-called innovative and ground-breaking educational policies and reforms adopted in Australia over the past 50 years, in the areas of policy, curriculum, pedagogy or assessment, have been copied from failed projects in the US or England. Neither of these countries is at the top end of the PISA rankings.'

He concluded, 'Australia is almost alone as a nation in the way it transfers responsibility for education from the public to the private, serving to further advantage society's elites'. The result in Australia is families with economic power use education to advantage their children. Referring to the system in Finland, Zyngier observed As the Finns have shown, high-quality staff, equitable funding and coherent systems are the key to a highly successful public education system.'

One could acknowledge that just about says it all!

Introducing its submission to the Gonski Review of Funding for Schooling the Nous Group (2011) emphasised the striking difference of Australia's school system from that of other countries, its division into three distinct sectors, each with significant market share, the Government subsidisation of the fee-charging, autonomously-run independent but publicly funded school sector (unique across OECD countries), the robust and competitive market for school education (the most competitive in the world by one measure) whereby parents with a reasonably high level of disposable income can exercise wide choice. As well, the ability of certain schools to attract enrolments by high-performing students was pointed out, indicating a high degree of academic selectivity.

Inasmuch as the Commonwealth Government now provides substantial funding for schools, and that constitutionally funding of schools is a matter for the States, the situation is complex to say the least. It is a situation where the Australian federation is tested as Ministers from the various jurisdictions argue about their prerogatives, promote the allegedly high standards their state expects and nothing much changes. It is also a situation where there is much attention to middle Australia and those able to afford private schools and little attention is given to children in regional and remote areas or to children with physical and mental disabilities. Yet it is the low performance of those groups that is of greatest concern in that, of course, it lowers the average achievement levels. It is a matter of equity to which PISA reports draw attention though that perhaps is of little concern to parents aspirational for their children *and* able to afford the fees for independent schools.

The NSW Government's Education and Communities Department response to the Gonski Report (NSW Department of Education and Communities 2011) pointed out, 'All schools in Australia are experiencing a trend of increasing enrolments by students with a disability'. The National Catholic Education Commission has reported that the fastest growing category of students in Catholic schools from 1985 to 2008 has been those with a disability and that this has occurred in every State and Territory. Independent schools are also experiencing the same phenomenon. In 2007, there was more than double the number of SWD [students with a disability] enrolled in independent schools than in 1997.

The Gonski Panel handed down its Final Report in December 2011 (Gonski et al. 2011). Unsurprisingly, the Report drew the same conclusions as had PISA 2009 reports: the most successful schooling systems around the world are those where students achieve to the best of their ability without their background or the school they attend impacting on their outcomes. Australia was achieving only average equity, meaning the impact of student background on educational outcomes is stronger in Australia than it is in many other OECD countries… students from disadvantaged backgrounds are consistently achieving educational outcomes lower than their peers.

The panel 'is of the view that Australia must do better to ensure genuine equality of educational opportunity for every child'. It said 'giving access to the best possible education and chance to [all Australian children] to realise their full potential can also be considered the moral imperative of schooling'. Governments must 'through addressing the facets of disadvantage, ensure that all children are given access to an acceptable international standard of education necessary to lead successful and productive lives'.

The Report noted the reduction in performance at the top end of the socioeconomic scale in Australia. It quoted studies (Chiu and Koo 2005) showing that 'Investing as early as possible in high-quality education for all students, and directing additional resources towards the most disadvantaged students, is a cost-efficient strategy that will have the greatest impact on improving overall performance.'

The complex and varied funding arrangements at the state and territory level made determination of actual funding for disadvantage difficult: those difficulties had flow-on effects in determining the needs of these students. Having noted all this and more, the Gonski Report stopped short of recommending the kinds of programs which have been implemented in Ontario or, indeed, which typify the school systems of high performing countries.

The panel made 41 recommendations, the principal one being that Commonwealth and State governments develop a schooling resource standard reflecting the agreed outcomes and goals of schooling and enable them to be achieved and improved over time capable of universal application. The anticipated capacity of parents to contribute financially towards school resource requirements should be a factor influencing funding of individual schools but non-government schools should be funded by the Australian Government on the basis of a common measure of need that is applied fairly and consistently to all. Reducing educational disadvantage should have a high priority. Teaching disadvantaged students, strengthening leadership, early intervention for students at risk, local parent and community engagement were all identified as important strategies in which to invest. Robust data about educational effectiveness were also considered necessary.

The government had said at the outset that no school would lose money as a result of the Inquiry! Hands were tied. Determination of the basic allocation for all schools will significantly influence the eventual total outlay: choosing the average expenditure of independent schools would increase that. However, noting that the

14.9 The Gonski Review

Gonski Report recommended continuing an SES funding scheme, but with schools on the same SES score receiving the same funding... Cobbold observed, 'The baseline funding in the Gonski model at each SES score must be that of most overfunded school in order to achieve the same level of funding for all. Otherwise, we will get another group of funding-maintained schools who get more funding than others on the same SES score, which contradicts the Reports recommendation.' (Cobbold 2012b).

Upon receipt of the Report Prime Minister Gillard praised its central recommendations without committing to implementing any of them. The Coalition, on the other hand, rejected the recommendations. Opposition education spokesman Christopher Pyne said they would drive up private schools' fees because the government hasn't promised to increase payments to non-government schools in line with inflation. 'We will make sure at the next election that parents and teachers and principals know the Coalition will continue the current quantum of funding plus real indexation', he said. The report was to be portrayed as a Labor attack on middle Australia (Tingle et al. 2012).

In the weeks following the release of the Gonski Report there were many comments from academics involved in education research. Several leading academics, including the University of Technology Sydney's Peter Aubusson, Melbourne University's Jack Keating and Richard Teese, Nobel laureate Brian Schmidt, David Zyngier from Monash University and others (Aubusson et al. 2012), expressed varying opinions. Zyngier observed that there was 'something amiss' with the public education system, with nationwide tests having a detrimental impact on children and families, Teach for Australia 'associates' leaving schools after 2 years, more than 18 % of graduate teachers unable to obtain ongoing jobs and principal and teachers refusing to participate in so-called performance bonus schemes. Government policies were being imported from the 'failed education systems of the USA and England.' He drew attention to the very different Finnish school system.

Keating observed that there was a problem with the timing of the report and that thought it was worthy the political climate might hamper its implementation. (He has been proved very right!) He described the Coalitions response as 'intensely negative and ludicrously political'. Richard Teese observed that 'Public schools have become a sector which is policed, while private schools have become a sector of preference'. The funding system was upside down, diverting resources away from schools that most needed them in favour of schools of choice. He also pointed out that much of the public funding on non government schools went to Catholic schools and less-than-notorious private establishments, opened in the past few decades or resuscitated from academic oblivion in the sixties 'that depended on this funding because their fee income was too low; these schools could not survive in the marketplace on their own: keeping these on life-support comes at a very high price because it uses up resources needed to eliminate under achievement in the public system and consumes cultural resources needed to make the public system work well.'

Aubusson observed that the fundamental problem with Commonwealth funding of the school system lay not in determining what is fair and reasonable but what is achievable. He criticised the 'simplistic dichotomy prevalent in the debate—public versus private schools that led to the argument being about whether one supported private schools or not. In this environment, with a mass media that increasingly sees its role as to advocate rather than to inform, and to inflame rather than calm, a nuanced debate is unlikely.'

Some commentators asserted that there would be no action on the Report by government. The independent schools lobby objected to funding schools on a needs basis claiming 3,200 schools would lose funding. This was despite pledges made already by the Prime Minister that no school would lose funding.

Opposition leader Tony Abbott promised that independent schools would get more funds under his government; that could cost an extra $2 billion a year according to others (Cobbold 2012c). Mr. Abbott had earlier implied that public schools received too much money. Coalition education spokesperson Christopher Pyne said that if they became government they would repeal any legislation implementing the Gonski recommendations.

Economics editor for the *Sydney Morning Herald* Gittins (2012) pointed out that failure to support the reforms result would be a 'lost opportunity to improve the future productivity of Australia's workforce'. That assertion was certainly supported by the OECD report on the economic impact of improving educational achievement (Hanushek and Woessmann 2010) and other research.

Ken Henry, a former Treasury secretary and the Prime Ministers special adviser on Asia, told a Canberra forum in August 2012 that Australia's education system had created ill informed Australians (Martin 2012): fewer high school students studied Indonesian now than in the 1970s. Henry also said universities were failing to prepare students properly for an Asian future, in part because the funding formula encouraged them to 'get as many bums on seats as they can'.

The Gonski Report gained huge media attention and much public comment. Response to the Report by readers of newspapers and electronic media reports was mixed. Readers of *The Australian* newspaper almost universally said that little would happen because the Gillard Government lacked vision and understanding, was profligate, the bureaucracy was bloated, the problem was the unions, the main aim of the government was to disadvantage independent schools and so on. Comments in other newspapers focused on disparities between different sectors, quality of teachers, the government's failure to make a commitment to the Report.

The Opposition had consistently criticised what they claimed was the Governments intention to reduce the funding to independent schools as class warfare! ABC economics correspondent Stephen Long (2012) observed, 'The sad truth is that the class warfare is being waged in the opposite direction—as public money disproportionately subsidises wealthy schools, while the disabled, the disadvantaged, and sons and daughters of low-to-middle income earners are left to languish in underfunded schools denied a fair share of the pie'.

Prime Minister Gillard announced the Government's response to the Gonski Panel's recommendations at the National Press Club on 3 September 2012. A new

14.9 The Gonski Review

funding model would be introduced and increased funding tied to concrete improvements (Gillard 2012). She asked for a commitment to a national crusade to ensure that by 2025 Australia is ranked in the top five in the world for the performance in reading, science and mathematics and for providing our children with a high-quality and high-equity education system. The aim of reaching this goal by 2025 will be legislated to galvanise our nations focus on improving schools. Australia's future prosperity depends on embracing a high-skill future and therefore depends on lifting the performance of our schools.

As part of its discussions with the states and territories and non-government school sectors, the Gillard Government will insist on improving schools by:

- Lifting teacher quality, including requiring more classroom experience before graduation and higher entry requirements for the teaching profession.
- More power for principals, including over budgets and staff selection.
- More information for parents through My School.

'Labor wants to make sure we have a school system that ensures all Australian children reach their full potential.

We will now start discussions with state and territory governments, and Catholic and independent schools, over the details of our plan. The Gillard Government is prepared to make a substantial investment over time to deliver this plan for better schools provided states and territories contribute their fair share and agree to the National Plan for School Improvement. There will be no blank cheques.'

The Prime Minister referred to the decline in the ranking of Australian students compared with those in other countries. The changes would deliver change as well as more resources to every school in the country and will be phased in over several years as recommended by the Gonski Report.

Under the funding model, funding for each school will be based on the needs of every individual student they enrol, determined through a new benchmark amount for every student—a new Schooling Resource Standard—based on the costs of schools that are already getting great results. Extra funding would be entitled to extra funding based on six categories including income, disability, English language difficulties, remoteness and Indigineity. This additional money would be a permanent feature of the new funding system. It would help pay for things like teachers aides, specialist literacy and numeracy coaches, and special equipment. These loadings, would be fully publicly funded so every student who needs more support will get it, no matter what type of school they attend.

Other features of the new school funding model include:

- All government schools would continue to be fully publicly funded.
- Special schools (like schools for students with disability) would also receive full public funding.
- Like the current system, the government funding provided to non-government schools would be adjusted based on parents capacity to contribute.

- Current annual indexation would be replaced by a new measure that reflects the real cost increases across all schools.
- Every school would see its funding rise every year.

The Prime Minister concluded, 'Funding would not be determined by whether a school is public or private—it would be determined by how much funding a school needs to deliver a great education. And as I pursue this work, as the Government drives for change, the centre of our plan will be the children, their schooling, their future.

'So the girl standing alone in the corner of the playground is noticed and the boy sitting silent in the back row learns. So words of encouragement and community applause are heard as often for the stars of mathematics as they are on the sports field and in the music hall. So the principal knows every student by name… and every parent knows their child's teachers names.

'Our plan will ensure that the humane goals of education will remain supreme. From a little boys first book to a decade later when he first finds an unexpected irony in a Shakespearean sonnet. From a little girl's first times-table to a decade later when she realises that a curve she's mapping describes a real world behaviour she's observed, but never understood. In a study group, unearthing a new fact about our past… and sharing new opinions on the historical controversies of today.'

The Prime Minister spoke passionately: she asked everyone to share that passion. Her proposals contained important and appropriate considerations. There were some elements that were not so appropriate including very positive references to My School and NAPLAN, both of which are of some value but not as much as ascribed to them.

This response has become the National Plan for School Improvement, described at the 'Better Schools' website, promoted as comprising five key areas reflecting the areas identified in the Prime Ministers response of 3 September 2012 and mentioned above:

- Quality teaching involving introduction of new, more rigorous standards for teacher training courses;
- Quality learning including implementation of the Australian Curriculum in all learning areas, improving literacy skills in early years, universal access to learning an Asian language (by 2025), addition of science to NAPLAN tests and greater access to quality vocational learning;
- Empowered school leadership giving more power to principals to make decisions over the way they run schools (building on the success of the Empowering Local Schools Program being implemented in 927 schools);
- Meeting student needs through providing support irrespective of location or school; and
- Transparency and Accountability through provision on the My School website of information about teacher expertise, opinion surveys, year 12 attainment rates and so on.

A number of aspects of the plan are contentious: standardised testing is to be an integral part of the plan, the authority of school principals relates to administrative matters and not curriculum issues and opinion surveys are to be introduced covering parent, teacher and student views.

The Coalition initially condemned the speech: spokesperson Christopher Pyne referred to it as 'all feathers and no meat' and Tony Abbott said it was 'vague and unworthy of the Prime Minister' (Ireland 2012). Later the Coalition expressed qualified support for some aspects of Gillard's proposals (providing they were consistent with Coalition policy). Garrett reported constructive discussions with some of the states in the week after the Prime Ministers speech.

But overwhelmingly, the response by many commentators in the media was to criticise Prime Minister Gillard's proposals as lacking detail; it was therefore condemned! Others criticised it because it would take too long to implement.

Then a few days later Mr. Pyne talked of the Coalitions plans that would cost only $4.2 billion compared with over $6 billion for the Government plan. Yet he promised the Coalition would not overturn the Labor Governments legislation if it was consistent with the Coalitions policy of supporting a robust curriculum, greater autonomy for school principals and ending discrimination against children with disabilities (Grattan and Topsfield 2012).

The Government's policies were incorporated in legislation, the Australian Education Bill 2012 introduced into the Parliament in late 2012.

The White Paper *Australia in the Asian Century* launched by Prime Minister Gillard in late 2012 has added significance in the context of the proposals for school reform. The goals of the Paper in forging closer relations with Asian countries to be achieved by 2025, addressed a range of areas, especially economic ones. All school children are to have continual access to one of five priority Asian languages (Mandarin Chinese, Hindi, Indonesian and Japanese); Business leaders are to be more Asia literate and the diplomatic 'footprint' is to be larger. Unsurprisingly, responses drew attention to the huge challenges and high costs; the Business Council of Australia and the Australian Chamber of Commerce reiterated their view of a need for greater competiveness and labour market deregulation! Did these responses address the goals of the White Paper or were they just the usual clamour?

Australia's relations with Asian countries are very contentious. Attempts to participate in Asian forums have not always been entirely successful. The strong alliance with the US drew comments from several experts in 2011 and 2012 to the effect that problems would arise in relations with China. However, especially after the US gained agreement from Australia in late 2011 in that a small number of American troops could be stationed in northern Australia as part of the new policy to contain the expanding influence of China, there was criticism of the alliance as likely to cause problems in Australia's own relations with China. Hugh White, professor of strategic studies at the Australian National University in Canberra, was particularly outspoken in a number of articles and speeches.

On 14 May 2013 The Senate Inquiry into Teaching and Learning, subtitled 'maximising our investment in Australian schools', was published (Australian

Senate 2013). Chaired by Senator Chris Black, Liberal, Western Australia), the Committee was a multiparty one. It heard from numerous witnesses and received many submissions. Its terms of reference included examining the effectiveness of current classroom practices, structure and governance of schools administration, 'the influence of family members in supporting the rights of children to receive quality education' and other factors. Its conclusions reflected much of what had been presented in various reports.

The submission by Professor Geoff Masters of ACER recommended raising the status and quality of student intakes to teacher educations, setting minimum standards for teacher registration, and recognising and rewarding development of specialist knowledge and skill (Masters 2012).

In their comprehensive submission to the Inquiry, the Australian Education Union (2012) drew attention to the 'failure to recognise that teaching is a complex professional activity which involves integrating a deep understanding of a knowledge base encompassing theoretical knowledge, pedagogy, subject discipline, child development and learning theory, in practical and unpredictable circumstances… Quality in teaching requires a sustained system-wide focus informed by empirical evidence rather than 'blaming and shaming' teachers, either individually or collectively.' They drew attention to the international evidence that better performing countries were successful because they developed the entire teaching profession. The submission rejected 'approaches to issues around teaching and learning which either implicitly or explicitly suggest that total responsibility for the quality of teaching and learning is exclusively borne by an individual teacher'.

The Committee's attention was drawn to submissions about independent schools. The Committee heard that many teachers were asked to teach subjects, including mathematics, science and technology, in which they did not have sufficient content knowledge; the Productivity Commission gave an estimate of between 15 and 25 % of maths teachers not qualified to teach the subject. Observations were made about the value of teachers participating in classroom observation; the Australian Education Union rejected any suggestion that such a practice be made compulsory and emphasised the need to properly resource all programs.

14.10 States Announce Their Own Education Policies

In May 2012, the New South Wales Government announced *Connected Communities*, promoted as, 'a radical overhaul of rural and regional education in a bid to lift results in Aboriginal and other disadvantaged communities'. Community hubs which will offer education, health, parenting support and anti-gambling measures will be created in some of the most disadvantaged areas of the State. Principals of the schools will be on five-year contracts paid $200,000 a year with a $50,000 performance bonus. Education Minister Adrian Piccoli said, 'With respect to health care for children, particularly school aged children and early childhood, we certainly do want to have a greater coordination between the schools and the healthcare providers'.

Executive principals would also be able to extend the hours of the school day and have a greater say over the employment of teachers. And in consultation with the local community, they may provide homework centres out of school hours, and also help parents improve their literacy and numeracy. The introduction of indigenous languages is a key part of this policy, as is preschool education. If a community doesn't have a functional preschool, the NSW Government says it's committed to building one on the existing campus. This whole of government approach to school communities will also include problem gambling. Does this initiative, such a break from tradition, suggest anything about future reforms in Australia?

Unfortunately, the New South Wales government's commitment to education was thrown into doubt by the announcement in September 2012 of substantial cuts to education funding affecting both public and independent—including Catholic—schools.

In late October 2012, Premier O'Farrell, using the National Partnership Agreement on Early Childhood Education which sets a minimum of 15 h of preschool in the year before school, announced that the hours children can attend government preschools would be capped at 15 h. Those schools currently offering 30 h would have to reduce their hours by the beginning of 2013. And TAFE courses that do not fill skill shortages and lead directly to jobs won't receive State government funding in the future. Private colleges will be encouraged but the Government will regulate fees.

The justification given for these funding reductions was the budget deficit; in November 2012 it was revealed by Auditor-General Peter Achterstraat that the 2011–2012 budget surplus had been underestimated by $1 billion! Unfortunately, New South Wales spending on education, including early childhood education, has been low, as revealed in Australian Bureau of Statistics figures (Cobbold 2013a).

In August 2011 the New South Wales government released its position paper, *Local Schools, Local Decisions* (NSW Department of Education and Communities 2011). Minister Adrian Piccoli proposed eleven reforms to increase the authority of local schools to make decisions about 'how they deliver education to students'! The policy followed consultations with principals, teachers, parents and the community.

Following the release of the Gonski Report and the Prime Ministers response, the governments of Queensland, New South Wales and Victoria announced their own versions of education reforms, dismissing significant aspects of the proposals of the Gonski Report in the process. In March Victoria announced *A New Era of Cooperation* giving school leaders more autonomy and making sure that the Education Department supported them in this. Minister Martin Dixon claimed his government was overseeing the beginning of major cultural change in Victorian education, focussing on schools to provide world-class education for all students. Student support Service Officers are to be moved from regional offices to school clusters, reporting obligations are to be removed and the school compliance checklist suspended!

In March 2013 Premier O'Farrell and Minister Piccoli announced *Great Teaching, Inspired Learning—a blueprint for action.* It was promoted as a detailed plan to lift the performance of the teaching profession in the State. Amongst the key reforms in the plan were raising the academic standards required to enter teaching degrees, a mandatory literacy and numeracy assessment that pre-service teachers would have to pass before they were accepted into the final year teaching rounds, ensuring teachers have induction programs and provide more rigorous formal professional learning that principals have to complete before appointment.

Queensland launched *Great Teachers = Great Results* in April 2013. Premier Campbell Newman claimed the direct action plan would build on the strengths of the existing school funding. He claimed up until now we have been unable to identify top teachers. (That is surely an extraordinary claim!) Educations Minister Langbroek said the plan focussed on professional excellence in teaching and boosting school autonomy. The plan called for a structured annual performance process, mentoring of beginning teachers, accelerated progression and paid post graduate study for high performing teachers. Disciplinary powers are to be enhanced. The selection process for staff is to be enhanced by giving a greater role to the community and removing union representatives for the process.

In making the announcement the Government specifically rejected the proposition that national solutions will achieve universally improved education outcomes. Efficient use of funds means 'funding for poorly targeted and untested programs' will not increase. Every dollar needs to focus on the things that work. 'Rather than becoming side-tracked by political slogans, the Queensland Government is delivering innovative solutions to achieve results.'

One of the themes common to all of these three policies is the placing of greater responsibility for decision making at the local and school level. The responsibility will mainly concern teacher recruitment and managing the budget. These are not the issues which the OECD in its PISA Reports has identified as critical in consideration of greater autonomy for schools and their principals. All emphasised the importance of teachers. All also claimed their systems were world class or would be.

14.11 Funding the Gonski Reforms; the National Plan for School Improvement

The Prime Minister released details of the funding proposed for implementation of the Gonski Panel's recommendations on 14 April 2013. The Commonwealth Government undertook to provide $2 for every $1 committed by State governments, all set out in the media release on the Prime Ministers website under the heading 'Resourcing All Our Kids, Classrooms and Teachers for the Future'. The total funds proposed, $14.5 million over 6 years were short of the initial amount of

14.11 Funding the Gonski Reforms; the National Plan for School Improvement

$6.5 million per annum. The Commonwealths share would be $9.4 billion or 65 % of the additional funding. Some referred to the plans as Gonski lite.

The funding ranged from $5 billion for New South Wales bringing the total public investment in that state to just under $87 billion over the 5 years (29 % of total national investment in schools) to $300 million for Western Australia of $38 billion over the period; $$300 million is to be provided for Northern Territory and $100 million to the ACT bringing total public investment in both Territories to $5 billion.

Extra funding would be secured should states and territories agree to more stable indexation of current school spending. The Commonwealth committed to 4.7 % annual growth provided states agree to 3 % growth. This funding represents, on average an extra $1.5 million per school and, on average, $4,000 extra for each student.

States would have to sign a new National Education Reform Agreement and maintain current spending to fairly fund every school. The new money would help schools pay for specialist teachers and resources. A School Resource Standard would be established based on the recommendation in the Gonski Report. The per student amount will be $9,271 for primary school students and $12,193 for secondary school students. Extra funding will be provided for students from low SES backgrounds, indigenous students, students with disability, students with limited English proficiency, small schools, and school location. 'All loadings will be fully publicly funded. Government and non-government education authorities will have flexibility to implement their own needs-based school funding systems, reflecting their own priorities and circumstances.'

Heads of Government, the Commonwealth, States and Territories, met as COAG on 19 April 2013. They left the meeting without signing on to the reforms. The Prime Minister said she would continue to pursue the agreement through June 30th. Queensland Premier Campbell Newman was reported by the ABC on 20 April as saying he would work through the proposals and was very enthusiastic about trying to reach agreement. Western Australian Premier David Barnett said he would rather talk about the nature of the proposals than the funding arrangements but that this was the first chance he had had to do that. Western Australia spends a larger amount on education per head than do other states. A couple of weeks later, New South Wales Premier Barry O'Farrell signed up to the reform proposals. Christopher Pyne acknowledged that NSW students would be better off. In late May 2013, the ACT government signed on to the *National Plan for School Improvement*.

Whilst some Premiers and Coalition politicians objected to the Governments Plan as leading to more control by Canberra, Minister Peter Garrett said school principals would be trusted to develop their school improvement plans without extra 'red-tape' but in consultation with the community. 'Schools and systems would be encouraged to share information about what is working and implement school improvement strategies in their schools', he said through a spokeswoman. 'There will be no "approval process"—schools and parents know best what will work in their school' (Hurst 2013).

Various versions of the Coalitions proposals concerning the National Plan were issued through early 2013. On a TV program Christopher Pyne said that the Coalition wanted to see a return to more didactic teaching and a move away from the child-centred approach of recent years. As an editorial in the *Sydney Morning Herald* on 22 April 2013 pointed out, Pyne had at one time branded the Gonski proposals as unworkable, later claimed that if they worked they would be retained, and in early 2013 he said that it was up to the States to decide. The editorial concluded that Mr. Abbott should short-circuit the ideological nonsense immediately and commit to retaining Gonski, subject to regular performance reviews.

The Victorian Government in its budget handed down on 7 May provided no funding for the Gonski reforms though a spokesperson said if Victoria did sign up to them, funds could be approved by the expenditure review committee and that would be reflected in the budget update later. The Victorian budget reduced funding on education by $80 millions or 0.7 %; the Commonwealth Government was blamed for reducing funding to the State. Prime Minister Gillard's Gonski proposals promise an extra $4 billion over 6 years.

The economic issues, as much as the social justice and equity issues, are compelling reasons for implementing the Gonski Reports recommendations (Cobbold 2013c). Low achievement rates amongst disadvantaged students in secondary school led to lower rates of year 12 completion and transition to employment. They impose higher costs on the economy through higher unemployment, lower lifetime earnings, lower productivity, higher health care and other welfare expenditure as well as high levels of involvement in crime. Trevor Cobbold (loc.cit) quotes studies by the US National Bureau of Economic Research which show that educated people enjoy greater work satisfaction, make better decisions about marriage and parenting; the pecuniary gains from an extra year of schooling may be as high as the earning gains to individuals or higher.

Cobbold quoted Productivity Commission estimates which show that increased skill levels contributed over 20 % of annual multi-factor productivity growth from the mid-1980s through the 1990s and that an increase in the average level of schooling of the workforce by one-quarter of a year would increase productivity by about 1.2 % The OECD has estimated that an additional year of schooling would raise productivity by 4–7 % in a country such as Australia.

In *The Education Policy Outlook on Australia* published mid April the OECD endorsed the thrust of the Gonski Report saying that the current system of school funding "lacks coherence and transparency". The *Policy Outlook* endorsed the Gonski Reports focus on reducing inequity in education: a key policy challenge facing Australian education is to reduce inequities between students from different socioeconomic and ethnic backgrounds (Cobbold 2013d).

The legislation, the Australian Education Bill 2012, implementing the National Plan for School Improvement was passed by the House of Representatives on 5 June 2013. As the debate in the House continued, the Independent member for Lyne in New South Wales, Mr. Rob Oakeshott, spoke of the importance of equity and of how the data on Aboriginal students and [children of] low-SES families was being addressed by the legislation. 'We either accept the education data or we do not. If we do accept the education data, we are accepting a massive failure of public policy... The Gonski process identified an 'intolerable link' between the education data and the funding formula. So either we accept that link or we do not. We accept that it is tolerable or intolerable, Once we have got across that very simple hurdle, we accept loadings and a new funding formula or we do not... Is the solution [to the intolerable link] to put in place loadings specific to regionality, Aboriginality and to socioeconomic status? That is the question before the House.'

Oakeshott joined with the Government to gag debate and the Bill passed the House. Opposition spokesperson on education Christopher Pyne responded that Mr. Oakeshott 'had abandoned any notion of proper scrutiny and any pretence of independence. This Bill hinges on there being a national agreement for school funding. There is no national agreement, with only one State and one Territory agreeing to the changes...'

Mr. Oakeshott retired from the House at the September 2013 election. In his valedictory address he described the Australian Education Bill as 'the significant reform of this parliament... I think to blow up a funding formula that was rubbish and leading to disadvantage is a credit to everyone involved.'

In a speech presented to a public forum in June 2013, Trevor Cobbold (2013e) spelled out what he saw as the positives and negatives of the School Plan as passed by the Parliament. Describing it as a 'watershed but not the full Gonski' he pointed to the 'the biggest increase in funding in living memory'. He said, 'If fully delivered and effectively distributed and used, it could make a major contribution to reducing the huge gap in school achievement between rich and poor throughout the country, which at age 15 amounts to 2–3 years of learning.'

'In adopting the Gonski model, the Gillard plan represents a marked change of direction in school funding in Australia. Instead of a primary focus on funding for school choice as in the Howard Government's SES funding model, the new model gives priority to reducing the effects of disadvantage on education outcomes. The focus of the new model is equity.'

He pointed to another significant feature, the breaking of the link between government funding for private schools and average government school costs which allowed that every time state governments increased funding for disadvantaged students in government schools, a portion of it flowed through to private schools.

However, as Cobbold pointed out that there will be at least two Federal elections before the bulk of the Gonski funding can be delivered. 'Consequently, there can be no guarantee that the full $7 billion for the final 2 years of the transition period will ever be delivered...' And the 'large part of the $2.8 billion increase to 2016–2017 is to be financed by the termination of existing programs... and their funding re-directed to the Government's Program. 'Thus, very little new funding will be allocated to the Gillard plan over the next 4 years.'

He pointed to the relatively small additional funding to be allocated to disadvantaged students and, 'in the case of low SES students, is to be spread over a much large number of students than proposed by the Gonski report'. For example, 'while the Gonski report recommended a funding loading for every student in the lowest 25 % of SES backgrounds, the Gillard plan spreads the funding much more broadly... more than 95 % of schools will receive low SES funding.' Cobbold also pointed out that Catholic schools will retain their current share of federal funding. 'The special deal will allow Catholic schools to receive additional funding to compensate them for any loss of enrolment share to government schools or other private schools.'

And the focus on improving equity in education in the Gonski model was diluted by a new "no losers" guarantee for medium to high SES private schools, the Government's promise that no school would funding under the new model.

'Unfortunately, the Gillard Government has not only 'delayed implementation for far too long and made it hostage to the election campaign, but it has not adopted the full Gonski'. He criticised the Plan as losing integrity and coherence by 'more special deals with private schools.' 'However', he concluded, 'the more states that sign up the greater its significance… It would provide the foundation for school funding in the future and offer the hope and opportunity for a "full Gonski". It would indeed be a watershed in the history of school funding in Australia.'

By the time the federal election was called by Prime Minister Kevin Rudd for September 7 four States—New South Wales, South Australia, Tasmania and Victoria—and the Australian Capital Territory had signed up to the National Plan for School Improvement. In the process there was some variation to the funding arrangements.

Prime Minister Gillard's call for a 'national crusade' in 2012 did not count for much. Despite numerous discussions Western Australia did not sign up to the Plan and neither did Queensland despite signs that it might. The Northern Territory did not sign up either. Students from the Territory have consistently achieved by far the lowest scores in all national and international tests, unsurprisingly considering the relatively high proportion of remote communities and high proportion of Indigenous families.

Leader of the Opposition Coalition, Tony Abbott, stated that he and Prime Minister Rudd were 'on the same page' in respect of the Plan and should the Opposition become government the Plan would continue to be supported through the present budget cycle. As the Australian Education Union's President Angelo Gavrielatos pointed out, this did not necessarily mean much since the 'budget cycle' was 4 years and the Plan was intended to be implemented over 7 years with major funding in the last few years, after the fourth year!

14.12 Education Reform: A Future of Equity or a Future of Privilege?

Countries in Europe, including Scandinavia, have been traversed by armies for centuries, public buildings and houses destroyed along with schools and churches, millions of people killed, landscapes ravaged, economies destroyed. All Nordic countries were involved in many conflicts from the thirteenth through the early nineteenth centuries culminating in wider conflicts in more recent decades.

South Asian countries such as Singapore and others such as Korea were colonised by European countries, occupied by Japan and involved in armed conflict. Chinese peoples suffered devastation through astonishing central government policies at a rate almost incomprehensible to most people in developed countries. Two generations ago South Korea had the standard of living of Afghanistan today and was among the lowest performers in education: today 97 % of all Korean 25–34-year-olds have completed upper-secondary education, the highest rate among the OECD countries.

Australia has suffered no such ravages, no such destructions through war, which is not to diminish the dreadful tragedy of losses suffered in wars elsewhere or the deaths and cultural diminution of Aboriginal and Torres Strait Islander peoples. Neither has the USA since the Civil War though it has devoted enormous funds to its various interventions in conflict around the globe.

Australia has, indeed, been the 'lucky country': most advances have been due more to good fortune than to effort. But though behaviours such as an independence of spirit, belief in a fair go and mateship are often cited as characteristic of Australians, in many instances Australia is all too ready to adopt the practices of other countries with much less than a critical eye. This is anything but independence of spirit! The increasing disparity in wealth consequent mostly on pursuit of market economics is hardly a fair go. Despite economic growth, poverty levels are increasing.

In the September 7 federal election a coalition of political parties—Liberal and National—was returned to government. The Coalition has shown a commitment to the economically and socially advantaged through policies on taxation and other areas, including education.

Actions in 2012 by state governments in New South Wales, as well as in Victoria and Queensland, in cutting funding for education are a demonstration of the ongoing failure of Australia to act as a nation. The question is of course whether the cuts will cease in the event that the States agree to the Commonwealth Governments plan.

The complex funding arrangements for government and independent schools alike, together with the continuing embrace of notions of accountability and transparency, advocacy about the shortage of skills, ongoing claims that student achievement is declining and predominance of views based on personal experience rather than reasoned analysis, all hardly auger well for success in education reform. The obsession with deficits and debt at all levels of government and the consequent reluctance to look to the long-term, as well as the influence of groups with narrow sectional interests, only add to the problems.

It is all made even more difficult by the vertical fiscal imbalance between the States and the Commonwealth which amplifies the dysfunctional Australian federation and the arguments that centre on accusations of overspending on the one hand and demands for a greater share of taxes on the other. It is not surprising that the public might remain confused when some of the media report the independent review of the GST (the Goods and Services Tax introduced by the Howard Government), which reported in early December 2012 that no major change was appropriate whilst another, *The Australian* on 1 December, claimed the review panel to have found that the tax is 'failing to provide the states with a stable source of revenue, and attacked the Gillard governments mining tax as unsustainable'. The Oppositions response was to say they would fix the problem by abolishing the mining tax, revenue from which is declining substantially.

Perhaps Australian education policy makers could learn something from the Australian wine industry. In a couple of decades Australian wine became the wine of choice in many countries, overcoming numerous obstacles. The achievement involved taking risks and learning from the best. Advocates like Len Evans took a long view that Australian wine had a world beating future. The industry is presently recovering from the takeover by large companies with no understanding of wine making, intent only on making a lot of money.

What does need to be emphasised is that the reforms proposed by the Australian Government in response to the Gonski Panel's recommendations are not some left wing plot to entrench unionism in schools, eliminate standards of achievement through ignoring judgements of student progress or cover up the failure of students and teachers. Indeed, from the earliest days of the Rudd and Gillard governments a number of the education reforms have been at odds with much of the research concerning standardised testing and other matters; some of those elements are no longer part of the National Plan for schools. That some commentators and politicians continue to parade these myths ought to be seen as the exercise in futility that it is. Unfortunately lies told often enough can become the truth.

If the level of caution shown in respect of the education reforms had typified US and European policies over the last 50 years in science and technology, there would have been no man on the moon, no probes to the outer regions of the solar system, all of which have generated economic returns vastly exceeding the costs of the programs. There would be no Large Hadron Collider exploring the structure of matter and the nature of the universe. And no less important, there would be none of the extraordinary discoveries in every branch of medicine which have revolutionised our understanding of the brain and the nature and treatment of major illnesses. And probably we would be travelling by motor transport preceded by a man carrying a flag, certainly not the very fast trains which so typify the transport infrastructure of many countries.

Apart from devotion to the notions of neoclassical economics, it has to be said that many in Australia in the media, business and politics have simply failed to make even the most basic efforts to understand the evidence about education, teaching and learning, not even reading the reports on the essential issues or understanding basic statistics. With a few notable exceptions, the media frequently fails to report important statements or reference important reports. Visits to Australia by leading educators go unreported, important conferences are not mentioned. But the myths of education reform promoted by people who have not bothered to read and think about the basic research which daily elucidates advances in education does feature. In these respects there is little difference from the situation in some other countries such as the UK and the US.

An example of how far conservative forces have been prepared to go is reflected in statements by Judith Sloan, economist and honorary professorial fellow at the Melbourne Institute of Applied Economic and Social Research at the University of Melbourne and former Director of the National Institute of Labour Studies and Professor of Labour Studies at Flinders University of South Australia as well as a Commissioner at the Australian Productivity Commission. In an article in *The Australian* of June 15 (Sloan 2013) Sloan asserted, 'The bottom line is that the implementation of Gonski is no way to conduct important public policy reforms. And if the key is the reform of school funding to reflect student needs, we should take note of [the] observation that "the funding formula Gonski recommended is already being used in various degrees by most states".

'But when it comes to leaving the control and management of public schools in the hands of the states and territories, the Labor government isn't having a bar of it. New controls, new bodies, new accountability measures, all 10,000 schools submitting annual School Improvement Plans—it is no wonder that the lagging states are a bit hesitant. And most of these new arrangements also will apply to non-government schools.'

In a blog on the Catallaxy website on 23 June 2013 Professor Sloan referred to child care workers as 'dim-witted graduates of second-class universities'; she asserted that the child-care arrangements of the government had not worked, that the sector was in disarray and referred to rising charges by child-care centres! She was asked about her comments on the ABC TV program 'Q&A' the following day and repeated the views she had blogged. No understanding of the pivotal role of early childhood at all is evident in her response. Her colleague Kevin Donnelly, a frequent contributor to *The Australian* and other media, commonly asserts that there is no relationship between educational achievement and socioeconomic status!

References

Aubusson, P. et al. (2012, February 20). Gonski review: full coverage. *The Conversation*.
Australian Education Union. (2010). *National symposium. Advice for ministers and ACARA on NAPLAN, the use of student data, my school and league tables*. Retrieved September 12, 2012 from http://www.aeufederal.org.au/Publications/2010/NS/papers.html
Australian Education Union. (2012, October*). Submission to senate inquiry into teaching and learning—maximising our investment in Australian schools. Southbank, vic*. Retrieved July 15, 2013 from http://www.aeufederal.org.au/Publications/2012/InvestAustschools.pdf
Australian Senate. (2013, May 14). *Senate inquiry into teaching and learning—maximising our investment in Australian schools*. Retrieved July 15, 2013 from http://www.aph.gov.au/Parliamentary_Business/Committees/Senate_Committees?url=eet_ctte/completed_inquiries/2010-13/teaching_learning/report/index.htm
Beder, S., Varney, W., & Gosden, R. (2009). *This little kiddy went to market. The corporate capture of childhood*. Sydney: UNSW Press.

Bonner, C., & Caro, J. (2007). *The stupid country: How Australia is dismantling public education*. Sydney: UNSW Press.

Business Council of Australia. (2007). *Action required to make education Australia's advantage. Media release 26 August, 2007*. Retrieved September 12, 2012 from http://www.bca.com.au/Content.aspx?ContentID=101154

Chiu, M. M., & Khoo, L. (2005). Effects of resources. Inequality and privilege bias on achievement: Country, school and student level analyses. *American Educational Research Journal, 42*, 575–603.

Cobbold, T. (2011, March 30). *Private schools make a brazen grab for more resources. Save Our Schools*. Retrieved April 2, 2011 from http://www.saveourschools.com.au/funding/private-schools-make-a-brazen-grab-for-more-resources

Cobbold, T. (2012a, January 25). Naplan results highlight the failure of governments to address education disadvantage. *Save Our Schools*. Retrieved January 27, 2012 from http://www.saveourschools.com.au/national-issues/naplan-results-highlight-the-failure-of-governments-to-address-education-disadvantage

Cobbold, T. (2012b, February 22). Gillard turns her back on the disadvantaged. *Save Our Schools*. Retrieved February 24, 2012 from http://www.saveourschools.com.au/funding/gillard-turns-her-back-on-the-disadvantaged

Cobbold, T. (2012c, August 31). Restrict funding increases for wealthy private schools. *Save Our Schools, 2012*. Retrieved September 4, 2012 from http://www.saveourschools.com.au/media-releases/restrict-funding-increases-for-wealthy-private-schools

Cobbold, T. (2013a, March 25). The parlous state of pre-school education. *Save Our Schools*. Retrieved April 17, 2013 from http://www.saveourschools.com.au/national-issues/the-parlous-state-of-pre-school-education

Cobbold, T. (2013b, April 2). New group to oppose NAPLAN tests. *Save Our Schools*. Retrieved June 2, 2013 from http://www.saveourschools.com.au/league-tables/new-group-to-oppose-naplan-tests

Cobbold, T. (2013c, April 23). The economic case for Gonski. *Save Our Schools*. Retrieved April 23, 2013 from http://www.saveourschools.com.au/funding/the-economic-case-for-gonski

Cobbold, T. (2013d, April 29). The OECD endorses Gonski. *Save Our Schools*. Retrieved May 12, 2013 from http://www.saveourschools.com.au/funding/the-oecd-endorses-gonski

Cobbold, T. (2013e, June 11). The Gillard school funding plan is a Watershed but is not the full Gonski. *Save Our Schools*. Retrieved June 21, 2013 from http://www.saveourschools.com.au/funding/the-gillard-school-funding-plan-is-a-watershed-but-is-not-the-full-gonski

Community Services and Health Industry Skills Council. (2011). *No more excuses industry skills councils call for action on adult literacy skills*. Retrieved September 12, 2012 from https://www.cshisc.com.au/index.php?option=com_content&task=view&id=660&Itemid=65

Dodd, T & Mather, J. (2012, December 12). Australian students get C on global report card. *Australian financial review*.

Dowling, A. (2007). *Australia's school funding system*. Melbourne: ACER. Retrieved August 28, 2012 from http://www.acer.edu.au/documents/PolicyBriefs_Dowling07.pdf

Ferrari, J. (2008, December 10). Doesn't add up: Borat kids beat Aussies. *The Australian*.

Garrett, P. (2011). Top teachers to be rewarded. *Ministers Media Centre*. Retrieved September 11, 2012, from http://ministers.deewr.gov.au/garrett/top-teachers-be-rewarded

Gillard, J. (2012). A national plan for school improvement. *Speech to National Press Club*. Canberra: Prime Minister of Australia Press Office. Retrieved September 10, 2012 from http://www.pm.gov.au/press-office/"-national-plan-school-improvement"-speech-national-press-club-canberra

Gittins, R. (2012, 27 August). Sabotage Gonski and productivity will suffer. *Sydney Morning Herald*.

Gonski, D. et al. (2011). *Review of Funding for Schooling*. Final Report. Canberra: Department of Education, Employment and Workplace Relations. Retrieved February 20, 2012 from http://foi.deewr.gov.au/system/files/doc/other/review-of-funding-for-schooling-final-report-dec-2011.pdf

References

Gruen, N. (2010). Where are the hordes of bad teachers? *Club Troppo* August 3. Retrieved September 12, 2012 from http://clubtroppo.com.au/2010/08/03/where-are-the-hordes-of-bad-teachers/

Hanushek, E., & Woessmann, L. (2010). *The high cost of low educational performance. The long-run economic impact of improving PISA outcomes*. Paris: OECD.

Hurst, D. (2013, 17 April). Canberra promises to take a hands-off approach on extra funding. *Sydney Morning Herald*.

Ireland, J. (2012, 4 September). PMs Gonski speech vague and unworthy, says Abbott. *Sydney Morning Herald*.

Jensen, B., et al. (2012). *Catching up: Learning from the best school systems in East Asia*. Carlton: Grattan Institute.

Long, S. (2012, February 22). Gonski. plutocracy and public policy. ABC The Drum Retrieved 12 September 2012 from http://www.abc.net.au/news/2012-02-22/long-gonski-plutocracy-and-public-policy/3843906.

Martin, P. (2012, 21 August). Education making us ignorant *Sydney Morning Herald*.

Masters, G. N. (2012). *Enhancing the quality of teaching and learning in Australian schools: Submission to the senate inquiry on teaching and learning (maximising our investment in Australian schools)*. Melbourne: Australian Council for Educational Research (ACER).

McAlpine, J, (2008, 13 October). National declarations blurred vision requires retesting. *Sydney Morning Herald*.

MCEECDYA. (2008). *Melbourne declaration on educational goals for young Australians*. Retrieved September 12, 2012 from http://www.mceecdya.edu.au/mceecdya/melbourne_declaration.25979.html

Nous Group. (2011). *Schooling challenges and opportunities*. Melbourne Graduate School of Education. Review of Funding for Schooling Panel. Retrieved September 8, 2012 from http://www.deewr.gov.au/Schooling/ReviewofFunding/Pages/PaperCommissionedResearch.aspx

NSW Department of Education and Communities. (2011). *Local schools, local decisions*. Report on the Consultations. Retrieved from May 12, 2013 from http://www.schools.nsw.edu.au/media/downloads/news/lsld/report-on-the-consultation.pdf

Perkins, M. (2010, 18 February). Low turnout skewing school test results. *The Age*.

Reid, A. (2012, 19 December). A dumbed down debate, but those tests still hold some lessons. *Sydney Morning Herald*.

Sloan, J. (2013, 15 June). Education's ominous national plan destined for failure. *The Australian*.

Thomson, S., et al. (2011). *Highlights from TIMSS & PIRLS 2011 from Australia's perspective*. Melbourne: ACER.

Thomson, S., Hillman, K., & Wernert, N. (2012). *Monitoring Australian Year 8 student achievement internationally: TIMSS 2011*. Melbourne: ACER.

Tingle, L., Freebairn, P., & Mather, J. (2012, 20 February). Coalition Rejects Gonski School Funding Plan. *Australian Financial Review*.

Tovey, J. (2012, December 12). Maths and English - nation could do better. *Sydney Morning Herald*.

Topsfield, J. (2012, 11 December). Australia's disaster in education. *The Age*.

Zyngier, D. (2004). A tale of two reports or how bad news for Australian education is mediated by the media. *Issues in Educational Research, 14*, 194–211.

Zyngier, D. (2011, 15 July). Here's a lesson for Australia's education policymakers: failure begets failure. *Sydney Morning Herald*.

Chapter 15
Concluding Essay: What Have We Learned and Where are We Going?

15.1 Centuries of Thought and Decades of Research: Critical Conclusions

We know a great deal about education and related matters. That is because there have been centuries of thought about it and decades of excellent research. Some people claim we do not know enough: that is true. But to suggest we do not know enough to identify the fundamentally important aspects of education and learning and what likely leads to superior learning outcomes is wrong. Though we need to understand more about learning in classroom situations, there is high quality research on effective teaching and on learning. A very important point is that relatively too much attention is paid to schooling: early childhood is the critical time. Children spend the vast majority their time out of school. Too little attention is paid to the influence of parents and the opportunities they can, but not always do, provide, influences which are far greater than that of the school.

It is equally unfortunate that ideology is imported to the debate from areas such as neoclassical economics and neoliberalism rather than from the best of our knowledge and understandings of organisational dynamics, human behaviour and behavioural economics, psychology and neurophysiology. As I said at the outset many issues, though they are part of other domains, affect educational outcomes. It is not the domination of economics but of a certain view of economics and its translation to neoliberalism and New Public Management which is the problem: and it is a major problem because it is all supported by little or no evidence! The education debate is just another of many issues ranging from the safety of vaccinations through evolution to climate change, the debates about which are distorted by reference to ideology and personal experience. These are debates driven by narrow self-interest and short-term gains with little regard for the greater good and the longer term.

In this concluding essay I summarise the major points from the preceding essays and identify the important policy issues and areas for further research to strengthen understanding and so better inform policy. I conclude with commentary on one of the major drivers of the debates about education and a summary of how ordinary people reach decisions about what they consider to be the truth. I conclude with a vision for what education might really aim to achieve.

A principal factor influencing education reform in many countries is adherence to market economics and its propositions that increasing prosperity rests on economic growth and that overcoming poverty depends on improving education. There is no doubt that education leads to improved economic prosperity. However, as the United Nations Human Development Reports show, improvements around the world in education and health have been due principally to cross border transfer of ideas: there is little if any correlation with economic growth! In other words we can learn a great deal from other countries and other domains: seeking out those lessons is vitally important. That is something that education administrators in Singapore do. Successful people and successful organisations gain enormously from exploring different ideas: that leads to innovation! Yet in Australia travel overseas by people employed in the public sector is considered a perk and something to be closely regulated.

Seven important points can be made in summarising what we think we know. These have been discussed in the essays. First, economic and social disadvantage severely limits the experiences and opportunities of those caught up in it, especially children. Experiences and opportunities enrich learning. That is why parent's socioeconomic background, including their own educational achievement level, is the principal predictor of the child's educational achievement. To ignore poverty and early childhood is to incur greater expenditure later in seeking reform and ultimately greater risk of limited success.

Second, 50 % of educational achievement once the child enters school is attributable to the understandings the child brings from home. The early years influence the exercise of creativity as well as the formation of relationships and the understanding of such things as the consequences of one's actions. The health of the child and the physical environment in which the child develops are strongly influenced by the social and economic environment.

Third, effective learning at school is principally influenced by the teacher through interaction with the student including exploration of ideas, argumentation and feedback, especially that which challenges the student through the setting of demanding standards. A high degree of control over the learning journey needs to be maintained by the student, rather than controlled exclusively by a teacher: even young children are quite capable of articulating what it is they feel is relevant. Too often the learning agenda is determined with little relevance to the child's goals.

Fourth, the educational achievement is influenced by peers and parents as well as teachers and a significant influence is, again, the social and economic context. Socioeconomic background of the class means that a student from a low socioeconomic background in a class from high average socioeconomic level performs significantly better than if they were in a class of low average socioeconomic status. Therefore maximum attention should be given to ensuring that socioeconomic inequity in the community is not visited upon the school. To assert, as some do, that socioeconomic status of the parents and the classroom and school environment is not important is to ignore the evidence.

Fifth, the extent to which the teacher can pursue a productive course is influenced by the nature of the school workplace including the way authentic leadership—behaviour consistent with expressed values—is exercised by senior teachers and especially the principal. Indeed the studies in South Chicago by Anthony Bryk and colleagues give prime attention to leadership as the feature on which other important 'supports' depend. And that is facilitated by a degree of control by school leaders over their agenda. Most particularly it is shown by the freedom they have to manage the curriculum. In other words, the principal's role in leadership is most important in respect of the learning and instruction which goes on there, not the control over budgets and staffing, thought those issues are not unimportant. Domain knowledge and transformational leadership are as critical in the school domain as in other domains. Managerialism has no place. The attributes of leadership which are critical concern the contribution to teaching and learning, not administrative issues of budget control and staff recruitment and promotion, important though those are!

Sixth, the constructivist nature of learning combined with the unreliability of memory and the uncertainty of the future mean that the most appropriate goal of education is the gaining of confidence in analysing and reasoning, questioning and refining ideas. Since in work life and personal life there is a constant call for cooperative relationships the education agenda should also develop an ability to work constructively with others. Thinking of the important contribution cooperation makes to complex science, technology and politics, as well as family life, is enough to show the truth of this. These are in fact qualities sought by employers who often express concern that their potential employees do not have these skills. People can be trained to acquire skills, developing social skills takes much longer and without them little else is likely.

And seventh, the contribution of skills to productivity and of expert knowledge and scholarship to major advances in every area of concern to society is such that, especially considering the substantial net contribution of graduates to the economy in later life, it makes sense for governments to invest in college and university rather than demand ongoing generation of significant funding through charging fees for attendance, the levels of which inevitably create substantial personal debt. Ongoing successive reductions in the name of encouraging entrepreneurship are disingenuous, debilitating, unproductive and destructive of the effectiveness of both the teaching and research function of universities.

That much of what has been learned from research is mostly ignored in policy discussions is not just regrettable but extremely unfortunate and in some cases, tragic. The disregard of evidence in favour of preconceived notions is a major feature of the world in the twenty-first century, facilitated by the development of 'web 2' and social media through its significant user-orientation and interactivity. Social constructivism and the notion that truth is what one wants it to be has invaded the blogosphere and hindered even further the gaining of agreement on what we think we know. Superior judgement is sacrificed. The costs are substantial and borne by the entire community, to be recognised in some cases too late.

15.2 Early Childhood

There is compelling and important evidence about early childhood. Very young children are intrinsically creative and diverse in their interests, they respond to encouragement and stimulation. The brain evolves over the person's life: it is capable of modification through stimulation almost up to the last minute of life, a feature which has led to the brain being described as plastic. This is recent research in one of the most active and exciting areas of science. The greatest gains in learning can be made in the earliest years. That is the most important time of life. Narrowing of experiences produces a narrow outlook in later life.

Learning is constructivist, modified by experience, precisely because the brain is so plastic and capable of adaptation through stimulation over time. Recent accounts of brain development and cognition include some recalling individuals experience in recovering brain function after stroke or other dysfunction such as that which may be evident at birth. Complementing these findings from neurophysiology are understandings from animal behaviour and behavioural economics.

Knowledge about early childhood informs policies about positive relationships between parent and child through time spent with the child and how that can be facilitated by parental leave, provision of high quality preschool available to all and so on. Deprived and unstable family relationships not only affect the child in their early years at school through adolescence but influence the behaviour of the parent, particularly the mother, when the child grows up and has children of her own. Vivid recollections of neglect or violence are likely to lead the parent, especially the mother, to revisit those experiences on her children. On the other hand, recollections of close and supportive relationships are likely to lead to positive behaviour: people successful in later life recall support of parent, close friend or teacher. The role of the mother is especially important for many reasons, not least because women usually take the major responsibility for child care.

These characteristics of early childhood and learning and the impact of social and physical aspects relating to the family's socioeconomic background are such that early childhood intervention is most critical for children from disadvantaged backgrounds. Those children are not inherently less intelligent than their more fortunate brothers and sisters. Rather they were *not* surrounded by a rich environment in their first few months and years.

Socioeconomic differences reflected in the home environment are evident in children's ability even at age 10 months (Lehrer 2012). For children of higher socioeconomic background growing up in the stimulating environment which more likely typifies their home means the parents sometimes frantic pursuit of cultural and sporting opportunities to enrich their child's life once they start school matters less than for less well-off young children. Diversity of experience is important for all: that some children lack that has profound effects. Children learning a language other than the one most commonly spoken, learning music, visiting museums and so on, gain enormously later on.

Early intervention has very large returns on investment and no downside risk. Children advantaged in the early years are more likely to be employed later in life, less likely to be involved in crime and substance abuse and so on. These findings on early childhood are unequivocal, perhaps more so than for any other aspect of education. In many countries every child attends preschool and if fees are charged by the preschool, government subsidises attendance by those children whose parents have difficulty paying.

Policies on urban planning including housing and recreation support of places of informal learning such as museums and zoos as well as opportunities for participation in creative and sporting activities are vitally important. They especially influence the development of creativity.

As at 2012 participation rates in Australia in early childhood education and public funding for it were relatively low. However, there are promising signs that greater attention will be paid to early childhood with new policies at Commonwealth Government level on parental leave and on standards for early childhood centres and their staff. Unfortunately, some state governments in Australia are yet to recognise this despite agreements signed by all state and territory governments as part of a national plan (Cobbold 2013a).

15.3 Schooling, Schools and Teaching

Once the child enters school the influence of the teacher is paramount but not exclusive. Quality teachers supported by strategic professional development leads to effective learning. But what it is that goes on in the classroom needs further research because of the dynamic nature of the classroom environment and the interaction of other factors including peers and parents. Leadership not only influences the effectiveness of the teacher but the development of vitally important relationships with the community, especially parents.

The pervasive influence of neoclassical economics has led to demands for accountability of schools and teachers through standardised tests and application of merit pay for superior achievement by teachers, as assessed by the test scores of the students they taught in that year. An emphasis on content knowledge also leads to demands for uniform curricula and intervention by groups such as school boards in the US, and sometimes in some other countries by governments in response to demands of some parents, that the content of the curriculum, especially in history and science, be closely controlled to ensure that the right views are taught. What is important is a rich curriculum well taught. Excessive privileging of facts leads to boredom, little takeaway knowledge and less understanding. Children don't like it!

In high performing education systems testing is used only to inform the teacher, schools do not compete with each other, teachers have considerable time for professional development and are assisted by extra staff where the class contains students with some disadvantage such as their native language not being the dominant language of the country. Additionally, teachers recruited from highly successful university graduates are paid more than average, highly regarded in the community and given considerable freedom in senior school years in curriculum development: they are trusted!

The search for the best school education has come to mean, in certain countries, the right of the parent to choose what school the child goes to. That is especially so in the US, especially evident after the 1954 Supreme Court judgement in Brown versus the Board of Education which in simple terms outlawed school segregation on the basis of race. Choice was a way of avoiding the consequences of that judgement so that white kids did not have to attend schools dominated by 'blacks'. Millions of dollars were spent bussing kids out of their neighbourhood instead of on better teachers and schools. The issue continues to this day in ongoing claims to legitimise discrimination and through support of charter schools in the Obama administration's program 'Race to the Top'.

The discrimination which characterised the early years of formation of the US continues with denial of voting rights to many who have committed even minor crimes and in some cases life imprisonment in states that have enacted 'three strikes' laws. For the most part those convicted and those incarcerated are from minorities, especially African Americans. Fifty years after 'Brown' the standards of schools and schooling for many minority children continues to be unacceptable and the same myths pervade the issues, that poor black children are neglected, not motivated, slovenly and prone to miss school and commit crime. Minorities dominate the poor and the homeless.

Support for independent schools is evident also in the UK where academies can be run by nonprofit organisations. In Australia early support for funding of Catholic schools has been transformed into government support for a variety of schools run by many different groups.

The reforms in the US have for the most part failed. Experiments in New York and San Diego and other cities and states have sought turnarounds in short order. Claims for success, when subjected to careful analysis, have turned out to be hollow. One time US Federal education administration official and education historian Diane Ravitch has been at the forefront of campaigns pointing to the failure of the reforms and the misinformed assertions about teachers and student achievement (Ravitch 2010). Her advocacy has been joined by many very high quality research studies by prominent education scholars, economists and statisticians as well as various NGOs. Successful reforms in south Chicago, California and many other places are seldom heard of.

There is no good evidence to support the proposition that independent schools achieve superior results; where they do it is because of selective enrolment of students from high socioeconomic backgrounds and substantially greater resources translated to higher paid teachers and better facilities of all kinds.

Studies of the reforms shows that standardised testing delivers no gains in educational achievement: it is accompanied by numerous other deleterious outcomes such as narrowing of the curriculum and gaming of the system as well as negatively affecting the health of students and family. Paying bonuses to teachers produces no gains in educational achievement either, no change in school attendance or teacher behaviour and indeed is considered by many teachers to be an affront to professionalism. Some schools game the system and some teachers have altered test scores in order to gain bonuses for themselves; of course these represent a small part of the system. Much more importantly, tests are only useful to the extent that they accurately reflect learning which achieves the overall goals of education: being able to answer multiple choice questions in reading, mathematics and science does not constitute an education! A broad and rich curriculum is an essential component of those educational systems which are successful internationally.

The research on these areas is close to unequivocal, yet ignored as recently as in the disputation with teachers in Chicago where recently elected mayor (and former White House chief of staff) Rahm Emanuel required standardised tests as part of the agreement with the union. It cannot be emphasised too strongly that opposition to testing is not to evaluation of students, or of teachers, but to the near exclusive use of so narrow a metric as student tests and the linking of the two.

Interestingly, there are numerous examples of reforms which attend to students having difficulties. They provide extra support, give special attention to professional development of teachers and encourage teachers to cooperate with each other. These reforms have produced interesting results and measurable improvements. But somehow much of the attention is paid to reforms that lack such characteristics. Too many people with influence in education policy seek quick results and are too ready to claim success when that is transitory or in fact absent!

American student's achievement in international tests has stayed steady or improved slightly in the last several years; however the scores of students from other countries have improved! As Ravitch (2012) has pointed out, 'A fair assessment of public education would acknowledge that high school graduation rates are today the highest in our history for every group, whether white, black, Hispanic, low-income, middle-income, or high-income'. It would also acknowledge that scores in reading and math on federal tests are at their highest point in history for every group of students.'

The concern in Australia with inequity brought about by the growth of independent schools as well as the effects of remoteness, magnified in turn by features such as indigeneity, have been principal concerns of public policy development through the Gonski Panel's Report (Gonski et al. 2011). Inequity was the principal focus of the extensive commentary upon the Report, the lead up to its release and the response by the Government to it culminating in Prime Minister Gillard's speech to the National Press Club by on 3 September 2012.

The research by Laura Perry and Andrew McConney of Murdoch University (McConney and Perry 2010; Perry and McConney 2010) shows that the differences between the scores in PISA assessments for a child in a low and high SES class represent about 2 years of learning and that this holds irrespective of the child's own SES background. The difference holds for reading, mathematics and science! Support for independent schools which enrol children from high SES backgrounds exacerbate the existing SES differences. Since the principal reason for low average educational achievement by a country's students is the achievement of the less advantaged this research must be considered amongst the most important. Perry and McConney point out, 'for the benefit of most children and larger society, balanced socioeconomic composition should be a primary aim of education policy, and… Reducing socioeconomic school segregation is not only equitable but also effective'.

It is surely extraordinary that despite the irrefutable evidence about the deleterious effects of disadvantage on the educational achievement of students, arguments continue to be strongly made for government support of independent schools! Such advocacy, in the face of this evidence and that from PISA and other studies, that choice of school lifts overall educational achievement is like supporting not just a flat earth but one created 6,000 years ago!

It is even more astonishing that politicians can claim that public schools which educate the vast majority of disadvantaged children are over funded, as has the leader of the Coalition then the Opposition in Australia, the Hon Tony Abbott, and that socioeconomic status is not important. It is equally astonishing that politicians such as the Coalition spokesperson, now Minister of Education, Christopher Pyne, can claim that an important needed reform is provision of autonomy to schools giving principals control over budgets and staffing: the evidence from countries such as Sweden and New Zealand shows that they are not.

The OECD in its PISA studies, based on data from all OECD countries and other countries participating in the studies, points out that there is no evidence supporting autonomy for schools in those areas. In New Zealand school teachers have become less cooperative and less prepared to share information and experiences with consequent losses in learning effectiveness. Mr Pyne also claims that teaching should return to didactic methods and move away from the child-centred learning that has typified the last few years. That proposition also flies in the face of the evidence! According to recent research on academies in England by the London School of Economics and Political Science 'the evidence that does exist at best shows only small beneficial effects on overall pupil performance and very little consistent evidence of improvements for tail students' (Cobbold 2013b). More than that, very recent research on charter schools in the US, cited by Trevor Cobbold of *Save Our Schools*, was at best inconclusive as to the aggregate effect of charter schools on student achievement. As reported in the review of Australian education policy (Chap. 14) policies adopted by Queensland, New South Wales and Victoria all emphasise strengthening the autonomy of schools in respect of staff recruitment and financial management but not curriculum!

As in many, many other organisations, the system for evaluation of performance and for promotion of teachers in many constituencies is inadequate. In the worst systems the goal is to make it easier for those judged to be poorly performing to be dismissed. Getting rid of bad teachers is advocated as the way to improve educational standards! Such a negative focus has its own 'rewards'. Any sensible system provides meaningful encouragement for successful performance. Performance management means close collaboration and mentoring, and clear benchmarks. Melbourne University's John Hattie and others emphasise that it is expert teachers rather than simply experienced teachers who make the difference.

The performance of the teacher is influenced also by the way the profession regards itself and how it is regarded by the community. In circumstances such as high poverty communities the links the school makes with the community are vital as shown by the pioneering studies of schools in south Chicago by the University of Chicago consortium including Penny Sebring, Anthony Bryk and others and the studies of Bill Mulford of Tasmanian schools.

The nature of the school organisation is a powerful influence on the performance of the teacher. The principal or, in a large school, other senior teachers, have as their principle focus the effectiveness of their teaching colleagues. Too often, however, as is the experience of professionals in many other parts of government, years of teaching lead eventually to assignment in instrumental roles such as timetabling and other administrative tasks. Support for teachers should translate to administrative support for them so that maximum time can be given to improving teacher effectiveness. All systems concerning rewards and promotion must have salience and credibility or they are doomed.

Whilst content knowledge is important it is pedagogical skill which is critical! Investigators like Stanford's Jonathan Osborne emphasise the importance of argumentation in teaching, gaining the confidence of the student in responding to questions about why things are the way they are. The feedback provided to the student is important and so is the recognition that in the end it is intrinsic motivation that makes the difference. That means genuine criticism rather than constant praise. After all, intrinsic motivation, the setting of personal goals, has greater salience in achieving engagement and achievement. And as is clearly established, learning must first engage at the emotional level!

The Gonski Panel's task of understanding and responding to the challenges of the current funding arrangements for schooling is complex and this has influenced the Australian Government's decisions. Differences in the way Australian schools are organised across sectors and their approach to collecting and recording data, differences in the demographics of student bodies and differences in the challenges faced by states all contribute further impediments to an outcome intended to be transparent, fair, financially sustainable and effective.

15.4 Community and Inequality

A major feature of the last 50 or so years has been the extraordinary increase in the average economic position of people in most countries, notably China and some other south east Asian countries such as Korea, lately Vietnam and also some South American countries. Millions have risen out of poverty. Gains in health and education have been substantial. No less dramatic, however, has been the simultaneous increase in disparities in wealth and income, in countries usually thought of as developed, such as the US and the UK, as well as some developing countries. The impacts on families and therefore on educational achievements are substantial, as pointed out above, because it is the out of school factors which contribute most to those achievements.

While the focus of concern and the campaigns for economic aid continue to be sub-Saharan Africa, increasing numbers of people in developed countries are falling into poverty. There are more people living below the poverty line in India than in all of sub Saharan Africa. The poor continue unheard and unrecognised. In fact: never mind the appeals and the promises. Then there are the extraordinary ongoing tragedies of intranational violent conflict generating millions of refugees invading other countries. The millennial goals are missed. The countries of the United Nations seem incapable of constructive decision. The fear of domestic criticism and precedent deny action to address issues of our common humanity. Refugees huddle at borders or starve in camps. And aid gets funnelled into private hands though developing countries are not the epitome of corruption, witness the daily reports of corporate mismanagement in western countries.

Politicians and some economists can talk of the importance of economic growth and every day inform us through the daily news of the movements of economic indicators and their interpretation. But little actual debate is had on why substantial absolute and relative poverty continues, why the usual groups, indigenous peoples, people from poorly educated and economically disadvantaged backgrounds, disabled people and surprisingly to some, veterans of wars, continue to struggle with needs for food and shelter, adequate health care and opportunities for education. Or even be persecuted and demonised! Domestic politics mirrors international failure. The rich hide behind their gates while the poor are moved on. Claims, invalid and unsustainable, continue to be made that unless Australia encourages population growth it will not prosper.

The two essays on community and inequity have brought out some of the major issues in those countries with which this book is mainly concerned. There are people who still argue that we should be celebrating the success of those who have gained economically: we should recognise that focusing on inequality is unproductive. A prominent business executive in Australia lamented the government's concern with wealth redistribution rather than wealth creation. Such rhetoric ignores all the circumstances which lead to the continuation, even growth, of substantial disparities which are so damaging to all.

The 'Great Divergence' has emerged in the US since 1980 as wealth moved up through the top 1 % of the population to the top 0.1 %. Government policies driven by the super rich determine the nature of health insurance, the basic wage, the activities of unions, the funding of colleges and so on. All contribute significantly to the divergence.

The propositions that economic growth benefits all and that education overcomes poverty are wrong. That is shown by the actual experience of the last several decades in developed *and* developing countries. Economic growth has tended to benefit the rich: the gap between rich and poor has widened in almost all countries. Poverty is exacerbated by unregulated or insufficiently regulated companies exploiting workers through low pay and by the many companies avoiding taxes though various devices including exploiting opportunities to transfer profits to countries with low tax rates. Poverty is exacerbated also by failure of governments to implement policies to benefit all sections of the citizenry, to do those things that otherwise would not be done.

Minimum investment by governments in infrastructure costs diminishes gains in productivity. When governments rely on economic growth to fund job creation they are failing in their responsibility to the community. And when they fail to invest in education systems, especially ones which promote equity, they are perpetuating the problems they now face. When governments outsource to the private sector areas such as health, housing and urban planning, transport and law and order in such a way as to abandon critical features of essential industry regulation then costs to citizens depending on those services are driven up and outcomes are by no means better. In particular, impacts on people disadvantaged socially and economically are further disadvantaged.

It is wrong to assert, as a generalisation, that the private sector is able to achieve both greater efficiencies and greater effectiveness in service delivery than governments. The issues concern leadership and management, not the profit motive! Importation of the principles of New Public Management has led to poorer service delivery by governments, not better. Frequently this has been accompanied by reductions in taxation levels for higher income earners who are able to afford private services and are not reliant on government services.

In many countries social mobility is more and more limited: the middle class affords the stimulating activities which enrich the life of the child whilst those at the bottom struggle. The banks get recompensed for the entirely unreasonable risks they took with their lending and executives receive their bonuses with little regard to actual performance. Throughout the European Union austerity is pursued despite its glaring failure and countries and citizens slide further down the economic ladder driving the young into long term unemployment with dangerous consequences in the medium to longer term, not least the rise of populist and discriminatory political views as seen in Europe after World War 1.

Social democracy in Europe has been sorely tested by the GFC. That in some countries governments have protected banks at the same time as playing an interventionist role to protect business and employees must not be forgotten. International agencies such as the IMF and countries like Germany take a very ideological and self-interested stand! Most recently that stand has been strongly criticised by Jürgen Habermas, influential Frankfurt professor, philosopher and sociologist who has helped shape Germany over the past 50 years (Traynor 2013). Asserting that 'Germanys handling of the euro crisis is awakening historical ghosts', Habermas criticises the disconnect between what needed to be done in economic policy and what was deemed to be politically feasible for voters as one of the biggest perils facing the continent.

The austerity measures adopted at the behest of the IMF (initially) and the European Central Bank by countries on Europe's periphery—Greece, Spain, Portugal, Italy and Ireland—have been strongly criticised by numerous economists including Nobel prize winners Krugman (2012, 2013a, b) and Stiglitz (2011), economic writers such as the *Observer*'s Hutton (2010) and the *Guardian*'s Elliot

(2013), the Australian McAuley (2012) and the Chief Economics Commentator of the *Financial Times* Wolf (2013). But so far the policies have persisted. Much of the policy is grounded in the populist belief that these countries must pay their debt because they overspent, a policy which in economic terms is simplistic nonsense.

That the theoretical basis of the austerity policy has been shown to be based on a spreadsheet error and that the IMF has more recently expressed strong doubts about the policy and its consequences all seem to make no difference. Substantial protests crowd the streets of European capitals as governments reduce their budgets and cut entitlements. Increasingly, a move to the political right is seen as protests grow about immigration to Europe from the east and from Africa. And education has been amongst the casualties of the budgetary tightening. In the US teachers have been sacked.

In Britain the government has embarked on an austerity program almost unprecedented and far exceeding those of the Thatcher Government (Curtis and Wintour 2010; Toynbee 2012). The program is grounded to an extent in notions such as the 'Big Society' for which read small government through reliance on volunteerism. Instead of greater freedom from bureaucracy claimed for the reforms, there has been an increase in central control in the name of accountability.

The Cameron government has faced down the criticisms of the Archbishop of Canterbury Rowan Williams and even the condemnation of political thinker, Anglican theologian Phillip Blond whose endorsement for the policies was claimed at the outset. The government has pressed ahead with drastic policies to reduce government and outsource services to community organisations. Williams challenged the government's approach to welfare reform, complaining of 'a quiet resurgence of the seductive language of deserving and undeserving poor' (Mulholland and Wintour 2011). Alongside this, right wing think tanks actively vilify public servants (Whelan 2011). Williams asserted, 'With remarkable speed, we are being committed to radical, long-term policies for which no one voted' and Blond (2012) wrote, 'a radical Toryism has been abandoned, the once-in-a-generation chance to redefine conservatism on something other than a reductive market liberalism has been lost'.

There are few better examples of how research evidence can be ignored than is shown by the way the relationship between poverty and education is dealt with. Many of the states in the US have child poverty rates of 25 % or higher (Anyon 2005; Edelman 2012); the consequences of growing up poor continue to be ignored. Nationwide a child is born into poverty every 25 s! In the UK poverty has trebled since 1979; in some places in 2005 over 90 % of children lived in poverty. In Australia, despite economic growth over the 7 years (averaging just under 0.8 % per annum) from 2003 through 2010 the proportion of people in poverty in Australia rose by a third of a percent. About 2.27 million people or one in eight people in Australia including 575,000 or 17 % of children are living below the poverty line (ACOSS 2012).

The economies of many developing countries have grown strongly yet poverty levels have remained unaltered or increased. Corruption is often blamed but tax avoidance practices of major corporations and failure of 'aid' programs to upskill the population by those countries supplying the aid employing their own citizens at high salaries is ignored.

The increasing departure of employment opportunities from inner urban and remote towns within countries as businesses relocate to upmarket suburbs and larger cities has meant declines in the local tax base and therefore the funding for education and community infrastructure. In the US especially, the jobs are now in upscale locations poorly served by public transport or far away from where workers live.

In the US especially, the campaign against unionisation has held back wage growth. Regressive tax policies favouring the rich and large corporations likewise diminish government funding. Children from poor backgrounds have difficulty obtaining text books and other curriculum materials. Even if they complete college they are unlikely to find employment. All this can be disguised by possession of the latest portable media and the wearing of fashionable 'threads'.

In Australia the situations facing Aboriginal and Torres Strait Islander communities are critical and have long been recognised as such. But research shows great importance to be attached to maintenance of connections with cultural background, ensuring that people themselves have control over their own affairs. And amongst other things, the research shows that early teaching of children gains from including substantial components in their own language: it is an integral part of their identity. Many communities are in remote locations poorly served by other facilities including libraries; shops may not even stock books, pencils and other writing materials which further magnifies the problems. Similar issues face many Aboriginal communities in urban areas.

Instead of addressing the inadequately trained staff in schools and woefully poor resourcing, conditions are imposed on Indigenous families that would never be imposed on non-Indigenous families except in the most extraordinary situations. Those conditions derive from generalisations about the reasons for poor attendance and poor achievement which don't stand up to sensible analysis. The parallel with situations facing people of colour in the US is strong. That includes the proportion of Aboriginal people in prison.

Adolescents are one of the sections of society often caught up in the inequality resulting from economic and political policies, most recently from the GFC and the austerity measures which have been the response. Though they are well able to articulate their wants and needs, as shown by the research of Stanford University's Milbrey McLaughlin and others, they are ignored. In truth the same problems have persisted over many decades. Unemployment rates amongst young people in the peripheral economies of Greece and Spain, for instance, have risen as high as 50 %. How can there be a future for the societies of those countries when that is so? Unemployment even affects university graduates.

A report by the European Union's research agency Eurofound showed in a survey in late 2012 that Europeans aged 15–29 not in employment, education or training had reached record levels (Malik 2012). This was costing the EU €3bn a week in state welfare and lost production equal to 1.2 % of the EUs GDP. And the OECD has said that Europe was 'failing in its social contract' and that rising political disenchantment could reach levels similar to those that sparked uprisings in North Africa and with the young. The likelihood is that young people will opt out of democratic participation in society.

Progress in educational achievement will require adoption of the kinds of policies which some European, including Scandinavian, countries and some southeast Asian countries have put in place: a focus on social democracy and support of the less fortunate in times of need. Those countries have not ignored the market but their governments seek to buffer both the individual and business enterprises from excessive fluctuations in economic conditions and, in general, promoted innovation and encouraged particular economic developments. For instance, without government programs, Sweden would have 26.7 of its population living in poverty, but with their social programs, the poverty rate is 5.3 % (McLaren 2012). Transport and communication infrastructure are seen as important government responsibilities.

In summary, as Daren Acemoglu and James Robinson of Harvard and MIT respectively show in their book *Why Nations Fail*, as mentioned already in these essays, 'No society which organizes the economy to benefit just 10 % of the population will generate prosperity'.

The reforms in the US and UK and some of the reforms in other countries have in fact ended up benefitting the already advantaged. This is especially so of support for independent schools. The reasons for poor average performance by students in various countries are most particularly related to the lack of satisfactory achievement by children from low socioeconomic backgrounds. And has been shown throughout many of these essays that means addressing the causes and the consequences of poverty! That has been pointed out for decades by such people as David Berliner and more recently Jean Anyon and many, many others. These issues have been extensively addressed in research particularly in the US and discussed at the 2013 annual meeting of the American Education Research Association. The problems are not due simply to lack of educational opportunities but result also from stereotyping and marginalisation, from treating the situation of poverty as a condition brought on by those in poverty rather than by the economic conditions developed and maintained by those in power. People treated as inferior end up believing they are inferior and behaving accordingly, something entirely ignored by many policy makers.

It is not just education which will continue to suffer in countries such as the US, the UK and others where great divergences continue. To achieve progress needs attention to all relevant areas simultaneously and an integration of relevant policies. These joined up solutions will not be achieved through arguments between different constituencies about primacies of authority and power. Rather they will emerge through trialling and building on strategic partnerships of constituencies who can form a common agenda. They will develop from what has been achieved already, not necessarily in the same country.

Economist Nicholas Gruen (2006), reviewing the work of one-time Australian government adviser and Ambassador to the OECD Fred Argy and his essays, 'Equality in Australia' (Argy 2006, 2009) observed that Argy had 'laboured long and hard to show the conjunction between equity, efficiency and equanimity and the fact that a range of measures that would make the world fairer would at the same time make it richer'. Gruen concluded, 'That we have not embraced them is both iniquitous and stupid.'

15.5 Universities and Other Places of Learning

Learning and education are lifelong experiences. Though schooling is the most common component, the progress of countries is increasingly being measured by the level of enrolment in post school educational courses of various kinds whether they focus on training and development of skills or whether they help advance scholarship. The benefits of higher levels of educational achievement to the community at large are substantial through increased employment enjoyed by graduates and the taxes they pay and their lesser dependence on social welfare. Those economic benefits far outweigh whatever it is that the taxpayer might contribute by way of tuition costs.

Despite the contribution by universities to the advance of knowledge contributing to progress in every part of society there continues to be insistence that universities generate their own income from commercial contracts and tuition fees. Colleges of technical and further education suffer reductions in funding and many close, university staffs shrink, class sizes grow, tutorials lose their significance and the community of scholars erodes.

All six people awarded the three Nobel prizes in science in 2012 work in universities or institutions associated with them, their research all started without any immediate economic benefit being obvious, yet that research is in every case now seen as enormously important in health and in communication! Where governments have seen the real gains from an investment in post-school education, there have been gains in all kinds of other areas. This is so in many countries including the US where now, astonishingly, more shrill voices dispute the value of universities!

All institutions and organisations which enhance the learning experience, such as museums and zoos and libraries, and even public broadcasting and some areas of commercial news media and the publishing industry, need like universities to be recognised for their contributions. A nation concerned about education would support such enterprises. The failure to invest will bring its negative return, as it has in other areas. It is unclear as to the extent that university administrations and academic staff and those in and supporting these places of informal learning might advance the agenda.

That the Australian Government, in the lead up to the announcement of the arrangements to fund the reforms recommended by the Gonski Panel, saw it as appropriate to (again) cut a few more millions of dollars from university budgets was a failure to understand the economic and societal gains from universities. The assertion, by Minister Craig Emerson, was that the sector was growing strongly;

some academics acknowledged that few people would in the end object to reductions in the funding. But the debate in the weeks following the Gonski funding announced on 14 April 2013 were full of criticism of the cuts to universities!

15.6 Misinformation and Its Consequences

A major conclusion from these essays is that too often policies are not informed by careful consideration of the evidence or even sensible discussion. Instead, views based on one's own individual experience often trump the findings of careful research, not just that which is so far inconclusive. People's world views play a hugely influential role in determining what is considered to be truth. In a carefully constructed, well written and strongly argued survey Stephan Lewandowsky of the University of Western Australia and colleagues (Lewandowsky et al. 2012) rightly assert that the widespread prevalence and persistence of misinformation is of public concern.

Because a functioning democracy relies on an educated and well-informed populace how people come to believe what they do is of great interest. It is not ignorance which is the focus: that is the absence of information. Or rather the near refusal to consider other information or even seek it out. It is the views transmitted through rumour, promoted by special interest groups, often through a compliant media focused on the 24 h news cycle, to advance their position at the expense of others. The adoption of policies of economic austerity, despite the fact that the analysis on which the policies were based has been shown to be wrong, as mentioned above, is just the latest example. Politicians on the right in Australia continue to maintain that Australia's additional spending in the face of the looming financial crisis was unnecessary despite the ratings of international economic agencies and the congratulations of many of the world's leading economists for the government's actions.

Through stories, especially those with emotional content, views can become amalgamated with already held beliefs, especially if the source is someone or some organisation already trusted. Individuals used to using rational argument have particular difficulties in this situation because of their lack of understanding that emotion is the way in which views first achieve salience and the tendency in their argumentation to repeat, and then contradict, the contrary argument in order to put the alternative case. Denial of strongly held views or threats to existing world views lead most people to reinforce their misinformed conclusions. It is far more effective to state the correct information with as little reference to the other views as possible. Will we ever learn?

15.7 The Future of Australian Education Reform

The prevailing response to Prime Minister Gillard's call for a crusade to reform schools when she addressed the Gonski Report in her speech to the National Press Club on 3 September 2012 was to ask where the money was coming from. That response reveals a profound and naive misunderstanding of the nature of policy formulation and implementation in the political environment of Australia. Eventually the reforms must involve state and territory governments as well as at least the major independent and Catholic school sectors as is being demonstrated in the first months of 2013. The immediate clamour about money reveals just how far Australia has come in giving primacy in government to financial issues, how best policy can be marginalised and considerations of long-term investment ignored: immediate and short-term considerations prevail to our eventual detriment. Yet to an extent it is consistent with the unfortunate tendency in Australia to reject any strong move for change shown, for instance, by consistent rejections of proposed changes to the Constitution.

It is widely acknowledged already that the present funding arrangements lack coherence. Whilst the substantial inequity in the system in the relative resourcing of many independent and most government schools is almost universally acknowledged, and certainly was a key point of the Gonski Report, Opposition leader, now Prime Minister, Tony Abbott suggested that government schools were not underfunded, or even overfunded! There are plenty of claims that funding of independent schools should not be reduced and the government had already made clear that, at the very least, no school would be worse off, which according to some has inflated the likely cost of reform by increasing the base rate of funding for all schools. There are multiple players and multiple demands!

Progress of any reform agenda requires agreement first on the vision and goals amongst which issues of equity and provision of special assistance to help overcome it are central. Consideration of strategies waits upon that agreement: the strategies will have to be agreed upon by every one of the constituencies and no doubt each will watch the others to ensure they do not get more than their perceived fair share. Numerous refinements of the strategies will be required through these negotiations until sufficient agreement—at least a consensus—is reached on them. In the course of that the levels of funding will be a feature but if the funding drives the strategy then the outcome will be more than unsatisfactory.

To appreciate the truth of this, one has only to recall that we have been there before: the Australian Schools Commission established in 1973 addressed many of the same questions addressed by the Gonski Panel including needs-based funding to ensure that all schools achieved minimum acceptable standards and disadvantage including special education. As well the Commission was to address teacher professional development and innovation. Forty years ago!

In the last 40 years Finland has completely reformed its education system, South Korea has come from where Afghanistan is now economically to be amongst the top educational achievers as well as highly successful economically and China, albeit at great cost in several areas, has overtaken Japan as the second most important economic nation!

Efforts in the US to achieve comprehensive agreement of the states to the No Child Left Behind failed when the states were left to determine the curriculum and manage the standardised tests. Reforms in that country have consistently failed because of a wish to see results quickly. No Child Left Behind failed also because it did not address the principal cause of poor educational achievement: poverty. The reforms in the Finnish system commenced with legislation in 1978 but criticism continued all the way to the publication of the first PISA results in 2001. Clearly then, to suppose that the reforms proposed by Ms Gillard can be accomplished within a few years is more than problematic.

It is not as if the arguments supporting the proposed reforms were not widely communicated or understood. An outstanding summary of the consequences of inequality for education outcomes in Australia was given by member of the Gonski Panel and distinguished Australian Carmen Lawrence in an article appropriately titled, 'Mind the Gap' (Lawrence 2012). Melbourne University's Richard Teese's excellent report 'From Opportunity to Outcomes' advanced the fundamentally important proposition that there should be equal education opportunity for all (Teese 2012). Lawrence's article carefully reviewed substantial research including that conducted in Baltimore linking educational outcomes with the special opportunities that advantaged children have through support by their family and, in summer, opportunities for visits to places of informal learning like museums and other activities.

Research in the US has demonstrated the gains which children from higher SES backgrounds make in visits to these places where they are taken by parents, especially during summer breaks. Karl Alexander and colleagues (Alexander et al. 2007) from Johns Hopkins University studied children from Baltimore over a number of years. Their widely quoted research reveals that the learning gains of children from disadvantaged backgrounds, which kept pace with their advantaged peers during the school year, decline relatively over summer weeks: few such children have the opportunities to visit various places like museums during the summer. The research also demonstrates the influence of parents and the home environment on literacy and numeracy.

In an extraordinary response to these findings UK Education Secretary Michael Gove is reported in *The Telegraph* for June 21 2011 (in an article by Neil O'Brien) as intending to reduce the length of summer breaks! The problem is the engagement of parents and the opportunity they have, a problem which is systemic and amongst the most important issues in education. Why do politicians keep getting things so wrong? Secretary Gove has shown himself to lack understanding of many issues concerning education and as prepared to invent 'facts' to support his assertions.

A detailed summary of the situation in the US was given by Professor David Berliner in a posting on the National Education Associations website, *Schools Matter* for October 17 2012. Berliner cited substantial research pointing out that the answer to school failures lay outside the school and was primarily a result of inequality, an argument he has previously advanced; social status has about 30 %

more effect on the test scores of American youth than for youth in Finland. These comments reflected the arguments advanced in the reports on PISA 2009. Berliner pointed to factors such minimum wages, housing prices, child well-being, mental health and so on and their contribution to low achievement by disadvantaged youth. High school dropout rates, low social mobility and rates of imprisonment amongst the indicators correlated with inequality. These are arguments detailed by Richard Wilkinson and Kate Pickett's *The Spirit Level*, Timothy Noahs *The Great Divergence* and many other writings including Acemoglu and Richardson's *Why Nations Fail*.

We can confidently conclude that the arguments that competition, choice and performance pay will improve educational outcomes are based on misinformation. The assertions that Australian education is in crisis, that public schools are failing, that teachers unions are preventing needed reforms, that teachers lack sufficient content knowledge, that it is too difficult to sack poorly performing teachers, even that teachers have an easy time of it because they have shorter working hours and longer holidays than other workers continue to be made. All are familiar and all are wrong.

The misinformation to bolster these arguments extends to wrongly reporting the conclusions of international surveys such as PISA. Declines in Australian students' scores are highlighted as if there was an education crisis. Certain evidence is ignored: school autonomy in respect of budgets and teacher hiring are asserted to be important when in fact it is freedom in teaching curriculum that makes a difference. The critical special support given in successful systems to students from backgrounds disadvantaged by language or economic circumstances, or the way in which unions in some countries including Canada and Germany have been critical to achievement of successful reform are not highlighted. There are even commentators who assert that socioeconomic status is not a factor influencing educational achievement. And they get heard! This misinformation and the influence of narrow sectional interests, so prevalent in Australian public life, have to be overcome to achieve reform. Is that impossible? Perhaps not!

The 'National Plan for School Improvement', the Commonwealth Governments response to the Gonski Report, and other reforms concerning early childhood and universities, deserve support because they address some of the most important issues affecting education outcomes and therefore, all of society, the period before school and after and the equity in quality education provision. However, there is a long way to go in reaching the level of support for early childhood education found in many other countries and that will require shifting the debate from the domain of child minding and work force participation where it continues to languish.

That like health, reforms in education are critical to the longer term mean that arguing that the economic situation is such that the reforms are too costly is plainly irresponsible! That is especially so in Australia because, contrary to the assertions of some on the right of politics, the economic situation is such that the investment in education can easily be afforded. Unfortunately, the political will to gather the funds through taxation reform is not there! And the self interest of the already privileged is arrayed against change.

It is fair to say that more attention is needed to understanding the learning that actually goes on in the school classroom and, especially having in mind the substantial time spent out of school, to the nature and value of learning in out of school, informal or free choice situations. Generally, present involvement of school classes in visits to museums and similar places, preserves the formal structure of the classroom with its emphasis on structure and immediately demonstrable knowledge gains. This is hardly exploiting the opportunities of such places and ignores the way in which they can encourage creativity precisely because they provide so many unstructured opportunities. Central to such studies is the views students themselves have of their experiences.

Two areas of formal education also require additional attention. The nature of teaching and the school experience changes from the primary school to the secondary school and then again from school to college and university. Much more is expected of the individual student and much less emphasis in appointing and promoting university staff is given to teaching skills in favour of competency in content knowledge and research achievement.

In primary school the one teacher teaches all subjects and in some countries, and in small schools, the same teacher may be with the student through several years of schooling; at secondary school every subject is taught by a different teacher. The personal rapport between student and teacher which contributes so much is not necessarily attended to. In universities competency in pedagogy—teaching and learning—is not privileged and lectures are assigned often to graduate students who do not necessarily have any training in teaching. Students expectations of these situations are not always met. The results for all but the better students speak for themselves.

What are the prospects for reform of education in Australia? Reluctance to sign up to the reforms, evident in the behaviour of some state governments represents one of the lowest points in the history of the Australian Federation! That State and Territory leaders can claim to have not been sufficiently informed about the reforms emanating from the Gonski Report is extraordinary. It seems that standing back and waiting for the Commonwealth to give details is considered good behaviour. Surely we are not expected to believe that officers of each government were not discussing the possibilities. Surely state government officials had views as to what might be achieved! Education has been and will remain a major responsibility of the second tier of government and is fundamental to the nation's future. That the funding now proposed is less than first recommended is not a reason to not proceed. Prime Minister Gillard has been unwavering in her advocacy of the reforms even though one can criticise the scaled-down version now proposed.

The debate can be seen in the same frame as other attempts at reform in Australia in recent years, another difficulty in coming to terms with the future: climate change and carbon emissions opposed by energy companies and the oil industry, a tax on mining companies super profits loudly criticised by super rich owners of big mining companies and the Mining Industry Council, rehabilitation of the Murray Darling River system opposed by irrigators, investment in urban public transport, a second airport for Sydney and fast trains—too expensive—all

15.7 The Future of Australian Education Reform

the way to superannuation reform, poker machine gambling opposed by clubs (and major retailers such as Woolworths who own more poker machines than anyone else), and recycling of containers opposed by the Grocery Council with arguments bolstered by statistics that even a primary school child would see were false. Australia seems stuck in the present like the scratch on an audio disc, just generating static, not going anywhere. Assertions about the style of the Prime Minister and claims, completely wrong, that Australia has some kind of fiscal crisis, are irrelevant and debilitating.

15.8 Everything is Connected

In late 2011 Geraldine Brooks, Australian-born former war correspondent and now successful writer, presented the ABCs Boyer Lectures. Brooks spoke of the many meanings of home, of her early engagement with activist environmentalism as a reporter for the *Sydney Morning Herald*, of the early engagement of Wampanoag Native Americans with English immigrants who occupied their lands on the island Martha's Vineyard off the coast of Massachusetts where she now lives. And much else. She recounted her daily life:

'These days, my work day begins with a short walk up a dirt track from my house to the main road, where I wait with my younger son for a yellow school bus to come to a halt.. My son climbs aboard, the stop sign folds back, and I wave. By the time I reach the house, I am already at work. I pause in the kitchen to brew a fresh cup of coffee, and as I wait, I pull a poetry anthology off the shelf and let the book fall open. I read whatever poem my eye falls on and, pump primed, climb the stairs to my study and step back into the past.'

Her day thus begins with ideas, ideas fuelled by the unexpected, one of the very stimuli that promotes the innovation on which our future has been built for millennia. Who knows what the poems will be, what they will say, what ideas might be described there and what thoughts they might provoke. But that they will provoke ideas is what counts. That is what education is. Brooks' novels are about people in different times. She recreates their lives through extraordinary research. Her thinking about the past, about home, about relationships, about human dignity, conflict and peace reflect all her research, her learning.

Education can bring home to us every day how everything is connected, how we cannot be better educated unless we attend to the physical, social and economic conditions in which we and others live, until we strive to overcome the political inequalities that hold back human society, how we ourselves are connected, that it is relationships with others which make us human. Unless we recognise the social and economic inequalities which divide us, preventing understanding of the past, forcing a retreat to fundamentalist ignorance. Education can make the past less a foreign country and help everyone choose their own future with more confidence.

The failure of governments to respond sensibly to what we know about education with a commitment to the longer term future and wider society through pressure from narrow sectional interests must frustrate those who have taken the time and made the substantial investment to elucidate the principal issues and questions, the people who have contributed their views in the hope of making a difference, the early childhood specialists, the psychologists and behaviourists, the economists, the social scientists, the education researchers in universities and research institutes, the school principals and teachers, the writers and ordinary citizens who have bothered to take an interest.

Think about the meaning of all the information, the reams of research reports and expert reviews. Notwithstanding that much remains to be further explored and that detailed universal solutions are inappropriate, there are very clear ideas about the most critical directions, the most sensible directions forward. That anyone in Australia, at a time of extraordinarily low interest rates, net government debt at levels that most countries could not hope to achieve in decades, can believe that the country cannot afford to invest in the education of future generations is ludicrous.

The reforms which the Australian Government proposes in response to the Gonski Report pay little attention to the kinds of things advocated by Rupert Murdoch and Joel Klein when they visited Australia in 2008. Instead they focus on issues such as equity and providing support for disadvantage and raising the standards of teachers. Clearly some gains can be made in government policy formulation! In fact many of the supports for the Gonski reforms are already in place through agreements by States and Territories at (COAG).There is a contrast with the lack of real progress in the education reforms in the UK and the US.

The Economics Editor of *The Age* newspaper Tim Colebatch on April 16 2013 wrote of the Gonski proposals by the Commonwealth Government, 'This is an opportunity for the nation to tackle one of its biggest challenges. We ought to grasp it.' Are Australians really going to reject that?

References

ACOSS. (2012). *Poverty in Australia*. Strawberry Hills, NSW: Australian Council of Social Services.
Alexander, K. L., Entwisle, D. R., & Olsen, L. S. (2007). Lasting consequences of the summer learning gap. *American Sociological Review, 72*, 167–180.
Anyon, J. (2005). What "counts" as educational policy? Notes toward a new paradigm. *Harvard Educational Review, 75*, 65–88.
Argy, F. (2006). Equality of opportunity in Australia: Myth and reality. *Australia Institute Discussion Paper* 85.
Argy, F. (2009, August). Equality of Opportunity. *The New Critic* 10.
Blond, P. (2012, October 3). David Cameron has lost his chance to redefine the Tories. *The Guardian*.
Cobbold, T. (2013a, March 25). The parlous state of pre-school education. In *Save Our Schools*. Retrieved April 17, 2013, from http://www.saveourschools.com.au/national-issues/the-parlous-state-of-pre-school-education
Cobbold, T. (2013b, May 24). New study shows that school autonomy increases the gap between top and bottom students. In *Save Our Schools*. Retrieved May 27, 2013, from http://

www.saveourschools.com.au/choice-and-competition/new-study-shows-that-school-autonomy-fails-to-increase-results-of-lower-achieving-students

Curtis, P., & Wintour, P. (2010, September 10). Coalition cuts will hit poor 10 times harder than rich, says TUC. *The Guardian*.

Elliott, L. (2013, April 28). Austerity-hit G8 leaders must not allow charity to begin and end at home. *The Guardian*.

Edelman, M. W. (2012). *The State of Americas Children 2012*. Washington, DC: Children's Defense Fund. Retrieved October 11, 2012, from http://www.childrensdefense.org/newsroom/child-watch-columns/child-watch-documents/the-state-of-americas-children-1.html

Gonski, D., et al. (2011). *Review of Funding for Schooling. Final Report.* Canberra: Department of Education, Employment and Workplace Relations. Retrieved February 20, 2012, from http://foi.deewr.gov.au/system/files/doc/other/review-of-funding-for-schooling-final-report-dec-2011.pdf

Gruen, N. (2006, December 11). Equality of opportunity in Australia. *Evatt Foundation Newsletter*.

Hutton, W. (2010, June 20). There is no logic to the brutish cuts that George Osborne is proposing. *The Observer*.

Krugman, P. (2012, September 27). Europe's austerity madness. *New York Times*.

Krugman, P. (2013a, April 19). The excel depression. *New York Times*.

Krugman, P. (2013b, June 6). How the case for austerity has crumbled. *New York Review of Books*.

Lawrence, C. (2012, July). Mind the gap: Why the rising inequality of our schools is dangerous. *The Monthly*.

Lehrer, J. (2012, March 5). Does preschool matter. *Wired*. Retrieved August 21, 2012, from http://www.wired.com/wiredscience/2012/03/does-preschool-matter/

Lewandowsky, S., et al. (2012). Misinformation and its correction: Continued influence and successful debiasing. *Psychological Science in the Public Interest, 13*, 106–131.

McAuley, I. (2012, May 7). Austerity breeds extremism. *New Matilda*. Retrieved May 13, 2012, from https://newmatilda.com/2012/05/07/austerity-breeds-extremism

McConney, A., & Perry, L. (2010). Science and mathematics achievement in Australia: The role of school socioeconomic composition in educational equity and effectiveness. *International Journal of Science and Mathematics Education, 8*, 429–452.

McLaren, P. (2012). The Poverty of Capitalism. Papers for AERA Annual Meetings 2013. Retrieved 11 October 2012, from http://www.aera.net/AnnualMeetingOtherEvents/EssayThemeCommentProject/ThePovertyofCapitalism/tabid/13500/articleType/ArticleView/articleId/1167/The-Poverty-of-Capitalism.aspx.

Mulholland, H., & Wintour, P. (2011, June 9). Downing Street hits back at archbishops broadside. *The Guardian*.

Perry, L., & McConney, A. (2010). School socioeconomic composition and student outcomes in Australia: Implications for educational policy. *Australian Journal of Education, 54*, 72–85.

Ravitch, D. (2010). *The Death and Life of the American School System—How testing and choice are undermining education*. New York: Basic Books.

Ravitch, D. (2012, June 7). Correspondence for do our public schools threaten national security. *New York Review of Books*.

Stiglitz, J. E. (2011, November 4). The globalization of protest. *Project Syndicate*. Retrieved November 27, 2011 from http://www.project-syndicate.org/commentary/the-globalization-of-protest

Teese, R. (2012, February 15). Gonski review: Tradition or reform for an upside down system? *The Conversation*. Retrieved September 12, 2012, from http://theconversation.edu.au/gonksi-review-tradition-or-reform-for-an-upside-down-system-5307

Traynor, I. (2013, April 28). German role in steering euro crisis could lead to disaster, warns expert. *The Guardian*.

Toynbee, P. (2012, September 17). David Cameron's men go where Margaret Thatcher never dared. *The Guardian*.

Whelan, J., et al. (2011). *The state of the Australian Public Service—An alternative report*. Canberra: Centre for Public Policy.

Wolf, M. (2013, July 11). How austerity has failed. *New York Review of Books*.

Chapter 16
Postscript: Australian Educational Futures After the 2013 Federal Election

16.1 A New Australian Government: Policies Compared

At the Australian federal elections on September 7 2013 the Liberal and National Party Coalition was returned to power after 6 years of Labor government. The New Prime Minister, the Hon Tony Abbott, and his spokesperson on education and now Minister, the Hon Christopher Pyne, had relentlessly attacked the Labor government's policies on school reform and also early childhood, at least in respect of 'child-care'. That there will be changes from the way the Labor government was heading is certain though here is not substantial detail just over a month after the election.

The previous conservative Coalition government of Prime Minister John Howard (1996–2007) had provided substantial funding to independent schools and the funding of universities had declined. During the term of the Labor government Mr. Abbott and colleagues had taken a 'market-based' approach to educational issues, asserting that the school funding system which had been put in in place by the Howard government was not broken and did not need fixing. The Coalition supported more independence in respect of financial management and staff recruitment for school principals; they also supported the establishment of school councils drawn from the local community. It also supported accountability in terms of standardised testing, and in that respect held much the same views as the Labor government. They also supported merit pay for teachers.

Before the election the ABC (Australian Broadcasting Corporation) posted on the web an analysis of the election policies of the major parties, ALP, Coalition and the Greens (Lane 2013). As noted in Chap. 14, in the run up to the election the Coalition, despite earlier criticism, agreed to support the Labor government's 'Better Schools Plan' through the present budget cycle, which meant the first 4 years. The Coalition said nothing about the later years of the Plan which involved substantial increases in financial support to those schools experiencing identified disadvantage.

Amongst the key differences in the policy of the two parties was the extent to which the States were expected to provide extra funding for the Plan. The Labor

Government intended that the States provide an extra 5.1b from the States and that the States index their payments for schools by 3.6 % until the 'new resource standard' was reached and by 3 % pa thereafter. The Coalition saw no need to provide extra funding and also said it would reverse any moves to centralise power with the Commonwealth. (Education Minister Peter Garret had stated that schools would be free to determine their priorities within the context of the Plan!)

The Labor government intended to retain the new National Curriculum introduced from 2013; the curriculum had been developed by ACARA, the body it had established to develop the curriculum and manage NAPLAN tests and the My-School website. The Coalition had never opposed testing or the communication of the test results for schools. Mr. Abbott and Mr. Pyne both had commented on certain aspects of the history curriculum, however, expressing concern about what they saw as 'balance'. Some commentators saw the possibility of a revival of the 'History Wars' though at least some historians doubted that.

There is little difference in respect of the commitment concerning the teaching of foreign languages. The ALP, in a 2012 White Paper, had already called for all school children to have continual access to one of five priority Asian languages. The Coalition said it wanted 40 % of year 12 students by 2023 studying a foreign language, preferably an Asian language. It would establish by 2014 a new two-way Colombo Plan, exchanging Australian students with students from Asia.

The ALP promised $2.5 billion through 2018 in additional funding for trade training centres to give greater access to skills training. It would seek guarantees from the States that there would be no further cuts to TAFE budgets; if States refused to do so then the Commonwealth would take over the funding of TAFEs. The Coalition also promised to invest in advanced job skills training including trade skills; it would provide a loan of up to $20,000 over 4 years to be repaid at the same income threshold for university students receiving FEE-HELP loans ($51,309).

The ALP intended that States determine how they would manage performance pay for teachers through their agreements to the National Plan; the Coalition asserted this amounted to an abolition of its previous promises. The Coalition promised a focus on improving teacher quality and 'implementing a robust national curriculum' in improving student performance. School principals would be given more control of their schools, 'devolving responsibility from bureaucrats'. The Coalition promised to work with States and Territories in supporting State Schools that choose to become 'independent schools' on the Western Australian model (That is dealt with in Sect. 9.2.).

The Coalition promised a capital infrastructure fund for schools 'when the budget is brought back to surplus'.

The ALP intended to continue the 'School Kids bonus' for primary and secondary students but the Coalition undertook to remove it because families did not necessarily spend the money on school related expenses.

And the Coalition said it would work with the higher education sector to reduce red tape. The Coalition had established a working group to investigate and recommend policies regarding Online Higher Education. (Online education by universities has burgeoned in recent years; however, it is transmission of information and not teaching and learning and also is based on a model which by itself is economically unsustainable! (Barber 2013)).

The Coalition also promised to instruct the Productivity Commission to review the entire child care system and costs. Coalition spokespersons and their supporters had complained of rapidly rising costs of child-care.

The consequences of some States—Queensland and Western Australia—and the Northern Territory having not signed up to the new School Plan remained unclear at the time the election.

The Federal Labor Government revamped some family payments, changed the private health insurance rebate and introduced changes to business taxation to help meet the cost of funding Gonski reforms.

The Coalition would continue the School Chaplaincy scheme, supported also by the Labor government despite legal challenge.

In summary, there are in fact some very important differences in respect of all of the stages of the formal education system. The Coalition's support for 'independent' schools, bringing with it more autonomy of principals in their management of schools, is grounded in their policy of removing Commonwealth government 'red tape'. Combined with the fact that there is no undertaking to support the School Improvement Plan beyond its fourth year makes it very likely that there will be no significant change from the present system of support for the independent school sector which was introduced by the Howard government. Though largely retained by the Rudd-Gillard governments the School Improvement Plan was to substantially amend that.

The early childhood policy differences are very significant. All governments through COAG had an agreement to deliver child care to all children and there was a commitment to professional staffing of child-care centres. Salaries of child-care workers are currently under scrutiny by the Fair Work Commission following substantial numbers of complains about payment of wages. The evidence on early childhood intervention makes clear the importance of properly trained staff, an inevitable consequence of which is higher salaries; how the higher costs would be met is not established and the fact that in most countries with extensive early childhood care, government provides the care free or partly subsidises it is seldom mentioned in the debate.

It should be noted that there is no evidence to support the view that independent schools increase student educational achievement. Indeed, the performance of Australian students has declined somewhat over the last 6 years! Studies of the Western Australian independent school scheme, to which the Coalition referred, has not found any evidence that it leads to improved student achievement (as reported at Sect. 9.2).

The evidence is clear that low socioeconomic status is associated with poorer educational achievement and that school systems which favour independent schools privilege the already advantaged and lead to poorer outcomes for children from less advantaged backgrounds. That is one of the principal themes of this book!

The election campaign again demonstrated the near obsession with schools in the context of the education debate on the part of both major parties. Early childhood is marginalised as a result. So are informal educational opportunities. Attention has been drawn to that already.

The new Coalition government's commitment to suspend the funding of programs related to early childhood whilst a Productivity Commission investigation is conducted is at least as worrying as is the likely developments for schools. Whilst that investigation is continuing an overly generous, in relative terms, parental leave scheme continues to be an important part of the government's program. Parental leave is being treated as a workplace issue instead of an education issue.

In the first month of the new Coalition government the Better Schools website was closed and grants for child care centres were suspended.

Two important reports must be mentioned in concluding this postscript. They are the Human Development Report 2013 and the OECD's survey of adult literacy and numeracy. Both serve as important indicators of sensible future government policy. Both indicate the failure of policy developments which marginalise government and which rely on neoliberal policies. Those policies have driven deep divisions between rich and poor and exacerbated existing problems in health, education and employment.

16.2 The Human Development Report

The Human Development Report, published every year is an independent report commissioned by the United Nations Development Program (UNDP) compiled by an independent team of experts including scholars and development practitioners. It analyses changes in the state of human development including education, health and employment. Special reference has already been made to the 2010 Report (see Sect. 3.2). The 2013 Report (United Nations 2013) is no exception. Subtitled 'The Rise of the South: Human Progress in a Developed World' it points to '… the broad progress in human development of many developing countries and their emergence onto the global stage … This growing diversity in voice and power is challenging the principles that have guided policymakers and driven the major post-Second World War institutions. Stronger voices from the South are demanding more-representative frameworks of international governance that embody the principles of democracy and equity.'

Projections in the 2013 Report suggest that by 2020 the combined economic output of three leading developing countries—Brazil, China and India—will surpass the aggregate production of Canada, France, Germany, Italy, the US and UK. That is not to say that human development progress is equitable in the leading developing countries.

The Report points out that the development of recent times has resulted from pragmatic policies that respond to local circumstances and opportunities including [importantly] 'a deepening of the developmental role of states, a dedication to improving human development (including by supporting education and social welfare) and an openness to trade and innovation.' Future progress', it says, 'will require policymakers to play close attention to such issues as equity, voice and accountability, environmental risks and changing demography'.

The Report makes some strong statements about the responsibilities of governments to ensure that issues of social inclusion and social welfare are not ignored. 'Individual achievements in health, education and income, while essential, do not guarantee progress in human development if social conditions constrain individual achievements and if perceptions about progress differ..' The promotion of social cohesion and social integration is a stated objective of the development strategies of a number of high growth countries in the 'global south'. Studies in both developed and developing countries show time and again that more equal societies promote greater progress and that unequal societies face major problems in health education and a raft of economic indicators related to those two issues.

A proactive state and determined social policy innovation are two of the three notable drivers of development identified by the Report: these drivers challenge 'the unfettered liberalization espoused by the Washington Consensus', policies which some developed countries have urged on developing countries. The Consensus, now generally understood as the substantial market-based approach to economic development, has come to dominate many developed countries: some have referred to it as representing in essence 'a neoliberal manifesto'. (The Consensus in the broad sense marks a displacement of Keynesianism and is sometimes considered to have begun about 1980. That is the date at which some commentators consider the increasing divergence of wages and salaries began in the US and some other developed countries that have adopted market economics.)

The Human Development Report asserts, 'Priorities need to be people-centred and to promote opportunities while protecting people against downside risks.' Whilst acknowledging that there are some risks of rent seeking and cronyism such policies have enabled several countries of the South to turn inefficient industries into early drivers of export success as their economies became more open. 'Investing in people's capabilities—through health, education and other public services—is not an appendage of the growth process but an integral part of it. Rapid expansion of quality jobs is a critical feature of growth that promotes human development.'

In respect of social policy innovation, the Report notes, 'Growth is generally much more effective in reducing poverty in countries where income inequality is low than in countries with high inequality'. Promotion of inclusion is critical for political and social stability. Even if the state does not provide the services it should ensure that everyone has secure access to the basic requirements of human development.

Amongst the most important findings of the Human Development Report 2013 concerns the importance of women and girls. 'Education also has striking impacts on health and mortality. Research for this Report shows that a mother's education level is more important to child survival than is household income. … This has profound policy implications, potentially shifting the emphasis from efforts to boost household income to measures to improve girls' education.' Accordingly, the Report says, 'Girls' education is a critical vehicle of a possible demographic dividend. Educated women tend to have fewer, healthier and better educated children; in many countries educated women also enjoy higher salaries than do uneducated workers.'

The Report observes, 'Projections also show that policy interventions have a greater impact in countries and regions where education outcomes are initially weaker'.

16.3 Adult Literacy and Numeracy

In October 2013, the OECD published a major survey of adult literacy and numeracy in all OECD member countries. The results largely supported previous reports on education including especially the PISA Reports. The Survey measured the skills of 16–65-year olds across 24 countries and related literacy, numeracy to problem-solving as used at work. The Survey 'provides clear evidence of how developing and using skills improves employment prospects and quality of life as well as boosting economic growth.' (OECD 2013)

Launching the Report OECD Secretary-General Angel Gurría said, 'Too many people are being left behind today. With effective education and life-long learning everyone can develop their full potential. The benefits are clear, not only for individuals, but also for societies and for the economy… Learning does not stop at school: governments, businesses and people can and must continue investing in skills throughout life.'

For people aged 16–24 Australia was ranked sixth in literacy ahead of Germany, Denmark, France, Canada, and Norway. Australia was ahead of South Korea in literacy for all adults but young Koreans ranked third. For all adults Australia was ranked fifth; Japan, Finland and the Netherlands consistently ranked in the first five.

In the case of numeracy, young Australians ranked 14th, ahead of Canada; Sweden, Austria, Germany, Denmark and Norway were among the countries ahead of Australia. The rankings for all adults in numeracy placed Australia 13th. The consistency between young and old in numeracy was a difference from England and the US.

Young Koreans are outperformed only by their Japanese peers whilst Korea's 55–64 year olds are among the lowest performing groups of this age. Older Finns are average but younger Finns are among top performers with Japan, Korea and the Netherlands.

'But in England and the United States, the literacy and numeracy skills of young people entering the labour market are no better than those leaving for retirement. England ranks among the top three countries surveyed for literacy skills among the 55–65 year-olds. But the country is in the bottom three when it comes to such skills among 16–25 year-olds. American 55–65 year-olds perform around the average, but young Americans rank the lowest among their peers in the 24 countries surveyed.' This substantial difference in literacy and numeracy between older and young people from England and the US is of great significance for the education programs and related factors!

Compared with other countries with similar average scores, the US had more people in the highest proficiency levels and more in the lowest; the gap in skills between the employed and unemployed was unusually wide (Pérez-Peña 2013). Amongst those who did not finish high school, Americans has significantly worse skills than their counterparts in other countries. England is the only country where the generation approaching retirement age is more literate and numerate than the youngest adults. A quarter of adults in England have maths skills of a 10 year old and one in four adults have only the most basic skills in math.

Italy and Spain scored badly in the Survey, coming last in the rankings for all adults in both literacy and numeracy. In considering the economic and social impact of skills the Survey finds that 'on average, the median hourly wage of workers scoring at the top levels (levels 4 and 5) on the literacy scale is 61 % higher than that of workers scoring at or below Level 1'. Adults with low skills are also more likely to place less trust in others and feel less civically engaged compared with the highly skilled.

The Survey also found that 'immigrants performed worse than the native-born, especially those who did not learn the language of their new country as a child. But skills proficiency improves with length of stay in the host country, pointing to the important role of integration policies… The highly skilled were on average three times more likely to take part in further training than the low skilled.'

16.4 Challenges for a New Government

The policies of the new Coalition Government are very much along the lines of the Washington Consensus, giving a major role to the market and to corporate business, as far as possible removing any government involvement which might hinder the progress of the business sector. As the Liberal Party website says, Australia's economy will be strengthened through a 'more efficient government, lower taxes, more productive businesses so that all Australians can get ahead in the global economy'.

The new government's policies are in general strongly supported by business groups such as the Business Council of Australia which promotes the proposition that the country will be a lot better when business is able to prosper. Though it has commissioned reports, such as that from ACER, which appropriately direct attention to the latest understandings about education, the Council pays little attention to the evidence in those reports. Instead, competition and financial incentives together with workplace deregulation are seen as the solution. It continues to advocate performance pay for teachers despite the evidence. (Cobbold 2013).

The major reports mentioned above and all the evidence brought together in the preceding chapters show that rising prosperity flows from attention to social cohesion and inclusion, through government policies to pursue those objectives. Critical to that is pursuit of strategies which seek to minimise economic and social disparities, most importantly strategies which address the critical time of early childhood and strategies which focus especially on girls and women, on improving conditions which contribute to social cohesion amongst families and which promote an equitable workplace.

In terms of inequality Australia is becoming more like the US and the UK rather than Scandinavian countries whose students and adults demonstrate such high results in international studies of educational outcomes. Of special concern in Australia are population centres outside the major cities and most especially Indigenous peoples. It is unclear how the Abbott government will address those issues.

The present policies concerning Indigenous peoples pay little attention to any of the international evidence, give little play to the issue of self-determination and do not address the ongoing totally unsatisfactory situation in housing, education and health which result to a significant extent from inequitable funding provision and a failure to institute genuine programs of skill development. Instead the situation is being addressed by social welfare approaches and is seen as an Indigenous 'problem'. Much of the funding of Indigenous programs goes to non-Indigenous bureaucrats, advisors and consultants and may not reach the communities that were intended to benefit. The model resembles colonialism.

The financial collapse of some Indigenous organisations will no doubt again focus attention of government and many of the population on the problem but ignore the similar failings which have beset non-Indigenous business corporations ranging from financial insolvency of financial institutions and energy generating companies through failures in infrastructure maintenance and negative environmental impacts as well as not infrequent rent-seeking and a failure to attend to workplace training and development. In both cases, the government regulating authorities have been strongly criticised.

As Professor George Williams points out (as mentioned in Sect. 4.5), 'The evidence in the US and Australia shows time and again that redressing disadvantage in the longer term depends upon indigenous people having the power to make decisions that affect them. They must be responsible for the programs designed to meet their needs, and must be accountable for the successes and failures that follow.' It is by no means clear that governments understand what self-determination actually means.

The evidence of the importance of women in social development, of girl's education and of the impact of the earliest experiences on later parenting behaviour all go to supporting the proposition that special support for Indigenous women is amongst the most important policy prescriptions.

In conclusion, it is quite possible that the progress made by the last 6 years of the Labor government in respect of education will be lost. That is not to say that there have not been mistakes and lost opportunities in the last 6 years. But it is not irrelevant to note that we have been there before. The policies adopted by the Rudd and Gillard government were very much like those pursued by the Whitlam Government from 1972 through 1975. They are very unlike the policies pursued by the US Government which successive Australian governments seem so inclined to follow. That the literacy and numeracy levels of young people from the US and UK (England) are significantly lower than those of older adults, as revealed by the OECD Survey, is the strongest indicator yet of the complete failure of those policies!

References

Barber, J. (2013, October 13). The changing face of university education. ABC RN 'Ockham's Razor'. Retrieved October 15, 2013, from http://www.abc.net.au/radionational/programs/ockhamsrazor/the-changing-face-of-university-education/5011596.

Cobbold, T. (2013, August 7). Business council ignores evidence on performance pay. *Save Our Schools*.

Lane, S. (2013, August 5). Education policy: Where the parties stand. Retrieved August 6, 2013, from http://www.abc.net.au/news/2013-06-21/education-policy-explainer/4744030.

OECD. (2013, October 8). Boosting skills essential for tackling joblessness and improving well-being, says OECD. Retrieved October 14, 2013, from http://www.oecd.org/newsroom/boosting-skills-essential-for-tackling-joblessness-and-improving-well-being.htm.

Pérez-Peña, R. (2013, October 8). U.S. adults fare poorly in a study of skills. *New York Times*.

United Nations. (2013). Human Development Report 2013. The rise of the South: Human progress in a diverse world. New York: United Nations Development Program. Retrieved September 26, 2013, from http://hdr.undp.org/en/reports/global/hdr2013/summary/.

Index

A

Abbott, Hon Tony
  government schools not underfunded, 299
  independent schools funding, 266
  on Prime Minister's response to Gonski report, 269
  on the 'same page' as PM on School plan, 276
  parental leave scheme, 88
  plan to appoint National indigenous council, 72
  promise on Indigenous affairs, 70
  socioeconomic status not important, 290
  Sydney morning Herald editorial, 274
Abecedarian project, 80
ACARA, 180, 257–259, 308
Acemoglu, Daron, 31, 45
Alexander, Professor Robin, 30, 124, 166
Alton-Lee, Adrienne, 106, 215
Anyon, Jean, 39, 296
Ariely, Professor Dan, 140
Aubusson, Associate Professor Peter, 182, 265
Australia in the Asian century White paper, 188, 269
Australian Education Union, 259, 270, 276
Australian schools commission, 9, 299

B

Bancroft, Jack Manning, 69
Baumeister, Roy, 28
Behrendt, 62, 64
Belongingness, 28
Berliner, David with Bruce Biddle
  impact of class size, 127
Berliner, Professor David
  criticises standardised testing, 164
  impact of poverty on educational achievement, 296
  importance of outside-of-school factors, 148
  notes incidence of suppurative otitis media in American children, 168
  refutes criticism of teachers, 165
  school failures a result of inequality, 300
Better schools plan, 307
Black, Professor Paul, 104, 105
Bonner, Chris, 137, 156, 160, 252
Bowlby, John, 86
Brooks, David, 26, 170
Brooks, Geraldine, 303
Bryk, Professor Anthony, 119, 285, 291
Building the Education Revolution (BER), 20, 157
Business council of Australia
  endorsement of bonuses for best teachers, 142
  report on school reform, 256

C

Cambridge primary review, 166
Caro, Jane, 156, 252
Children's defense fund, 39
COAG, 9, 68, 89, 273, 304
Cobbold, Trevor, 90, 141, 156, 259, 274, 290
Common core, 177, 178
Consortium on Chicago school research, 121

D

Darling-Hammond, Professor Linda, 143, 164
Dinham, Professor Stephen, 142
Dircks, Ruth, 182
Direct instruction, 115, 116
Dockery, Michael, 66
DuFour, Ricky, 115, 125

E
Early years study, 81
Ehrenreich, Barbara, 50, 57

F
Follow through project, 115
Fullan, Michael, 137, 148, 220

G
Gardner, Howard, 4, 193, 199
Garrett, Hon Peter, 142, 273
Gillard, Hon Julia
  bonuses for best teachers, 141
  extra funding for disadvantaged schools, 259
  government response to Gonski report, 266
  intiates review of funding arrangements for schooling, 261
Gonski AC, David, 157, 262, 289
Gonski Panel, 262, 291
Gonski report, 246, 251, 263, 264, 266, 271, 299
Gopnik, Professor Alison, 77
Gove, Rt Hon Michael, 160, 178, 222, 300
Grafton, Anthony, 232
Grattan institute
  report on benefits to the community of university attendance, 243
  report on better teaching appraisal, 140
  report on learning from the best school systems in East Asia, 262

H
Harvard project, 55, 67
Hattie, Professor John, 97, 100, 102, 104, 290
Head, Simon, 235
Heckman, Professor James, 80, 81
Heppell, Professor Stephen, 201
High/Scope Perry Preschool Project, 79
Hoyles, Professor Celia, 186
Hughes, Professor Helen, 62
Human development report, 40, 41, 92, 307, 310, 311
Hutton, Will, 15, 24, 32, 293

I
IMF, 24, 293
Ingvarson, Lawrence, 138, 261

J
Jackson, Professor Tim, 26, 194
Judt, Tony, 6, 29

K
Kahneman, Daniel, 25, 27
Killen, Professor Roy, 98
Kleinhenz, Elizabeth, 138, 261
Klein, Joel, 10, 30, 118, 304
Krugman, Paul, 17, 21, 23, 31
Krugman, Professor Paul, 21, 23, 32, 293

L
Ladwig, Professor James, 103
Lazaridis, Mike, 200
Lewandowsky, Stephan, 298

M
Marceau, Professor Jane, 244
Marmot, Professor Michael, 44
Martin, Professor Andrew, 168
Masters, Professor Geoff, 254, 256
McAuley, Ian, 7, 8, 25, 294
McCain, Margaret, 81
McConney, Andrew, 156, 289
McLaughlin, Professor Milbrey, 49, 295
McNamara, Robert, 38, 39
Melbourne Declaration, 255, 261
Mirror neurons, 27
Mischel, Walter, 170
Mulford, Bill, 127, 146, 147, 291
Murdoch, Rupert, 10, 30, 156, 289, 304

N
National board for professional teaching standards, 139
National early childhood development strategy, 89
National partnership agreement on early childhood education, 90, 93, 271
National plan for school improvement, 267, 268, 273, 301
National professional standards for teachers, 261
Nelson, Brendan, 238, 239, 244, 247, 248
Newfield, Christopher, 236
New public management, 70, 30, 33, 283, 293
Noah, Timothy, 44, 301

No child left behind, 10, 51, 118, 125, 131, 153, 163–165, 300
Nous group, 263
NPM, 7, 30, 31, 33
Nuthall, Graham, 106, 108, 129, 203

O
Obama, Barack, 11, 93, 141, 288
OECD, 2, 7, 8, 10, 19, 26, 37, 40, 43, 46, 56, 77, 78, 89–93, 98, 100, 117, 126, 129, 142, 143, 148, 160, 161, 163, 165, 209–214, 218, 220–222, 224, 226, 240, 244, 246, 252, 263, 264, 266, 272, 274, 277, 290, 296, 297, 307, 310, 312, 315
Osborne, Jonathan, 111, 169, 176, 184, 203, 291

P
Perimeter institute for theoretical physics, 200
Perry, Laura, 156, 289
Piccoli, Hon Adrian, 61, 270, 271
Pickett, Kate, 42
PIRLS, 253, 254
Productive pedagogy, 102, 103
Productivity commission, 68, 90, 128, 141, 259, 270, 274, 279, 309, 310
Professional learning communities, 115, 125
Project STAR, 127
Pyne, Hon Christopher, 265, 266, 269, 273–275, 290, 307, 308

Q
Queensland school reform longitudinal study, 102, 147

R
Race to the top, 141, 288
Rand corporation, 91, 140, 141
Raudenbush, Professor Stephen W., 119
Ravitch, Diane, 118, 130, 176, 223, 224, 226, 288, 289
Resnick, Professor Lauren, 112, 115, 118, 122, 124, 125, 131
Robinson, James, 31, 194, 195, 197, 296
Robinson, Ken, 11, 30, 104, 129, 171
Rocard, Michel
  report on science education, 186

Rosenzweig, Roy, 180
Rothstein, Richard, 85
Rowe, Kenneth, 130, 162, 168
Rudd, Hon Kevin
  education revolution major plank of 2007 election, 255
  speech to National Press Club 27 August 2009, 255

S
Sahlberg, Pasi, 11, 214, 224
Sanger Unified School District, 126
Sebring, Penny Bender, 121
Self-control, 170
Sen, Amartya, 22, 28, 40
Sen, Professor Amartya, 22, 28, 42
Share the World's Resources, 46
Sloan, Professor Judith, 279
Smith, Adam, 28, 29
Stiglitz, Joseph, 22, 23, 25, 32
Stiglitz, Professor Joeseph, 22, 23, 32, 293
Survey of adult literacy and numeracy, 307, 310, 312

T
Taleb, Nassim, 22
Taylor, Professor Tony, 181
Teese, Professor Richard, 9, 157, 265, 300
TIMSS, 43, 104, 110, 170, 252, 253
Torrance tests of creative thinking, 195, 196
Tovey, Noel, 70
Toynbee, Polly, 48, 49, 294
Tucker-Drob, Eliot, 84
Tytler, Professor Russell, 169, 183

U
UN, 292
UNICEF, 47, 55, 56, 88
UNDPR, 40, 92, 209, 284, 310

V
Vygotsky, Lev, 4, 79, 199

W
Washington consensus, 311, 313
Watkins, Cathy, 116

Whiting, Beatrice and John, 87
Wilkinson, Professor James, 237
Wilkinson, Richard, 42, 301
Williams, Professor George, 67
Wylie, Cathie, 215
Wynhausen, Elisabeth, 57

Y
Yates, Professor Lyn, 3, 178

Z
Zucker, Jessica, 87
Zyngier, David, 124, 129, 252, 262, 263, 265

Printed by Publishers' Graphics LLC